T0367166

From Philosophy to Sociology

FROM PHILOSOPHY

TO SOCIOLOGY
The Evolution of French Liberalism, 1870-1914

William Logue

NORTHERN ILLINOIS UNIVERSITY PRESS·DEKALB, ILLINOIS

Part of chapter 8 is reprinted from Logue, W., "Sociologie et politique: le libéralisme de Célestin Bouglé," *Revue française de sociologie* 20 (1) 1979, 141–61. Editions du C.N.R.S., Paris, with permission of the publisher.

Library of Congress Cataloging in Publication Data

Logue, William, 1934–
From philosophy to sociology.

Bibliography: p.
Includes index.
1. Liberalism—France—History—19th century.
2. Sociology—France—History—19th century.
I. Title.
JA84.F8L575   1983   320.5'1'0944   82-22263
ISBN 0-87580-088-2

Copyright © 1983 by Northern Illinois University Press
Published by the Northern Illinois University Press, DeKalb, Illinois 60115

All rights reserved
Design by Joan Westerdale

For Carol

Contents

Preface

*T*he works of historians grow out of their experience in ways that are often unexpected and unintended. It may be helpful to the reader to know a bit about how the present work came to be. I have long been interested in writing a general history of French political thought in the nineteenth century which would supersede the now fifty-year-old work of Roger Soltau, *French Political Thought in the Nineteenth Century* (1931). In investigating this topic I soon discovered that there was one major lacuna in the secondary literature. There was no satisfactory interpretation of liberal thought after Tocqueville; indeed, there were few works dealing with later nineteenth-century liberalism at all. Henry Michel's magisterial *L'idée de l'Etat* (1895) was, for all its scholarship, a partisan work produced during the era in question and lacking the necessary perspective. John A. Scott's *Republican Ideas and the Liberal Tradition* (1951) seemed to me more a caricature than a history. Georges Burdeau's recent synthesis, *Le libéralisme* (1979) is an excellent, thought-provoking work but does not go deeply into any individual thinkers.

American scholarship in particular has produced a number of good works on the extreme Right in France and even more on the extreme Left, but its neglect of the middle-of-the-road liberalism that dominated the political life of the late nineteenth century gives a false picture of the period. It became clearly evident that if I was going to understand the development of liberal thought I was going to have to study the period closely myself. In the course of that effort I discovered the phenomenon of a transformation of French liberalism, a transformation which furnishes the theme of this book. What emerged from

ix

this transformation was a New Liberalism which was interesting not only because it repudiated extreme individualism in favor of social action but also because in the process it was shifting the intellectual foundations of liberalism from philosophy to sociology.

This theme began to exert its own influence on the direction of my research. Because it led me to be concerned not merely with the political ideas of the liberals but also with the intellectual underpinnings of those ideas, I naturally gravitated toward the more "serious" thinkers—many but not all of them academics—who were more apt to be concerned with the foundations of their own thought and therefore more apt to shed light on this problem which had drawn itself to my attention. I also tried to find figures whose reputations among their contemporaries indicated that they were regarded as influential thinkers. When you study any period intensively you get a feeling for who was regarded as important and influential, even if you cannot produce quantitative evidence for your conclusions. A different approach from the one I have taken, an approach which concentrated on the social history of ideas, would no doubt be able to turn up other sorts of evidence about the importance of the people studied here, but it would also have produced a different sort of book. It would be interesting to have such evidence, but I do not think it is essential to my argument.

On the whole I think the reader will be able to decide whether he or she agrees with my argument in this work on the basis of my discussion of the thinkers I have chosen for close study. Other scholars would no doubt have chosen somewhat differently and some would have approached my subject in a different manner. Indeed, I hope they will, for I am convinced that the thinkers studied in this work would repay study from different perspectives. I have, for example, drawn some assurance about the validity of my thesis from the fact that something of a parallel phenomenon has been found in English liberalism by such scholars as Melvin Richter in his study of T. H. Green and by Michael Freeden in his examination of the English New Liberalism. It might be well worthwhile to attempt to do for the French what Freeden has done for the English, but what I have attempted here is quite different. In part this difference results from differing conceptions of intellectual history, but it also reflects something of the national differences between the French and the British. It is commonplace, but correct, to observe that ideas have always been more important to the French, while the British have been more concerned with results. What follows here is not, therefore, a social history of ideas, but neither does it treat ideas as timeless abstractions. The political thought I am studying has a very definite historical context which has not been ignored, though others may wish I had given it greater emphasis.

I am, nonetheless, convinced that the liberal thought of the late nineteenth century has an enduring interest and that studying it can help us to think about the issues of today. A respect for historical context should not be incompatible with an effort to draw some attention to the ongoing interest of the ideas being studied. This is certainly one of the legitimate uses of intellectual history. The approach I have taken in this work is certainly one which is particularly congruent to my own intellectual inclinations, but also, I think, particularly appropriate to my subject matter.

The manner in which this work developed exposed me to a familiar danger of intellectual history, namely, that of selecting figures for inclusion on the basis of whether or not their ideas fit my thesis. Since I could not pretend to have studied all the liberal thinkers of the period, I had to accept the fact that readers would always be able to ask, "Why didn't you study X?" or, "How does Y fit into your thesis?" But the more individuals I did study, the more I found who confirmed my hypothesis, and I became more convinced that I had found one of the major features, perhaps the major feature, of French liberal thought in the later years of the nineteenth century. I do not claim, on the other hand, that all French liberals of the period can be fitted neatly into my scheme.

French intellectual life has always been too diverse, and even important thinkers have not always fit smoothly into their times. Older views do not necessarily disappear, as is demonstrated by the French school of economics—currently being studied by Boris Blick and Dan Warshaw—with its attachment to laissez-faire. Another obstacle to any comprehensive study of French liberalism is the difficulty in agreeing on which thinkers should be considered liberals. From some points of view, for example, the theorists of crowd psychology—headed by Gustave LeBon—who have been so well examined by Robert Nye, Susannah Barrows, and others, can be considered influential liberals. These men were certainly representative of an important trend in their day, and no picture of French intellectual life in the Belle Epoque would be complete without them; but in my opinion they were outside the main direction in which French liberalism was moving—to the point that it could be said that they had abandoned liberalism for something else, which perhaps still needs to be defined.

Readers who have some familiarity with French political thought may also wonder why I have not included a couple of quite diverse figures. One of these is Emile Littré, perhaps the best-known disciple of Auguste Comte and even more famous as a lexicographer. Littré was certainly an interesting character, whose career would repay more study, especially from non-positivists, but it seems to me that his philosophical influence was confined to a certain sect of Comteans and had little impact on the development of the liberal sociology I am examining. The other figure I am referring to is the philosopher Alain (pseud. of Emile Chartier), who offers quite a different case. I have justified excluding him from consideration on the grounds that his influence fell mostly after 1914. I am, indeed, not sure that he should be considered a liberal; I am sure, however, that the usual tendency to treat him as the major liberal intellectual of his time is greatly mistaken. Alain might better find a place in the history of individualist anarchism, in the tradition of Max Stirner. I suspect Alain would prove to be a more interesting subject for the psychohistorian than for the intellectual historian.

In sum, the work which follows does not claim to have the last word on the history of French liberalism in the late nineteenth century, but it does claim to shed new light on a too much neglected subject. I will be more than rewarded for my effort if it stimulates others to take an interest in what I have found to be a fascinating topic.

Acknowledgments

I especially want to thank W. Paul Vogt of the State University of New York at Albany for the generosity with which he gave of his knowledge and understanding of French liberalism. This is a much better book because of his unstinting advice. Without the efforts of my wife, Carol Baur Logue, this book would probably still be hiding in my boxes of fiches. Not only did she hold my nose to the IBM and insist that my inspired first drafts be converted into readable English, she led me, in the course of many hours of discussion, to think more clearly about what I was trying to say. Finally, a word of thanks to the Bibliothèque Nationale, her chief rival in my affections. Without its unrivaled collections and the scholarly atmosphere of its great Salle de Travail, this work would never have been completed.

·I·

French Liberalism, Old and New

Il y a en France un courant de libéralisme et d'idées libérales beaucoup plus
fort qu'on ne le croit souvent.[1]   Albert Thibaudet

*O*f all the diverse currents of French
political thought in the nineteenth century, liberalism has been the
most neglected and least well understood. Paradoxically, the principal
reason for this neglect may be precisely that liberalism was the main
current, and students of ideas are more attracted by the extremes,
where thinkers are less concerned about practical consequences. This
tendency has led to the development of a bipolar image of French political thought in the late nineteenth century which is by no means
faithful to the character of the age. In France the political thinkers of
the center have often suffered a fate similar to that of the political
leaders of the center, but modern French history cannot be understood
without reference to the political center. This work will attempt to
show the contemporary importance and the enduring interest of the
centrist political thought which was the liberalism of the early decades
of the Third Republic. It will also attempt—as Herodotus advised—to
honor the memory of worthy men, whom we have neglected at our
own cost.

Among the great upheavals and exciting developments of the
Belle Epoque—emergence of an industrial economy, rise of an important socialist movement, revolutions in painting and music—one of the
most important but least remarked was the appearance in France of a
new liberalism.[2] The nature of that new liberalism will be one of the
main themes of the chapters to follow. As we shall see, this new liberalism was an effort to overcome the deficiencies of the old laissez-faire
individualism without sacrificing the rights and interests of the individual to the community. Determining the proper balance between the

individual and the community has been the central—and the most difficult—problem of liberal political philosophy. It was viewed as the most pressing issue by liberal thinkers at the turn of the century. For the French liberals this was not merely a pragmatic problem, but one which demanded a coherent intellectual solution; such a solution was of general interest, for ideas have consequences.

Thus any consideration of the practical shortcomings of the old liberal individualism led to the conclusion that the philosophical foundation of liberalism had to be profoundly changed. The emergence of the new liberalism was therefore of great importance to the development of French social and political thought. Put in the broadest terms, that development was nothing less than the replacement of a liberalism based on metaphysical philosophy by a liberalism based on sociology. Of course, this transition did not take place overnight, and the transitional steps between a reliance on philosophy and a reliance on sociology are of particular interest. The problems which the French liberals confronted have lost surprisingly little of their importance; their attempts to solve those problems have a more than historical interest.

The history of the French liberal tradition in the past 170 years has yet to be written, though parts have been explored with great skill. The task is a formidable one because some of the greatest figures— Tocqueville is the prime example—are in many respects marginal to the main lines of development. Our aim here is much more modest, yet it is critical to the whole enterprise. For if liberalism has almost seemed to disappear in twentieth-century France, except as an anachronism, it is because most observers have failed to see the emergence of the new liberalism and to give it the attention it deserves. Part of the problem is one of vocabulary. The term "new liberalism" was not much employed in France and, indeed, no one term describing the new phenomenon achieved acceptance. This is good—or at least not bad— insofar as it stresses the continuity between the old and new in liberalism, but a terminological distinction is sometimes needed in order to make clear the changes being discussed. So, new liberalism it will be, to indicate in a very general way a liberalism emerging in the later nineteenth century, which stressed the social as well as the individual, and which admited a role for the state that was not merely one of necessity but one justified by liberal theory. Our task here will be to describe and to analyze (and perhaps to a certain extent explain) the emergence of this new liberalism in the period 1870–1914.

Because this topic is sufficiently coherent in its own right, only a bare minimum of historical background seems necessary to situate it in the larger history of the liberal tradition. To go back no further than the eighteenth century (and one could find reasons to go back to the very beginnings of Western philosophy), the modern liberal tradition first flowered in the Enlightenment. Freedom of thought, long nourished in and nourished by the Western mind, began more urgently to seek to exteriorize itself in such diverse areas as freedom of religious practice and freedom of economic enterprise. It entered the realm of politics, at first to protect the individual from the arbitrary exercise of governmental power, then to see government as an expression of the needs and interests of society as a whole, leading to the demand for government to take certain actions which would bring about socioeconomic changes (abolition of monopolies and "feudal" privileges). It is indeed in the enlightened despotism sought by many of the philosophes that we have the most obvious ancestor of the welfare state. Henry Michel was largely right in calling the new liberalism a return to the liberalism of the Enlightenment over the selfish individualism of the nineteenth century.[3] Indeed, one of the most important aspects of twentieth-century politics has been the attempt—partly successful—to put into practice the ideal of the enlightened despot, or even more grandly, of the philosopher-king. But that effort has led us far away from liberalism.

With the Revolution there appeared an important division in French liberalism between those who stressed control of the centralized state power—in order better to fight the enemies of liberty and progress—and those who sought to reduce state power in order to promote the vigorous development of liberty at the grass roots of society. The tension between these Jacobin and Girondin strains in French liberalism would persist into the twentieth century, not so much as two separate lineages, but as an inner division which affected most French liberals.[4] The Revolutionary era contained the seeds of almost all the political issues of the nineteenth century. In addition to the tension between centralization and decentralism, there were the issues of representation (restricted vs. universal suffrage; delegation of power vs. *mandat impératif*), of human rights (the Declaration of the Rights of Man and the Citizen proving one of its most durable accomplishments), of the foundations of sovereignty (people? nation?). The practical experience of the cycle of upheavals exposed the different questions of the relations of order and liberty, or authority and responsiblity. Differing views of that experience would greatly affect liberal attitudes throughout the century.

Something of the same could be said of the Napoleonic Era, though the experience was, to be sure, less varied. Napoleon was in many respects an ideal enlightened despot who brought to fruition some of the aspirations of the philosophes, especially those tending to a more rational structure of the legal system and of taxation, to the suppression of regional and local privileges, to a greater opportunity for individual advancement (the emperor himself being the prime demonstration of the "careers open to talent"). But his rule also exposed the dangers to liberty inherent in this version of liberalism, and liberals were increasingly to be found among the opposition to the Empire. That (major) aspect of liberalism which insists on the limitation of government, on the careful definition of its legitimate authority, and on the constitutional structure most likely to ensure the respect for those limits received a powerful impetus from the Napoleonic experience.

The immediate fruit of that experience was the political regime of the Restoration, or more accurately, of the *monarchie censitaire.* Often cited—especially in its second act, the July Monarchy—as the apogee of French liberalism, it could be more accurately considered the high point of the liberalism of the *grande bourgeoisie,* the one in which an explicit relationship between wealth and political power (or at least political rights) was recognized (and contested). It had, indeed, the unfortuante effect of identifying the word "liberalism" with the social power of a tiny minority and with the parliamentary monarchy and limited suffrage. This identification makes it awkward to use "liberalism" to describe political forces and movements of ideas later in the century for which "liberalism" taken broadly seems the correct label. For example, most of the *radicalisme* of the nineteenth century should be called liberal, even though it was a liberalism defined in no small part in opposition to the governmental liberalism of the July Monarchy. For it is in that period that the merger of liberalism and democracy began to take place, which would form the liberal democracy of the turn of the century. Both the "old" and the "new" liberalism of the period 1870–1914 were democratic.

Intellectually, the period of the *monarchie censitaire* also produced the first liberal philosophies which we will later examine in detail—the *spiritualiste* liberalism of Victor Cousin and his immediate disciples. It was a liberalism based on a mixture of philosophical and religious (though not sectarian) concepts. It began as a sort of official philosophy, legitimizing the existing social and political order—accepting the legacy of the Revolution as transmitted by Napoleon to Louis XVIII and embodied in the Charter of 1814. But it proved capable of moving beyond this beginning, forming the foundations of the *radicalisme* of the liberal philosopher-politician Jules Simon, whose career and whose ideas bridge the gap between the July Monarchy and the founding of the Third Republic. Furnishing the intellectual foundation for the liberal opposition during the Second Empire, spiritualist liberalism became democratized, leading the way to the Third Republic.

While most histories of political thought treat Alexis de Tocqueville as the representative French liberal of the mid-nineteenth century, he was more of an aberration. There can be, indeed, no one "typical" liberal for that dynamic period, but Tocqueville is representative neither of the satisfied liberals (Guizot would be a better choice) nor of the dissatisfied (J. Simon). Tocqueville had, perhaps, a more remarkable mind than either Guizot or Simon, but it is doubtful that he was as influential—in France—as either of them. He was greatly admired but had not much of a following. If Tocqueville represents anything, it is the recrudescence of the aristocratic liberalism of which Montesquieu was the great figure in the eighteenth century.[5] The curious enthusiasm with which he has been taken up by his American admirers has exaggerated his importance in the history of French liberalism, and it is possible to understand the developments which are the subject of this work without much reference to him.

Intellectual developments do not conform neatly to the chronological framework of political history, and our subject overlaps the period 1870–1914 at both ends. The first figures we will deal with in detail began their careers and formed their ideas well before 1870. They give us, so to speak, the state of liberal thought at the beginning of the Third Republic. The last of our thinkers were born almost with the republic itself and carried the new liberalism into the interwar period and beyond. But before introducing them and outlining the plan of this work it is necessary to say a few more words about the meaning—or meanings—of the word "liberalism" as it will be applied here.

No more than in other places, no more than in other times, no more than other political terms, did the word "liberalism" have a single, clear, commonly accepted meaning in the France of the Belle Epoque.[6] Rather it carried a number of distinct meanings which were sometimes in harmony with one another, and sometimes in isolation if not in actual conflict. Quite often it was used in the narrowest sense of economic liberalism, describing the advocacy of the most complete policy of laissez-faire possible. This was the liberalism of Bastiat's *Harmonies économiques*, closer to Herbert Spencer than to Adam Smith in its advocacy of the unregulated economy. Opponents of liberalism—on the Right or the Left—were apt to speak as if this were the only kind of liberalism there was, perhaps because it was easy to refute or at least easy to make seem immoral and heartless. But many who thought themselves to be liberals rejected the extremes of laissez-faire economics. The partition between the old and new liberalisms is not quite upon this line, though the advocates of the new did promote a more extensive economic role for the state. Except for the narrow circles of professional economists, convinced of the scientific validity of laissez-faire, very few liberals of the late nineteenth century believed that it was tenable.

This is not to say that they rejected in any way private enterprise and the competition of the market but that they did not believe that the market alone could produce the best of possible worlds, accepting that some elements of social oversight and regulation were needed— differing among themselves on exactly what was appropriate. And these differences were sometimes significant. Liberals would continue to distinguish themselves from socialists by their commitment to the virtues of private property; how far private property could be subject to social regulation and still remain effectively private property was a serious question, not easily answered. There was, as a result, in practice a somewhat unclear borderline between socialists and liberals which the exigencies of political life led them sometimes to obscure and sometimes to accentuate. One of the major problems of liberal political philosophy was to establish the grounds on which this distinction could be clearly based.

A second meaning of the word "liberalism" was generally unquestioned, though of course there were differences over interpretations and applications, that of adherence to and advocacy of the Rights of Man. To be a liberal meant to support freedom of speech, of the press, of assembly, of religion, and so forth, without, however, the peculiar twentieth-century illusion that any of these rights could in practice be absolute and unlimited. This was not just a commitment to the value of these freedoms; it was also a rejection of the society and government of the ancien régime, a positive expression of the opposition to the costly privileges of the aristocracy, the irresponsibility and profligacy of the court (not to mention its immorality), and the moral and intellectual hegemony of the church. To be for the rights of man was in the broadest sense to be a progressive, a man who turned his back on the unenlightened past and looked toward a more rational future. It was an emotion, a state of the soul, as well as— sometimes more than—an intellectual conviction. The philosophers we will be studying would of course give greater attention than the average man to the logic of the liberal commitment to the freedoms, but they, too, were not unmoved by the feeling of being progressive. The practical application of these rights would be an important issue on several occasions during the early history of the Third Republic. The press laws were a particular object of controversy, retaining too much of the authoritarian attitude of the empire yet often inefficacious against the enemies of the new regime.[7] Liberals were particularly wracked by government efforts to repress anarchist propaganda as well as deeds in the 1890s. The church-state question would force them to examine the meaning of freedom of religion on more than one occasion. The Dreyfus affair, the most famous civil rights case of the Third Republic (and perhaps of the last century), found genuine liberals on both sides because there were so many competing factors that entered into each individual decision. A *cause célèbre* of world interest, it was surely of less importance for the development of civil liberties in France than the more fundamental issues of rights of press, of religion, and of association.

In the narrower sphere of politics, liberalism throughout the nineteenth century stood for representative government on the parliamentary model. At the beginning of the Third Republic liberals were still divided as to whether a monarchical or a republican version of parliamentary government was the best choice. Both had spectacular failures to their debit in the previous half-century, but the monarchy, in addition to being burdened by the divisions of the monarchists, was too clearly linked with memories of the ancien régime to command a majority of liberal support. It appealed most to the members of those prominent families who had flourished in the less democratic era of the 1840s, whose liberal ideal was that of eighteenth-century England. Most liberals were convinced by 1871 that the republic offered the best combination of stability and progress, whatever sentimental attachment to the glories of France's monarchical past they may have still felt.

The monarchy was also doomed because its model of parliamentary government was too closely associated with the highly restricted suffrage of the *monarchie censitaire*. Though many liberals still had qualms about universal manhood suffrage—and virtually none were willing to contemplate women's suffrage—qualms reinforced by the excesses of the Commune but quieted by the vigor of its repression, no one doubted that political democracy had become so much a part of the *moeurs* as to be beyond challenge. Minor differences over how elections should be organized apart, liberalism meant the democratic republic—full power confided in a parliament responsible to its electorate alone, choosing and dismissing ministers at will. In the mid-century, democrats and republicans alike had come to favor a single-chamber legislature because the appointive upper house was a feature of the monarchical regime and an elected upper house made logical sense only in a federal system like that of the United States. But having accepted the Senate as part of the price to be paid for securing any republican constitution, liberals soon gained control of it and found it a valuable lever of political power, therefore no longer anti-democratic in their eyes.

The issue of self-government which caused the French liberals the most difficulty in the nineteenth century (in both a practical and an intellectual sense) was that of local self-government. In its historical origins French liberalism was very tightly associated with the idea of the self-government of the nation. The possibility of local self-government on the English model was entertained by some, but in French experience, political authorities independent of the national government were apt to be more, not less, illiberal—as Voltaire had recognized of the *parlements*. The intellectual conviction that local power was a source of freedom, a bastion of resistance to tyranny, could not overcome the experience which suggested it would be easier to liberalize the national government than local ones—and this continued to be the feeling of most liberals despite the Reign of Terror (which sent many liberal advocates of local rights to the guillotine) and the Napoleonic autocracy.[8] As liberalism became more widely implanted in provincial France in the nineteenth century, the question was revived not only by Anglophile intellectuals but in political circles. The communal movement which surfaced with the fall of Napoleon III was probably a lost cause from the beginning but showed a direction liberalism might have taken in the coming decades.[9] In effect, communal liberties would be only a marginal issue (with the case of Paris, as always, distinct) when provincial France gained control of the Third Republic. In general, historical experience led French liberals to fear the "state within the state," whether based geographically or functionally (the Catholic church), more than they feared the power of a central government responsive in some measure to the popular will. The sociological approach of the new liberals would open a new chapter in this story, presenting a view of society in which freedom and order both depended on a multitude of associations and organizations besides the national state—and yet in which the role of the national state was not diminished but reinforced.

Finally, there is one other major element which must be included in any definition of liberalism in nineteenth-century France, an element more difficult to present with precision, an element perhaps more consciously if not more accurately perceived by liberalism's enemies than its friends: liberalism as the expression of bourgeois society. It is not necessary to accept the idea that liberalism is merely the ideology of the dominant bourgeoisie to see that the rise of the middle classes in Western society has been accompanied by—in a relation of reciprocal reinforcement—the rise of both liberal ideas and of the liberties which liberalism has advocated. Liberalism has, nonetheless, a fundamental aspiration to universality, and the effort to render that universality increasingly effective has been one of the driving forces behind the evolution of liberal thought. Liberalism's great realism shows clearly in its commitment to a perpetual struggle for greater liberty, avoiding the utopianism of these philosophies which seek to establish a perfect society once and for all.

The linkage between liberalism and middle-class society is not that of ideology to infrastructure, but a kind of synthesis of theory and practice. Liberalism is the political expression of the middling, centrist view of life. It is the humanism of moderation, modesty, and morality. It is the expression of a desire to life above the brute existence of the poorest and below the idle luxury of the richest. Indeed, French liberalism suffered from the persistence of aristocratic values among the middle classes. Political liberty and economic development both felt this handicap.

Liberalism is less an expression of the ownership of property than of the simple values of home, family, and labor. It flees from extremes of all kinds—even moral ones. It is a philosophy undergirded by a sentiment of the fundamental dignity of man, which refuses to sell man short in spite of his weaknesses. Its values are in conflict with those of the ancient military nobility as they are with the *conformisme totalitaire** of today. It is true that even middlingness and modesty of ambition can be carried to extremes, as some Frenchmen would demonstrate, but French liberalism as a whole was to avoid this snare, too. None of the thinkers we will deal with was simply content with the world as he found it; liberalism was for all of them an aspiration toward a fuller realization of man's capacity for good.

The bourgeois life-style, self-government, the rights of man, laissez-faire can all be distinguished from one another in the realm of theory and, as we have seen, late nineteenth-century liberals did increasingly reject laissez-faire in practice, while an autocratic ruler—Napoleon III—moved toward the laissez-faire goal of free trade. The balance of elements in liberalism varied from time to time and, indeed, from thinker to thinker. Most would insist on their necessary interrelationships. However much liberals would concede the necessity of social controls on the exercise of property rights, property remained one of the fundamental bastions of liberty and the necessary support of the independent family life they so valued. At bottom what the French liberals of the nineteenth century sought to make possible was for the average man to live a moral life—to be free to live a moral life, because without freedom you could have only the morals of the slave or the morals of the master. Not an heroic aspiration? But we have come to know only too well in the twentieth century those heroic aspirations that lead to massacre—the heroic aspirations of a Lenin or a

---

**The term is Jean-François Revel's.*

Hitler—far worse than those the liberals of the nineteenth century were in rebellion against.

For while individual liberals were on occasion defenders of the status quo (but the staus quo changed too often for anyone to always defend it in nineteenth-century France), there can be no doubt that liberalism was a force for political change in that era—even the main force, since French nationalism did not have the unsatisfied goals of Italian or German nationalism. Having achieved a major part of its aspirations in the first decades of the Third Republic, liberalism entered a new era, without ceasing to be the major reformist force of the twentieth century. With the rise of left- and right-wing extremisms in this century, liberalism remained virtually the sole surviving repository of the aspirations of universalism and rationalism which the French themselves thrust upon the world in the eighteenth century. This makes the question of what happened to French liberalism at the turn of the century a question of more than historical interest.

The opening two-thirds of the history of the Third Republic, from 1870 to 1914, were of the greatest importance in the history of French liberalism, both intellectually and in the political arena. On the political scene the liberals took the first steps toward the conversion of liberalism from a doctrine of hostility to governmental action in social life toward the welfare-state liberalism which has characterized the Western world in the twentieth century.[10] In speeches, in electoral programs, in bills proposed to the Chamber of Deputies, yes, even in legislation actually enacted, French liberals moved—with their historic caution, but more rapidly than their critics have admitted—toward the welfare state of today. It is true that the liberals in power enacted less of their program than they might have done, but it would be a mistake to see only the gap between the campaign rhetoric and the legislative action and to fail to see that there really was legislative action. An adequate history of what was done to lay the foundations of the welfare state before 1914 needs to be written, but that is not my purpose here.[11]

That purpose is rather to trace the emergence of the new liberalism which served as a rationale to justify these and later welfare measures. It is an exercise in intellectual history which will trace the development of French liberal thought as shaped by some of its most brilliant and original proponents and by some of its most influential popularizers. Not only did the political doctrine of liberalism undergo important changes, but the philosophical foundations on which that doctrine rested went through an even more profound transformation, the consequences of which are with us yet. This latter transformation is the heart of our investigation, and we hope to explain clearly and convincingly a development that has not received its due. It might be rash, but I think justifiable, to insist that our subject was at that time—and in retrospect—the most significant aspect of French political and social thought in the period 1870–1914.

No period can be characterized, especially briefly, with 100 percent accuracy, and there are individual exceptions to every generalization we can make about the period 1870–1914.[12] Ideas that might later seem of the greatest importance appeared, but were without great significance at the time. Other ideas that seem identified with periods well in the past had not disappeared as completely as their opponents had expected. But the attitudes and efforts most characteristic of a period are neither these anachronisms nor the self-styled waves of the future. What we are concerned with here are the attitudes and ideas which had the widest resonance in the milieu under consideration, which is the intellectual community and, more broadly, the republican middle classes that had received a secondary education.

With these qualifications understood, we can say that the dominant characteristic in the political life of the period was the effort to reconcile the rights of the individual as proclaimed in the eighteenth century and given historic force by the Revolution, with the needs of modern society, which appeared to be evolving fairly rapidly and which, should the liberals chance to ignore them, were the center of attention of much illiberal social thought. The main political thrust of this liberal effort at reconciliation was to make room for more state action than had been approved by the classical liberalism of the earlier nineteenth century. Liberals were moving away from the concept of the minimal or nightwatchman state in which the best of possible worlds would result naturally from the free competition of individuals.[13] A few economists like Jean Courcel-Seneuil might lament that the experiment of a truly laissez-faire society had never been made and insist that the antidote to the evils of a little freedom was more freedom, but by and large liberals were convinced that this ideal harmony could not be achieved in the world of real men. Some would even begin to challenge the intellectual argument behind that theory of natural harmony—and yet do so from a liberal viewpoint.

That the state should be the protector of common social interests was of course not a new idea in France, nor even one that liberals had always rejected, as the Revolutionary experience showed. Those liberals who were actively engaged in politics were no doubt more prone to think of the good uses to which state power might be put than were those whose interest was more exclusively intellectual. And since liberals found themselves out of power during much of the first half-century, it was natural that they had tended increasingly to see the state as the enemy of freedom and to mistrust any paternalistic exercise of power outside the immediate circle of the family.

With the establishment of the Third Republic the relation of the intellectuals to the state necessarily underwent a change. So much was the republic in harmony with their views that discussion of forms of government largely disappeared. There was of course considerable discussion during the period of prolonged constitution-making from 1871 to 1875. The dangers of majority rule seemed to cause less concern than in 1848. In short, the republic appeared to be the most favorable milieu for solving the problems of the individual and the society.[14] Without guaranteeing a liberal outcome, it nonetheless provided the means for the solution of social problems in ways compatible with the dignity of free men. The essential thing became then to provide the republic with the direction, the impetus, the inspiration, the will, and, most of all, the philosophy needed to solve its problems.

Intellectual interest in the relations of the individual and society was thus given new urgency by the establishment of the republic. Liberal intellectuals felt strongly the obligation to provide the intellectual leadership the new order would need. Conscious that the problems facing society were complex, difficult, and in some cases new—and that they could not be solved by habit and tradition alone—the intellectuals believed themselves especially competent to furnish a direction appropriate for the times.[15] The political leadership—even seen in the most favorable light—was too much preoccupied with day-to-day concerns to be able to provide the necessary reflection and the new ideas.[16] It would be counted upon, however, to implement those ideas, and few of the intellectuals aspired to political power for themselves.

Seeing themselves rather as educators of the political elite, the intellectuals were naturally concerned with the propagation of their ideas as well as with their development. Questions of education, therefore, frequently make their appearance in this study of political thought. It is only natural that the intellectuals' solutions to social and political issues should stress the importance of knowledge—even Bergsonism was not that anti-rational—and the liberals held a common view of human progress as essentially the result of the accumulation of knowledge, every temporary setback the result of its loss. Our concern here is of course with knowledge about man and about human society. It was generally recognized that knowledge about the physical universe had expanded much more rapidly than knowledge about man, and it was agreed that this was because man and society were much more complex and difficult subjects which could not be fully grasped until a later stage of man's history. Everyone was confident that time was arriving and that comparable progress in the human

12

sciences was getting under way. There was, however, considerable disagreement about just how this progress was to be made. The flourishing, multifarious social philosophies of the first half of the nineteenth century had made it clear that speculation on man and society, though productive of autointoxication to the point of madness and leading to insights of great originality, was not as productive of solid, scientific results as earlier generations had imagined.

Liberal philosophy, if it was to defend its ascendant position, needed to become more rigorous after the vagaries of Cousinian eclecticism. Social science—however conceived—needed to free itself from the dogmatism of its founding fathers and to seek to become truly scientific. In both cases, not only did theory need to be perfected and the question of the relations of philosophy and social science to the natural sciences resolved, but also the concrete empirical knowledge of man— the workings of his mind, the functioning of his societies—needed to be greatly expanded in order to put speculation on a more solid foundation. It was not possible to wait for some hypothetic future state of perfect knowledge, for action in the present was vital. The need for scientific caution remained balanced by the social need for results, a need to which the intellectuals were by no means indifferent, a need to which they might be tempted to make sacrifices of the intellect, as the post-1914 era would so cruelly reveal.

This work will be primarily concerned with the liberals' effort to develop and to propagate the new understanding of the relations of the individual and society (and especially the corollary question of the role of the state in a free society) in response to the feeling that this was the pressing issue of their time, both intellectually and practically. The new liberals agreed that an extremist individualism could not be tolerated as a practical policy or justified intellectually.[17] Where they could not agree was on what should take its place, on how the needs of society could be met in harmony with the interests of the individual. This was more than a policy question, for policy questions could not be resolved in a consistently liberal manner without a solid theoretical position from which to attack them. It is the effort to build a solid theoretical foundation for the new liberalism which occupied some of the best minds of the epoch and which is at the heart of our enquiry here.

That effort underwent a fundamental evolution in the course of the period 1870–1914. It was an evolution which had begun before 1870 and which would certainly continue after 1914, but its major turning points clearly occur within that period. There were three principal approaches to the problem of giving liberalism a new intellectual foundation—approaches which overlap in time, but which nonetheless form a sequence with a clear succession of predominance. The first phase is that of the second generation of the eclectic or spiritualist philosophers; the second, that of the idealist or neo-Kantian philosophers; the third, that of the positivist social scientists.[18] Each arose in response to the perceived inadequacies of its predecessors; each believed that it had found the only solid ground on which liberalism could rest.

Many factors entered into the making of this evolution of ideas; for it was such a fundamental question that it was affected by virtually the totality of contemporary experience. There was to some extent a conflict of generations (but there were fundamental disagreements within generations, too); there was an element of response to changing social conditions and political alignments; there was perhaps even an element of personal ambition; there was certainly an important element of response to the critics of liberalism. Not less important was an element of evolution intrinsic to the flow of ideas in Western civilization, a gradual but substantial shift in what constituted knowledge with respect to man, in what kinds of arguments carried conviction; it was a sort of epistemological revolution in the domain of *sciences humaines*. Ideas are by no means mere epiphenomena and cannot be reduced to reflections of material conditions, and the element of internal evolution was certainly strong in the transformation of liberal philosophy. Liberalism's capacity to evolve is not a manifestation of some hypostatized capitalism, fertile in expedients to stave off inevitable decay, but a testimony to its fundamental commitment to the rational comprehension of man and his world.

In the chapters which follow we will attempt to trace the evolution of French liberalism by means of an examination of the works of an appropriately middling number of intellectuals—with one or two exceptions, not as well known today as they deserve to be. We will not attempt anything like a definitive treatment of each individual but will consider his thought and, to a much lesser degree, his action as they relate to the overall purpose of our investigation. In some cases this may well be the most interesting aspect of that individual; in others it will represent a more secondary aspect of his work. We will begin with a group of eclectic philosophers, direct students of Victor Cousin, whose defense of liberalism took form around the middle of the century, but who continued to promote the spiritualist vision into the early Third Republic. They formed, so to speak, the base from which the liberal evolution of 1870–1914 took its departure; yet they already marked a change from the liberalism of the 1840s. Middle rather than upper bourgeoisie, they had moved toward the democratic republic and had begun to mark their distances from an exaggerated individualism whose antisocial character they deplored. Paul Janet, Elme Caro, Adolphe Franck, and Jules Simon will not figure greatly in the intellectual history of the nineteenth century; none can claim a great originality of thought. But they were all men of considerable intelligence. A sampling of the best products of the Cousinian school, they will give us a good idea of the strengths and weaknesses of mid-century liberal orthodoxy.[19]

In the third chapter we will turn to one of the most important critics of eclectic philosophy, Charles Renouvier. A contemporary of the quartet above, he was repelled by the lack of rigor which he found in their philosophy and by what seemed to him a complaisance of the Cousinians for the existing political order. As initiator of the neo-Kantian movement in France, Renouvier would have a great influence on the general philosophic movement of nineteenth-century France. One of the more original and creative minds of the century, Renouvier was also vitally concerned with the fate of liberalism, and much of his philosophic effort aimed to give it the solid yet flexible foundation which eclecticism could not provide. He would also address himself to the political applications of his neo-criticism to the problems of the Third Republic.

The following chapter will evoke the impact of the founding of the Third Republic on French liberalism, with particular attention to the stimulus it gave to the question of moral education, which became one of the pressing issues of liberalism. It will especially examine the work of two men, trained as philosophers, who had considerable impact on the development of the moral education of the republic: Ferdinand Buisson and Gabriel Séailles. Activists, publicists, and popularizers, they were nonetheless serious thinkers of the second rank.

In the fifth chapter we will examine at length one of the most original philosophers of the second half-century, Alfred Fouillée. Creator of a synthetic methodology aimed at rendering philosophy scientific, Fouillée applied his key concept of the *idée-force* to virtually every subject of contemporary philosophical interest over his long career. One of his main concerns was to furnish an unshakable foundation for political liberalism. Fouillée stood, consciously, at the very crossroads of the intellectual and political forces that were shaping France in his day. He embodied the tensions which were propelling the evolution of liberalism.

Across that border between philosophy and social science which Fouillée so adroitly straddled we find in the next chapter three unequally important advocates of a social scientific liberalism. Standing above the others was Gabriel Tarde, magistrate from Sarlat, Durkheim's chief rival for the direction of French sociology at its birth.

Tarde's sociology was first and foremost a social psychology, and it offered a promising path for the socialization of liberalism. Alfred Espinas and Jean Izoulet demonstrate the variety of paths a socialized liberalism might have taken in this phase of its flux and birth.

The emergence and triumph of Durkheimian sociology, considered in the seventh chapter, mark the definitive conquest of a liberalism founded on sociology. We will see that Durkheim, despite some interpretations, must be considered a liberal; that, indeed, only by doing so can we understand that evolution of liberalism from eclecticism through neo-Kantian idealism to sociology. The implications of Durkheimian sociology for liberalism appear somewhat more clearly in the work of one of the team assembled around the *Année sociologique*, Célestin Bouglé, whom we shall consider in the eighth chapter, along with the legal theory of Léon Duguit, a rather heterodox Durkheimian.

The thinkers we will study, philosophers and sociologists alike, were all moralists, and the new liberalism was a phenomenon of the Left, if we apply the definition of Agulhon and Nouschi:

> the Left is the mental attitude of those who, in the name of a total and unifying humanism, attempt to apply the same laws to collective relations as to private relations, in other words, to subordinate politics to morality instead of distinguishing between them.[20]

If we accept the usual view of the spectrum of French politics, it would be better to say that the new liberals belonged to the *centre-gauche*—and it was this Center-Left which was the vital pivot of political life in the Third Republic. By way of conclusion we will venture some observations of a speculative as well as historical nature on the significance of the evolution of liberalism as we have described it. We will compare the contributions of philosophy and sociology to liberalism and briefly consider their respective interest in the light of today's problems.

II

Eclecticism and Individualism

*E*clecticism—or spiritualism, as some of its proponents preferred to call it—was a peculiarly French philosophical movement which rose to prominence at the beginning of the nineteenth century. The influence of its founder, Victor Cousin (1792–1867), did not extend outside French circles, but within France it was for a long time all-powerful; he and his pupils controlled the official teaching of philosophy until nearly the end of the century.[1] Cousin's eclecticism owed its domination not so much to its intrinsic philosophical merit as to its ability to respond to the needs of a large part of the French intelligentsia. This was particularly true at the beginning of the century, when eclecticism stood in a relationship to the Enlightenment which closely paralleled the relationship of the Restoration monarchy to the Revolution: both were legatees but also drew on earlier traditions and earlier sources of inspiration. They accepted that the Revolution had done some good things which deserved to be preserved, but they also believed that it had fallen into terrible excesses which had to be understood in order to be avoided in the future. Eclecticism was thus in its origins the philosophical equivalent of the Charter of 1814, and indeed the early eclectics believed in the political wisdom of the Charter.

In the ensuing decades the eclectics became the defenders of a mildly progressive liberalism which was the dominant form of French liberalism on the eve of the Third Republic. The main tenets of their liberalism were clearly expressed by Jules Simon in 1859:

I believe that one can sum up all the conditions required for political liberty in three principles: first, written law replaces arbitrary authority in all matters; second, law consecrates and respects the natural and imprescriptible rights of man; and third, which is almost identical to the second, is that government never regards itself as having rights and interests of its own, but rather that it always acts as the servant and minister of the general interest.[2]

The struggle against arbitrary government which had taken the center of the political stage in 1789 was by no means a thing of the past, as the experience of the Second Empire had shown and as the early decades of the Third Republic would continue to make evident, but it was not enough simply to establish a government of laws. Those laws had to be based on principles which assured the protection of the inherent rights of citizens; this was perhaps the main task facing the leaders of the republic in the view of the eclectics. The intellectual foundation on which the eclectics based their liberalism was a variety of natural law doctrine. A liberalism so founded necessarily put a very high value on the rights of the individual, but it was by no means an anarchism or, to use a twentieth-century term, a libertarianism. The liberalism of the eclectics tried to situate the individual in the context of the social order, but the individualist penchant of its philosophical basis made it difficult for them to adapt to the changing needs of that society and thus paved the way for the rise of a new liberalism.

French philosophy had been stung by the charge—hurled from across the channel by Edmund Burke, himself a liberal of sorts, and at home by the decidedly illiberal theocrats Maistre and Bonald—that it was responsible for causing the Revolution and all its unfortunate consequences. Rejecting this charge, Cousin and his associates and pupils (and his pupils quickly became his associates) set out to prove that philosophy was the necessary basis for a stable social order.[3] To do so they reached back into the traditions of seventeenth-century philosophy, foreign as well as French, seeking to recover the Cartesian temper and to revitalize natural law philosophy. They also hoped to reverse the trend which began in that century to separate religion sharply from philosophy:

[Cousin] broke both with the tradition of the 17th century which, by isolating philosophy from religion made it no more than an incidental or accessory matter in the life of humanity, and with the tradition of the 18th century which, banning religion in the name of philosophy and reason, made it inexplicable and incomprehensible.[4]

But by no means did they intend to repudiate all of the eighteenth cen-

tury. Political gains had been made through the Revolution and intellectual gains through the Enlightenment.[5] The political settlement
of the Restoration gave philosophers the opportunity to incorporate
these intellectual gains into the larger legacy of Western philosophy.
Eclecticism was a means of finding what good there was in every
tradition (but its opponents would charge that it lacked a rigorous and
consistent method of deciding what was good and what was bad).[6]

The eclectics wanted to preserve both the political and civil liberties gained through the Revolution and thus opposed any return to
the royal autocracy or the aristocratic privilege of the ancien régime.
They were particularly concerned to oppose the revival of clerical
influence which had been one of the fatal weaknesses of the old
society. But against the almost universal sentiment that it was the religious unbelief of the philosophes which had led to the excesses of the
Revolution they wanted to reaffirm the importance of religion for
society. This put them in that centrist position typical of nineteenth-
century liberalism. It was no small accomplishment on the part of
Cousin to have, in a period of exasperated Catholic extremism, upheld
the banner of religious freedom and intellectual inquiry. Naturally,
the anti-Catholic extremists of the Left would accuse the eclectics of a
base capitulation to the religious authorities, but they were comprom-
isers rather than defeatists, not men who would sacrifice everything to
retain their official positions as Cousin himself proved, but neither
men who abandoned them lightly, with hypersensitive consciences.[7]

Nothing less than the reconciliation of religion and philosophy
was their aim, a position which they considered to have been long
fundamental to Western philosophy.[8] In an age which saw all sorts of
efforts to create new religions (whether avowed as such or not),[9] they
held to the—multiplicity of—existing religions, insisting that religions
are sui generis and cannot be created by intellectual effort. They felt
strongly the unity of the Western religious tradition and were open to
Jewish and Protestant as well as Catholic participation. The bridge
between religion and politics was morality. Pure philosophy could
suffice as a basis of morality for a few superior souls—experience
proved this—but for most men religion remained essential for morality.[10] Morality in turn was the basis of social relations, including
those of the political order.

The second generation of eclectics, with whom we are dealing
here, was less content than the first that the Charter embodied the last
word in political wisdom. They were increasingly attached to the idea
of the democratic republic, considered it a viable possibility for
France, and welcomed it when it came. But they never felt that they
were repudiating their mentor in this deviation from his politics.

Cousin inspired an extraordinary degree of loyalty and admiration in his pupils, which endured throughout their lives.[11] A true philosopher, whose thought was a guide for living rather than an exercise in intellect, Cousin knew how to inspire his pupils with a profound sense of their own individual worth.

The eclectics were particularly faithful to Cousin's example in their determination to treat philosophy primarily as a guide to living well. They were erudite men by the standards of any age, but their erudition was always a means rather than an end in itself. They addressed themselves to a wide public and believed that what they had to say would be meaningful to any educated man. Much of what they wrote was frankly polemical, for they were vigorous critics of all rival philosophies and spent much of their effort trying to stem the rise of both Kantian idealism and Comtean positivism. Given the nature of eclecticism it is not surprising that they were generally more acute in their criticism of others than in the construction of their own system. Many of their objections to positivism, which caused them to be seen as conservatives, have been validated by later experience. Perhaps a future generation may come to admire the austere life of moral dignity which they preached and which, to a remarkable degree, they also practiced.

In order to see the political dimension of eclecticism better we are going to look in detail at four of this second generation: Adolphe Franck (1809–93), Jules Simon (1814–96), Paul Janet (1823–99), and Elme Caro (1826–87). What follows is not meant to be a thorough study of the thought of any of these men (though I hope others will be encouraged to look more closely at them), but rather an attempt to convey the general character of the liberalism of the eclectics. At the same time, I want to convey something of their distinctive interests and viewpoints as individuals and not simply to present a disembodied school of philosophy. It is not possible to say that any one of these was more typical of the movement than the others, and we will try to use their particular cases to illustrate various aspects of the eclectics' liberalism.

For a general view of the liberalism of the eclectics we can do no better than to turn to Adolphe Franck, whose life's work illustrates the unity of the eclectics' moral and political philosophies. Franck was born on 9 October 1809 at Liocourt, in Lorraine.[12] His family was apparently middle class because he was able to pursue a secondary education at the Collège royale of Nancy, where he was quickly marked as a brilliant pupil. His higher education is uncertain but probably took place in a provincial Faculty of Letters, for he did not meet Victor Cousin until he had passed the *agrégation* in philosophy in

1832 or 1833 and had been appointed professor of philosophy at the Collège of Douai.* Franck's professional itinerary brought him to Paris and the Collège Charlemagne in 1840, after he taught at Nancy and Versailles. He attracted enough attention to be elected to the Académie des sciences morales et politiques in 1844, and in 1847 he taught a course in social philosophy at the Sorbonne.

From 1849 to 1852 Franck was a *suppléant* to Barthélemy Saint-Hilaire at the Collège de France† and in 1854 succeeded him as chargé de cours in natural law and international law, becoming titular holder of that chair in 1856. Franck usually devoted one of his annual courses to the analysis and critique of ancient and modern legislation and philosophy pertaining to the relations of peoples. His favorite period was the eighteenth century, where he found ideas and aspirations closest to his own hopes for humanity. In 1863 he became one of the editors of the *Journal des savants*, and he was also a long-time contributor to the *Journal des débats*. An honored member of the educational establishment through four regimes—from the July Monarchy to the Third Republic—he combined, like Cousin, a rectitude of personal life, an independence of opinion, and an adaptability to changing external circumstances.

As a young man, Franck was educated in the Talmud, and he remained a practicing Jew throughout his life. Jewish studies formed an important part of his scholarly work, and he published, among other things, a well-regarded study of the Cabala. Active in the affairs of the Jewish community, Franck would serve terms as vice-president of the Consistoire Israélite of France and as president of the Alliance Israélite Universelle in addition to being chairman of the Société des études juives. His public activity was not confined to Jewish organizations, however, and he was active in a number of groups promoting religious and political causes. The most important of these was probably the Ligue contre l'athéisme, in which he served as founder and director of its official organ, *La paix sociale*. Franck clearly believed that philosophy was of the highest relevance to everyday life, and he

---

* *The agrégation was a competitive examination for selecting men for teaching posts in higher education and in the upper ranks of secondary education. A collège was a secondary school not funded directly by the national government.*

† *The Collège de France, however, was a most prestigious institution of higher education. It awarded no degrees, had no students, though the professors gave a couple of series of lectures each year. Its main purpose was to promote scholarly research.*

practiced what he so eloquently preached. His public defense of religion and morality made him welcome in all but the most reactionary circles; he would, for example, be called upon to lecture under the very Catholic auspices of the Empress Eugénie during the Second Empire.[13] Despite his adaptability, Franck was not a man whom even his enemies—if he ever had any—would have thought of calling a hypocrite, so transparent was his sincerity and goodwill.

Franck's liberalism clearly had its roots in the age of Locke and the Glorious Revolution; it was still in the tradition of what Macpherson has called "possessive individualism."[14] For Franck, the idea that the individual was the owner of himself was at the origins of both moral and political philosophy. Both were clearly expressed in his dictum that one must be neither a master nor a slave if one is to live a moral life or to be free.[15] Without moral liberty, political liberty would be meaningless, even incomprehensible.[16] From this followed his view of government, that it existed for the purpose of helping men to be free and to lead moral lives. This was, so to speak, the psychological base of his thought, the feeling about man's nature from which he started; it was foundation capable of supporting more than one super-structure—as his differences with Locke and the utilitarians would show—and Franck built upon it in a way typical of the eclectics.

The direction taken by Franck was certainly not that of his English contemporaries; one might even say that it was the example of the English which impressed upon him the necessity for a more defensible individualist philosophy on which to base political rights. English utilitarianism was anathema to the eclectics; the effort to found society on the naked self-interest of its members seemed both base and unlikely to succeed. Franck charged J. S. Mill and Herbert Spencer with confusing duty with the general interest, thus losing the idea of duty.[17] From the philosophical point of view, their empiricism was a fatal flaw. We can see here a conflict of national traditions—perhaps somewhat abated in the later eighteenth century with the rise of French sensationalism, but still very much alive—which would shape one of the main French efforts to solve the liberal dilemma of how to reconcile the rights of the individual and those of society. Franck joined the English liberals in defending the free market economy as both right and expedient, but not on the grounds of the sovereign independence of every "empirical" individual.

"Concrete" individuals were too diverse for a felicific calculus to compute a common good out of their diverse desires. Moreover, for Franck, no invisible hand could guarantee to make public good out of all private vices, and all social and political philosophy had to take into account the evil endemic to mankind (as all religions did). A

philosophy which consecrated the rights of the individual could succeed only if it took as its base a kind of abstract individuality: *la
personne humaine.*

> The human personality is also the foundation of political and
> civil liberty; for it is opposed to all despotisms, ... The value of a
> society, of its institutions and laws, is determined by the value
> placed on the human person in that state.[18]

With the eclectics emerged one of the persistent traditions of French
liberalism, the tradition in which the element of religion would be an
enduring fixture: *personnalisme.* For Franck, English extremist individualism was scarcely a lesser danger to liberty than the new authoritarianism which he saw proceeding from the positivistic social
sciences. It would be the great shame of the nineteenth century, he
remarked, if Herbert Spencer should go down in history as its most
representative thinker.[19]

The concept of the human personality was, then, the keystone of
Franck's liberalism, respect for it the "foundation of civil and political
liberty."[20] It was this personality which was the bearer of human
rights, and societies were to be measured by the respect they accorded
its rights: the right to life, to individual freedom, to property, of conscience, of thought.[21] Liberty did not consist of each actual individual
being able to do whatever he desired—whether he thought it right or
wrong—but was an action shaped by duties and obligations which
were also part of the intrinsic character of the human personality.[22]

It was also in this manner that Franck attempted to solve the
liberal problem of the relations of the individual and society. One
could, in the abstract, conceive of a concrete individual, genus homo
sapiens, in isolation from all society—though in practice efforts to do
so usually sneaked society in through the back door, just as Robinson
Crusoe carried it with him, though alone, to his desert island. The
human personality, on the other hand, could only develop in society,
relations with others being part of its intrinsic character.[23] At the same
time, Franck held, society could exist only because the human personality existed and society existed to serve the human personality, so
that there could be no grounds for its absorption into or sacrifice to
society.[24] Thus, as individuals, we had obligations to serve the common
good, and society, through its organ the state, had the right to intervene in our lives for certain purposes. And this necessary harmony
could be established without leaving us open to either the risk of
anarchy or of tyranny.

This would, to be sure, not seem a secure foundation to all other liberals, especially those of a later generation who were no longer convinced by the natural law arguments on which it rested. Toward the end of his life, Franck congratulated himself because there were still defenders of natural law among younger generations,[25] but there can be no doubt they were rather few and scattered. It may be that natural law, like the religious faith that often accompanied it, responds to a human need for which the positivists have not found an adequate substitute. In any case, it would certainly be eclipsed in the nineteenth century.

Within Franck's personalist philosophy there were three key terms which he felt defined the person, the human soul or spirit (*âme*): right, duty, freewill (*droit, devoir, libre arbitre*). These were characteristics of man *qua* man, in all times, places, circumstances, though of course differently realized in actual societies. Human societies, like human individuals, were vastly unequal in value—and likely to remain so in Franck's opinion—but that did not destroy the fundamental equality and identity. Franck was convinced that blacks were and would remain inferior to whites in most respects—beauty, intelligence, moral character—but that this inferiority in no way gave whites a right to enslave blacks.[26] To do so was to fail to respect the universality of the human personality both in the blacks and in oneself. To abase others below the level of men was to abase oneself.

To take Franck's three key terms in reverse order, let us first consider free will. All arguments for and against the existence of free will seemed largely superfluous to him, so necessary was its assumption as a given. Without free will there could be no morality; the very concept of morality made no sense if men were only automatons, unable to make a meaningful choice between good and evil.[27] Christian tradition seemed to ratify philosophy in this conclusion: God's grace and man's choice must move together in the highest matters. Without liberty, then, no morality; without morality one could not speak of the dignity of man. And it was on that dignity that the whole edifice of political and civil rights rested in Franck's philosophy.[28]

From freedom came responsibility, and duty was an equally important word in Franck's social and political philosophy.[29] Not quite so austere a concept as Kant's duty for duty's sake, it was nonetheless central because duty—the obligations every human has to himself and to others—was the distinguishing characteristic of mankind, the one respect in which all men were indeed equal.[30] Both individuals and races were highly unequal in every other respect and likely to remain so. Franck accepted Pascal's remark that there was as great a difference between some men as between men and beasts. The equality of mankind's common parentage had lost its practical force as a result of its subsequent differentiation; equality of duty remained the sole concept capable of maintaining the unity of mankind. Duty and rights were indissolubly connected in this view; equality of rights rested on the God-given equality of duty.[31] Both were necessarily universal and eternal.

That this view of the human person did not support an atomistic individualism can be seen when we turn to Franck's views on property rights.[32] He started from the Lockean base that property rights were natural rights, a consequence of individual liberty. But this did not seem to him a safe or adequate ground for property.[33] Property was a necessity. Without it the family could not exist; without the family there could be no civilization. Society was indeed composed more of families than of individuals.[34] The complex of individual duties had its center in the relations of husband, wife, and children. Franck's repugnance for any communism rested most strongly on his conviction that it destroyed the family even before sweeping away the last vestiges of individual liberty.[35]

Franck's economics were on the whole those of the classical economists. He had reservations about the labor theory of the origins of property, but individual effort, motivated by the needs of the family, seemed to him the only effective motor of prosperity and progress.[36] It was in society's interest to promote and reward effort and not to adopt policies which reward idleness. Because men were unequal in intelligence, talent, industriousness, and luck, the free economy would result in wide differences of wealth, which were therefore not in themselves bad.[37] Effort to create equality of fortune must fail.[38] The capitalist, to the extent that he was a moral man, was a public benefactor, increasing the wealth of society as a whole through his essentially self-regarding activity, and the entrepreneur was a force for the material advancement of civilization. But Franck was far from admiring the pursuit of wealth for its own sake, of its pursuit by all means possible. It must never become more than a means to an end—and the most appropriate end in his view was the security and independence of the family.[39] His mixed feelings were something like those expressed in Zola's *L'argent*.

Not envying the surplus of the rich, his own ideal was of a more modest comfort and independence.[40] The real rewards of this life came from the knowledge of fulfilling one's obligations, whatever one's station in life. In a free society it would be possible for talented individuals to rise above their backgrounds, but those who could not had equal opportunities for satisfaction. More wealth, after all, also meant more responsibilities. Like many successful bourgeois, Franck may have underestimated the difficulties facing those at a lower economic level, but his middle-class ideal was probably closer to the real aspirations of most workers than were the utopias of contemporary socialists.[41] He did agree with the socialists that property needed the protection which society offers it; property was therefore obliged to make sacrifices to society.[42]

His view of individual responsibility for economic welfare was strongly shaped by his moralism. He agreed with Malthus that people had an obligation not to have children whom they did not have reasonable expectations of being able to support.[43] But he could not follow the English extremists who insisted on letting "nature" take its course of eliminating this human surplus. He did suggest that society might have some right to regulate marriage but drew back from pushing this idea very far.[44] Charity was never the bad word in France that a minority of English liberals tried—unsuccessfully even in their own country—to make it. As Jules Simon observed,

> If there are men hard enough to insult poverty, ignorant enough of the conditions of life to believe no one falls into poverty except through their own fault, rigorous enough in holding to the pitiless right to deny that the State has a right to show compassion, they are—thank God—only a tiny minority; society as a whole rejects and condemns such disheartening exaggerations.[45]

Franck even admitted that private charity might not always be adequate and that state charity—though requiring the state to limit the liberty of those who have in order to aid those who have not—was legitimate. French liberals would never accept the *right* of individuals to be succored by the state, but they never repudiated the *moral obligation* of society to attend to the needy.[46] Socialists would insist that men's equality required the recognition of such a *droit au travail;* liberals believed that to accept such a right opened the door to the suppression of economic, and, then, of all liberty, and they argued that the socialist position was more humanitarian than their own in appearance only.

Despite his profound respect for the sanctity of the family, Franck did not claim that it was immune from the intervention of the state. While the family was a refuge from the pressures of society and a defense for the individual against the state, there were inevitably cases in which the rights of family members needed to be defended by the state. The protection of children from abuse and ignorance was a particular concern, not merely for their sakes but because society has a stake in the family.[47] Franck insisted on the necessity of civil marriage, both to mark the separation of church and state and to

make clear that marriage involved the assumption of social obligations, to provide the legal grounds for the exercise of the social interests involved.[48]

One of the obligations of the family, according to Franck, was to
provide the moral education of its children; nowhere else could this
be as effectively done.[49] Beyond this the society was obliged to provide
a certain minimum of instruction necessary to prevent children from
becoming its wards through lack of ability to support themselves.[50]
Moreover, in the increasingly democratic society of the nineteenth
century, the state had an obligation to provide a basic civic education,
to prepare future citizens to understand their rights and responsiblities:

> Public education is, moreover, the education most appropriate to
> free nations and democratic states; it is the education most suitable
> for building citizens and for emplanting the principle of equality
> before the law in the *moeurs*.
> Public education ought to build citizens; domestic education
> ought to make men.[51]

The development of public primary education was an important measure of the progress of the century. Franck believed that it should be
made obligatory.[52] The teaching of philosophy in the secondary and
higher schools was also important to the eclectics because it promoted
social stability and progress.

No believer in automatic progress or in any of the philosophies of
history that sprouted with such great profusion in his day, Franck
embodied the eclectics' interest in history and the particular emphasis
they gave to the history of philosophy. He tried to be familiar with all
of the latter; references to all periods abound in his work. He was
particularly interested in the history of social and political thought,
and he situated himself with respect to its development. It was this
historical perspective which enabled Franck to avoid the pitfalls of
extreme individualism, which gave him confidence that despite both
intellectual and practical difficulties the state had an important role to
play in a free society. The state had, after all, a *mission civilisatrice*.

Unlike his fellow spiritualist Jules Simon, Franck was sufficiently
detached from everyday politics to accept a chair at the Collège de
France under the Second Empire yet interested enough in contemporary issues to turn his lectures to the subject of framing a new constitution after 1871. Early in 1871 he had published a series of three
letters in the *Moniteur universel* in which he vigorously denounced
Prussian militarism and aggressive expansionism, while charg-
ing the late imperial government only with failing adequately to

prepare for the war.[53] There can be no doubt, however, that he favored a state rather more liberal than the Second Empire, though he seems to have approved the direction it was taking in its later years.

Franck did not, however, advocate a state that was weak or was narrowly circumscribed in its activities, and he chided other liberals for limiting the range of state action too drastically.[54] The state's very responsibilities, its fundamental purpose, of protecting the rights of its citizens ensured that it would have a lot to do.[55] There was much which private initiative was not able to undertake yet which was necessary to society. Franck was not thinking merely of immediately practical matters, either; he insisted that the state had obligations to support scientific research, exploration, the arts; it had a cultural as well as a moral responsibility, well in the French tradition:

> There is a third opinion, according to which the State, while insuring respect for the rights of the citizen and those of the whole society, while leaving everyone free to look after their own interests to the best of their intelligence and powers, has yet another task to fulfill. That task consists of satisfying by means of public institutions those sentiments and those higher needs which run the risk of declining or even disappearing if left to private initiative, and of giving an impetus to, and lending support to, those noble faculties which are the honor of a nation and of mankind. This opinion of which we speak does not belong to a school or to a party; it is the practice which has long been followed by the governments of all civilized nations.[56]

The French liberals did not share Jeremy Bentham's opinion that "pushpin was as good as poetry."

In the crisis of regime which followed the collapse of the empire, Franck largely followed the course of which Adolphe Thiers was the political leader.[57] The republic was now the only viable form of government and it would have to be based on universal manhood suffrage. On the other hand it would be necessary to ensure that political leadership remained in the hands of the enlightened middle classes—whose responsibilities could include raising the rest of the country to the level where it could wisely and effectively exercise its rights of citizenship.

The constitution which Franck proposed in 1871–72 was designed to limit the dangers of democracy—particularly of instability and demagogery—while granting it formal recognition.[58] He proposed a chamber of deputies elected by more or less universal manhood suffrage.[59] The chamber's power would be checked by an upper house organized in a sort of corporatist fashion to represent the various great

interests of the nation rather than geographical areas.[60] Franck proposed this as a means of providing the necessary stability to protect the
long-run interests of society in the absence of the monarch who had
played a corresponding role in liberal opinion at the beginning of the
century. The inherent conservatism of this functional upper house
would balance the inherent dynamism of the popular lower house, making possible progress without disorder, stability without stagnation.[61]

Franck's proposal called for a parliamentary executive, chosen by
the legislature and responsible to it alone.[62] He thought that such an
executive would be strong enough to carry out its responsibilities but
unable to become tyrannical. If France had had bad experiences with
republics twice in the past, she had now learned the necessary lessons
and could put into place a regime both stable and progressive, capable
of enduring and capable of being improved. Franck's general contentment with the republic and his concern to keep it on the true liberal
path can be seen in his major work of political philosophy—his *Philosophie du droit civil* of 1886—which summed up the teachings of a lifetime.[63] For the liberal, civil law remained more important than public
law;[64] an era of foreign and domestic peace would offer the opportunity to further liberalize France.

Conscious of being attacked as rearguard defenders of an out-
worn, sentimental creed in an era of hard facts and science, Franck
and the other eclectics devoted a larger part of their published works
to the critique of other intellectual movements. Believing as they did
in the practical importance of ideas, they kept a close watch on the
thought of their contemporaries, sought to work out its consequences,
and bestowed praise or blame as the situation required. Holding to
the supremacy of rational argument, they welcomed the expression of
conflicting ideas, responded with forebearance to bitter attacks, and
practiced the toleration they preached. A vigorous critic of positivism,
which seemed to him little more than a revival of the errors of pre-
Socratic materialism, Franck nonethelesss lamented that the Académie
française had withdrawn its prize from Hippolyte Taine's *Histoire de
la littérature anglaise* (1865) and that it had rejected (an error later
redeemed) the membership bid of Emile Littré, compiler of the century's greatest French dictionary.[65]

The eclectics' battle against positivism seems in retrospect a lost
cause, a swimming against the current of their century, but this does
not mean that they had the worst of the argument or that they were
less rational or even less scientific than the positivists, from Comte on
down. For a sampling of the eclectics' defense against what they saw
as intellectual threats to the foundations of liberalism we are going to

turn now to another philosopher, unknown today, who was a brilliant and widely read critic of positivism and scientism: Elme-Marie Caro.

Caro came from a Catholic family of Breton origin and he would remain loyal to the faith of his youth, although his immersion in philosophy would make him a very undogmatic Catholic.[66] He was born in Poitiers on 4 March 1826, where his father was a professor of philosophy in the local *collège*. Though not the only one of our subjects to grow up in an atmosphere where ideas were valued, he was, I think, the only second-generation philosopher; his own career was directed in his father's footsteps from the beginning. After brilliant studies at the collège in Rennes, Caro was sent to the Collège Stanislas in Paris, where his professors included the liberal Catholic leader Frédéric Ozanam, one of the founders of the Society of St. Vincent de Paul. Caro's secondary studies were crowned with the prix d'honneur of philosophy in the annual Concours général. In 1845 he entered the prestigious Ecole normale supérieure, which marked him among the nation's elite intellectual youth.

On completing his studies at the Ecole normale, Caro won third place in the national competition for the *agrégation* in philosophy. He then taught at a series of secondary schools while preparing his doctoral theses on Seneca and on Saint-Martin, "le philosophe inconnu." Caro received the doctorate in 1854 and was appointed to the Faculty of Letters at Douai, but the ambition to come to Paris led him to take a post at the Lycée Bonaparte in 1858. He became, almost at once, also a Maître de conférences at the Ecole normale and a *suppléant* to the titular professor of philosophy at the Sorbonne, Adolphe Garnier. In 1861 Caro became an Inspecteur de l'Académie de Paris—an influential post in the direction of public education—and in 1864 he succeeded Garnier as professor of philosophy on the Paris Faculty of Letters (Sorbonne). Caro's successful career was crowned by election to the Académie des sciences morales et politiques in 1869 and to the Académie française in 1874.

In addition to writing the many books cited in the bibliography, Caro was a frequent contributor to the *Revue européenne*, the *Journal des savants*, and, especially, the *Revue des deux mondes*, where he appears to have been on close terms with its famous director, François Buloz. Mme Caro (née Pauline Cassin, 1835–1901) was also a contributor to the *Revue des deux mondes*, having published there (pseudonymously) her very popular first novel, *Le péché de Madelaine* (1864). She subsequently had a very successful career writing romantic, but highly moral, novels.

Caro was an excellent writer, still quite readable today; he was so successful as a public speaker from his chair of philosophy at the Sorbonne that his reputation and career were damaged by his popularity. He was so embarrassed by being caricatured in Pailleron's popular comedy *Le monde où l'on s'ennuie* that he henceforth spoke only to his students; even in the classroom, his later years were marred by the political harrassment he suffered from some ill-timed remarks at Edmond About's funeral.[67] But the image of the worldly orator whose audience was sprinkled with fashionable ladies does a great disservice to Caro, as does the fact that he was an outstanding stylist in the French tradition at a time when the rebarbative obscurity of German philosophy was taken as the exterior sign of profundity. Caro was no more highly original than others of his generation of eclectics, but he had an acute mind and was a vigorous and effective controversialist.[68]

In the forefront of his work was the defense of metaphysics as valid, independent, and important. The main enemy of metaphysics was no longer authoritarian theology, but rather materialism—which denied the existence of the subject matter of metaphysics—and positivism—which professed an agnosticism and indifference with respect to metaphysical questions, but which was at bottom also materialistic.[69] Situating himself as a defender of rationalism—"reason is the guide"— Caro sought to demonstrate on philosophical grounds alone the falsity of positivism and materialism.[70] Although as convinced as Franck that those doctrines were dangerous to morality and society, Caro thought that they could be more convincingly refuted if questions of practical impact were set aside.[71] In any case, he insisted, spiritualism did not claim that ideas were true because their consequences were good.[72] He obviously also wished to avoid the charge of attacking the "new" ideas purely in the interest of conserving the existing social order. It was a frequent enough accusation, and one which irritated the eclectic liberals because they believed that they stood for progress, while materialism, claiming to be the latest word in science, was really a retrogression to the early days of Western philosophy.[73]

For the eclectics, metaphysics responded to a fundamental need of the human spirit. No matter how often it was argued out of existence, it kept coming back.[74] Though the realm of scientific knowledge had grown immensely throughout history, and the boundary between physics and metaphysics had been a shifting one, man had persisted in his desire for rational knowledge of matters that remain "beyond physics."[75] Metaphysics had always to respect science but was in no way tributary to it, and Caro insisted that the two should always be in harmony.[76] Metaphysics was nonetheless for him a higher form of knowledge, one which touched, on its other side, on religion. It remained distinct from religion and theology, too, because it relied exclusively on the tools of reason—logic and intuition—without re-

course to revelation. The most important truths of the historical religions were also subject to rational proof, but the nineteenth-century
version of deism did not seek to replace religion, except perhaps for
an elite of philosophers.[77]

Caro's attack on positivism centered on its claim to be scientific
(indeed, to be all science), to describe the domain of the knowable, to
direct all future research, and to be the only method of genuine knowing.[78] His was a two-pronged attack, attempting to show on the one
hand that positivism did not describe in fact how science had worked
in the past or how it worked in the present and, on the other hand,
that the whole colossal edifice of Comte's work led ineluctibly not to
the crowning achievement of positive social science (let alone the
moral science which Comte announced but did not live to expound)
but to the absurdities of his Religion of Humanity—"the strangest of
religions complementing the most arid of sciences"—with its incoher-
ent mysticism.[79]

That science led inescapably to atheism was easily refuted by the
examples of the great scientists of the past and present who were be-
lievers or who even asserted that their science was conducive to faith,
a group easily more numerous than those, like Laplace, who claimed
to do without "the hypothesis of God."[80] More fundamentally, for
Caro, science was simply incapable, because it was a method for understanding the *natural* world, of having anything to say for or against
the existence of God—and Comte clearly went beyond this position.

Even within the legitimate domain of science, Caro thought, the
positivists failed to understand the role of reason and subscribed to a
kind of naive empiricism which was altogether contrary to the true
methods of experimental science.[81] Science was by no means simply
composed of "facts." If it were, it would have been sterile and impotent to develop, which has obviously not been the case. To defend
his view of science Caro could turn to the writings of great scientists
themselves, and Claude Bernard's *Introduction à l'étude de la médicine
expérimentale* (1865) furnished a convincing demonstration of what
the eclectics had been saying throughout the century—that science
proceeds by hypotheses, not simply through the compiling of facts,
that its core of "facts" must always be surrounded by a larger body of
"probabilities" and even "possibilities," that the whole of what is
known would become an unmanageable chaos without the enveloping
framework of speculation.[82] The subsequent progress of scientific
knowledge has overturned some of the eclectics' views on specific
subjects—as it has those of everyone else—but it has only confirmed
their view of the scientific method against that of the positivists. Without being able to stem the positivist tide, the critique leveled by the

eclectics may have helped make the later heirs of Comte more circumspect, more scientific.

The defense of metaphysics against the monopolistic claims of positivism and materialism was certainly important to Caro for reasons that were not purely intellectual. His view of man, especially of man's freedom and responsibility, rested on a metaphysical foundation, an intellectual conviction that amidst the material world conditioned by the laws which science did not cease to discover, man possessed a freedom of thought and action which materialism would deny. Human existence would be indeed meaningless if it could be reduced to a mere play of mechanical forces. This could not be true; man's very conscience revolted against such an idea. Science, whatever surprises it might yet have in store for man, could not destroy human freedom and therefore could not destroy metaphysics.[83]

The concept of human freedom was basic not only to Caro's philosophy but also to his politics. He was a defender of the same sort of moderate liberalism as Franck and the others; like them, he moved away from the *haut-bourgeois* self-satisfaction of the doctrinaires like Guizot and Royer-Collard toward political democracy, convinced that the fullest possible liberty must be extended to all.[84] Caro did not hesitate to take Cousin to task for insisting that France was by temperament a monarchical country.[85] While there were such things as national temperaments, they were not fixed, eternally the same, and indeed they were seldom simple and unified. There was a monarchical tradition in France and there was now also a republican tradition; in the course of the nineteenth century the latter had clearly become predominant. It was wrong to insist, as some monarchists persisted in doing even after 1871, on flouting the present will of the people in the name of some "deeper" national attachment to the monarch.[86] The French, Caro observed, no longer had that feeling for any of their past dynasties which makes monarchies possible.

Caro was deeply shaken by the events of 1870–71, which made the risks of democracy seem greater, but his fundamental ideas were not altered. His first reaction was one of patriotic exaltation and optimism, and he was filled with hope that national sentiment had been revived and partisan conflict stilled, that France would learn from its chastisement and renew itself as Prussia had done after Jena.[87] Disappointed in this hope, saddened by the Commune—he supported Thiers— Caro was not weakened in his commitment to the democratic republic.[88] Like many moderates, he was highly critical of the manner in which the government of National Defense came into existence and conducted itself.

Caro's analysis of the revolution of Quatre Septembre, while not flattering to the exalted republicans who carried it out, was largely confirmed by the subsequent experience of the Third Republic. The national quarrel over the continuation of the war, the trauma of the Commune, and nearly five years of constitutional interregnum could have been avoided, he thought, if the republicans had been willing to consult the nation in 1870 and had not insisted on the revolutionary dictatorship of Paris, that is, themselves. There were, he argued, two kinds of republicans: republicans of principle and republicans of party. For the latter, the republic was the property of a party which possessed a divine right—though of course they could not call it that—to establish the republic in France, to establish it in the name of popular sovereignty, but against the explicit will of the current majority if need be.[89] Caro noted, but did not dwell on, the fact that many of these republicans were lawyers who had chosen to make a living in politics rather than at the bar and that personal ambition and egoism were often evident in the attitudes they took toward the "people" they claimed to represent or, better, to incarnate.[90]

Caro described the revolutionaries of 1870 as guided by historical myth and self-deception. Refusing to believe—perhaps sincerely—that the republic could be established by any hands other than their own, seeing all of France outside Paris as ignorant and reactionary, and with the historical model of the "proper" revolution ever present in their minds, the *exaltés* broke up the hesitant legislature, proclaimed the republic from the Hôtel de Ville, and relived—*in petto*—the great days of 1792 and 1848.[91] If that second version had been—as Marx tartly noted—a farce, what could be said of this third one? That no one should have been surprised to see it suffer the same fate. The French would pass one last time through the cycle of Girondins, Jacobins, and Hébertistes.[92] Caro did not doubt that the fall of the empire had to be proclaimed; the dynasty had in effect abdicated. But he knew the value, the practical political value, of respect for legality. The republicans had continually reproached the empire for the crime of its origins; did they think they could stage their own Second of December with impunity?[93] Had they possessed the courage of their republican convictions and a respect for the nation, they would have found it possible, he thought, to persuade the National Assembly to vote itself out of existence through a call for new national elections and the establishment of a provisional executive which included representatives of the whole nation and not just of the Paris insurrection.[94] The elections would have been no more difficult to conduct than they were a few months later, Caro argued, and the sense of national unity would have been more effectively preserved than it was by the later efforts of self-appointed *représentants en mission*.[95] The fatal gap between Paris and the rest of France would have been avoided, the exaltation of Paris to revolt given a less fertile soil in which to work, and perhaps even a more favorable peace concluded.

Convinced, like Thiers, that "the republic will be conservative, or it will not be," Caro believed that, contrary to the fears of the republicans of party, a republic, not a monarchy, would have emerged from this course of action, one perhaps even more open to reform because lacking the scar of civil war.[96] This view of an *homme de cabinet* rather than an *homme d'action* was full of a sober realism based on a profound knowledge of his countrymen. The sacrifices which a sobered-up Gambetta would make for the republic in 1874–75 would have been more effective in 1870–71, Caro thought. There was no better evidence that France in 1870 was ready for the republic than that she did not turn away from it after the failure of the republican revolutionaries and the bloody upheaval of the Commune, as she had done after the parallel trauma of June 1848. Even the misdeeds of the republicans could not this time prevent the triumph of the republic.

The attitude of Caro toward the Commune of 1871 was typical of the liberals of his generation. He had no sympathy for the revolt but blamed both the leaders who promoted it and the government of National Defense which, unintentionally, prepared the way more than he did the average participant.[97] He severely criticized a government which armed the populace in the face of the Germans out of proportion to the military possibilities of Paris but gave this amateur army nothing to do but draw its *solde*, adding material loss to loss of status when the inevitable day of disbandment came. Demoralization was unavoidable in such an armed force, which may never have been intended to face the foreign enemy, only to serve as a rampart for the republic. The rigors of the siege only added to the psychological gulf between this dubious force and the rest of the country. The Government of National Defense left behind a powder keg which it might not have been able to defuse and which its successors were not altogether unhappy to see explode.

Caro also observed that the leaders of the revolt did not for the most part come from the working class (unlike those in 1848) but rather from the fringes of bourgeois society, from the *bohème* celebrated by Murger in 1852.[98] This new phenomenon of the nineteenth century provoked an interesting analysis from Caro, though he thought wrongly in 1871 to have seen its end. This marginal society of people who played at being writers, artists, philosophers, but who used more of their wits at enjoying life on as little money as possible than in their presumptive vocations, evoked the scorn of the serious thinker, whose life was shaped by his chosen work. More talk than performance, the *bohème* naturally preferred being applauded to the labor of being right. It was a fertile soil for the nourishment of streetcorner demagogues—and of those who would follow them, like the Maurice of Zola's *La débâcle.*

It is true that Caro did not do justice to the liberal element in the Communal revolt or recognize the middle-class elements in it and the degree to which similar sentiments existed in major provincial centers. The question of centralization and local rights was clearly evoked by the Commune at its beginning, but in such a fashion as to make it difficult for most liberals, whatever their views on local government, to pay much attention to it. Caro had lived through this all once before, in 1848; he had no desire to see 1851 repeated as a consequence. The Commune could only appear to him as another effort to rule France by means of the Paris mob; it was certainly not a proletarian revolt against capitalism; it had to be defeated if a liberal France was to emerge.

Even in the throes of national defeat and civil war, amidst all the intellectual threats to liberalism, Caro and the eclectics carried a buoyant optimism into their old age. They exhibited no sense of the impending doom of Western civilization. Men of the mid-century, they carried into its closing decades something of the measure, the *bon sens,* the modesty and self-restraint of an earlier civilization.[99] The frequent charge that they were doctrinaires, blind to the rapidly changing realities of their society, does not stand up to a reading of their works. It is true that they were not enthusiastic about everything they saw going on around them, and their forecasts of disasters to come have only too often been verified by experience. As well as most, they strove to be realistic and hopeful.

It was the rootedness of their ideas in the Western tradition which made this combination possible in an age of upheaval. Caro had a strong sense of the continuity and unity of Western history which was the backbone of his distrust of proposals for rapid change or for the rejection of the ideas of earlier centuries. For him, that continuity was a progress, obviously a progress in science and in the industrial arts, but also a moral progress, the gradual elaboration of individual freedom and the construction of a more just society.[100] But it was a progress that was far from unified and continuous, and which was certainly not guaranteed.[101] Caro saw a stream of fatalism issuing from Hegel's philosophy of history which was false to all experience as it was unsound in metaphysics. The intellectual inconsistency of those socialists who adopted related philosophies of history while proclaiming an activist struggle for a freer society seemed incomprehensible to him. But reason had suffered its setbacks in the past, and man's long experience gave him hope for the future as well.

All the eclectics were immersed in the history of philosophy, but the one whose liberalism was most shaped by and reflected in his historical study was Paul Janet.[102] Janet was one of the few native Parisians among the subjects of this work (Buisson and Séailles were the others), having been born on the rue St.-Honoré on 30 April 1823, the youngest of four children. His father, who died when Paul was only nine, kept a bookstore and also sold music. Janet's interest in philosophy was awakened at the Lycée St.-Louis. In 1841 he entered the Ecole normale supérieure, where his most important philosophy teacher was Emile Saisset, a collaborator of Victor Cousin. Janet was received first in the nation in the philosophy *agrégation* of 1844. Cousin, who was president of the jury, took the young man as his secretary during the next academic year. Janet later remembered that he had not found the great man a very warm personality, but there is no doubt that the experience gave a considerable stimulus to his career.

Janet's first teaching position was at the Collège royal of Bourges (1845–48), where he became a close friend of Michel de Bourges, a prominent leader of the republican opposition to the *monarchie censitaire*. The year 1848 was an important year personally rather than politically for Janet, for he gained his second *agrégation* (in literature this time), was awarded his doctorate, and married a cousin he had known since childhood, beginning fifty-one years of exemplary married life. With the doctorate in hand, Janet now became a professor of philosophy on the Faculty of Letters at Strasbourg, where he had an enormous success, especially with a series of lectures on the family, first delivered in 1855.

In 1856 Janet returned to Paris to accept the chair of logic at the Lycée Louis-le-Grand. In 1864 he was named professor of the history of philosophy at the Sorbonne and was elected to the Académie des sciences morales et politiques. According to Emile Boutroux, who would himself become one of the leaders of the neo-Kantian movement in the French university, Janet's lecture course of 1867 marked the beginning of the serious study of Kant in France. Janet would be especially appreciated by generations of students for his ability to render the philosophies of Kant and Hegel clear and comprehensible. The closest Janet came to being involved in politics was a brief period of service as an advisor to Jules Simon when the latter was minister of public instruction in 1871. That year also marked the beginning of Janet's participation in the Ecole libre des sciences politiques, perhaps the most important training ground for public servants during the Third Republic.

The eclectic succession passed to Janet in 1887 when he followed Caro into the chair of philosophy at the Sorbonne. In addition to his teaching and writing, Janet served the Republic on the Conseil supérieur de l'Instruction publique from 1889 until 1896, when his health began to fail. During the last two decades of the century he was probably the dominant force in philosophy education in France, a role in which his openness to novelty and his encouragement to the young contributed to the flourishing interest in philosophical study. While he appeared to the younger generations as a survival of the past, the last of the eclectics, he and they were on rather good terms of mutual respect. Janet seems to have seen in the young neo-Kantians a commitment to the search for truth similar to his own, and they did not cause him to despair of the future of philosophy.[103] To a degree, he admitted the justice of their criticisms of the eclectics and regretted that Cousin had not imparted a more clear-cut direction to the movement.[104] He felt that it was unfortunate that the eclectics had not drawn more inspiration from the metaphysics of Maine de Biran, who appeared in retrospect to have been the outstanding French philosopher of the beginning of the century.[105] Perhaps, had they done so, their eclecticism would not have been so readily eclipsed by the criticist and idealist wave that became dominant in the early Third Republic.

An examination of the modern history of Western philosophy shows, Janet insisted, that the eclectics were the direct heirs of the eighteenth-century Enlightenment, rather than a reaction against it or a throwback to the seventeenth century as some had claimed. This was especially true of their political philosophy, where they carried on the defense of the natural rights of man.[106] He was particularly at pains to associate them with the Revolution of 1789, whose principles they wholly approved; the Declaration of the Rights of Man was the charter of their politics.[107] As he pointed out, this tradition was exempt from the exaggerations of later extremist individualism, never proclaiming unrestricted rights but always insisting on the social obligations of individuals.[108] Like the other eclectics, he seems to have been satisfied that the assertion that the individual's exercise of his rights is limited by his obligation to respect the identical rights of other individuals is sufficient both practically and theoretically to solve this basic issue. He was certainly not unaware of the antisocial character of some extreme claims of the autonomous individual.

There is no doubt, however, that the focus of the eclectics was on the grounding of freedom and that they saw this emphasis as continuing a long tradition of Western thought. The principal modern contribution to this effort was the concept of the human personality, bearer of certain natural rights.[109] It was this idea which had proved so fruitful in the American and French revolutions and which reached its fullest theoretical expression in the metaphysis of Maine de Biran.[110] When this ground for freedom began to seem insecure to younger generations, liberal thought would begin to turn away from the path taken by the eclectics.[111]

In his historical study of political philosophy, Janet concluded that there were really only two main schools, both present throughout history: the absolutist and the liberal.[112] While each of these could be subdivided into various branches, the fundamental dichotomy still reigned. In nineteenth-century France, he recognized on the one side the aristocratic and royalist school and the socialist school and on the other, the democratic school and the constitutional and liberal school.[113] The steady pressure of political events in France tended more to produce political parties than schools of political thought.[114] The eclectics, with members in both of the liberal camps, appeared to him as the main intellectual supporters of liberalism, and this judgment was certainly correct for the opening two-thirds of the century.

Outside all the schools of his day was Alexis de Tocqueville. Janet, who was probably his greatest admirer among the eclectics, credited Tocqueville with reviving concern for the threats posed to individual liberty not merely by governments but also by the mass of society.[115] As Caro observed in 1876: "Right is menaced today not so much by the tyranny of individuals as by that of anonymous and irresponsible masses."[116] While Tocqueville tried to view the rise of democracy from the heights of his aristocratic detachment, the eclectics felt more keenly the ambiguities in the relations of middle-class liberalism to democracy. Janet situated Tocqueville intellectually in the tradition of the great observers, men like Machiavelli and Montesquieu.[117] In an age given to broad theoretical constructions, to generalizations embracing the whole of human history, Tocqueville was a man of middle-range generalizations, trying to develop the importance for his own age and the decades immediately ahead of what he had observed.[118] His weakness as an observer came from his being less well nourished in historical observation than the other great members of this tradition.[119] But all liberals had now to be concerned with the problems of democracy, and they owed a debt to Tocqueville for opening a new stage of the discussion.[120]

For Janet, the most pressing question—and one for which he felt he lacked a sure answer—was whether socialism was an inevitable by-product of democracy or whether it was a passing phase, one of the birth pangs of the new democratic order.[121] It was certainly an important question, which might decide whether liberty would survive the rise of democracy.[122]

Looking at the history of political thought, Janet was impressed by the persistent close association of questions of morals and politics. It was a reciprocal relationship, each influencing the other from time to time. The question of the proper relationship between private and public morals was a perennial one and had received every possible answer from total disassociation to total identification. Janet thought that there was an important distinction to be made, one which did not deny their interrelationship but insisted on a difference of roles. The goal of the individual was virtue; the goal of the state was justice.[123] Virtue is a quality which may be possessed by individuals; their moral freedom enables them to pursue it. But virtue must not be the goal of the state: "nothing is more dangerous."[124] The state which takes virtue as its goal must try to impose it on its citizens, but by its very definition virtue cannot be imposed and the effort to do so necessarily makes the state tyrannical, suppressing the freedom of conscience of all. Past attempts to impose an official religion on a minority—the sad record of Louis XIV, for example—were good examples of this. The growing recognition of equality of rights, Janet believed, closed this path to the state, which increasingly recognized an obligation to create a world in which people of differing opinions may seek to live virtuous lives.

Nineteenth-century French liberals did not go so far as to say that matters of private morals must be beyond the range of governmental concerns. But a government should not go beyond the promotion of a morality based on reason—which is alone universal—to support a morality based on revealed religion, however much supported by a majority.[125] The liberals agreed with the ancient observation that virtue was necessary in a republic; a virtuous citizenry was necessary to the survival of a free society.[126] For unless individuals have a mastery of self that fits them to live amongst their equals, they will prove unable to govern themselves and will inevitably surrender their liberty to one despotism or another. One reason the liberals were suspicious of everyday materialism as well as of the philosophic variety was their fear of its tendency to dissolve social obligations in the pursuit of individual pleasure.[127] They were not ascetics preaching withdrawal from the world, but moralists who insisted upon the difference between freedom and self-indulgence.

Janet was still optimistic enough to believe that the excesses of individualism the nineteenth century had witnessed were not fatal, that they were part of the process of adjusting to a degree of freedom new in human experience. The justification of the excesses in the name of reason was a matter for concern, but not for alarm; the cure for the excesses of reason was more reason, not less.[128] The eclectics carried through the nineteenth century the faith in reason of the eighteenth. New irrationalisms might arise, often proving to be old ones in new clothes, but the past gave hope to the future. The advance of reason had often been checked but was always resumed. In the present dark age that hope seems dimmed, but it will be infinitely worse to lose sight of it altogether.

Of the eclectic philosophers descended from Victor Cousin only one had an important political career as well as notable success as a writer: Jules Simon, who has become almost the symbol of the pre-1870 republican, carried to the heights of success at the end of a career, when he was already somewhat démodé in thought and manners.[129] Like the other eclectics, Jules Simon was of middle-class origin. His father was a cloth merchant who had converted from Protestantism in order to marry a Breton Catholic. Perhaps because of his physiognomy, anti-Semites like Edouard Drumont would later claim that Simon's father was Jewish. Born François-Jules Suisse on 27 December 1814 at Lorient (Morbihan), Simon grew up in the Catholic conservative atmosphere of Brittany, receiving his secondary education at the Collège royal of Vannes. He showed a marked interest in religion as a youth and might well have developed a vocation had it not been for the influence of his father. His ambivalence about his origins led him to adopt the name Jules Simon, marking the break with his upbringing.

Instead of entering the church, Simon went to Paris and entered the Ecole normale supérieure in 1833. In that studious atmosphere, philosophy came, quite gradually, to replace religion as the guiding force in his life. Simon became a collège professor of philosophy at Caen in 1836, moving to Versailles in 1837, when he also began to write for the *Revue des deux mondes*. Simon's academic career would soon give way to politics, but throughout his political career he maintained an interest in educational questions. Elected to the chamber from the Côtes du Nord in 1848, he resigned in 1849 to accept appointment to the Conseil d'Etat. Active among the moderate republicans who held power for a time in 1848, Simon refused the oath of loyalty to Louis Napoleon after the coup d'etat of 1851 and remained in opposition throughout the Second Empire.

Deprived of public employment, Simon lived, at least in part, by writing extensively on topics of political and social interest.[130] During this self-imposed internal exile, he articulated the ideas he would later have the opportunity to try to put into practice. Never considered a particularly profound thinker, though serious and well-informed, he was a publicist of ideas rather in the manner of the lesser philosophes of the eighteenth century. His voluminous writings made him perhaps the most widely known advocate of the liberal republic during the empire. No one presented the liberal position with greater clarity and simplicity.

Writing was not enough to satisfy Simon's ambitions, however, and he returned to political action during the "liberal empire," winning election to the Corps législatif in 1863, the same year he was chosen by a rather more exclusive electorate to be a member of the Académie des sciences morales et politiques. After the revolution of 4 September 1870 he joined the Government of National Defense as Minister of Public Instruction, Religion, and Fine Arts. Elected to the National Assembly in 1871, he served as minister of public instruction under the presidency of Adolphe Thiers. When the new constitution was adopted in 1875, Simon was chosen by the Assembly to be one of the life senators. The same year brought him another life honor, election to the Académie française. The climax of Simon's political career came in December 1876, when he became premier and minister of the interior. His dismissal by President MacMahon precipitated the Seize Mai crisis, one of the decisive episodes in the formation of the Third Republic.

In addition to his many books on social, political, and religious questions, Simon was an indefatigable political journalist, serving as editor of the *Siècle* (1875–77) and of the *Gaulois* (1879–81). He also contributed to many other papers and periodicals, such as the *Matin*, the *Temps*, the *Figaro*, and the *Journal des débats*. All the eclectics believed that thought should make a difference in men's lives; all of them were activists as well as intellectuals. Jules Simon was undoubtedly the most activist and the least intellectual of the group studied here, but through his activism he brought the eclectics' liberalism to a much wider audience and gave it a political as well as an intellectual influence.

The "self-evident truths" of natural law occupied the same central place in political philosophy for Simon as for the other eclectics. These truths were considered universal and accessible to all men. Their application had, of course, to vary with circumstances, and it was the task of statesmen to determine what was appropriate at a given moment.[131] But it was also the task of statesmen, as Simon saw it, to move toward the ideal, to seek to bring positive law more closely into harmony with natural law.[132] This was not an easy task, as revolutionaries often forgot; man's ignorance and immorality posed obstacles at every step, and they could be vanquished only gradually. To reach the goal of maximizing liberty, the statesman, Simon argued, must be reconciled to taking many little steps; the great leap forward always ends in backward motion.

The key task of the statesman was to discover how much liberty his compatriots were prepared to exercise, and one of the great practical advantages of representative government was that it facilitated this determination. For Simon, it was historical experience which shaped the situation of a people. A people accustomed, as were the French, to relying on the central authority in the least of public affairs had to acquire greater habits of self-responsibility before they could do without the tutelary power.[133] Liberty being, however, the only school of liberty, the statesman would seek to lead his countrymen to take more responsibility for themselves. One way to do this—little tried in France—was through the promotion of local government.[134] Rather than by a gradual process, though, France had progressed in liberty through a series of fits and starts, oscillating between extremes of liberty and of repression.[135] There were rare historical moments when men seemed to rise to the full capacity which was in them. For Simon, the earliest stages of the Revolution of 1789 were such moments—reaching a culmination in the night of the fourth of August—but even there the French soon overreached themselves and the resulting anarchy gave way to a renewed tyranny.[136]

This position was clearly consistent with Simon's measure of the legitimate activity of government, which was *necessity*.[137] Government had the right, indeed the obligation, to do what needed to be done and which individuals and voluntary groups of individuals were unable to do.[138] This body of activities was thus historically determined; Simon's message was that with the growth of freedom the range of governmental activities would be progressively reduced, though it would never disappear entirely, for evil and the need to repress it will always exist.[139] Simon did not, any more than did the other eclectics, advocate an unrestricted individualism, which would be an immoral anarchy. The individual had obligations which required him to make sacrifices to the common good; he could even be coerced to do so if need be.[140] Liberalism required the conciliation of the individual and society.[141] But for this generation of eclectics, the practical problem presented by French conditions was not to reconcile the individual to his collective responsibilities but to urge him to accept more individual responsibility and to diminish the sphere of authority.[142] The excess of individualism would be a greater concern of later generations. This marked a significant difference between them and the later generation of liberals formed in the society of the end of the century, but it was a difference of degree, not a reversal of values.

Because of Simon's more pressing interest in the issues he had to face as a politician, we can see more clearly in his work something of the social and economic factors which influenced the liberalism of the eclectics. The question of property found a larger part in his work

43

than in that of the others. Liberty and property, Simon insisted, were related in theory and in practice. Every man understood intuitively (for the eclectics intuition was an important aspect of reason, not an enemy) that he was his own property. All infringements on liberty could be shown to involve a denial of this basic truth. Historical experience, in Simon's opinion, showed that attacks on property have been one of the main means by which liberty has been attacked. Indeed, this had been one of the leitmotifs of history.[143] The socialism of 1848 thus seemed to him merely a revival of past errors rather than an expression of new needs.

Simon followed Locke in basing the right of property on labor, not sharing Caro's views of the dangers in this argument, and he found no difficulties in moving from this to the defense of accumulation beyond individual needs, transfer, and inheritance. The existing unequal division of property did not imply any inequality of rights, and it seemed to Simon to flow naturally from the differences in capacity and effort of men, compounded by the long historical experience of those differences. It was a natural inequality, and any social efforts to redress the balance seemed likely to destroy property, and with it, freedom.

This is not to say that he thought the existing distribution of property to be ideal or to be the only possible distribution compatible with freedom. The very relation between property and freedom made it necessary for all men to have some property if they were to develop their capacities to the fullest, and the social problem was now to render property *accessible* to all.[144] The Revolution was important precisely because it took the basic first steps in this direction, destroying the privileges of aristocratic property and the *mainmorte* of the church, leading to the establishment of common property rights.[145] On the practical level, the distribution of the *biens nationaux* also contributed to the spread of property. While the Revolution primarily affected landed property, the nineteenth century would also see the increasing liberation of other forms of property, with obviously stimulating effects on the economy.[146]

The majority of the French population were still peasants in Simon's lifetime, people to whom property meant land, and he thought that it was to France's advantage to remain primarily an agricultural country. The variety and fertility of her soils, the obliging character of her climate, the experience of her people, seemed to him to predestine France to an agricultural vocation. Industry was needed, but should remain secondary; there was no reason to imitate England, whose situation was quite different.[147] Germany was not yet an industrial threat, and Simon did not suspect that his recommendation would have gravely threatened France's position in Europe, a position of which he was as jealous as any other patriot. Simon recognized that not everyone who wanted land and was willing to work for it would be able to acquire it within France and that an excessive subdivision would be economically harmful. He was inclined to think that for those to whom land ownership remained the highest value there were still sufficient opportunities in the world. (He did not live to hear the prophecies of the dangers to come from the "closing" of the American frontier.)

So industry was necessary, and indeed one of the advantages of modern society was that it increased the forms of meaningful property. For an increasing proportion of society, the *mobilier* would take the place of the *foncier,* * adding not only variety but flexibility to property holding, spreading wider the foundations of individual liberty.

Simon did not attach any special advantage to owning the "instruments of production." It was in the nature of the modern economy that most would never be able to possess this kind of property—though it would in fact become more widespread than he foresaw. He believed that liberty could be supported on other forms of property, some of which were only beginning the great expansion they would see in the next century: a house or an apartment, a savings account, an insurance policy, rights in a pension fund. He was among the first to recognize that these, too, are forms of property and that they can assist men to a greater independence. Simon did hope that many workers would acquire a share of ownership in business through their savings and investment and through the actions of farsighted entrepreneurs. He was also an active supporter of cooperatives, though he suspected they would lack the drive of individual entrepreneurship and the motive for risk-taking which played such a role in modern progress.[148] He even expressed a limited support for trade unions.[149] On the whole he seemed to have found mid-century assaults on property no more than the growing pains of a freer world, pains which would not prevent the progress of liberty.

Simon's arguments about the unity of property and liberty serve to remind us of the historical origins of nineteenth-century liberalism, origins of which the liberals were well aware, and which must be taken into account if their positions are to be understood. A sense of the oppression exercised by the privileged aristocracy and by the divine-right monarchy of the ancien régime was still very strong in Simon, though he had never lived under it himself.[150] He and his fellows understood very well the feeling of their elders that under a regime which could tax and spend and regulate without any accounta-

---

*Foncier is real estate; **mobilier** covers all other forms of property.*

bility to or consent from the governed there could be neither freedom nor property.[151] That situation had come to an end because enough men became convinced that it was both unjust and unreasonable. The fact that this Revolution contained a revolution of the peasantry as well as a revolution of the bourgeoisie was further evidence for the liberals' claim that the liberal view was based on a natural understanding accessible to, and equally valid for, all men.

Natural law also dictated for Simon the organization of the family appropriate to a free society: the monogamous paternalistic family. Drawing his inspiration from classical antiquity as well as from Christianity, Simon propounded a view in which the family was the locus of moralization, the place in which each new generation learned the responsibilities and rights of human beings. He thought that the production of moral beings required the combination of the love of the mother and the authority of the father—a division of labor created by nature, rediscovered by some twentieth-century psychologists. The moral function of the family was not confined to the task of child rearing; the relations of husband and wife were also a school of morality. Of all the relations among adults this one is given a special moral character by the nature of the perpetual obligations—the only perpetual ones recognized by most liberals—which were assumed by both spouses.

Because Simon believed that there was no difference between private and public morality, men would have to become self-disciplined in order to be worthy of freedom in the public sphere.[152] The family was the best school in which they, as children and as adults, could acquire that self-discipline. Yet there was, Simon insisted, a fundamental difference between the family and the state. Those authoritarian social philosophers who justified the divine-right monarchy on the model of the patriarchal family were altogether in the wrong.[153] It was precisely because authority existed in the family that it ceased to be needed in the state. "The liberty of the citizen rests on the authority of the father. A man must be powerful and respected in his family if he is to be powerful and respected in the State."[154] Paternal authority could only be exercised over unequals. Otherwise it was oppression and servitude. Once men were mature, it became an offense against their rights. Just as nature had destined males to political rights and duties, so, according to Simon, had it given them the responsibility of exercising order within the family.[155] Women and children had rights, but they were rights of an inferior order. The exercise of paternal authority was not without its limits; Simon was no advocate of the Roman *patria potestas*, and he agreed that society can and must intervene within the family to protect the rights of women and children—

to the extent, for example, of forcing fathers to send their children to school.

Simon did not think that women would or should ever have a place in public life. Nature had not given them the virile qualities needed for such an arduous life, and he would make no exception, even for exceptional cases. The social role of women was very important, but it was essentially subordinate to that of the man. He did lament that the women's role was not being filled as effectively as it might be and argued that society would benefit from giving women a better education, though certainly a very different one from that which men needed.[156] Simon's views on the inequality of women were largely shared by the other eclectics, indeed, by virtually all males of his time. There were some nuances, however; Franck, for example, insisted that parental authority must be a shared responsibility and in general (perhaps because of his Jewish background) was prepared to grant women more power within the family if not within the state.[157] Seeing marriage as a vital protection for women, without which they would be subjected to the cruelest oppression (certainly true for the nineteenth century), Franck nonetheless favored divorce, within fairly strict limits.[158] On the other hand, a great gap separated the eclectics from that idolater of women Auguste Comte, who insisted that marriage should indeed be a perpetual vow to the extent of prohibiting physical separation or even the remarriage of either spouse after the death of the other. The greatest problem of the early liberals' view of the family was not that they were altogether wrong about the social role of the family—they may have been largely right—but rather their conviction that only a certain internal model of it was "according to nature." For the most part they did not push their examination very deeply, being content with what few contemporaries would have thought to reject; but this would be a weakness, for what people would see as "natural" is subject to change, and the very concept of natural law could be undermined if stronger arguments were not prepared to support it.

The values of the eclectics' liberalism were middle-class values, not in the sense of promoting the economic and social interests of the middle classes, but in the sense that only the middle classes had yet been able to move very far toward realizing them in practice. They were values which were meant to shape domestic life as well as the political sphere; the political philosophy of liberalism was not something totally abstracted from everyday life. The freedom which the liberals sought was a way of living, and it seems to me appropriate to make some observations about what liberty meant to them in everyday terms: (1) First, and perhaps foremost, it meant not being a dependent; the economic goal was not riches so much as independence. (2) Independence also meant having a home of one's own, a place of security from the pressures of the outside world; the "bourgeois interior"[159] was as distinct from the noble's palace as from the workman's hovel. (3) Having a home meant having a family, which gave a man the opportunity to exercise his capabilities through the exercise of authority over others but counterbalanced this power with the responsibility for their welfare. (4) The profession and the home also provided opportunities for the individual to develop his capacity for moral life; freedom was the essential prerequisite for moral action in all aspects of life. Living in accord with the moral law produced a justified contentment, which sometimes degenerated into self-satisfaction. (5) The free man also possessed the opportunity to become involved in public life—if he so chose, for liberals had mixed feelings about politics, and for many involvement was a duty but a somewhat unpleasant one. (6) Liberty entailed education: knowledge (not necessarily formal schooling) was essential to the individual's self-government; it enabled him to give his informed consent in public and private affairs. Education also was essential to that form of liberty which is freeing oneself from the domination of the passions (of all kinds). (7) The free man had to learn to practice moderation in all things. In politics as in domestic life this meant recognizing that all things desirable are not possible for the individual or the society at any given moment; they accepted that we must be content with the relative good. In domestic life this meant living within one's means; in political life it meant accepting the wisdom of Edmund Burke's observation that "liberty, too, must be limited in order to be possessed." (8) Liberty also meant having the possibility of planning and making provision for the future, which was one of the distinctive features of the modern world. (9) Far from providing a license to live in any conceivable fashion, liberty as the eclectics conceived it required men to live a life of inner and outer dignity, of a seriousness worthy of man's character as a rational animal. (10) Finally, it should be evident from many of the above points that the eclectics considered liberty to be essentially a masculine attribute; to be free involved a degree of effort and struggle of which they did not think women capable, indeed, from which they thought women ought to be protected. From an intellectual point of view their natural law philosophy was a shaky ground on which to base this prejudice about woman's place in home and society. But we should not forget that the birth of liberty in Western society was a struggle which would probably never have been launched if equality of the sexes had been a prerequisite; only later would that equality become a widely shared aspiration of liberty.

In French liberal circles it may be, however, that the paternalistic model of the family outlived the natural law philosophy as a basis for liberalism, at least in advanced intellectual circles. The natural law argument for human rights, despite the objections raised against it in the nineteenth century both by liberals and their opponents, certainly made the greatest practical contribution to the advancement of individual liberty of any philosophic school.[160] Long after it ceased to satisfy the intelligentsia, it remained the most effective way of conveying ideas of rights to the masses. It is intuitively graspable with no great philosophic training; it has both a scientific and a moral sound that has never lost all its appeal. In this work we are concerned precisely with that intelligentsia which found the idea of natural law too vague, which indeed found no proof that there was such a thing.[161] To Kantians and positivists alike it seemed a metaphysical chimera, not a solid ground of liberty. The ideas of what constituted freedom would not change so much as the arguments by which those ideas were defended.

The philosophical weakness of eclectic liberalism was probably that the restraints which were imposed on the individual were not really effectively grounded in natural law philosophy but depended on the continued strength of a place in the Judeo-Christian religious tradition, which enjoined consideration for others.[162] This philosophical weakness may have been a practical strength, and religious tradition the most effective counterweight to the anarchist tendencies inherent in liberalism. The eclectics had the additional advantage of knowing that religions cannot be fabricated by the intelligence and that the philosophical spiritualism which guided their lives would not be effective with the masses. They understood the power of transcendence better than the sociologists would later. They already saw that the rejection of the transcendent meant making man into his own god, and that far from being a liberation, this opened the way to a new tyranny, one from which there might be no escape.[163] Auguste Comte offered them this glimpse of a possible future for man, when human society should come to be regarded as the highest thing there is in reality.[164]

This was a question which would become increasingly important with the rise of democracy. If the masses in a liberal democracy became convinced that there was nothing higher than self-interest, liberty would decay into anarchy, making certain the return of tyranny. The eclectics were aware that people must believe in the essential justice of the society in which they live, and they perhaps underestimated how hard this would be in a period of more rapid social change, but they were so convinced of the universality of man's aspiration for freedom that they could not imagine that recent progress would be lost.[165] Their universalism may have made them less attentive than following generations to the socioeconomic transformation of French society, but in compensation it gave them a clearer perspective on the long-term consequences of ideas.

Adolphe Franck, Jewish social philosopher and reformer; Elme Caro, Catholic moralist and literary critic; Paul Janet, historian of philosophy; and Jules Simon, philosophy professor and eminent republican politician—these four men have illustrated the main facets of the liberal philosophy dominant at the birth of the Third Republic. Our rapid sketch of their thought should be enough to convince us that the conventional picture of the French liberal is defective on several points, though accurate enough on others. The free and responsible individual was certainly their highest ideal, as it must be in any philosophy that can be called liberal.[166] But this value was not pushed to logical extremes at the expense of all other values. There was no equivalent of Herbert Spencer among the French liberals, no Max Stirner; nor was there an equivalent of Social Darwinism.[167]

In many ways the eclectics had become conservatives by the 1870s and 1880s, but there were things worth conserving, not least of them an individual freedom unprecedented in the experience of continental Europe. They were defenders of a social order in which the middle classes were predominant, but these were middle classes much more broadly based than in the past, more open, more active, and with an activity which brought moral and material benefits to a greater proportion of society than ever before, a process that was only beginning.[168] Enemies of efforts to bring about radical transformations of the human condition, yes; but we know by experience today what they understood by reflection then—that such efforts are more likely to lead to tyranny than to liberation.[169] Rather straightlaced moralists who challenged the indulgences of the flesh (though not without a sympathy for man's weakness), they would certainly be out of place among the intelligentsia of today's hedonistic society, but then we seem bent on proving the truth of their observation that license is not liberty. Defenders of reason and rationality, they recoiled at efforts to make man the plaything of natural forces beyond his control, fearing this would undermine his sense of moral responsibility. Men of a somewhat austere dignity whose time had passed by 1870, certainly; but it is less certain that we have altogether benefited from its passing or that the twentieth century has understood liberty better than they did.

III

Charles Renouvier: Critical Philosophy
and Liberal Democracy

*I*t has often been observed that the French, more than any other people, refuse to be content with pragmatic solutions to empirical problems and always seek a theoretical foundation upon which to build their understanding and—if need be—their action. They have even been charged with preferring the neat theoretical formulation to the possibility of practical action. But if this has sometimes been true, it is also true that the French have understood better than others that action proceeds from thought and that if man is ever going to substitute—even in a limited fashion—reason for emotion in the conduct of his public affairs he must develop an intellectual foundation for his action.

This need was certainly felt acutely at the turn of the century among those members of the middle classes who felt the inadequacy of the old egoistic individualism and the threat of the new collectivist socialism. As Henry Michel observed in 1897: "They are quite right, these worried observers of the present day who typify its appetite for doctrine in asking for at least a choice between collectivism and something else, something else than the chill theorems of orthodox political economy."[1] In Michel's opinion that "something other" was already available in the critical philosophy of Charles Renouvier (1815-1903). The political implications of Renouvier's neo-Kantianism had already been worked out in his *Science de le morale* (1867), which remains the unrecognized masterpiece of nineteenth-century political philosophy.[2] Renouvier had himself gone on to illustrate the concrete applications of his theory in a series of almost-weekly articles for his *Critique philosophique* (1872-89). For his part, Michel, beginning with his justly celebrated thesis, *L'idée de l'Etat* (1895),[3] spent several years propagandising the idea that Renouvier had furnished a basis for what might be called a "democratic liberalism" which could compete with the democratic socialism that was being developed under the leadership of men like Jean Jaurès, who was also influenced by Kantianism. Much the same line was taken by Jules Thomas when he reedited Renouvier's *Manuel républicain de l'homme et du citoyen* (originally published in 1848) in 1904.[4]

If Renouvier was ever to be recognized as the "philosopher of democracy" he certainly needed help in popularizing his ideas. It was not that he wrote badly or obscurely but that he lacked the elegance and wit, the style, which enabled lesser minds like Renan and Taine to win an audience in the circles that controlled fame and public honors. Leading a withdrawn life, Renouvier was unknown in the intellectual salons of the Second Empire and the Third Republic. A private income freed him from the need to teach but cut him off from the opportunities from recognition that a position in the university provided. His frequently expressed contempt for the "philosophes salariés" would have certainly made it awkward for him to have accepted any position from the republic. Nonetheless, he felt as strongly as the academic philosophers that the philosopher has a civic responsibility, and he sought through his writings to provide the democratic republic with the philosophy it needed, a practical philosophy which would reconcile the exigencies of reason and morality with the no less pressing, but often contradictory, exigencies of everyday life.

Liberalism badly needed the intellectual grounds for the conciliations that political life imposes if it was to be able to claim a continuing validity, to be something other than a historic creed whose time had passed. Renouvier had from an early date consciously set himself this task of intellectual conciliation. In 1848 he wrote: "I am not dreaming of an ideal community or of a total devotion, but I am trying to harmonize liberty with equality, the independence of individuals with the power of the Republic, property with the public welfare."[5] Though his approach to these problems would change after 1848, Renouvier remained devoted to this program.

Charles Renouvier was born at Montpellier into a prosperous and politically active middle-class family which had been generally identified with liberal causes.[6] He was taken to Paris in 1829 to study at the Collège Rollin by his father, then a member of the Chamber of Deputies, and he soon became involved in the intellectual circles of Saint-Simonianism. Still uncertain of his ambitions, Renouvier entered the Ecole Polytechnique in 1834, where he had Auguste Comte for a mathematics instructor. Declining the position in the navy to which his ranking in the graduating class of 1836 entitled him, Renouvier remained unsettled about his career until he was persuaded in 1839 to enter an essay contest on Descartes, sponsored by the Académie des sciences morales et politiques. The fruit of that effort (which received an honorable mention) became his first book, the *Manuel de philosophie moderne*, published in 1842. Between 1843 and 1847 he contributed a series of articles on philosophy to the Saint-Simonian *Encyclopédie nouvelle*, founded by Pierre Leroux and Jean Reynaud.

Although writing with the confidence of youth, Renouvier had not yet found his own approach to philosophy. The social-reforming motivation for philosophy which he had taken from—or shared with—the Saint-Simonians dominated his thinking, and indeed it would be present throughout his career, though he would later bring it under more intellectual control.[7] The concern with the relations of mathematics and philosophy, which Comte had helped awaken, would likewise be prominent in his mature thought.[8] Like most of his contemporaries Renouvier was also touched by the romantic religiosity of the age, an orientation which would return with particular force toward the end of his life. All of these factors, combined with the civic-mindedness of his family, insured that Renouvier's philosophy would never lose its concern for the concrete problems of man in society. He remained, however, dissatisfied with the intellectual foundation of his thought, and after the disappointments of his involvement in the political struggles of the Second Republic, he turned to the studies that would make his reputation as a philosopher.

Unlike his elder brother Jules, now a deputy, Charles Renouvier was not active in the reform campaign which led to the February Revolution of 1848, but he soon became active in republican politics. One of the Saint-Simonian circle, Hippolyte Carnot, having become minister of public instruction, named Jean Reynaud to head a committee on scientific and literary studies; Reynaud in turn made Renouvier secretary to the committee. The minister invited the composition of civic manuals for the instruction of the newly enfranchised masses in their republican rights and duties, and Renouvier wrote his *Manuel républicain*, which was printed up in 15,000 copies for distribution at government expense. When conservatives in the chamber attacked it as socialistic, Carnot, who had not read the manual, though he had dismissed the rector of the Academy of Caen for refusing to distribute it, was forced to resign.[9] Renouvier was surprised by the bitterness of the attacks against his work and published a second edition in December 1848. He then joined a group preparing a program for the reform of the political organization of the *commune* and after that became an editorial writer for a left-republican weekly, the *Feuille du peuple.*

Renouvier had never been engaged in the socialist groups of 1848 (though he appears to have been more sympathetic to Proudhon and Fourier than to Louis Blanc), and his emphasis now turned more to politics and to the need for political freedom.[10]

After the coup d'etat of 2 December 1851, Renouvier retired to the country near Fontainebleau, convinced more than ever of the need for a republican education which would free men of their dependence on the authoritarian forces of church and state.[11] He was also convinced that this education would require a sounder philosophical foundation than he had so far been able to give it. The need to give his thought a greater rigor drove Renouvier away from the uneasy combination of Cousinian eclecticism,[12] Hegelianism, and Saint-Simonianism that had seemed adequate before the failure of the 1848 revolution and turned him back to Kant. Before his return to Paris in 1861, Renouvier produced the first two of his four *Essais de critique générale,* which would be his most important work of pure philosophy and which would establish the philosophy of neo-criticism. Renouvier had felt it necessary to establish a coherent position on all of the basic questions of philosophy before he could attack the problems of political and social philosophy. If the philosopher was going to change the world, he needed first to understand it.

Renouvier had come to the conclusion that the problems of society hinged on the problems of morals. He explored this relationship in depth in his *Science de la morale,* which we will examine at length in this chapter. After the fall of the Second Empire, Renouvier once again threw himself into the defense of liberal republicanism. Most of his later career was taken up with the elaboration and defense of the philosophical and political ideas he had developed during the 1850s and 1860s. Like Comte and Saint-Simon, his last years were marked by a turn toward religion. Increasingly despairing of man's ability to progress morally through his reason alone, Renouvier concluded that men needed a motivation which could be provided only by faith. After arguing for a time that only Protestantism could supply a faith which was compatible with man's liberty,[13] he evolved his own religious philosophy, which he called *personnalisme.*[14] Not surprisingly, some of Renouvier's sympathizers have found this last phase of his thought inconsistent with the ideas of his mature philosophy, while others have seen it as a logical development. From the point of view of the history of political ideas, it does not much matter what position one takes. Renouvier's contribution to the development of liberalism rests on his earlier work.

Because Renouvier's moral and political philosophy was firmly rooted in his general philosophy, it is desirable first to take a very brief look at that general philosophy before entering the heart of our subject. The term "neo-criticism" indicates Renouvier's filiation with Kant; it also indicates that he was not merely a continuer or follower of Kant but differed from the master in important ways. Renouvier shared Kant's apriorism and, like Kant, employed a system of categories to explain how the human mind interprets reality, though his categories differed in important respects from Kant's.[15] Renouvier thought that Kant had not altogether freed himself of the old metaphysics which he had subjected to such a destructive analysis in the *Critique of Pure Reason*. In an attempt to avoid this pitfall himself, Renouvier rejected Kant's distinction between *phenomena* and *noumena*: there were only phenomena. Rejecting the unknowable and the *Ding-an-Sich* which he identified with the substance-philosophy of the old metaphysics, Renouvier sought to remain in the realm of everyday experience: even the categories were to be interpreted as phenomena. He thus opposed the idealist metaphysics which was nurtured in France and Germany by many neo-Kantians. At the same time Renouvier set out to refute materialism, which he called an "unconscious pantheism."[16] Rejecting both idealism and materialism, he sought to construct a phenomenology, thus entering a path which would become better traveled, if under different auspices, in the twentieth century.

Renouvier's attack on metaphysics was not inspired by any contempt for vain theorizing. Rather it was because these metaphysical views had practical consequences—harmful influences, he thought—that he tried to supplant them with a philosophy which upheld the reality of contingence against the determinism of either absolute ideas or brute matter. As Gabriel Séailles has remarked, Renouvier's philosophy was above all a philosophy of liberty.[17] He based his defense of contingence on what he called the "law of number" and the discontinuity which it introduced into reality. The world of phenomena, the real and only world, was a world created, finite, discontinuous. In order to defend man's moral liberty, threatened by the determinism associated in most minds with modern science, Renouvier carried his attack into the camp of science itself with an effort to show that materialism could not explain our scientific knowledge of the material world and that at the heart of all our certitudes—even in natural science—there was an act of will and therefore of contingence and liberty.[18] These views led Renouvier further to the rejection of two of the favorite ideas of the nineteenth century: progress and evolutionism.[19]

It is easy to see in this brief and necessarily incomplete overview that Renouvier's main concern was always with practical reason, with moral philosophy. He fought unceasingly against his contemporaries' preference for unitary solutions, even going so far as to flirt for a time with polytheism as a basis from which to defend his pluralism.[20] This is not to say that his practical motives vitiate his critique of materialist and idealist metaphysics; it is easier to find drawbacks in his own system than to refute his criticisms of others. The changing attitudes of his later years show that Renouvier was dissatisfied with his own solutions, but he carried on his battle for liberty to the last day of his life.[21]

The key questions for social and political thought in the nineteenth century centered on the nature of society and the relations between society and the individual.[22] Philosophies which consider society a real entity usually concede to it rights as well as obligations and have difficulty justifying the defense of individual freedom against social oppression. Indeed, in many cases such philosophies resulted from a desire for strong social control. But even when the thinker's intent was liberal—as would be the case with most later French sociologists—he would find it difficult to escape the natural inclination of his theory; he would find it easier to develop excuses for the exercise of coercion than solid grounds from which to resist it. On the other hand, intransigent defenders of the individual were not scarce in nineteenth-century France, and Renouvier would not have been significant had he been merely another of them. Holding that only the individual was real, they tended to push this philosophical position to the extreme of virtually negating all social solidarity. This left them easy prey to the temptation to abandon philosophy for the ferocious biologism which elevated the "dog-eat-dog" of everyday life to the dignity of a scientific principle. This Social Darwinian individualism did not merit the name of liberalism since it sacrificed the liberty of the individual to the automatism of biological impulse. The eclectic liberals had seen this and pursued a more moderate individualism. But they as well as the extremists of individualism were intellecually defenseless against the criticism of sociology when it demonstrated the dependence of the individual upon society. Any viable liberalism would have to show that this dependence was compatible with the freedom of the individual, for "the bond [between the individual and society] is very strong and it is necessary."[23]

Renouvier tried to meet this problem by conceiving of the individual as a moral conscience.[24] His philosophy was thus based on a conception of the individual, but of the individual in society, not in isolation. At the beginning of his moral treatise Renouvier briefly considered man in relation to himself and in relation to the world of animals, but he moved quickly to the realm of man in society. While admitting that man had certain obligations to himself[25] and to Nature,[26] Renouvier found that these were not properly moral obligations, for that term applied only to relations among men.[27] His moral ideal was the automony of the will.[28]

Only individuals had wills; but he insisted that the autonomy of the individual will was possible only in a society where every individual recognized the autonomy of all the others. Such a judgment could apply only in the realm of pure theory, but clearly even in the realm of pure theory Renouvier's moral philosophy was a social philosophy, as becomes even more evident when we follow him into the sphere of practical morals. Renouvier's individualism was a large individualism more akin to that of the eighteenth-century philosophes than to the narrow egotism promoted by early nineteenth-century liberal economics.[29] He aimed at furnishing a philosophical basis for a revitalized, socially conscious liberalism.

In order for liberalism to be revitalized it had not merely to show a greater concern for "social questions" in the political arena but also to show an ability to deal with these questions intellectually, without self-contradiction or question begging. This was not an easy task. Liberals who had long been content with the question-begging doctrine of the automatic harmony between individual desires and social good found it difficult to abandon this faith.[30] Even when they became aware that their view was incompatible with current reality, they feared that it could not be given up without abandoning liberalism to its enemies of the Right and Left. Thus, the practical success of any attempt to revise liberalism hinged on its being able to convince the liberals that it provided an adequate defense of individual liberty and to convince the non-liberals that it took adequate account of the individual's obligations to society and his fellow man. Without a new theoretical basis liberalism could not hope to make this transformation on the practical level. Renouvier would try to show that liberal theory could be given an intellectual sophistication in no way inferior to that of rival social views.

The problem of morals was at the heart of Renouvier's intellectual effort. For most liberals there was an intimate connection, on both the theoretical and practical levels, between moral philosophy and politics. Even most of the new generation of sociologists thought that they could— and needed to—replace the old ethic of moral laissez-faire with a new, scientifically justified ethic. They would find that the increasing tendency of sociology toward empiricism made this a difficult task, but some would persist in the effort. While empirical sociology would eventually get bogged down in the morass of the real world, traditional philosophers had trouble leaving the pure realm of theory. Renouvier cannot be credited with definitively disposing of this perennial problem of the gap between moral theory and practical reality, but he realized the necessity of a two-level construction: "Just as there is a pure mathematics and an applied mathematics so there ought to be a pure morals and an applied morals."[31] He had the merit of being one of the few philosophers to tackle this difficulty head on; the sociologists, of course, met the problem in an entirely different way—by denying the value of the pure theory.

Renouvier's effort to distinguish within the realm of a science of morals between the domain of pure morals and the domain of practical morals—and to provide a bridge between them—was certainly heroic. He insisted on the importance of constructing a system which would be "independent," its validity not depending on the validity of a religious creed or of a metaphysical theory.[32] For Renouvier, this meant a moral philosophy had to be founded on reason alone. In his stand one can see a reflection of his early admiration for Descartes, but it was from Kant's *Critique of Practical Reason* that Renouvier's theory derived its fundamental inspiration. In his opinion Kant had started in the right direction but had failed to go far enough because he had been unable to free himself from certain attitudes of the old metaphysics. In the end, Kant had contented himself with a moral system which was inapplicable to the real world and had resigned himself to this incompatibility. Renouvier would not accept what he justly regarded as a defeat.

The principles of Renouvier's pure moral theory came rather directly from Kant, though he rejected Kant's idea of duty for its own sake and tried to find some way of incorporating man's desire for happiness into his moral theory without falling into utilitarianism.[33] At the center of pure morals lay the categorical imperative, which was the expression of man's obligations and rights, based on his intrinsically moral character. Renouvier formulated the categorical imperative, which he preferred to call the "practical obligation," in the form of a precept: "Recognize the person of others as your equal by nature and in dignity—as an end in itself; and as a consequence, never use it as a simple means to reach your own ends."[34] This clearly called for a system of morals based on justice rather than on love or charity, and justice was seen to flow from the recognition of the equal dignity of all persons and of the person as an end in itself.[35] But when this maxim was reformulated to serve as a practical guide for action—so act that the maxim on which your action is based could be erected into a universally applicable law—it became apparent that the imperative could only be followed in a society of more of less perfectly rational and moral individuals. In the real world, where other men do not treat us as ends in ourselves but as means to their ends, the imperative becomes not inapplicable but contradictory. This was the dilemma which Kant failed to escape and on which Renouvier concentrated much of his effort.

Renouvier insisted on the moral and rational validity of the imperative, remaining eternally true in the realm of pure morals which he called the "state of peace."[36] The actual corruption of man, the impossibility of applying Kant's maxim in real life, must not lead to its abandonment as the measure of moral truth lest man sink into the relativism of accepting whatever is as right.[37] But at the same time moral philosophy was obligated to furnish practical guidance for this life lest it become a sterile intellectual exercise. These twin problems could be solved, Renouvier thought, by conceiving of actual society as a "state of war" ("We do not have peace, we have war, . . . "[38]), in which man could justly depart from the strict rule of the imperative so long as the imperative was preserved as the highest ideal and every departure from it tested by the yardstick of necessity.

Necessity was, of course, a singularly elastic yardstick, and Renouvier recognized the need to impose some rational criteria on it. Thus he argued that in the state of war a new right appears, a sort of applied right which does not negate the validity of the pure right but is nonetheless a right itself, a right which helps to set standards by which to measure departures from pure rights. This device he called the "right of defense." Since the individual was at the base of all values, he could not be morally required to will his own destruction, but this was what would result from the rigorous application of the categorical imperative. Though the highest goal of moral autonomy was not fully attainable in this life, the individual could at least seek to preserve as much of his own autonomy as the real world permitted and as much respect for the autonomy of others as was possible.[39] Unlike the categorical imperative, the right of defense was applicable only in the real world; in the state of peace man could by definition expect moral conduct from others and therefore himself act rationally toward them without the *arrière-pensée* of self-protection.

To fulfill its moral function, the right of defense obviously had to be something other than a rationalization for the pursuit of self-interest in a hostile world. Renouvier consistently condemned utilitarian efforts to build a moral philosophy of self-interest.[40] The Stoics and the Epicureans had endeavored to teach man how to live in a world of evil, but their solutions in Renouvier's opinion had sacrificed morality and offered man only the counsels of prudence. It would, of course, be possible to abuse the right of defense, and he recognized that the line between legitimate defense and immoral offense was easily crossed. But he believed that the idea of a right of defense at least provided the basis for rational judgment and discussion, whereas the principles of love or altruism were more easily corrupted and furnished no basis of measure unless regulated from without by rational considerations.[41] Rational considerations, however difficult, were always possible because reason was as deeply rooted in man's nature as was love. Renouvier did not deny the importance of the emotions in determining behavior, nor did he deny that they could make a positive contribution to moral action; they were simply inadequate as a foundation for moral action.[42] Renouvier was first and foremost a rationalist.

In practical terms the right of defense was closely related to the right of property.[43] Renouvier held the right of property to be inherent and to have existed in the first primitive societies—a fundamental part of the human personality and the extension of the self: "property, once settled, should be inviolable as is the person, of which property is an external development."[44] To deny the right of property would be to deny not merely man's outer liberty, but his innermost autonomy. Renouvier's views on property were thus part of his view of man, but his concern for property also had a more practical side. While he realized that property was guaranteed by society, he also held, with other liberals, that it was one of the most effective practical guarantees of individual freedom from the pressures of state and society.[45] But if property was a practical as well as an intrinsic good, it was a good for everyone, and a society of free men was not possible unless all had the protection which property gave.[46] The problem of maximizing liberty thus became linked to the problem of providing the opportunity for everyone to possess property.

From his early contacts with the socialists, Renouvier had learned how the lack of property deprived the working man of freedom. But he would reject most socialist solutions to this problem. Collectivism in particular offered no answer, for although it might offer material security (though not necessarily), it could not offer any support for the autonomy of the individual. The equal division of existing forms of property, he thought, was no solution either; if everyone had his little plot of land or his government bond, the portion of each would be so small as to be useless. The more equitable distribution of existing forms of property was desirable; it would, for example, largely do away with the need for public assistance while making it more feasible in the remaining cases.[47] Existing forms, however, would have to be supplemented by the development of new forms that were equivalent in their contribution to autonomy.

New forms were especially important to avoid damage to existing property. Renouvier insisted that existing property had to be respected in order to preserve that limited measure of peace which was possible among men in the world.[48] He was prepared to accept measures which would limit the growth of inequalities deriving from the existing distribution of property, for example, a progressive income tax.[49] This would not, however, be enough to turn the tide in the other direction.[50] Another method would be the creation of social guarantees which would provide the worker with a security equivalent to that provided by property. The revolutionaries of 1848 had been groping in this direction with their slogan of the *droit au travail*.[51] But while this offered a possibility in theory, Renouvier found it difficult to settle on a means of implementation which favored the development of the individual, and he hesitated to recommend any specific action.[52] When it came to the art of adapting political theory to the concrete problems of the day, he remained more cautious than his theory required.

Unlike his contemporary, the socialist Louis Blanc, Renouvier did not think that the state could or would help much, at least not until such considerable changes had already taken place in society that the state itself would have to change.[53] "No religion or revolution has ever been able to bring about a rapid and voluntary change of the social customs regulating work and property; no State whatever can have the least hope of succeeding where they have failed."[54] Voluntary action, especially the formation of voluntary associations, was the only possible path toward social reform.[55] If the goal was individual autonomy, it could not be reached except by methods which did not negate the goal: "To seek to resolve the opposition [of capital and labor] through the exercise of [governmental] authority would be to abolish liberty."[56] Like most liberals, Renouvier clearly feared that state action was by nature coercive and thus unlikely to cultivate the spirit of individuality.[57] The effort of individuals, grouping together in cooperatives, seemed a more promising path to him, as it did to most liberals.[58] His personal sentiments and his reflection on what the French state had so far shown itself capable of led him further in the direction of deprecating state action than his theory strictly required.[59]

Renouvier's critique of state action was directed against the advocates of socialist revolution as well as against the authoritarians of the Right. His critique of the messianic hopes which the revolutionaries placed in the seizure of the state power was trenchant and to the point.[60] He showed that their proposed means were incompatible with their proposed end of universal freedom and that many of them were merely perpetuating the old authoritarian error of justifying the means by the ends.[61] Freedom as a goal, he justly insisted, was attainable only through freedom as the means.[62] In pure logic, of course, this view led to the paradox that the only liberty which was attainable was that which already existed and that progress toward greater liberty was impossible; but Renouvier insisted that this was a paradox in logic only and not in life, where partial gains were always possible, where partial increases in liberty had been made and therefore could be made, where growth by stages was the rule.[63] The problem of politics for the liberal was how to promote these partial gains, how to progress without destroying the good that one had by the means one chose to reach for the better that one desired. This was a problem that most reformers have preferred to skirt for fear that it would blunt the reforming impulse. Renouvier had the merit of attempting to meet it squarely.

Renouvier brought to his political theory the same useful distinction between pure and applied ideas that was basic to his moral system. For him, politics and morals were indivisibly united at both the theoretical and practical levels. As in morals, it was necessary to begin at the level of pure theory in order that practical theory might be as rational as possible. Man could move with some assurance amidst the ambiguities of the real world only if he had a practical philosophical position which maximized its accommodation to the demands of pure theory.

On the level of pure theory, the only rational form of social bond which Renouvier recognized was the contractual bond.[64] Because society was composed of autonomous individuals (in theory, remember, not in practice), their relationships could only be based on consent, both tacit and explicit. Government as such would exist in such a society only insofar as the size of the society compelled the delegation of certain tasks which were vital to the common interest. At this level of pure theory the concepts of consent of the governed and the rule of law offered no difficulties. The problem of political obligation would be simple: man's moral obligation would be only to that government which had his rational consent.[65]

In applied politics the question was of course different. The real political world was not rational, and the individual who tried to base his behavior in it on rationality alone would soon be lost. The social contract was thus a rational rather than a historical conception; all actual society was to some extent coercive.[66] If rational consent were the only basis for political obligation, there could be no such obligation in the real world. But this conclusion was as unacceptable to Renouvier in politics as was a moral relativism based on man's practical inability to reach the ideal. A meaningful political obligation was obviously necessary to the life of any society.[67] This obligation was different from, but related to, obligation in the realm of pure theory. Political thought could not rest content with pure theory; it had to seek to answer the question of the nature and extent of political obligation in the real world.

> The *petitions de fait* [begging the facts] of theoretical morals are not permitted in applied morals; to avoid those *petitions de principe* [begging the questions] common to moralists, the facts of experience must be taken into account by theory and one must establish the modes of transforming precepts [from pure morals to applied morals] and how to measure these transformations.[68]

For Renouvier, the answer lay in the application of the right of defense, which permitted us to live in an irrational world while seeking at the same time to maximize the elements of rationality and the sphere of liberty in that world.[69]

Because he placed the autonomy of the individual at the core of his moral philosophy, it is evident that Renouvier would be concerned with the problem of political liberty. The liberal state was not merely a subjective value-choice for him; it was the necessary consequence of his whole picture of man's nature and destiny. He applied the ideal of maximizing freedom to the question of the best form of government and to the problem of which policies to pursue within a particular form of government. As we should now expect, Renouvier insisted that in the real world there could be no single correct answer to either of these questions. The options which were presented to men in everyday life rarely appeared in the simple and clear-cut terms that could be developed in the world of pure theory. The main function of government was to safeguard individual rights, but this was easier to state in principle than to apply.[70] In practice, man's choices are governed both by his theoretical principles and by the correctness of his analysis of the given situation. Political philosophy ought to offer some guidance, at least, on how to choose between possible alternatives.

Any philosophy of political obligation had to deal with the extreme form of the problem: the question of the right of resistance. "In principle, the duty of obedience to the law is conditional on the respect for political justice by the State."[71] For Renouvier, there could be no doubt of the moral right of resistance to oppressive government: "the most just of wars is obviously that declared by men deprived of their most essential liberties against those who have despoiled them."[72] But the choice of the means of resistance was conditioned by the nature and degree of the oppression and by the viability of the alternatives.[73] Revolutions were justified if, and only if, the revolutionaries were acting in good faith and if there was some reasonable hope they would lead to a less oppressive condition—and Renouvier doubted that this condition often prevailed.[74] He cited as examples of justifiable revolutions only the Reformation, the English Revolution of 1640, and the French Revolution of 1789.[75] The right to active resistance was, as for Locke, a collective right. The isolated individual could not exercise it without creating more injustice than he destroyed.[76] He might, however, have recourse to more passive forms of resistance which did not sacrifice the right of others.[77] Renouvier's discussion of this question showed him to be skeptical of the virtues of revolution, and though his position was no doubt influenced by his experience in 1848, it was also the logical conclusion of his moral philosophy. Ever since Locke set out to apologize for the Glorious Revolution of 1688, liberals have had difficulty reconciling their distaste for revolution—justly felt to be irrational and illiberal in most cases—and the necessity of justifying it in particular cases. For those who do not partake of a messianic faith which justifies their imposing their will or opinions on others by force if need be—that is, for liberals—the problem will always evade a neat solution. Renouvier, with a longer historical experience of revolutions to draw on, was able to carry the examination of the problem further than Locke had done.

Social contract theory was of course compatible with varying forms of government,[78] but in the nineteenth century it tended to become identified with the defense of republicanism and especially of the democratic republic. Certainly for Renouvier the democratic republic offered the greatest possibilities for a government compatible with the dictates of reason.[79] But the democratic republic also brought more sharply into focus certain difficulties inherent in the contractualist scheme when one attempted to apply it in the real world.[80] The morality of consent required unanimity, but unanimity never exists, can never exist in the real world, and any substitution was artificial: "neither a majority nor a minority, as such, lends itself to that convention which treats them as equivalent to an expression of a general will."[81] Unanimity belonged to the state of peace, majority rule to the state of war.[82] Hence, in democracies, the resort to the rule of majorities (or in practice to the rule of elites speaking and acting the name and with the consent of majorities).[83] Nineteenth-century liberals were acutely aware that majorities could be oppressive; the French Revolution had shown them that absolute monarchs had no monopoly on the will to suppress individual freedom.[84] Moreover, from the point of view of morals, oppression was still oppression whether the majority that supported it was 51 percent or 99 percent. Renouvier's right of defense furnished a basis for individual resistance to the oppressions of any form of government, though it would call for greater discretion in its application under a democratic government. But no state, much less the democratic state, was an entity possessing rights of its own; there was no sovereignty, even popular sovereignty, above man except that of the moral law—and that was not so much above man as within him, above any given individual perhaps, but within man as man.

Renouvier was thus a republican, but not one who expected the form of government alone to solve all the problems that had existed under previous forms of government or to usher in the best of possible worlds. The important thing was to establish the rule of law, however imperfectly.[85] The only possibilities for improvement in this world lay within individuals, and the republic was the form of government most conducive to the development of these possibilities, because "the greatest progress which man has been able to make in his social life has been to regulate his conduct by the voice of reason derived from deliberation in common."[86] Given a certain level of enlightenment and a sufficiently widespread belief in the primacy of justice, a society could attempt to offer guarantees to its members. A society in which the members had taken and continued to take an active part in their self-government, not only through their participation in the activities of the state but also through voluntary association, would be more likely to extend the freedom of the individual than would a society in which all authority was considered to fall from above.[87]

It was not enough, then, to have a republic in form; there must also be a republic in spirit. The liberals sought to infuse the republic with an ideal, but few grasped as clearly as Renouvier the difficulty of implanting new traditions in a country which had broken with its old ones.[88] His criticism of other moralists foreshadowed the attitude of the sociologists toward moral philosophers in general: they "have treated morals and even law or right as if it were sufficient to promulgate abstract duties."[89] Renouvier's concepts of the distinction between a state of peace and a state of war and of the right of defense offered a means by which to bring at least something of the categorical imperative down from the empyrean to which Kant had assigned it and into men's lives. From the standpoint of man's freedom and dignity almost any of the liberal philosophical positions would have been preferable to the coarse utilitarianism which reigned in the political world most of the time.

Had Renouvier enjoyed the advantages of academic position, had his personality fitted him for a teaching career, could he have done more for republican reformism than either of the reigning viewpoints—transcendental philosophy and, subsequently, positivistic sociology—managed to do? This is necessarily a moot question, but one that naturally poses itself in the context of this investigation.[90] He would certainly have given republican practical philosophy, especially the doctrine of solidarism, a greater sophistication than it had, but solidarism did not fail for lack of subtlety.[91] What Renouvier had to offer liberalism was not merely a moral theory which stressed the obligations of the individual to his fellow men without sacrificing the individual as the ultimate value, but also a moral passion, a commitment to social justice that a liberalism grown complacent with the progress of the middle classes needed if it were to recover the strength and the openness which had given it force in the eighteenth century.

The university was not lacking in men who would teach an elevated moral code and teach it in a way which would make a profound impact on their students, nor was it lacking in men of moral courage as the Dreyfus affair would show. But the reaction of the academic liberals in the Dreyfus affair was largely a defensive one, a struggle against what were perceived to be dangers coming out of the past—the authoritarianism of the army and the church.[92] Some of the more far-sighted realized that liberalism was less well rooted than they had assumed it to be, that it would have to reexamine its premises and renew its effort.[93] In part they had been the victims of the illusion of progress; this was one reason the Dreyfus affair was such a shock to them; it was one reason why the Great War would be an even greater shock. Here, certainly, liberalism would have done well to have paid greater attention to Renouvier.

Faith in progress had been if not an essential element of the liberal creed, at least a common element in the creed of most liberals. The example of Rousseau or even of Voltaire should be enough to show that even in the flowering of the eighteenth century they were anything but blindly optimistic. In the nineteenth century Guizot, the historian of the rise of the bourgeoisie, had a strong sense of man's limitations, of his capacity for regression. Nonetheless, belief in an automatic and benevolent progress continued to spread in the nineteenth century, a spread much aided by the rise of Comtean positivism with its simplistic view of history. Renouvier fought continually against this blindness as he directed his critique against all philosophies of history, whether of progress or decline or recurrence.[94] All were deterministic, and determinism as applied to man was both demonstrably false and morally corrupting.[95] It was a disguised version of the doctrine that might makes right.[96] Moreover, the deterministic doctrine of progress flew in the face of the empirical evidence. There is change in history, and, for Renouvier, some times and places were better than others, not only materially but also morally.[97] This change, however, could not be reduced to any law of history, let alone a law of progress. To take only Western civilization as an example—and Renouvier clearly valued it more highly than any other—there had been at least one very long period of regression: the Middle Ages.[98] And there could be no guarantee that the progress which had been made in modern times, mixed as it was, would continue, no guarantee that a new age of regression might not be before us.[99] The possibility had to exist because man is free, free to make wrong choices as well as right ones, free to pursue evil as well as free to pursue good. This understanding, which was one of the key points of Renouvier's political philosophy, was essential if liberalism was to face the mounting challenge of social determinism. When philosophy gave way to sociology as the mainstay of liberal political thinking, liberalism would find it easier to adjust to the needs of society, but it would also risk losing its sense of the vital importance of human freedom.[100]

Renouvier also strongly criticized concepts of the organic foundation of the nation, what he called "natural nationality," as a doctrine offering only permanent strife and war. This was, he thought, the inevitable consequence of trying to build a social system of "involuntary social facts" which denied the role of reason and the will in shaping the state.[101] The politics of positivism led in directions which were inescapably illiberal: "Let us consider the theories which spread during the reign of the determinist spirit; in religion these are systems of grace, in morals, systems of utility, in politics, systems of authority."[102] The sociologists of the twentieth century would try to show this last, at least, to be false. We will try to see how far they were successful.

The same deterministic view of progress marked, he thought, most socialist systems. It gave the socialists confidence in the possibility of a radical cure for today's evils through the transformation of man's environment.[103] It was true that society corrupted men, but it was also true, Renouvier insisted, that society is corrupted by men.[104] There can be no easy way out of this vicious circle, only a long-term effort of amelioration. Indeed, to the extent that man was shaped by his environment, change was not made easier, for no one was endowed with a special power to transcend the conditions to which others must submit. (Experience would show that belief in such an elite leads to the Leninist party, a powerful force for the repression of progress, and helpless to bring it about.) Renouvier's liberalism did not promise any easy solutions. The more deeply rooted an evil was in society, the more difficult it was to remove without creating other injustices.[105] One could not push too far ahead of contemporary conditions, and there were times when it was necessary to compensate those adversely affected by changes, but Renouvier also cautioned against too great a fear of the risks reform always involves.[106]

When the Second Empire was overthrown in 1870, Renouvier sought to return to the political arena—not to participate as directly as he had in 1848, but to attempt to influence affairs through journalism. His philosophy had outgrown the utopian enthusiasm of his youth; he now needed to translate his mature system into terms that would be both relevant and intelligible to the educated lay public. His instrument was the *Critique philosophique,* begun as a weekly in 1871, and written almost entirely by Renouvier and his disciple François Pillon. Their announced purpose was both to explain neo-criticism to an audience that could not take the time or make the effort to master his massive *Essais de critique générale* and also to demonstrate the relevance of that philosophy to the issues of the day—political, religious, literary.[107] Renouvier proposed to take the offensive, announcing that one of his aims was

> to combat common tendencies which show themselves under so many names and in so many forms in our century: pantheism, Hegelianism, Saint-Simonianism, positivism, communism, altruism, evolutionism, monism, Buddhism, religious utilitarianism, sacerdotalism, transcendental immorality, rehabilitation of the Middle Ages, justification of evil as a necessary cause of good, abandonment of the historical and moral principles of the Revolution, all tendencies that are harmful and threaten to sweep everything away.[108]

It was a program which he largely fulfilled.

Defense of the democratic republic was the underlying political purpose of Renouvier's journalism, but as it was a preaching directed at convinced republicans, he did not spend much time explaining why the republic was the best form of government.[109] Rather, he was concerned with how best to secure it, to make it enduring, to avoid the errors of the founders of the ephemeral First and Second republics. The most important thing for the republicans to learn was the necessity of establishing a regime of legality; monarchy had lost forever its aura of legitimacy; Caesarism appealed to force and necessity—if the republic could don the mantle of legitimacy, its future would be assured.[110] Renouvier regretted that the leaders of the revolt of Quatre Septembre had not simply proclaimed the restoration of the constitution of 1848, and, in so doing, avoided all the problems created by the election of a National Assembly dominated by the desire of the country to end the war, a circumstance which enabled monarchists to control the assembly though a minority in the country.[111] But while railing against the monarchist conspiracies, he counseled the republicans to prudence and patience.[112] There was indeed some advantage in a situation where the Right would be forced either to accept the republic or to resort to open illegality, relieving the republicans of the onus of being the party of violence and disorder.

Renouvier applauded the decision of the republicans to accept a constitution made, more or less in ill-faith, by the monarchists, abandoning the policy of all or nothing.[113] He even advised them to go slowly in revising it once they came to power—as they would—in order not to appear to be raising the question of regime.[114] Once the republican regime was firmly implanted it would be possible to talk of improving its mechanisms—within the framework of legality which it created.[115] This caution was especially needed in France where, in the nineteenth century, so many political questions had become questions of regime. Though he rarely mentioned Gambetta by name, Renouvier's admiration for his leadership (after Gambetta's comeback from the disasters of the Government of National Defense) shone through in his praise of a properly understood opportunism.[116] His frequent condemnations of the Jacobin tradition showed a certain nervousness about the maturity of the republicans, but having lived through both 1848 and 1871, he seemed to have felt that they had learned their lesson.[117]

Thus Renouvier faced the Seize Mai crisis calmly. Though he was vigorous in his denunciations of the quasi coup d'etat staged by President MacMahon and his prime minister, the Duc de Broglie, he felt that the republicans had only to remain firm and united, to behave calmly while the Right showed itself to be the party of disorder.[118]

Rather than attempt to comment on all the issues of the day, Renouvier used particular issues to draw attention to what he saw as the major underlying questions. Thus the larger part of his articles in the years 1872–78 was devoted to the question of church-state relations, or to put it less neutrally but more accurately, to what he considered the clerical menace.[119] Because the philosopher believed that political action was ultimately shaped by a people's religious and philosophical attitudes and ideas,[120] he was convinced that the battle of ideas would ultimately decide whether the republic would live or die, regardless of immediate victories or defeats in the assembly. From this perspective the Catholic church appeared as the greatest threat to the republic,[121] and Renouvier worked to show how the republic could defend itself against this threat without betraying its own liberal principles.

Underlining the antiliberal, antinational character of the church's official doctrine, expressed in the previous decade in the Syllabus of Errors, Renouvier argued that it was a false liberalism which felt that the church must be allowed a liberty of action that it would not accord to others. On the old issue of tolerance of the intolerant, he argued forcefully that the liberal had a positive obligation to defend liberty against those who would destroy it.[122] While it was necessary to avoid interfering with the religious freedom of individuals, this did not leave one defenseless against the efforts of the church to overthrow the republic and to abolish the religious freedom of others.[123] Renouvier's picture of the political position and aspirations of the church in nineteenth-century France may have been exaggerated, but it was no caricature. The church had not only reinforced its stand against freedom of religion and of thought in the Syllabus of Errors (1864) but had also moved to stifle divergences of opinion within the church by the declaration of papal infallibility (1870); it had clearly turned its back on all efforts to liberalize. It is not difficult, at any rate, to see why republicans were disturbed by the political stance of the church.[124]

That Renouvier's liberalism was far from a laissez-faire libertarianism emerges clearly in this context. Not only did he reject the Catholic claim of the superiority of the church over the state, but he asserted the supremacy of the state over all other associations.[125] The powers of the state were not unlimited, but because the republic was the political expression of society, it had a large right of action in the interests of that society; it was an instrument of freedom. Furthermore, the republican state was a moral association in its own right, not merely the enforcer of a moral code validated from outside, for example, by a church.

The republic had a right to determine a morality compatible with its principles, which were those of liberty, and an obligation to teach that morality to its young people.[126] In a country where the only other possible source of a moral education reaching the whole population—namely, the Roman church—taught a morality of obedience, of submission to priests, of heteronomy rather than autonomy, the state was under an even heavier obligation: it had not only to provide its own moral education but to prevent the dissemination of a hostile moral education.[127] A state monopoly of primary education was thus justified by the right of defense and shown to be a genuinely liberal position. The theme of the two youths—one republican, one Catholic—was a familiar one for republican writers of the early Third Republic; all were agreed that this national disunity needed to be overcome, and most looked to a system of national education as the means of overcoming it, but many were unsure whether liberty could be respected in the process. Renouvier tried to reassure them that it could, provided that the state did not teach a dogma of its own but rather a morale of tolerance and mutual respect.

Republicans, he knew, would have to face the charge of irreligion, indeed, of persecuting religion, but they could actually interfere less in the internal affairs of all churches than previous regimes had done; they could certainly cease to promote Catholic interests by restricting Protestant evangelism.[128] But the republic must not disarm itself against the political activities of the church.[129] Renouvier had no objection to the state paying salaries to clergy if it was in the state's interest to do so under given conditions, and he warned against thinking that ending the *budget des cultes* would solve the problem of church-state relations.[130] For the separation of church and state to be truly effective, the state would have to cease to deal with the church hierarchy as if it were another power and simply deal directly with local congregations of all faiths.[131] Only when the privileges of the Roman church were ended could religious freedom be considered established.[132]

Leftist historians have often accused the liberal republicans of creating a false religious issue in order to distract the working class from the real issues and from the failure of the republic to enact needed social reforms. This accusation may have been warranted on occasion, but it was often itself disingenuous, the expression of a secular version of ultramontane Catholicism, equally hostile to individual liberty. Between liberals and socialists there was certainly a difference of priorities. Renouvier was quite conscious of this; he believed that the republic had to be firmly established before it would have the moral authority and the popular backing to undertake more radical reforms.[133]

The political problems of France were not merely religious or intellectual in origin, and Renouvier was quite explicit about what he saw as their socioeconomic base. France, he argued, had been under the rule of a narrow oligarchy, an oligarchy comparable to that of the ancient Greek city-states in its hatred for the people, though today that hatred was hypocritically concealed.[134] Their record destroyed all hope that this elite could lead the country anywhere except to civil war and foreign invasion. Their economic interests had not determined this, but rather the failure of their morals, a failure reflected in a tendency to subordinate everything to their caste interests—*après nous le déluge*.[135]

The republic must therefore rely on different social elements than those which supported the July Monarchy or the Second Empire, and Renouvier adopted Gambetta's famous appeal to the "new social strata" to provide the foundation for the liberal republic.[136] He expected the republic to have the support of the working classes and the peasantry but did not think that their political development was sufficiently advanced to provide the leadership needed.[137] Fortunately there was a liberal bourgeoisie as well as a reactionary one.[138] What was left of the old oligarchy ceased to be a grave menace when Thiers succeeded in forming a conservative republican party, a group which Renouvier considered a useful, even necessary, counterweight in parliamentary politics.[139] Liberalism did not express a class interest but offered a means of overcoming class division and of building a truly national society.

To do this it would have to prove to the workers and peasants that it was capable of operating in their interests, that it could put into practice the principles of 1789: make taxes really proportional, make conscription equal for all, liberate judges from the administration, make public instruction really liberating.[140] Renouvier's Saint-Simonian past showed through in his call for a "modern policy for the *physical, intellectual, and moral amelioration* of the most numerous and poorest class."[141] This was clearly in the interests of society as a whole, for if it were true that society was divided into two irreconcilably hostile classes, freedom, he thought, would indeed be impossible.[142]

Renouvier's liberalism did not expect the state to bring happiness on earth or, indeed, even to be the principal force for improving the human condition. He rejected both those who expected miracles from its action and those who expected only disasters. In the state of war, which was the lot of mankind for the foreseeable future, the state was necessary to the existence of that measure of freedom and justice which was possible. Necessary not merely to provide protection from external attack and internal disorder, vital though both of these were to all classes of society, but also because it was one of the means men have of dealing with their common problems—the only effective means they have of dealing with some of those problems. In the historical situation of France only the state could provide the kind of elementary education that was needed. Only the state could see that equity was respected in the private relations of individuals. The difference between Renouvier and the eclectics we have studied was in practice relatively small—he was if anything more sensitive than they were to the authoritarian abuse of state power—but he grasped better the need for a new philosophy of liberalism. Driven both by an awareness of changing social needs which his career as outsider and political opponent of the nonrepublican regimes reinforced and by an intellectual search for something more rigorous and systematic than the reigning eclecticism, Renouvier sought to establish a purely rationalist liberalism. His will to be systematic sometimes led him into excesses in his theoretical work; his firm grasp of everyday realities sometimes led him to be overly hesitant in his proposals for practical reform. But democratic liberalism had no more effective defender.

Renouvier's liberal philosophy would be the last important attempt in France to defend liberalism from within the traditions of Western philosophy which had been dominant for centuries. It marked a high point and at the same time an end point of the rationalist tradition (which has paradoxically found its firmest defenders in the twentieth century among the neo-Thomists). Leadership in the effort to rebuild the intellectual foundations of liberalism now passed to the positivist sociologists—not without intermediate steps, but decisively.

IV

The Triumphant Republic: Liberalism and Education

*T*he fall of the second Napoleonic empire in 1870 and the founding of the Third Republic, which dragged out over the next five years, raised a number of questions for French liberals, questions that were both practical and theoretical. The viability of the new regime was—and remained for a long time—in doubt. Experience suggested rather strongly that a durable liberal regime could not be established by *fiat*, even in the form of a coup d'etat staged by the classic alliance of the intelligentsia and the Paris mob. Paris had found it easier to overthrow governments than to establish a new legitimacy that would be recognized by the whole country. But by 1870 the liberals had ceased to underestimate the task before them: they were going to have to rally the nation to the liberal republic. This would require both organization and ideas.

Like every other modern French regime, the Third Republic was born in conflict, in this case foreign as well as domestic, and the dimensions of that conflict which had an impact on liberal thought were various. The foreign war, hailed at its beginning by an enthusiastic populace (at least in Paris), turned quickly to disaster. Moltke's guns at Sedan swept away the Second Empire as a prelude to the establishment, by Bismarck's pen at Versailles, of the Second Reich. In the time between those two events the radical republicans of Paris seized power in the time-honored manner and attempted to relive the miracle of 1792–93. But the God of Nations was on the other side this time: German nationalism triumphed in a paroxysm of race-hatred (which French liberals accurately predicted would one day prove Germany's nemesis); French nationalism self-destructed in a paroxysm of internecine hatred before the very eyes of the smiling victors.

The failure of the Government of National Defense and of the Paris Commune demonstrated—once again—that Paris was not France and that its unwillingness to respect the rest of the country was self-destructive. The nationalist emotion released in 1870–71 would remain one of the major dimensions of the political life of the new regime. That emotion was often hard to distinguish from the emotion exposed by the social conflicts which were also a part of the revolution of 1870 and the revolt of 1871. Though by no means the proletarian revolution that some socialists would try to make of it, the Commune of 1871 did create an atmosphere of social conflict which, after the relative calm of the plebiscitary dictatorship, registered on all consciousnesses.

The protracted struggle to endow France with a new form of government (1871–75) revealed further dimensions of conflict. Though the quarrel between monarchy and republic was little more than a survival of a dead past, made possible only by the circumstances of 1870 and the social position of a few monarchists, the related quarrel between Catholic and revolutionary France was still a live issue whose effects would long continue to perturb the republic.

All three of these dimensions would have an influence on liberal thought. Nationalism would have the least impact because it was already well integrated into the liberal position. Liberal convictions were reinforced by the events of 1870–71, and many emerged feeling that the sentiment of national unity needed to be reinforced. Some disagreements about how best to accomplish this goal would play a role in the evolution of liberalism. The Dreyfus affair and the growth of a pacifist-internationalist liberalism at the turn of the century would reveal that liberal unity was less strong on this question than it had seemed in 1870.

The sense of developing social conflict would have the greatest long-run effect on the evolution of liberalism. The effort to modify liberalism to enable it to better face that conflict, indeed to resolve it, would become the major issue of the twentieth century. Socialists would of course say that the liberals had not feared class conflict in the days when it was a question of the ascension of the bourgeoisie, but only when it became a question of the ascension of the proletariat. This may have been true enough of those middle-class elements which rallied to the Second Empire, but the social peace provided by that authoritarian regime came with too high a price tag for most liberals. Liberals accepted that the middle classes had been the main vehicle for the rise of liberalism; they did not accept that liberalism was a middle-class doctrine.

The conflict which dominated liberal concerns at the beginning of the Third Republic was the politico-religious conflict which pitted monarchists and Catholics on one side against republicans and defenders of religious liberty on the other. The problems which stemmed from this division in French social and political life were in a sense the continuation of the conflicts born in the Revolution of 1789. They account for the relative stability of liberal concerns before and after 1870. And in the period before World War I, they were the source of more concrete difficulties for republican political life than the social issues which liberals are often—exaggeratedly—charged with ignoring.

More and more, liberals and republicans had come to interpret their past failures as the result of the existence of an opposition which possessed both organization and ideas: the Roman Catholic church. The republican political system and the liberal faith were both confronted with the hostility of the church, which had lent its moral authority to every autocratic regime and mobilized its educational institutions to combat the spread of liberal ideas. The liberals' main intellectual weapon against the Catholic influence in French political life—rationalism—had won considerable successes among the educated, but the educated were as yet too narrow a stratum on which to found a durable political regime. Many, perhaps most, liberals had been hesitant about putting those powerful weapons of rationalism and individualism into the hands of the masses, but it was becoming evident that the social basis of liberalism would have to be expanded if it was going to survive. Liberalism's aspirations to universality were going to be put to the test.

Liberals were naturally reluctant to expand the authority and role of the state, but only the state could provide what they now realized was needed to counteract the influence of the church—a mass education. The key issue of the early Third Republic was public education: how it was to be organized, how it was to be staffed, how it was to be financed, what it was going to teach. It was this latter question, of course, which is of interest to the theme of the present book, though at one remove, so to speak. Our concern has been—and will continue to be—with the underlying ideas of the liberals. The interrelationship between this basic intellectual development and the very practical problems of the new republic is evident. Without the stimulus of those practical problems, the evolution of liberal thought would have been much slower. The antisocial potentialities of the old individualism would have to be faced sooner or later; the fall of the empire made it sooner. French liberals were in need of a socialized liberalism, and one was already in the process of development.

The same circumstances which made the establishment of the republic so difficult also dictated that one of the most acute problems of the new regime would be how to establish a laic state in a society that was traditionally Catholic and in which the authority of the church, though much eroded, was not negligible. The degree to which the idea of the laic state was at war with traditional Catholic concepts of proper church-state relations would have made this a difficult problem under the best of circumstances. But the situation in France was hardly the best of circumstances. Catholics had just been reminded by the assassination of the Archbishop of Paris, held hostage by the Communards, that the tradition of republican violence toward the church was not dead; liberals had just been reminded of the church's continuing claim to a guiding role in political life by the activity of Catholics and of the Catholic hierarchy in the effort to restore the dynasty of "most Christian kings." Liberalism had its origins in the struggle for freedom of religion, a struggle older than that for political freedom, and liberals saw too much evidence that the Catholic church had still not accepted this freedom. Even the most conciliatory of liberals could not ignore the message that Pope Pius IX was bent on sending them.

Catholic political authoritarianism had been diluted by the division between Legitimist and Orleanist royalists and in part discredited by the support it had given to Bonapartism. Churchgoing was in decline; attendance at mass was increasingly dominated by women and the elderly; priestly vocations were inadequate. But liberals would feel that their victory risked being only temporary so long as the church played a significant role in the education of the nation's youth. Many republicans were convinced that the Catholic domination of education was a major threat to the survival of the.republic. They set out first to create a state system of primary education on a truly mass scale and then adopted measures which were aimed at bringing most pupils— some hoped all pupils—into the public schools. The church, taking advantage of the fact that many liberals were torn between their commitment to intellectual freedom and their conviction that Catholicism was the greatest enemy of intellectual freedom, protested that the liberty of Catholic parents was being violated by the drive toward a state monopoly of education. Most liberals' reactions to this problem were pragmatic, but they continued to feel the need for a sound theoretical justification for their position. If traditional liberal individualism threatened to play into the hands of the Catholics, it is not surprising that many liberals would be looking for a more socialized liberalism which, among other things, would justify the state's new role in education.

In the eyes of the rising generation of liberals, both public and church-controlled education in the decades before 1870 had grave faults—indeed some of the same grave faults. The method of those schools was dogmatic, and their goal was indoctrination; they were designed to turn out good subjects, not good citizens. As a result, the educated elites were not much better off than the ignorant masses; their potentialities were stifled as surely by bad education as the others' were by none at all. This loss was not merely an individual loss, and liberals did not approach the question of education purely from the point of view of the interests of the individual. What was at stake in the education question was seen to be the future of the collectivity. Political liberty and national sovereignty depended on the existence of citizens who were prepared not merely to defend their rights but also to assume their duties. What distinguished the citizens of a republic from the subjects of an authoritarian regime was not simply that they saw their rights as springing from the human condition and not as gifts of authority, but also that they saw their duties as self-assumed rather than imposed from without.

Thus it is not surprising that for most French liberals the provision of public education for the entire society was one of the highest obligations of the state, ranking not far below defense against foreign invaders and domestic criminals, nor far below the protection of individual rights. This expresses a far more positive attitude toward the role of the state than French liberals are usually credited with but one which was not inconsistent on their part. The accusation often hurled from the Left, that this liberal acceptance of state action was merely a matter of expediency, of forging a tool for the indoctrination of bourgeois ideology, is not altogether in error; but it misses the essential point on which liberalism is different from other "isms." However much liberals might sacrifice their ideas in pursuit of private or group interests, liberalism remained attached to its belief in the virtues of rationality and science, its belief that the free exercise of the human spirit would lead to the best possible world for the individual and for society.

Because they agreed on the importance of public education, however much they differed over its details, the liberals were able to move ahead rapidly after 1875 with the creation of a public school system on a scale which would make it a major strain on the financial resources of the young republic. Their hopes for the future of the republic rested on this effort at national education. The enormous burden which the liberals placed on education was not the result of a naive overconfidence in the efficacy of ideas. If they had any such illusions in the beginning, the practical work of building a national education soon forced them to recognize the difficulty of translating ideas into practice. The pedagogical debates of the period are full of expressions of the sterility of purely abstract thought, and liberals were more apt to find an excess of intellectualism among the socialists than in their own ranks. On the other hand, liberalism was a movement of ideas; it was not in its essence an effort of a class to overthrow the domination of a superior class or to hold down the aspirations of a lower one. Liberal ideas could be, and were, used for such purposes, but this usage was always a corruption of their basic intent. It was, however, the social, more than the intellectual, interests of liberals which shaped their concern with education. A movement of ideas which, like liberalism, aspires to cut vertically across the real social strata of any society must, to be effective, find a base in everyday life which will compensate for its lack of "natural" base in some social class. For religion, which has the same aspiration, this base had been the church; for liberalism it could only be the state. As an instrument for the propagation of ideas the state can act in many ways, but for liberals the most legitimate of those ways, the one least likely to threaten individual rights, is through the education system.

Because of the nature of liberal ideas, this state education could not, without self-contradiction, become an ideological indoctrination. The liberals did not fear that they might be establishing the mechanism through which some new tyranny might emerge; they were confident that the democratic character of the new regime and the mission with which the educators would be imbued guaranteed that republican education would be an instrument of liberation. They were indeed eager to prove that the kind of education program they were building would not infringe on the rights of even liberalism's bitterest opponents. They did think that state education would, and should, in the long run tend to eliminate the bases of opposition to liberalism, but it would do so by spreading rationality through all levels of society and not by any forced conversion.

The immediate practical problem for the founders was to build up an education system physically and mentally capable of bearing the burden that was to be put upon it. By and large, the republic succeeded in this monumental task fairly rapidly, though the realizations often lagged behind the legislative authorizations. It is not our purpose here to trace the history of that effort, but we do need to note that it had several dimensions. The effort to provide the rudiments of intellectual, moral, and civic culture to the entire population involved the creation almost from scratch of a public primary school system, including the Ecoles normales primaires needed to train the teachers on a grand scale. These primary schools differed from our conceptions of elementary education today (though less from our nineteenth-century practice) in being conceived as complete in themselves. They led to a certificate of primary studies at age twelve or thirteen and did not prepare pupils for any higher studies. Most graduates began to earn, at least in part, their own livings. For those with further aspirations—

and means—there were some Ecoles primaires supérieures and technical institutes.

The secondary schools remained, as before, a separate path open largely to those whose families could afford a substantial tuition and, often, the cost of boarding, for such schools were only available in larger towns. Elementary grades were organized by the secondary schools to prepare their own future students, and movement from the primary to the secondary system was very rare. The secondary schools, known as *lycées* or *collèges*, were thus the preserve of the middle classes, though efforts would be made from time to time to broaden access through government scholarships. The secondary system did not lead to a school-leaving certificate but to an examination administered by the Faculties of Letters and of Sciences: the baccalaureate. In the early years of the republic this was the major function of the faculties, which were thus diverted from their other function of providing higher education. Being able to afford the lycée was no guarantee of ability to pass the baccalaureate examination, which became the essential qualification for most middle-class careers, as well as for higher education. Not surprisingly, the secondary schools received as much attention from the liberals as the primary system; the secondary system was the training ground of the national elites.

The secondary school programs terminated, after the first form, with a special year devoted either to mathematics or to philosophy, in preparation for one of the two forms of the baccalaureate. The last few years at the lycée was the time when French youth received the higher general education which we usually allocate to the first two years of college. Teaching positions in the lycées were thus more prestigious than our high school posts, and most of the subjects of this book began their teaching careers in lycées. Teachers in the lycées were known as *professeurs* and generally had a minimum of three years of post-baccalaureate study in a faculty, where they received essentially professional training. The elite among them—like most of our subjects—received their training not in the faculties but at the Ecole normale supérieure, the most exclusive teacher-training institution in the Western world. Whatever the path, fitness for teaching was certified by passing an examination for the *licence*. Teachers in the faculties and the Grandes ecoles (Normale supérieure, Polytechnique, etc.) were recruited through the *agrégation*, a competitive examination where the number of passes was determined by the number of posts available in a given year. Many professors in secondary and higher education also spent years working toward the doctorat d'état, which required original research leading to the production of two dissertations (one in Latin) which were then defended in a public examination. The liberal republicans were especially interested in upgrading the intellectual levels of secondary and higher education, but as we shall see, they were also very much concerned with the moral and civic impact of these programs.

When leaders in the construction of the republic's education system like Léon Bourgeois stressed the national goal of rebuilding the unity of France and emphasized the need for a unity of spirit in the schools in order to give unity to the nation, they were more often thinking of the secondary schools than of the primary. The hitherto ignorant and superstitious masses were seen in those early years as less formidible potential enemies of the republic than those middle- and upper-class youths who had received their education at the hands of priests, lay brothers, or—worst of all—Jesuits. It was disunity within the elite which most worried the liberals of the late nineteenth century, not disunity between the elite and the masses. Even when the latter danger began to appear, especially when it took the form of socialist pacifism, liberals were still mostly concerned with unity at the top; a united elite was the best guarantee against a divided country. A truly republican and liberal elite would be the natural leaders of a democratic people.

The growing social and economic importance of the French middle classes in the late nineteenth century made a new understanding of the relations of the individual and society more pressing than ever. It would do little good to use the primary schools to convince the masses of their obligations to the *patrie* and of the solidarity which should overcome all distinctions of class and status if at the same time the secondary schools produced a bourgeoisie that was self-satisfied, pleasure loving, and narrowly individualistic. Liberals found themselves with a problem of moral education for the middle classes as well as for the working classes, and they pursued this task with an equal vigor in the schools and in the "cultural media." The theme of the liberal message addressed to the middle classes went through a major shift in emphasis after the fall of the empire. Where it had seemed vital to persuade them to assert their rights more vigorously, to be less dependent on the public authorities, it was now necessary to combat their egoism and to remind them that an elite has many responsibilities to society.

The elite of the nation's youth seemed to most liberal thinkers to be imbued with an egoism which the current secondary education had tended to reinforce. Yet the question of national unity was as relevant for them as for the rest of society and was thus a concern to the secondary as well as the primary schools. The sons of the middle classes needed to be taught that being an elite of talent was not a license to parade one's superiority, but a greater obligation to work for society as well as for oneself. Where primary students were to be catechized, the secondary elite would be exposed at the end of its education to the intellectual grounds of its obligations. The *année de philosophie* preceding the baccalaureate examinations was the particular focus of this intellectual concern. Philosophical studies in the postsecondary institutions would be responsible for providing the secondary schools with the ideas and the men they needed to fulfill their social task.[1]

While the eclectic philosophers were dominant in the secondary and postsecondary institutions at the beginning of the Third Republic, they were already facing a challenge from those who found them both politically compromised and intellectually outdated. The defeat of 1870 and the opening of a new regime both seemed to call for new ideas and new leadership in education as well as in government. Even before the dimensions of the new needs of the new era could be clearly seen, a vague but strong urge to renewal was evident. In part, it was a renewal of generations, which is a force for change in philosophy as elsewhere. At a moment when philosophy was under increased assault from positivism, it proved still capable of exciting interest, even inspiring vocations, among young men. It should be noted that this interest was not all pragmatic, as the focus of the present work might suggest, for there was a great deal of attention paid to the more technical and abstruse, to the oldest as well as the newest problems of philosophy.

On the practical side, attention was undoubtedly focused on the problem of developing a view of man which would reconcile the ultimate value of human freedom with the individual's debt to society. The growth of more vigorously anti-individualist social philosophy outside the university was not ignored by the philosophers and indeed may have strengthened their determination not to sacrifice freedom. That the intellectual challenge was also reflected in political movements of both Right and Left no doubt reinforced the commitment of the Third Republic's academic philosophers, but it did not close their minds to the rise of social science, which was, after all, largely the work of men trained as philosophers in the republic's schools. The idealist philosophers who succeeded the eclectics and the sociologists who would—in this domain at least—succeed them in turn, knew each other well. They provided that continuity within change in the domain of political philosophy which corresponds to the mobile centrism which is vital to the health of all democratic politics.

This concentration on the humanistic unity of the elite was a major reason that so much attention was drawn to the conflict of ideas. Outmoded ideas and allegiances to dogmas that had no place in the modern world seemed the most pressing dangers to the survival of the liberal democratic republic. Such ideas and allegiances could be combatted through education; the lycée would have a prime role in establishing the new order. Salvation through education also requires the possession of the ideas and knowledge which will guide the republic's teachers. Money can set up the apparatus, build the schools, send the inspectors on their rounds, but it cannot decide what is to be taught and how. The thinkers we are concerned with were mostly engaged in the search for the social and political ideas on which to base republican education. Some were more engaged than others in converting ideas into curricula and lesson plans, some with shaping the spirit of the teachers and infusing them with a sense of their high mission; the latter part of this chapter will deal briefly with two of the most influential popularizers and implementers: Ferdinand Buisson and Gabriel Séailles. We need to know a little about the character of their effort so that we may put the work of the deeper thinkers into its social and intellectual context. It was a sociopolitical *conjoncture* which placed an unusually high value on the role of social and political ideas, helping to call forth the significant work we will examine in the following chapters.

The problems raised by Catholic opposition to the republic also guaranteed that much of liberal thought would be directed to the question of morals. The relationship of politics and morals was already deeply rooted in the liberal tradition, but Catholic criticism drew attention to an aspect of the problem which had not been of such great importance before the establishment of the republic—namely, the role of the secular state in the promotion of public morality. Catholics had always insisted that this was a responsibility of the church which only the church—indeed only the true church—could fulfill, since it alone possessed the doctrine and the men qualified to teach it. This was a pretension which the liberals could not possibly accept and which they could not ignore.

There was a certain republican tradition which fed on historical reminiscences of republican Athens and of republican Rome and which associated the republic with the reign of private virtues in public life. The experience of two republics had forced some modification of that image, though there were, no doubt, still some who thought Robespierre was a greater patriot than Danton because he was surnamed the "incorruptible," while Danton's venality was well known. But no one really thought that the act of establishing a republic was sufficient to inaugurate a reign of virtue in France. Republicans who had long denounced the corruption of the authoritarian regimes do not seem to have been much embarrassed by the scandals which reached high in republican political circles in the late nineteenth century. These seemed survivals of the political *moeurs* of earlier regimes, which the republic would have to live with for a while, just as it had with a host of less than liberal laws bequeathed in the Codes.

What did stir republican thinkers to action was the question of the impact of the republic on the morals of the whole of society. The republic would survive the misdeeds of a few deputies, but its long-run prospects depended upon a virtuous citizenry (which among other things would keep governmental corruption from getting out of hand). It was not what the republic was but what it did that mattered; it provided the ideal context for public and private virtue, but its responsibilities did not end there. The republic had an obligation to see that all its future citizens received the moral education that would fit them for their future social roles.[2] The liberals' determination to fulfill that obligation was the spark for the most acute phase of the conflict between church and state.

Regardless of their own religious convictions, the republican leaders could not contemplate leaving moral training in the hands of the church. The church's continued anti-republican position made such an abdication equivalent to suicide, or at best to the acceptance of a permanent *foyer* of national disunity. The Third Republic would do what the first two had not had time for—mold a republican citizenry through a republican moral instruction. Fortunately, this would not take long; one generation of republican education, Jules Ferry thought, would be sufficient to guarantee the stability of the new regime.[3] The basic minimum of instruction which the republic undertook to provide for every child was, then, reading and writing and calculation—but especially civic morals.

If that instruction was to be free and compulsory, it had also to be secular. Liberty of conscience stood too high in the liberal scheme of values for the state to give its support to any sectarian program, however much it was approved by the majority of the population. Debate centered rather on whether this primary moral instruction should be presented in the form of the nonsectarian deism of the spiritualist philosophers or whether even that was a partisan position which had to be avoided. Jules Ferry, the leader of the movement for free, compulsory public instruction, was a positivist for whom the eclectic philosophy was as outdated as Catholic theology, but he adopted the argument that it was the religiously neutral character of the state which made it improper to mention God in the classroom.[4] Moral instruction would not be less effective, and no one would be justified in saying that his religion had been offended (except insofar as its absence from the state schools was itself an offense, as it was to many Catholics). Everybody, after all, agreed on moral questions; it was only over how these common moral precepts were to be grounded and how they were to be taught that opinions diverged.

How were the *instituteurs* to teach "the good old morals of our fathers" if they could not refer to any philosophical or religious conceptions?[5] By the use of their common sense, Ferry insisted. For this, no special training was required, though the republic would soon decide to provide some, if only to bolster the morale of the *instituteurs* who had to defend their moral instruction against the vigilant hostility of the local *curés*. The schools were expected to make patriotism and national unity part of this moral instruction. Whether or not the moral instruction of the republican school was successful is no doubt an unanswerable question; that it was a factor—though not the only factor—in the development of national unity seems well established.[6] Liberal intellectuals were no doubt dissatisfied with this commonsense foundation, but the kinds of questions they wanted to raise found a more appropriate arena in the secondary and higher education realms. The method of the catechism may have sufficed to inculcate republicanism at the elementary level; it was beneath the dignity of the secondary schools.

The problem at the secondary level was not that of integrating the masses into the nation; the masses did not go beyond the elementary level. The politicians were therefore less urgently concerned, and the intellectuals had a wider margin of action. What was at stake here was nonetheless important to the republic—it was the preparation of the elite, the leaders of tomorrow. They were the audience for the effort to revitalize the foundation of French liberalism.

The intellectual defense of the republic presented different, and in some ways more difficult, problems under the republic than it had during the empire. As is often the case in human affairs, promise and reality were at variance: "How beautiful the republic was during the empire" was not an unusual reaction. Republican principles were often easier to defend than republican practice which could not suddenly transmute them into reality. The Bonapartists and the monarchists were now able to attack the republicans not only with Bonapartist and monarchist ideas, but they could also find occasion to use liberal arguments for their own purposes. This had at least the intellectual advantage of forcing liberals into examining their own principles; it had the disadvantage sometimes of tempting them to abandon those principles when they seemed to work for the advantage of the opposition.

In this context, the intellectual questions involved in the defense of the liberal republic naturally assumed a greater importance. Was the context of these questions much changed by the establishment of the republic? Certainly the general forces we discussed at the beginning of this chapter were felt in the more elevated realms of thought, but there were also some more specific issues which need to be introduced here.

Certain basic political questions seemed to have passed from the stage of controversy. The most important of these was that of sovereignty. Virtually everyone, even in the monarchist camp, accepted popular sovereignty and agreed that the will of the people was the ultimate source of authority. They differed on how best to consult it, and their willingness to consult it at any given moment was conditioned by the results they expected. Even the republicans were guilty of this distrust of the sovereign. The Third Republic was established not merely without a constitutional referendum, but with a general rejection of such an appeal to the people by the republic's own defenders.[7] In the four-year interval between general elections the legislature was in effect sovereign, even possessing the right to alter the constitution under certain circumstances. The executive power was at its mercy every day.

The liberals had plenty of opportunity to learn that the possession of power does not necessarily elevate an assembly. The system of small, single-member constituencies proved effective in giving everyone a stake in the republic's success and in giving it a grass-roots foundation that earlier republics had lacked. But it also meant that the national government would devote a disproportionate amount of its time to local matters. The republican system did not promote long-run consistency in national affairs, either. It was not so much that the republican governments were unstable—there was often much continuity from ministry to ministry—as that they were so often petty and lacking in dignity. It was not the Right alone which often felt that the deputy considered it his highest obligation to assure his own reelection.

But if in the liberal conception, government existed for the furtherance of the interests of individuals, how far could liberals object to this development? Some, no doubt, were quite satisfied. But most liberals, especially while the memory of 1870 was strong, were unwilling to abandon the defense of French *grandeur* to the authoritarians. French liberalism never consisted merely of the defense of individual interests, but the coming of the republic forced it to focus more clearly on the question of the general interest and its relations to particular interests. They had to confront the question of whether the regime which offered the best protection for individual and minority *rights* might not risk becoming the servant of individual and minority *interests* at the expense of society as a whole. The liberal Third Republic certainly served a much broader constituency than the class-bound July Monarchy. Liberals did not intend to create a regime of privilege; could they assure that it would not turn out that way? The meaning of the marriage of liberalism and democracy had now to be worked out.

Liberals saw in their acceptance of democracy no reason to weaken their commitment to individual liberties; indeed, in some ways it would have to be strengthened in order to counter the different threat posed by democratic conformism. Neither did democratic liberals see any reason to weaken their attachment to private property or to the idea of individual merit and responsibility. These ideals could be applied to all strata of society, and liberals had not waited for the coming of the Third Republic to begin thinking about how access to property could be broadened. Liberal democrats were convinced that the republic did not diminish the need for leadership and for elites in society, and the French middle classes had not lost their conviction of being the natural leading elements of society, an elite more open than any other in history.[8]

Without sacrificing their commitment to self-reliance and personal effort, French liberals were increasingly aware that all the problems of the poor could not be blamed on their moral failings. Competing explanations of the origins of poverty abounded. The rise of evolutionary biology naturally led to an emphasis on the role of genetic differences. This would seem to have limited individual responsibility since no one can choose his parents, but it also had the tendency to suggest that there was no solution to the social problem, except perhaps through a compulsory Malthusianism at one end and eugenics at the other. The extremes of the biogenetic view, such as Lombroso's theory of the born criminal identifiable by physiological traits, led to a reaction, in which the sociologists figured prominently, which stressed the role of the social environment in shaping the individual and which could with equal ease also lead to a diminution of personal responsibility. Philosophical liberals could obviously not accept any of these lines of solution.

The practical problem was closely related to the theoretical one. The mode of action for dealing with social problems is inevitably conditioned by the idea one accepts of their causes. When those causes increasingly seem to be social in nature, then more appeal must be made to the organized action of society in dealing with them. While liberals thought first of voluntary organizations, most realized that these would be insufficient to meet the needs of contemporary society. The question of state action had therefore to be faced, both in those instances where the state was itself the source of the problem and in those where the accumulated effects of private actions were at fault. This was an important and difficult step for liberals, who were coming to recognize that the claim of individual rights had been too often used as a cover for social evils:

> You will not find anyone now who would republish these formerly
> much admired articles in the *Journal des débats* [Buisson ob-
> served] protesting in the name of the dogma of liberty, the "social-
> ism" of Jules Simon who had dared demand the intervention of
> the State in favor of eight-year-old workers.[9]

This new attitude was itself in part a result of changing circumstances.
The original liberal inclination to hold the individual entirely responsible for his situation had its origins in an era of relative social stability.
The degree and rapidity of social change evident in the last half of the
nineteenth century made this conviction seem less self-evident than it
had to earlier generations. Most liberals accepted the changes of that
era as progress, as on the whole beneficent, but they did not deny that
many suffered from them in the short run. If society wanted to enjoy
the benefits of change, did it not have a responsibility to help those
who were paying a disproportionate part of the bill? This semiconscious perception was the necessary foundation for the changes that
would take place in liberal thought.

The older liberalism had never denied that the better-off had an
obligation to assist the "less fortunate," but it seldom had occasion to
emphasize this point. The obligation was not incorporated into liberal
philosophy because it antedated liberalism; earlier generations of liberals were still imbued with the Christian tradition of charitable concern for the poor and took this attitude for granted, not questioning
whether it could be reconciled with their philosophy. French liberal
philosophers had never argued that the unlimited pursuit of self-interest was the best way to serve others; self-sacrifice was always honored—
if often in the breach. It was not the existence of social obligations but
their nature that was changing at the end of the century. It was no
longer a question of private charitableness or of honest dealings with
clients or employees. It had become a question of organized state
action to deal with problems which had become prominent in the
public consciousness.

The transition from private charity to state welfare programs presented great difficulties for the eclectic philosophers, not only because
many of the new programs conflicted with their deepest feelings about
the liberty of the human person, but also because their philosophical
position was hard to adapt to the exigencies of the new situation without falling into contradiction. The neo-criticists, following Renouvier's
example, had a somewhat easier task insofar as his theory of the "state
of war" offered a principled position from which to adjust to the reality

of a "solidarity in evil." Whatever its other defects, social science was by its very nature better prepared than either philosophy to cope with the new issues of social responsibility. But social science would have to demonstrate its intellectual credibility before it could be called on to assume the direction of liberal consciences. The need for immediate action would produce, at the level of popular discourse, a kind of amalgam of philosophy and social science that functioned as a more or less adequate stopgap.

The two activists we are going to look at briefly in this chapter illustrate some important characteristics of the intellectual milieu in which the developments discussed above took place. While having widespread interests, they were both especially active in the popularization of secular moral education for the new era. Ferdinand Buisson (1841-1932) and Gabriel Séailles (1852-1922) were so permeated with the idea of progress—evolutionary version—that it almost took the place of systematic thought for them. They dismissed the dogmas of religion and the doctrines of philosophy equally with the statement, "It is no longer possible to believe that ..." or, "Humanity has passed the stage in which it was possible to believe that...." They were concerned, in other words, not so much with specific ideas as with *mentalités*. Séailles gave this viewpoint its most coherent expression in his *Affirmations de la conscience moderne* (whose very title was a program), while Buisson illustrated it in almost every speech. Their rejection of the past did not mean that they were primarily negative thinkers. On the contrary, what mattered most to them was that humanity had now passed through those earlier stages of thought and had reached a level where unprecedented good was possible.

Their mode of thought was thoroughly permeated by the evolutionist, relativist mentality so feared by the metaphysicians. Buisson's view of religion is a clear example of this. For him, all religious beliefs were respectable in their time and place, but not elsewhere.[10] This approval covered everything from the most primitive fetishism to the Catholicism of the High Middle Ages. But Buisson held that the Reformation had marked the beginning of the end for all of these earlier forms of religion and that man had now reached a final stage beyond which no further evolution of religion was possible. The Reformation had brought the right of the individual conscience to examine all dogmas, all sacred texts, all religious organizations, and that examination had inevitably shown them all to be merely human devices—not impostures, but not divinely inspired either—that could no longer be justified.[11] They belonged to the infancy of the human race, to its childhood and adolescence, but maturity had at last liberated man from them.

Their support was no longer needed, for man could face the world as it was. Buisson did not, however, simply wait for religion to disappear, and he justified his vigorous anti-clerical campaign as "the unrelenting revenge of reason against faith, of freedom against authority."[12]

Beginning his career among liberal Protestants in Switzerland, where he had taken refuge after refusing the oath to the empire, Buisson would spend a lot of his time in later years trying to convince his erstwhile hosts that free thought was the logical conclusion of their Protestant position and that they should give up their last ties to a dead past: belief in a personal God, in the divinity of Christ, in immortality.[13] Such beliefs, Buisson thought, served only to compromise the true role of religion today, and today it was possible to see what the true and eternal meaning and purpose of religion was, and always had been. Religion was simply the expression of man's eternal aspirations, aspiration to know what was yet unknown, aspiration for a better life, both moral and material.[14] One could not find the essence of religion, as Durkheim proposed, by studying its most elementary forms, but only by studying the evolution of its highest forms.[15] Today, Buisson argued, man's aspiration could effectively manifest itself only in the effort to bring about social and political reforms.

Buisson's long career was indeed a kind of lay ministry in which a minimum of key ideas furnished the base for an unwearying evangelical campaign of exhortation. The first and last phases of that career were devoted to the cause of international peace, an effort that—despite interruption by two major wars—was crowned with the Nobel Peace Prize in 1926. That campaign does not directly concern us here, but it does clearly illustrate that virtually unlimited optimism which characterized the mentality of many turn-of-the-century liberals.[16] The progress which Buisson saw, the triumph of rational thought, the spread of domestic freedom, made it impossible for him not to believe that an era of world peace was now possible. The modern conscience could not accept war any more than it could accept miracles, since both were equally irrational. Given the sort of biological analogy of growth on which this idea of progress rested, it was equally impossible for Buisson to believe that mankind could take a step backward; having put aside childish things, to take them up again would be madness.[17] It is certainly one of the interesting features of the modern era that the powerful drive to avoid the naive beliefs of the past can lead to the most unrealistic views of the present.

The phases of Buisson's career that most concern us here are the thirty years he put into the service of the establishment of free, compulsory, laic primary education in France, and the following twenty years of activity in national politics. Returning from Switzerland after the fall of the Second Empire, he entered the education ministry under Jules Simon in 1871 and served there in various capacities, the most important being that of director of primary education, until assuming the chair of pedagogy at the Sorbonne in 1896. Buisson was Jules Ferry's right-hand man in the drafting and implementation of the laws which shaped the primary school system of the Third Republic, and he campaigned vigorously in defense of the three principles of laicity, gratuity, and compulsion.[18] He sought to convince the middle classes that far from being an assault on liberty, this legislation was its veritable foundation.

Buisson was perhaps less interested than other republicans in the contribution to national unity of the primary schools, though his internationalism did not reject love of the *patrie*.[19] His greatest interest was in the schools' potential for freeing the country from the domination of Catholicism, the most important obstacle to the development of free thought. Gambetta's battle cry, "Clericalism, there's the enemy," seemed to Buisson not a partisan stratagem but the highest statesmanship.[20] While admitting that Catholics were disturbed by the rise of state education, he blandly denied that they had any legitimate reason for concern.[21] It may be doubted that he expected to convince the Catholics on this point, however, and his main concern was rather to quiet liberal fears that the general principles of liberty might be harmed in the attack on the power of the church.[22] The most complete secularization of education, he argued, would not violate anyone's rights; the removal of all religious personnel from the schools was justified because priests and nuns were ipso facto unqualified to be teachers.[23] None of this constituted an offense against freedom of religion in Buisson's opinion, because government measures merely removed privileges which the church had unjustly enjoyed; France was at last ceasing to treat the church as a sovereign power and forcing it to obey the common law.[24]

On the question of the teaching of a secular moral code in the public schools, Buisson was equally fervent. The pretensions of Catholicism or any other religion to be the foundation of morals were absurd, he insisted, for morals were the foundation on which religions rested, not vice versa.[25] Now that the errors of religion were no longer necessary to man, morals could stand openly as an independent force. Buisson does not appear to have been much interested in the social-science argument behind this position, though since he considered himself a positivist in scientific matters, he was certainly more inclined in that direction than toward any philosophical construction of *la morale indépendante*, such as Renouvier's.[26] At base, morality was self-evident and self-sufficent for Buisson. The example of Christ's life was all the motivating force a man needed, but even that should not be referred to in the schools lest the naive associate it with His presumed divinity. Buisson even suggested that liberal Christians avoid using the word "God" until people were better prepared to understand its real meaning.[27]

Entering into politics as a result of the Dreyfus affair, Buisson was elected to the chamber from Paris in 1902 and sat among the Radical-Socialists. He played a prominent role on several important issues, serving, for example, as chairman of the committee on education and the committee on the separation of church and state.[28] Buisson considered the separation legislation to have been the climax of the process of secularization and thereafter began to work for religious appeasement, one of his main motives in the founding of the Ligue française d'éducation morale in 1911 and the Union pour la culture morale in 1914.[29] In 1912 he fought against those fellow Radicals who wanted to continue to use the schools as an anticlerical weapon, and he even opposed the state monopoly of education that had been the logical outcome of his earlier position.[30]

In putting aside religious issues, Buisson turned his attention to social and political reform. He became prominent in the effort to lead liberals to accept a large number of reforms in the interests of the working classes, especially the minimum wage and other forms of social insurance such as unemployment and retirement benefits.[31] The attitude of free thought which rejected authority in religion, also, he insisted, opposed privilege in politics and the power of capital in economics.[32] The intellectual foundations of Buisson's advocacy of social reform were somewhat sketchy; in general, he spoke of society's obligation to enable men to be men.[33] His position was no doubt closest to that of Léon Bourgeois' *solidarisme* (and Bourgeois contributed a preface to Buisson's 1908 manifesto, *La politique radicale*), but he had some reservations about the foundations of solidarism and continued to emphasize that society was composed of individuals who possessed rights against the collectivity.[34] His vision of man remained at heart closer to that of the philosophical liberals than to that of their sociological rivals. Yet clearly he was seeking that middle way between individualism and socialism which characterized the new liberalism.

Buisson's interest in political reforms was also significant. As vice-chairman of the chamber's committee on universal suffrage, he promoted the adoption of proportional representation. Buisson was also the most important political figure of the early Third Republic to support women's suffrage, which was not a popular cause among old or new liberals in France.[35] Introducing a women's suffrage bill into the legislature, he warned fellow deputies that France was falling behind the rest of the civilized world and risked becoming a laughingstock because of its resistance to women's rights. The liberal commitment to the universality of rights, he insisted, had long since undercut all the various arguments against women's suffrage.[36] Not to be "progressive" remained the cardinal sin in Buisson's world view; in other words, he was the complete twentieth-century liberal activist, even to the extent of being a little ahead of his time in certain of his opinions. Not notable for his intellectual contribution to the new liberalism, he was an important example of the temperament which made it a political force before World War I.

A similar activist view and temperament were represented within the university by Gabriel Séailles, who succeeded Paul Janet in the chair of modern philosophy at the Sorbonne in 1898. Séailles belonged to the new generation of philosophers brought up on the Kantian revival.[37] He collaborated with Janet on a massive history of philosophy and wrote a solid book on Renouvier.[38] While following Renouvier in his critique of metaphysics, Séailles did not exactly become a neo-criticist himself.[39] It would indeed be difficult to assign him to a particular school of thought, because his temperament was more activist than reflective. While well aware of the problems raised by the confrontation of science and philosophy, he did not think it worthwhile to make an all-out effort to resolve them in the manner of a Renouvier or a Fouillée. From Séailles' point of view both science and philosophy had practical weaknesses as well as strengths. Science was the means to truth, but it did not supply us with enough knowledge to live on; philosophy tended to confuse its abstract conceptions with reality, but it provided some of the values and inspiration which men need in order to live. Séailles hacked his way out of this dilemma with what might be called a philosophy of action or of will:

> Since we do not find in nature or in history the facts which correspond to the moral order, since that order risks becoming only a vain fiction if divorced from reality, it is left up to man to posit by his actions the facts which will start to prove that it is possible for the moral order to be in accord with reality.
> Ideals are born in action and find their justification in it.[40]

This philosophy supplied Séailles with the motivation for a social action well beyond his responsibilities as a professor.

By his example more than by his doctrine, Séailles sought to liberate middle-class youth from its complacency and egoism.[41] The most notable aspect of his action was his involvement in the campaign to bring higher education to the working classes. Séailles played a prominent part in the founding and operation of the first of the *universités populaires*, the "Coopération des Idées" of the Faubourg St-Antoine, and he served as president of the Société des universités populaires.[42] The *universités populaires* were meant to build bridges between the middle-class intelligentsia and the workers—to show the intellectuals that they and the workers belonged to the same society, that their interests and aspirations were *solidaire*.[43] This was certainly more important than introducing the workers to the outlines of the history of philosophy or the rudiments of higher mathematics, though such courses could be the vehicles for the accomplishment of his social goals.[44] Contrary to socialist suspicions, his aim was not so much to co-opt the workers as to radicalize the middle classes.

Séailles' particular target was that middle-class intelligentsia whose numbers were being swollen by the expansion of public education. The young educators involved in the *universités populaires* were mostly of relatively modest origin and not altogether anxious to deny their origins.[45] While there may have been an element of condescension in the hand they extended to the workers, there cannot have been much, or they would not have found an audience. Audience there was. A small minority of French workingmen had always been interested in higher learning; the spread of public primary education, though it did not prepare anyone to enter the system of higher education, can only have diffused that taste more widely. The professors of the republic were determined to show that the regime responded to the needs and interests of all the people; where public instruments for such action were lacking they tackled it by private action, calling on the purses of their fellow middle classes to finance the *universités populaires*. Attacked by the Right on the grounds that they would make dangerous malcontents of the workers, and attacked on the Left for trying to absorb the workers into the capitalist system, the position of Séailles and his colleagues was eminently characteristic of twentieth-century liberalism.

Like Buisson, Séailles was a kind of lay preacher for the democratic republic. His religion was equally secular, God having become a synonym for the spirit of justice. He advocated tolerance but was vigorously anticlerical, concerned to destroy the power of the church.[46] He defended private property and condemned revolutionary socialism, while castigating the egoism of the rich and promoting cooperatives and syndicalism.[47] Like most liberals he preferred voluntary institutions over governmental ones as instruments for building the new solidarity lacking in modern society.

Séailles campaigned for public morality without attempting to ground it in either philosophy or sociology. Science offered no moral direction for mankind; religious dogma was dead and could not be revived, even in a modernized and secularized version; philosophy offered little practical guidance; men would just have to look to their consciences for the inspiration needed for moral life.[48] This would not threaten social solidarity, for the individual conscience was not a thing apart, isolated from the society of its fellows; in any given time and place certain possibilities and those alone were open to it. The modern conscience was committed to individual liberty, social equality, and justice; man through his action would find, bit by bit, the means of translating this understanding into reality.[49] It was not carefully reasoned arguments, in any case, but the evolutionary advance of the modern consciousness that prevented thought—and mankind with it—from making any retrogression.[50]

With the "Century of Progress" about to close in 1914, French liberals had embarked on a course of social and intellectual reform that would have seemed in the eyes of many earlier liberals to have threatened liberty by its emphasis on collective action and the obligations of the individual to society. Public spokesmen for the new liberalism like Buisson and Séailles had identified many of the social issues of the new age and eagerly attacked them. These activists were aware of the underlying intellectual issue of the relations of the individual to the society but chose a course of action rather than of the reflection characteristic of most of the other thinkers covered by this study. The activists were nonetheless part of the same intellectual milieu, as Séailles showed when he remarked, somewhat hesitantly: "... Perhaps it is possible by rising from the idea of the individual to the idea of the person to find that which justifies both respect for man and devotion to society."[51] Others who were not content with such a "perhaps" would seek to establish more solid intellectual grounds for the socializing of liberalism than seemed necessary to Buisson or Séailles. The story of their effort will fill the rest of this work.

·V·

Sociology and Liberalism: The Challenge

*T*he rise of sociology was undoubt-
edly one of the main features of intellectual life in the Western world in
the nineteenth century. Surprisingly, the relationship of the growth of
sociology to the evolution of liberalism has been little studied in France
despite the considerable attention given the parallel phenomena in the
Anglo-Saxon world. That relationship was, nonetheless, of considerable
importance in France, as the remainder of this work will try to show.
In the early years of the Third Republic there were a number of important efforts to give liberalism a social scientific foundation which
would enable it to adapt to the changing problems of a new era. The
most influential of these efforts turned out to be that of Emile Durkheim; but this was by no means apparent (or assured) before the Great
War, and we are going to look in the next two chapters at some of the
major varieties of sociological liberalism which emerged at that time:
those of Espinas, Izoulet, and Tarde in this chapter, that of Fouillée in
the following.

It can hardly be surprising that the nineteenth century should have
seen an effort to include politics in the domain of science, to replace
political philosophy with political science. For many it had come to
seem evident that no field of thought need any longer be considered
outside the reach of scientific method. Or if anything was resistant, it
could be dismissed as mere metaphysics, a survival of man's intellectual infancy. As far as political thought was concerned, this movement
had its origins in the effort to separate political theory from ethics, to
make it a field of study in its own right. This was one of the characteristics of the intellectual side of the Renaissance and was evidently

95

linked in a general way to the rising interest in science of that epoch. The effort to construct a political science based on observation went back at least to Machiavelli and, in France, to Jean Bodin.

In the eighteenth century this empirical approach gave way to a more rationalistic scientism which sought to deduce the features of the ideal social order from a few postulates which were taken to be scientifically established. The sense-psychology propounded by Locke and brought to its fullest development by Condillac furnished the grounds for most of this line of thought. The scientific ideal was to be found in the deductive methods of mathematics, which with mechanics and astronomy was the most advanced and successful branch of science. The social systems of Mably and Morelly belonged in this category.

Another fertile source of ideas which came into increasing prominence was natural history, which seemed a promising source of ideas which could be applied to man. The growing accomplishments of the biological sciences, which seemed at last to be following in the path laid down by the physical sciences, gave biology a predominant influence on social scientific thought in the nineteenth century. Acquired results and promises for the future were often inextricably confused in this borrowing, and the grounds for the transfer of ideas from one domain to the other were rarely examined with any seriousness. Biological metaphor worked its way so deeply into the Western languages as to appear even in the writing of people who rejected the validity of that metaphor for the study of man and his society. The most influential aspects of biological science were cell theory, which opened a door into the workings of living things that had previously been seen only in gross anatomical terms, and evolutionism. Both supporters and critics rightly saw in evolution the principal novelty of nineteenth-century thought. For those with some knowledge of modern philosophy, the ascendancy of evolutionism began with Hegel.[1] Even for the rest, it was well established before Darwin; and the *Origin of Species* (1859) supplied what evolutionists had been looking for, a plausible explanation of the mechanics of biological evolution.

The impact of this development on French thought was to promote a search for the biological foundations of politics. This search went in several directions, not all of which are of interest to us here because they led to clearly antiliberal conclusions. The most obvious of these is racism. Nineteenth-century liberals were by no means immune to racial ideas or even to seeing racial conflict as one of the great motivating forces of history.[2] What they rejected was any effort to build political and moral philosophy on racial differences. To do so could only justify the domination of some over others, offering no foundation for the liberty of all. Racism could serve as a base only for authoritarian politics—it was probably this conclusion which enabled liberals to pierce the scientific veneer of racism to see the irrationalism underneath. The other direction rejected by French liberals was Social Darwinism, which would enjoy a greater vogue in England and the United States than in France. The French, while not denying the existence and indeed the ampleness of conflict in nature, insisted that it also furnished examples of harmony, of cooperation, of organization for mutual benefit. Any attempt, therefore, to model political philosophy on biological science had to take into account the latter as well as the former. Moreover, the fact of struggle in the animal world did not prove that struggle for survival ought to be law for the human world.[3] Social Darwinism of the Anglo-Saxon variety, whatever its advocates may have thought, was not a philosophy of liberty; the French rightly placed it among the antiliberal schools of thought in the nineteenth century.[4]

In France, the search for a biological foundation was primarily a search for models of cooperative organization. This search could lead to liberal as well as to authoritarian conclusions, depending on the searcher's prior inclinations (which should have been enough to bring the scientific character of the work into question, but seldom was). Evolutionism was used as a model to explain the historic changes of human societies, and, equally importantly, to justify the value-relativism implicit in this view of history. Here is where the French found the conjunction of Hegelianism and Darwinism, reinforcing one another. If no universal measures could be justified by science, if society evolved in a determined pattern, then there were different truths for different eras and peoples; and the search for the absolute was reduced to a passing phase of the human experience.

This trend, perhaps the major one in nineteenth-century French thought, led irresistibly to the rise of social-scientific political thought. The particular conditions of the early Third Republic also contributed to its implantation in France: the social problem that was brought most insistently to the attention of the makers and supporters of the republic was the lack of national unity. Whether they stressed the religious division between Catholic and secular society or the economic division between the rich and the poor, political leaders and political thinkers returned again and again to the question of how to unite this fragmented nation. The defeat of 1870–71 made this a question which even those most satisfied with the existing social order could not ignore. There was a tendency for older republicans to accentuate the religious question and for younger ones to worry more about the socioeconomic, but there was no really clear-cut division on a generational basis—an overlapping in any case.[5]

The conflicts surrounding the foundation of the Third Republic gave an emphasis to the religious question. The church and some Catholic politicians had figured too prominently in the monarchist camp for it to be otherwise. The result, as we have seen in the previous chapter, was an attempt to build national unity from the base by a program of moral and civic education at the elementary level founded on a liberal philosophy, which its proponents considered to be compatible with the rights of all citizens because it was based on reason alone and did not infringe on the domain of religious differences. Acceptance of the legitimacy of this effort could almost be taken as the distinguishing mark of a liberal in the 1870s and 1880s. But experience showed the failure of this effort to win the assent of all consciences and, rather than treat this as the result of the malevolence of the priests clinging to the last vestiges of their authority, some liberals began to argue that it was a result of the weakness of the philosophy on which this education was based. The philosophers of neo-criticism entered into this debate; and as they increasingly occupied places of influence in the educational system, they would try to make the program even more rationalistic. But one could not teach Kant to third graders—or even try to explain the difference between spiritualism and criticism—so that the impact of their effort was greater on the philosophy classes of the secondary program, which reached only a small minority of all children. What they could teach to the elementary grades was, after all, not much different from the spiritualist program—or, for that matter, from the positivist program.

The social sciences offered another way out of the problem. If metaphysics remained controversial in spite of all efforts, then clearly it was not the long-sought grounds of unity. But social science, by rejecting all issues of religion and metaphysics as irrelevant, basing itself on "facts" that could be understood and accepted by everyone—how could they not be, since they were facts?—offered the real way to unity.[6] Since science alone was universal, science would have to produce the *morale* which the country's educational system needed, which the country needed if it was to recover from the divisions of the past and avoid the new divisions looming in the future. For social science would claim to offer the path toward the reconciliation of not only the rights of the individual and the interests of society but also of the classes within modern society. Thus the overall trend of ideas and the stimulus of specifically French problems came together to bring to birth the new social scientific liberalism.[7]

In addition to the biological sciences the other major influence on the direction taken by French sociological theory was that of Auguste Comte's positivism. Though Comte had a set of loyal disciples—who indeed supported him financially in his later years—his influence did not depend on any strict fidelity to his ideas. The disciples themselves were split between those who followed him to the end in the Religion of Humanity and those like Emile Littré who accepted the first part of his work and repudiated the last as an aberration. This latter group was, obviously, the more respectable and influential. More than any specific ideas, it was the general drift of Comtism which seemed to many to sum up the new age—especially his proclamation that henceforth man could live entirely by the light of science. That he offered more of an encouragement to scientism than to science was no obstacle, since few yet saw this distinction. Also vaguely influential was his "scientific" representation of the idea of progress in the famous "Law" of Three Stages. This gave an aroma of necessity to his proclamation of the end of theology and metaphysics. What on top of this assured the respectful attention of social scientists in the following generations was his classification of the sciences, which put sociology—the word he is credited with coining—at the summit, arguing that man had now reached the stage where this most complex, difficult, and important of sciences could take flight in its turn. The promise of finding oneself at the summit of man's intellectual history is a heady one; if not everyone was so unbalanced by it as Comte himself, it was surely nonetheless a powerful spur to the imagination.

As a sociologist, Comte himself remained in the prescientific age. His was still the era of heroic individual effort, the erection of enormous comprehensive systems in which deduction from a small number of postulates was the method of work, in which the quality of the results depended on the encyclopedic grasp of one man and his ability to avoid getting lost in abstraction or in detail. A mathematician by training (not an original or important one—Comte's forte was telling other scientists what they ought to be doing, an attitude he inherited from his nonscientist mentor Saint-Simon), Comte was inclined to deduction and abstraction, despite his professed reverence for induction. When he turned to sociology, Comte was certainly no longer at his best, but he showed one direction in which a positivist political philosophy could go—and it was certainly not liberal.

It was not Comte's appeal for the support of the conservative backers of Louis Napoleon that made him an anti-liberal. Even Proudhon had been tempted by this possibility at appealing to the enlightened despot. It was rather the deduction which he drew from his scientism. By eliminating the unknowable from human concerns, man would deal only with questions which could be answered definitively, where the answers of science would compel agreement. Questions of freedom of conscience disappear when there is only a question of being right or wrong. And for Comte all scientific knowledge had the analytic certainty of two plus two equals four. When science had uncovered the laws of society and explained the right organization of government, there could be no longer any room for differences of opinion, for the very word "opinion" would be a "non-sense." Comte, it is true, was inclined to rush things, to believe that he had already found all, or almost all, the necessary answers; and a social organization was part of his Religion of Humanity. Yet, all of Comte's mental aberrations aside, was he not right to see that belief in a science of society offers the highest license to suppress differences of opinion and, indeed, all other kinds of freedom?

For the most part, the heirs of Comtean sociology did not think so. Their concept of science was more sophisticated than his; their view of the accomplishments of social science was more modest; they were more respectful of the complexities of the problems involved since they started from natural history or from philosophy (which Comte had banished) rather than from mathematics. The key separation came over the nature of society. They could all praise Comte for reacting against the extreme individualism of his time and for recalling the individual's dependence upon society (a call in which he was echoing the theocrats Maistre and Bonald), but they balked at his insistence that only society is real. Yes, society was real; and some, like Espinas, would go so far as to consider it a living organism possessed of a consciousness distinct from that of its members. But the individual was real, too, and society existed for the benefit of the parts as well as the whole.[8] It would remain to be seen whether a liberalism could be built on this foundation.

That the effort would be made seems inevitable in the political, social, and intellectual context of the early Third Republic. The declining credit of spiritualist liberalism and the difficulties of the criticists in getting themselves accepted as scientific seemed to call for an effort to found liberalism on science. The idea that individualism had been taken to extremes was accepted in all the liberal camps; the problem was how to bring it back into harmony with society. The efforts to do this were not new, as we have seen—spiritualism itself having always tried to avoid extremes of any kind—and criticism seeing the unshakable foundation in reason for this harmony. These efforts can all be called attempts to socialize liberalism, to bring about the "socialization of the idea of the 'self.' "[9] There remained an alternative approach, and that was to liberalize sociology. In the remainder of this work we will try to see what happened when liberalism and sociology came together. This chapter will examine three quite different efforts, two by well-known figures, Alfred Espinas (1844-1922) and Gabriel Tarde (1843-1904), the third by the briefly influential, quickly forgotten Jean Izoulet (1858-1929).

Alfred Espinas was born on 23 May 1844 at Saint-Florentin (Yonne), where his father was a pharmacist; if his father was a typical member of his profession in nineteenth-century France, he was probably the origin of the liberal and anticlerical attitudes that Alfred would later profess.[10] Circumstances also had their impact, for just when Espinas was reaching the later years of his secondary education, the philosophy program was abolished by the government of Napoleon III on the grounds that it was promoting political dissent and irreligion. It seems likely that Espinas' militant atheism dated from this experience of clericalism in politics, or at least was reinforced by it. There was not any secondary program in the natural sciences at that time, so Espinas turned to the study of French literature. He was usually at the head of his class at the lycée of Sens, where he had as a classmate and friend the poet Stéphane Mallarmé. To prepare for the Ecole normale supérieure, Espinas transferred his studies to the Lycée Louis-le-Grand in Paris; he was admitted to the Ecole normale in 1864 and studied philosophy under Albert Lemoine and Jules Lachelier.

Despite his evident talent Espinas was clearly not in good favor with the education authorities of the Second Empire. His first teaching assignment as a philosophy professor was in the lycée of Bastia (Corsica), and his acceptance in the *agrégation* competition was delayed until 1871. He had, nonetheless, moved, in 1868, to the lycée of Chaumont, where he began the independent study of natural history which would greatly influence the formation of his sociology. With the outbreak of the Franco-Prussian War, Espinas joined the National Guard of Chaumont, which marched but never saw battle. The war and the Commune stimulated his interest in social questions, and it led Espinas to set for himself a course of study designed to produce the science of society needed for the revitalization of France.

After the fall of the Second Empire, Espinas taught in the lycées of Le Havre (1871) and Dijon (1873) while working on his doctoral theses. His principal thesis, *Des sociétés animales,* made quite a stir (see below) both intellectually and politically, attracting the interest and approval of politicians as diverse as Léon Gambetta and Louis Barthou (1877). Despite the controversy, he received an appointment to the Faculty of Letters at Douai and then at Bordeaux. Espinas would remain at Bordeaux for a number of years, becoming titular professor of philosophy in 1881 and doyen of the faculty in 1887. In 1882 he inaugurated the course in pedagogy in which he would be succeeded, with greater éclat, by Emile Durkheim. All told, the years in Bordeaux were the happiest and most productive of Espinas' career.

The call to Paris finally came in 1893. His importance as an innovative thinker was recognized by the creation of a chair of the Histoire d'économie sociale for him at the Sorbonne, endowed by the Comte de Chambrun in 1894. What might have been an apotheosis became a disappointment. Though named to the chair, he only held the rank of Chargé de cours, and Espinas was not elevated as titular professor of his chair until 1904. He had in the meantime failed to build a student following, became disenchanted with his position, and virtually stopped teaching in 1907. After repeated leaves of absence he was forced to relinquish the chair and retired in 1911. Espinas was honored with the succession to Tarde's chair of the Académie des sciences morales et politiques in 1905, but by then biosociology's day was over in France. In some ways Espinas had the misfortune to have been born too soon. As a pioneer he had spent too much of his effort in securing recognition for the legitimacy of his work. As a result he did not reach Paris, the vital center for the exercise of intellectual influence, until his views were already being outmoded. Though the path he opened up for social science undoubtedly led to a dead end, Espinas deserved greater recognition for his innovative work.

In general histories of sociology, Alfred Espinas is usually presented as an important precursor of Emile Durkheim, a sort of intermediary between Durkheim and Comte, and as the author of a curious thesis on animal societies, which has a certain status as a "classic" even though sociology everywhere has taken an altogether different direction.[11] None of this is exactly false, but neither does it give us an adequate picture of his role. Our concern here, of course, is not the history of sociology but rather the impact of sociology on liberalism.[12] In that context, though, Espinas occupies a similar position; he took an abortive direction, but one not without influence because of the quality of the man and his work.

Espinas did indeed help pave the way for Durkheim's sociology, but with an approach basically different from Durkheim's.[13] Rather than a continuer of Comte, he aspired to introduce into France a sociology derived from Herbert Spencer.[14] But French sociology proved as resistant to Spencer's biologism as French liberalism did to his extreme individualism. Espinas himself rejected this extremism, which seemed to him an inconsistency in Spencer, and sought to draw the scientific consequences of the Spencerian approach, which made social evolution merely a specific case of organic evolution, more rigorously than the founder.[15] For he saw this as the path to make sociology finally scientific, as Comte had failed so signally to do.

For Espinas, science and politics were never very remote from one another. Just three years into his career as a philosophy professor in 1870, he was determined to find in science the means to the revival of France.[16] The biological justification of the nation figured prominently in his work, with the consequent impetus to subordinate the individual to the goal of national revival.[17] He quickly drew back from the antiliberal implications of this position, however, and espoused a liberalism which derived from the evolution of societies. Biological sociology proved capable of supporting—at least in the minds of its proponents—a rather diverse, even contradictory, set of political positions.

With Espinas, the drive to be scientific and the drive to be useful were equally strong.[18] Indeed, they seemed to him to be inseparable: only by being scientific could one hope to be really useful. Experience would later convince him that this was not so true in practice as it seemed in theory, but his commitment to science did not waver. Espinas agreed with Comte in situating sociology as the science which follows biology in the natural hierarchy of knowledge. An important part of his effort was to better mark the dividing line between the two sciences. Following Littré and rejecting Comte, he also allowed psychology a similar position, but he considered it essential to science to clearly distinguish the three from each other.[19] Though he collaborated in some experimental psychology research, Espinas later came to the rueful conclusion that the popularity of experimental psychology had been a hindrance to the advance of sociology.[20] He nonetheless adhered to his conviction, absorbed from Spencer, that a unity of principles bound all the sciences together and that therefore sociology and philosophy would develop necessarily out of biology.

The principle which bound them together was that of evolutionary development: differentiation and organization.[21] Without this continuity there could be no hope for a scientific sociology (a possibility which Espinas could not admit). Societies themselves had to be products of evolutionary development out of simpler forms; one could only discover where the science of society began by retracing this development. This was what Espinas set out to do in his thesis, which became his most famous work, *Des sociétés animales*. Trained as a philosopher, he had to educate himself as a naturalist and present his thesis to a jury of philosophers, including Paul Janet and Elme Caro. It is easy to imagine the consternation this fiercely positivistic work caused among the spiritualist philosophers, but their habitual tolerance found a way to award him a doctorate.[22] Certainly *Des sociétés animales* supplanted the dualism of the eclectics with a rigorous monism.

Espinas began by tracing the (presumed) evolution of multicellular animals out of simpler forms until he arrived at the level of what he called "societies of nutrition" (or *blastodèmes)* in which a differentiation of cells plus their inseparable interdependence for nutrition marked what he at that time considered the beginning of society and the domain of sociology.[23] The course of evolution was then further traced to show the emergence of higher forms of societies in which the linkages of the component parts were more psychological than physical. Despite this distinction, Espinas insisted that there was an absolute continuity between higher and lower societies. All higher organisms were shown to be societies of societies.[24] Just as an individual of a higher species was really a society of lesser individuals, so might we consider the society of higher individuals itself an individual.[25] The higher one went, the more the bonds of this society were psychic, and the psychic predominated at the level of human society.[26]

While this course of evolution obviously made the relations of human individuals to their society rather different than the philosophers had ever imagined, Espinas did not think that it threatened individual liberty. Understanding the character of the individual and his limits in relation to society—that is, understanding the real nature of liberty—was necessary if man was to maximize his potential liberty. One of the most important (and controversial) steps, according to Espinas, was to conceive of human society as an individual, one whose most striking characteristic was the possession of a *conscience collective*.[27] Insisting on the absolute reality of this *conscience collective*, Espinas argued that the consciousness of the individual human is itself a sort of *conscience collective*, lacking that absolute unity and distinctiveness attributed to it by philosophy. The physical base of the *conscience collective* of society—it had to have one—was the brains of that society's intellectual elite. This physical dispersion seemed no obstacle to Espinas, but rather a logical evolutionary development.

Espinas would never abandon his conviction that the reality of the *conscience collective* was absolutely necessary if there was to be a science of society. Those who denied it were usurping the name of sociologists, following the fad for sociology without accepting its scientific discipline. He rejected the objection that it led to the suppression of human liberty. Liberty was not the source of modern societies, as political philosophers had imagined; it was a product of those societies. The complex psychic interrelationships of human beings—having its biological roots, but reaching a new level with the emergence of consciousness—produced a social order which alone made possible what men have come to think of as freedom.

While Espinas' argument hinged on analogies between human and other animal societies, and while he insisted on the validity of those analogies, he was well aware of the abuses which had been made of organismic analogy and was determined to avoid such pitfalls by a careful analysis of the whole process of evolution.[28] He hoped to avoid establishing mere rhetorical similarities through the demonstration of evolutionary continuity. Despite his affiliation with Spencer, Espinas' evolutionism was not purely in the English school: he was more of a Lamarckian than a Darwinist.[29] While refusing to find any finality in the evolutionary process, he did not see it as a blind fatality, either. An element of choice and consciousness entered into the process of selection—of real, not merely apparent, alternatives—at all but the lowest levels. Unconscious forces were dominant, even at the level of man, but they were not exclusive.[30]

Espinas was anxious to avoid the pitfall which the eclectics had seen in evolutionism: he did not want to be taken as a materialist. Repudiating transcendence, he followed the monist solution of finding consciousness immanent in the real world of phenomena. It was its quality as a product of evolution that made consciousness real for Espinas, giving it a reality which philosophy had sought in vain to demonstrate.[31] He even went so far as to call his position "idealist." Where his philosophy teachers had gone astray was in their emphasis on rationality. Both psychology and sociology showed that it played a secondary role in human affairs; habit and instinct (which were closely related) were much more powerful.[32] There was a continuity between man and the lower animals, a difference of degree but not of kind. Espinas did not think that his view sacrificed man's distinctiveness; it merely put that distinctiveness on a more solid foundation.

Recognizing the force of the spiritualist arguments that fatalism and materialism undercut morality, Espinas was concerned to show that his linkage of man and animal did not have the same effect.[33] This led him to find evidence of morality among animals, commensurate with their limited degrees of consciousness, though he insisted that actions may be moral without conscious motivation.[34] This conclusion was necessary if he was to demonstrate an imminent source for morality. In this effort he certainly followed the Comtean tradition: morality was defined as altruistic action and its source was found in sympathy.[35] More specifically, it was found in the intrinsic sympathy which all animals have for others of their kind (explained as a sort of identification—a recognition of themselves in others).[36] It was this sympathy which permitted the positivist to pass from the more fundamental (because appearing earlier in the evolutionary process) sentiment of egoism to altruism. Altruism was a kind of egoism which had broadened its base to include others of the same kind.[37] The kinds of arguments on which philosophers tried to found morality were all clearly later products of the evolutionary process. Espinas did not come to grips with the arguments against trying to explain morality in terms of sympathy; there could be no other way to explain it, given his basic assumptions.

Moreover, this approach to morality accorded with Espinas' initial impulse of national regeneration. The sympathy of likes for likes no doubt extended to all of humanity, but only in very diluted strength. The basic unit of human society was the nation, and it was this identification which Espinas wanted to reinforce.[38] He was not offering a racist concept of the nation, however; the biological roots of the sympathy which Frenchmen felt (or should have felt) for each other were covered by a thick layer of social experiences. Blood and soil did not rule so imperiously for Espinas as they did for Barrès.[39] Espinas was inclined to deny the title of society to groups less "organic" than the nation; they were associations which lacked the quality of inclusiveness necessary to the existence of a *conscience collective*.[40] It was this latter consideration which prevented Espinas from seeing the nation as a society of societies of societies, a view possible under the Durkheimian idea of "social fact" but not in Espinas' initial idea of "social fact." He did later conclude that society was composed of families and would not have its organic character without them.[41] Twentieth-century sociology has remained divided on the significance of social units smaller than the nation; so has twentieth-century liberalism.

Espinas must be credited with being among the first to understand the potential relationship of sociology and liberal politics. He clearly grasped the transition which we have been trying to demonstrate and gave one of the clearest expositions of the question as early as 1882. Espinas always placed himself firmly in the liberal camp; if he had been active in politics, it would probably have been with those who called themselves Radical-Socialists, that is, the left wing of the liberal movement. This was not the main distinction which separated him from the more conservative liberalism of the eclectics, however; for they were in agreement over most of the spectrum of liberal values. Espinas parted company with the older generation over the question of how that liberalism was to be defended and on what grounds its claims were to be justified.[42]

Conceding that on the whole the liberal philosophy had been effective in practice in the past, he argued that by the coming of the Third Republic it was losing its effectiveness.[43] Philosophical liberalism was in decay because it was ceasing to be intellectually tenable; because it could not provide adequate answers to the problems of the day; because, simply, people were ceasing to believe in it, and its efficacy rested on that belief.[44] Espinas called philosophical liberalism the "revolutionary religion," and he meant literally that it had the intellectual character of a religion, whose credo was the Declaration of the Rights of Man. Its doctrine was held to be above criticism, and with good reason, he thought, since, like other religions, it could not stand scientific examination.[45]

Espinas traced the rise of the idea of absolute rights of the human person to reaction against the oppressive regime of Louis XIV.[46] That regime's very absoluteness made the idea of rights an effective political weapon, and once it was sufficiently diffused in the population, it brought down the ancien régime. But the idea of absolute rights failed, he thought, as a grounds for justifying liberal government and society. Its absolute character encouraged a tendency to go to logical extremes, and the doctrine of absolute rights could lead in two opposite directions, both fatal to liberal society.[47] Both of these directions were already to be seen in Rousseau's *Social Contract*. Taken in one direction, the doctrine made government impossible, creating an anarchy of individual rights with no possibility of effective association among them. Taken in the other direction, it did succeed in founding society, but only at the price of the total sacrifice of natural rights and with no means of connection from them to the social rights which replaced them. In practical politics liberals would oscillate between Rousseau's proclamation that men are born free and his suggestion that it could be legitimate to force them to be free.[48] French political experience showed this was no mere possibility.

Because their political doctrine was a religion rather than a coherent system of thought, the liberals, Espinas thought, were able to paper over its weaknesses and internal contradictions. They could speak of absolute rights without fear of their logical consequences because of a whole complex of Christian beliefs which restricted the application of those rights, because of the social experience of a whole society which accepted many curbs on individual expression. But within itself liberal philosophy had no grounds for effectively curbing the excesses of liberty.[49] Espinas did not go so far as to say it, but he clearly suggested that the ideal position for a liberal politician, like Jules Simon, was to be in opposition, where he could throw his absolutes at the head of the government without having to fear that they would be enacted. The behavior of the Radical party in power would seem to confirm such a view. It was not that the liberals did not understand the need for gradualism and pragmatism—they clearly did—but that their justifications for them were intellectually unsound.

As a sociologist, Espinas would readily concede that a coherent intellectual justification is not necessary to a successful politics. But belief in the existence of such a justification was necessary, and Espinas could not believe that he was alone in finding the liberal philosophy without force. The whole positive trend of the century toward scientific thought was inescapably eroding the conviction which had supported liberalism. It was, therefore, an urgent necessity to put a scientific foundation in its place, and this was the mission he envisaged for biological sociology. In the beginning, he seems to have expected sociological theory to bring immediate practical support to liberal politics.[50] Later he would admit to having been excessively sanguine, that his own views should have told him the process would be long; the gap between social theory and the art of politics was not unbridgeable, but it was wide. There were dangers in demanding too much too soon.[51]

First and foremost, he explained, sociology was better equipped than philosophy to solve the problem of the relations of the individual and society because it was not handicapped by the abstract idea of the isolated, distinct, autonomous individual.[52] Espinas' whole evolutionary sociology was focused on this problem, explaining how individuals and societies were related through the workings of one and the same evolutionary process. In this view the individual could not be abstracted from society; indeed, he owed his very existence to that of the society, and the qualities which distinguish men from other animals are the products of social relations for which the individual can claim little credit.[53] Espinas hotly denied that the primacy of society thus conceived was a threat to individual liberty; he attempted to show that, on the contrary, it was the best possible defense.[54]

Those who jumped by analogy from primitive animal societies to human society might argue that the individual was nothing and society all, but this was not Espinas' method. His evolutionary approach attempted to show the distinguishing characteristics of higher societies and of human society in particular. The *conscience collective* of human society did not negate, he insisted, the individual consciences that were parts of it. If they were zero, so would it be zero.[55] The more complex the society, the more complex the individuals that make it up.[56] And the complexity of human society was not just in the economic division of labor which made everyone materially dependent on the whole; it was in the whole mass of mental relations—intellectual, religious, moral, esthetic—which men have with each other. It was in this complexity rather than in some innate character of the individual, some metaphysical substance, that liberty had its origin. Liberty was nonetheless real for being a later product of evolution.[57] In Espinas' view, it was impossible to set up the value of the individual against society, for the nature of that society safeguarded all the *possible* liberty of the individual.

Liberty, in Espinas' view, was not merely an illusion; indeed, it was the liberty of the philosophers which was illusory. To proclaim that human rights consisted of what a society had come to admit as human rights did not appear to him to threaten the future of those rights.

It is certain that the idea of rights is not abolished or even diminished according to the evolutionary hypothesis, but rather it is transformed and reinterpreted. For the spiritualists, rights are inherent and individual; for the naturalists, they result from social action and are facts of opinion. . . . Society is not limited to defining and safeguarding rights; it creates them, since rights are nothing but the value attributed to the human person by public opinion in a given country.[58]

Understanding the true origin and nature of rights would not cause men to disbelieve in them, but it would make it easier to see how to apply them in the present. There was, nonetheless, a change of focus here from that of the older liberalism, for Espinas' approach offered a cure for the excesses of individualism more than a protection against the excesses of government.

Clearly, Espinas favored more government than did the eclectic philosophers, including a greater role for the state in economic matters. Against the economic doctrine of the eclectics, which he called a revival of the Physiocrats, he tended to favor a revival of mercantilism.[59] This was a by-product of his conception of the nation as the highest organic society, and he was attracted by the national economics of Friedrich List (perhaps swayed here by his memories of 1870).[60] He rejected the socialist movements as utopian—Marxism as antisocial— but argued that the working of economic laws would in the long run convert certain enterprises into public services because that was their nature.[61] What evolutionism taught in this matter as in others was the necessity of gradualism; social evolution was not as slow as organic evolution, but it was subject to the same requirement of going through intermediate stages.[62] Welfare-state liberalism would illustrate in practice the kind of development Espinas favored, though he did not explicitly formulate the concept.[63]

Representative government—republican under modern circumstances—also seemed to flow naturally from his biosociology.[64] What it did not support was any sort of leveling egalitarianism. The collective consciousness of modern societies was so complex that it could not be effectively lodged in the brain of one man. A broad representation was necessary to get an accurate expression of it, and the more successful a government was in expressing the *conscience collective*, the more effective and stable it would be.[65] The executive power, on the other hand, needed the authority to carry out the laws decided by the representative organ—moral authority, mostly, but coercion as well. Animal societies showed that the necessity of leadership was deeply rooted in life, and human societies had to have elites to survive, and the *conscience collective* had to be personified in individuals if it was to function.[66] But modern society had a larger complex of elites, and the social analog of the individual brain was highly dispersed.[67] In Espinas' opinion, this again was an advantage of the sociological view. All the eclectics believed in the existence and necessity of elites, but the only grounds that their doctrine offered for justifying such elites were the superior merits and abilities of individuals—which clearly were inadequate to account for reality and which were in any case fundamentally at war with the egalitarian conception of absolute human rights.

In Espinas' opinion, the eclectics faced a similar problem when it came to the question of property.[68] They were aware that the labor theory of the origins of property could be made to lead to conclusions which they considered oppressive—abolition of inheritance, of rents, and so forth—but they could only hedge property rights with qualifications, not arriving at anything else compatible with their individualism. They certainly repudiated any absolute conception of property rights, recognizing such as destructive of society; it was hard for them to find any grounds other than sheer necessity for the restrictions they favored. Even the eclectics recognized that property rights require the sanction of society in order to be effective; Espinas thought that liberals could then accept that property had its origin in the functional development of society. While depriving property of its sacred character, the sociological view still defended its existence with the practical force of experience. Espinas did not agree that this was a less secure defense; it certainly suppressed some of the problems of justifying property's inescapable limits.

The thing that the eclectics perhaps feared most of all was the destruction of morals. Any *morale* not founded in the transcendent seemed to them both to risk falling into relativism and to risk being ineffective in motivating men. Insisting, on the contrary, that the record of transcendental morals in practice was not so wonderful—that, for example, the sanction of eternal punishment had never had much deterrent force—Espinas held that a sociological *morale* would be even more effective.[69] For one thing, its scientific character would eliminate one cause of conflict—disagreement over *morales*. The philosophers seemed to him to be using the question of morals as a smoke screen behind which to conceal the indefensibility of their metaphysical or theological positions. He had every confidence in a future *science des moeurs.*

Espinas was no Voltaire in style or temperament, but he sometimes betrays a regret that it had taken so long to *écraser l'infâme.*[70] In 1901, a moment when the future of sociology was beginning to be assured, he fell into a depression at the persistence of an opposition which by all rights should have been growing weaker, and he attributed sociology's lack of success to a sort of philosophical *cabale des dévots*.[71] Religious prejudice against sociology was unyielding; even people who professed to be sociologists refused, he thought, to draw the necessary conclusions (especially that society was an organism), and that refusal stemmed from their being—however liberated, like Tarde—Christians.[72] The fact that Espinas was an unwavering atheist may no doubt have cast some shadows on his sociology in the minds of the spiritualist philosophers, however much they appreciated the sincerity and seriousness of his quest for truth.[73] But for Espinas, the triumph of sociology meant the triumph of *his* sociology, not out of personal vanity, but because he could see no other path to science.[74] In the end it was the criticism of the Durkheimians rather than that of the philosophers which eclipsed biosociology.[75]

In a more optimistic mood, Espinas grasped the real situation, the evolution of ideas that would give sociology the succession to philosophy at the heart of French liberalism. Philosophy had been an effective foundation for liberty, he observed, as long as people believed in it. Now they no longer did. Sociology would be an equally powerful support when men came to believe in it, as they sooner or later must.[76] The evolution of mentalities at the turn of the century was on the sociologists' side. It was only a semiconscious process (which Espinas could appreciate as well as anyone) in which the quality of arguments, despite their high level on both sides, was less conclusive than the appeal—quasi-rational—of modernity and progress.

Despite Espinas' assertion that his sociology had reached the level of a science, with many researchers in different countries applying the same methods, biosociology was far from presenting a united front, even in France.[77] Starting from the same assumptions (that society was an organism and that its development was ruled by the laws of evolution—that is, differentiation and organization), Jean Izoulet (1858–1929) devoted his career to promoting the revival of France by means of a civic religion. Biosociology could apparently lead to both of the modern temptations feared by the spiritualists: atheism (Espinas) and pantheism (Izoulet). Even within the liberal camp, biosociologists could arrive at quite varied prescriptions for current problems. Izoulet was drawn to the common questions of the relation of the individual to society and the role of elites in modern democratic societies; he sought solutions to those questions which would leave intact the values of liberalism while being compatible with the lessons of modern biological science.

Jean Izoulet came from a family of country doctors, members of the rural bourgeoisie.[78] He was born in the village of Miramont-de-

Quercy on 20 August 1854. When he distinguished himself in secondary studies at the lycée in Montauban, his family sent him to Paris to study at the Lycée Louis-le-Grand in preparation for the Ecole normale supérieure, which he entered in 1874. Emerging as an *agrégé* in philosophy the usual three years later, Izoulet received his first teaching position at the lycée of Bourg-en-Bresse.

The young philosopher quickly distinguished himself as an advocate of a natural, civic religion which—at first—appeared attractive to those republican leaders in search of a laic *morale* for use in the schools. Izoulet attracted their interest at an early age, and he served as personal secretary to Paul Bert, minister of public instruction in Léon Gambetta's short-lived cabinet of 1881–82.[79] While continuing his career as a lycée professor of philosophy, Izoulet was called upon by Jules Ferry to give a series of lectures on "the psychology of morals" to large numbers of primary-school instructors.[80] Izoulet's popularity in republican circles reached its peak with the publication of his doctoral thesis, *La cité moderne et la métaphysique de la sociologie* in 1894.[81] Political patronage had probably contributed to his advancement, as, between 1886 and 1897, he was professor of philosophy in two prestigious Parisian institutions, the Lycée Henri IV and the Lycée Condorcet.

Izoulet was rewarded for his doctoral thesis in 1897 when, through the initiative of the liberal politicians Raymond Poincaré and Léon Bourgeois, a chair of social philosophy was created for him at the Collège de France.[82] Though he would hold this position for the rest of his life, it soon proved a hollow honor. He apparently fell out with the republican educational leadership in the course of the Dreyfus affair, and he lost his opportunity to become a leader in the development of republican social thought. The teaching of sociology was gathered into the hands of the Durkheimians, whom he denounced—without understanding—as teaching a defeatist and pessimistic sociology which could only lead to the ruin of the nation.[83] His considerable oratorical talent enabled Izoulet to continue to draw a sizable audience for his public lectures at the Collège de France, but he had been shunted to a side track and was embittered by it.[84]

Izoulet's quarrel with the republican leaders came to focus on the religious question, for his sociology led him to conclude in the necessity of a civic religion with its corollary, the restoration of God into the state and its schools.[85] While the liberal leadership was united on the need for a laic moral education in the public schools, they had concluded that religious neutrality required the exclusion of any mention of God and were not convinced that Izoulet's pantheism was any more scientific than traditional religion. Despite its evolutionist foundation, Izoulet's civic religion was obviously inspired by the city-states of classical antiquity, though the scale was quite different.[86] Izoulet followed the historian Fustel de Coulanges in seeing state religion as the central characteristic of the Greek polis and as the only force capable of overcoming individual egoism and integrating the individual into the state.[87] Izoulet was indeed not afraid to call his position a revived paganism; but of course it was not a revival of Zeus and Athena, and he preferred to call it a modern pagano-Christian religion.[88] Its pagan characteristics included the cult of the dead and the cult of heroes.[89] Once Christian dualism had been overcome and the monism of the pre-Socratics restored, Izoulet was prepared to recognize some moral value in Christianity, although "Nature, source of life and of laws, is essentially the fount of morality."[90] Izoulet also acknowledged his (and our) indebtedness to Moses, whom he saw as the greatest Western religious figure, not only for the clear-cut moral code of the Decalogue, but also for the Hebrew vision of salvation in this world: for Izoulet vigorously rejected the possibility of personal immortality, which made it all the more important for the individual to be able to find his reason for existing and his satisfaction in this world and this society. Politics thus became the true religion.[91]

The intellectual foundations of Izoulet's civic religion were to be found in his biosociology. Originally trained in philosophy, he had undertaken considerable postgraduate work in biology; but the conclusions he drew from both these branches of learning were subordinated to the demands of a monist and pantheistic temperament. Izoulet was not content to trace the origins of human solidarity back to the earliest animal societies; he insisted on the even more basic "affinities" of the chemical elements and spoke of a "chemical solidarity."[92] While he did not claim to draw direct conclusions from this for human society, he did demonstrate with such language that his pantheistic inclinations were stronger than his scientific ones. There was the same almost mystical overflowing at the opposite end of the evolutionary scale, for Izoulet's evolutionary construction did not stop at the level of human society but went right on to what might be called, in the language of a different philosophy, the "world-soul."[93] Just as the individual was an organism with its consciousness focused in the brain, and society was an organism with its consciousness focused in the state (taken broadly), so was the universe an organism whose consciousness was a necessarily omniscient God.[94] This was not quite classical pantheism; for Izoulet, God was immanent in Nature but at the same time transcended it.[95] This view of God and the universe was more than a speculative curiosity for Izoulet; it was essential to his social doctrine in its effort to build social solidarity and defend liberty.[96]

After completing his thesis, Izoulet was more concerned to communicate the practical lessons of biosociology than he was to further its scientific foundations. Like everyone else he admitted that sociology was in its infancy and then proceeded as if the essentials were in fact already known.[97] The lessons seemed of such vital importance to contemporary society that the methods were not always strictly examined. These lessons were two, in Izoulet's opinion. First, society was an organism greater than the sum of its parts, and those parts owed virtually everything to society, even their freedom.[98] Second, as an organism, society was subject to the rule of differentiation, which meant that different groups played different roles and that there was a directing elite whose role was analogous to that of the brain in the human organism.[99] The evolution of social elites was comparable to that of biological organisms:

> Ideally, one can in this respect reduce its evolution to three stages:
> 1) A vague and precarious distinction between leaders and the led;
> 2) The formation of governing centers, or the feudal network;
> 3) The establishment of the centralized State.[100]

The social organism was the nation; its brain was the state: "A dog's head is to its trunk (in this *physical body*) what the state is to the nation (in a political body)."[101] For Izoulet, as for Espinas, each nation was thus radically distinct from all the others, though it was not fixed and eternal, and the individual's highest loyalty was owed to the nation, not—as Comte had thought—to humanity. Neither preached *revanche*, but 1870 had exposed the dangers of French disunity, and they were worried by the continued lack of civic spirit among Frenchmen.[102] The "cerveau social," whose relations to the body of French society so concerned Izoulet, was not conceived as limited to the organs of formal government; it included the entire intellectual elite, which furnished the real leadership of society, which was the source of all progress.

This concern with the question of elites was a common one at that stage of this democratic era.[103] The presumed democratic tendency to leveling was widely seen as destructive of society and of progress: "Egalitarianism is killing us."[104] The biosociologists thought they could prove what the philosophers could only assert, that elites are a natural and essential ingredient of all society.[105] "The thinking elite is the necessary and powerful leavening of our great democracies."[106] Natural law philosophy, with its emphasis on individual rights, seemed to the sociologists to encourage the egalitarian trend, or at least to offer no grounds on which to resist it. On the other hand, people should have no difficulty accepting the biosociological demonstration as fact, making it possible to eliminate one of the dangerous tensions in modern society.[107] And

114

modern intellectual elites were democratic in that they were open to talent from below.[108]

Izoulet went beyond this common sociological position to focus his attention on the role of great men in history. The elites, if not the masses, of the Third Republic were clearly hostile to the very idea of great men, which they associated with the autocracy of Louis XIV or Napoleon I; but Izoulet thought that great men were compatible with democratic society and with liberty, that they were even needed. The great man, after all, could only be one who effectively incarnated the *conscience collective* of his time and showed it where it was going even before it was aware itself of the consequences of its thoughts. To make up for the lack of French works presenting this view of history, Izoulet translated Carlyle's *Heroes and Hero-Worship*, Emerson's *Representative Men*, and Theodore Roosevelt's *The Strenuous Life* into French. Though the nation as an organism possessed will and intellect, it was the peculiarity of the social organism that these qualities had to be personified in human individuals. Given the complexity of modern society, the elite had to be fairly large to do all that was needed; this led to the risk, in Izoulet's opinion, that the leadership of society would be inadequately unified. Subject to the checks of representative government, the great man offered the most effective path for the realization of the common will and personified it most clearly for the rest of society.

Lest one think that Izoulet's concern to the role of elites or of great men led him in an illiberal direction, we need to look at the pyschology and *morale* which he attempted to construct on the basis of evolutionary biology. Izoulet's psychology sought to be totally immanentist. All of man's mental capacities could be accounted for by the association of cells as evolution had produced it. All of man's complex of inclinations could be reduced to an inherent egoism; man differed from other animals in that, whereas they sought only pleasure, he sought the more complex and more difficult ideal of happiness.[109] Happiness was a state that no individual could fully possess unless it was possessed by all; it was thus the bridge between man's egoism and his altruism.[110] Justice, as in so many systems of morals, turned out to be a higher form of interest.[111] But, for Izoulet, materialist psychology could not lead us to this goal because it made reason no better than a form of instinct, while spiritualist psychology cut man off from the society in which morals had their meaning.[112] Both were antisocial, and Izoulet called for a social psychology which would make reason immanent in this world.[113] Reason was not prior to society, and a rationalist moral theory would start from this fact.

This approach to morals did not do away with individual responsibility, as the eclectics feared, but it certainly cast it in a somewhat different form. The liberty of moral decisions existed, but it did not derive from the independence or autonomy of the individual soul. It was a product of social evolution; and the individual owed his possession of it solely to the society into which he was born, just as he owed his reason to that society: "The soul is a daughter of the city."[114] Where other *morales* had to struggle to find ways to lead this autonomous soul they predicated to recognize its obligations to others, biosociology eliminated the problem: social solidarity coming first in fact and in logic, there was no antinomy to be overcome. This *morale*, Izoulet thought, since it was purely rational, could be easily taught and indeed ought to be placed at the very beginning of education.[115] The republican idea that religious neutrality barred the teaching of a *morale* in which God was mentioned seemed as ridiculous to Izoulet as it had to the spiritualists.

The political consequences of his philosophy, Izoulet insisted, were far from being despotic.[116] On the contrary, his philosophy supported the diffusion of liberty—and of power—in modern society. His pan-theism was the religious counterpart to the pan-archy which had replaced monarchy in the modern world.[117] Izoulet considered modern constitutional government with its representation, its separation of powers, its guarantees of rights to be one of the greatest gains made by modern man.[118] Property, too, was part of this evolution toward liberty. Izoulet joined the other liberals in considering it the practical basis of freedom—"Property alone establishes liberty"—and in arguing for its extension.[119] He looked favorably on the rise of industry, which he believed was destined eventually to free all men from the servitude of physical labor.[120] Like many defenders of private property on the French Left he was not afraid to call himself a socialist, but he found contemporary French socialists to be operating from a philosophy of individualism while ignoring the value of liberty.[121] What he thought they needed was a really *social* viewpoint, and Izoulet offered his political philosophy as a metaphysics for socialism, a doctrine of "libertarian solidarity."[122]

This hybrid expression paralleled the way in which he described his philosophical position: *monisme idéaliste* or *monisme finaliste*.[123] Such an approach offered, he thought, the only path for the restoration of philosophy in a world of science.[124] It has indeed proved to be an approach which appeals to the scientific but not mechanistic mind. Izoulet's principal disciple, Emile Bocquillon, had pointed to the affinities between Izoulet's vision and that of Teilhard de Chardin; there are also echoes of Izoulet in the philosophy of social evolution of Julian Huxley.[125] Izoulet saw human society as somewhere in the early stages of a long evolution from an imperfect condition to a perfect one:

> Therefore *mental culture* is the daughter of *leisure,* which is
> the son of *abundance,* which is the daughter of *industrialism,* him-
> self the son of *science,* herself daughter of the *division of labor,*
> that is to say of *association* or of the city of man.
> There is the true sacred genealogy.[126]

Only about 10 percent of humanity had yet reached the stage of mental culture, but the rest would do so some day. Clearly, Izoulet's vision
too easily took on a cosmic dimension which lost touch with the effort
to construct a social science from which he had started. The evolutionist approach to sociology was, in general, vulnerable to a tendency to
proceed deductively from a few central principles; the biosociologists
could be nearly as *a prioristic* as any philosopher. French liberalism
would not find in Izoulet or Espinas the scientific foundation toward
which it was groping.

The sociology of Gabriel Tarde had relatively few points in common with that of Espinas or Izoulet, but this did not prevent him from
arriving at a similar political position. He, too, defended the growing
role of government and offered a sociological explanation of the need
for and the role of elites in a democratic society. Tarde stressed both
the historic role of the individual and the need for social integration;
he reconciled liberty and authority. Tarde, however, justified these positions in a very different manner; indeed, he totally repudiated the
biological sociology of Espinas and Izoulet. His conclusions about
elites were derived from the observation of human society—mostly
contemporary—rather than from considerations based on the observation of animal societies. He launched a devastating attack on the ahistorical character of all efforts to reduce human experience to a single
evolutionary model. But he, too, sought to make sociology a science,
capable of determining the laws of human social behavior, a science
with its own subject matter and its own methods, not simply copied
from some other science. And he, too, thought that such knowledge
would be of great practical value.

Gabriel Tarde was born into a very old Perigord family whose
services to the state had earned them the particle of nobility, but Gabriel would never refer to himself as "de Tarde."[127] By inheritance he
was predestined for the law: his father was a judge at Sarlat (Dor-
dogne), and his mother was the daughter of an *avoué* who would later
become mayor of Sarlat. Tarde was born there on 12 March 1843. He

was an only child, his father being already forty-six years old. His father would die when Tarde was only seven years old, and as a result he became and remained very close to his mother until her death in 1891. He was a very sensitive child, and even a non-psychohistorian will recognize that there was probably some relation between these early experiences and the mysterious vision troubles that plagued Tarde from 1862 until 1867. The young man received his secondary education in the Jesuit college in Sarlat, passing his baccalaureate in 1860; he then did his *année de philosophie* with a Jesuit professor.

In 1862 Tarde enrolled at the Faculty of Law of Toulouse but in fact pursued his studies at home, a curious practice which was not uncommon at the time. He did not confine his reading to the law but ranged widely; his future ideas were probably most influenced at this time by his reading of Maine de Biran and of A.-A. Cournot. After going through something of a crisis of mysticism in 1864, Tarde went to Paris with his mother in a partly successful effort to complete his legal studies.

The completion of those studies—back in Sarlat—coincided with the end of his worst visual disturbances, and Tarde began his legal career as assistant to a local judge. In 1869 he was named a juge suppléant to the parquet of Sarlat, beginning the career on the criminal bench which occupied most of his life. After serving briefly as substitute for the procureur de la République at Ruffec (Charente), Tarde was named juge d'instruction at Sarlat in 1875. He married the daughter of a local lawyer in 1877 and settled down to a dual career as jurist and writer.[128]

Tarde's first publication (soon withdrawn) was a volume of poetry and stories written in his student years. He would continue throughout much of his life to write bits of imaginative fiction, some of it for publication, some—such as his plays, composed for amateur performance in Sarlat—not. He began to write more seriously on social and criminological topics for the *Revue philosophique* in 1880 and for the *Archives d'anthropologie criminelle* in 1887. His reputation in social science circles grew rapidly, especially as a result of his polemic against Cesare Lombroso and the Italian school of criminology, but he achieved a wider fame only with the publication of his *Les lois de l'imitation* in 1890.

By now Tarde had acquired friends and admirers who felt it was a disgrace to the republic that his talent should be domiciled in Sarlat and not in Paris. After two years of effort, they got him appointed Directeur de la statistique judiciaire in the ministry of justice. In the ten years that he survived this transplantation to Paris, Tarde drove himself relentlessly. He filled the hours left over from his work at the ministry and from his research and writing with a strenuous social life, for he was in great demand as a conversationalist. Though his ideas were already largely formed, Paris brought him into contact with many of the important sociological thinkers of the day: Espinas, Lucien Lévy-Bruhl, René Worms, Fouillée, and Durkheim, in particular.

For the first time in his life, Tarde also turned to teaching, giving courses at the Ecole libre des sciences politiques in 1896–98. In 1899 he declined the chair of modern philosophy at the Collège de France because he wanted it changed to a chair of sociology. He gave in, however, the next year, a year which would also see his election to the Académie des sciences morales et politiques. Having reached the summits of the academic world late in life, Tarde would not be able to give the full measure of his talent, for he died, prematurely worn out, in May 1904. His seat in the Académie would go to another sociologist—Espinas—but his chair on the Collège de France would revert to the philosophers—he was succeeded by Henri Bergson.

His experience as a criminal court judge gave Tarde a familiarity with a wide range of contemporary social problems unmatched by rival social theorists. While this experience probably accounts for much that was distinctive in his thought, and while Tarde was very open to experience, his bent of mind was not merely empirical.[129] Possessed of a broad erudition which he wore very lightly, from his youth he displayed a reflective disposition which drove him to seek to bring intellectual order to his ideas and experiences. The systematizing urge of the nineteenth century was still very much alive in Tarde, and he would aim to create a general sociology that was applicable to all societies;[130] but this urge probably did less harm in his case than in many others because he did not lose sight of the complexity of reality and therefore sought to make his system as flexible as possible. While convinced of the validity and importance of his sociological theory, he was anything but a pontiff by temperament. One is tempted to say that had his literary style been less popular and his personality less genial, Tarde might well have been taken more seriously than he has been by most historians of nineteenth-century thought. He was a complex figure whose importance extends well beyond the scope of this work.

Tarde became a sociologist largely by way of his interest in criminology.[131] He first made his mark as a criminologist when he emerged as a leader in the opposition to the Italian school, the pseudo-biological theory of the criminal type, made famous by Cesare Lombroso. Out of the negative effort to expose the unjustified nature of Lombroso's claims to scientific objectivity—which he did thoroughly and convincingly—Tarde was led to develop his own theory, not merely of criminal behavior, but of social behavior generally. We will not be directly concerned with his criminological work, but we need to recognize that it left its mark on his general sociology, even though it is not easy to distinguish this influence from that of his judicial career. Both combined to protect him against the facile optimism of many liberals.[132]

One can see the influence of Tarde's reflections on the nature of crime in his conviction that the larger part of human behavior is to be explained in sociological rather than biological terms.[133] In the criminals that came before his bench, Tarde had learned to read the workings of social influences; his conviction of the importance of social imitation was probably born there. As he came to see the responsibility of society in most criminal activity, so was he led to see the decisive impact of society on most noncriminal activity as well.[134] As a judge, he would undoubtedly not be rated a "coddler of criminals" by today's standards, and he always insisted that society's share of responsibility did not deprive it of the right to blame criminals for their acts;[135] but he does occupy an important place in the development of more humane attitudes toward society's criminals. On the other hand, one deep, fundamental conviction which underlay his hostility to Durkheim was Tarde's refusal to accept any incidence of crime as normal, even healthy, in all societies.[136] Criminality was a fact, indeed a universal fact, but one that we ought always to seek to eliminate.

One other aspect of the influence of Tarde's work as a criminologist on his sociology which deserves mention was his interest in social statistics. Through his experience with the statistics of French (and to a lesser degree foreign) criminality, he became a sophisticated user and interpreter of social statistics. Though he would never demonstrate their utility in as influential a fashion as Durkheim did in his *Suicide,* Tarde was convinced of the importance of statistics for social science and postulated that quantification could be extended usefully into many areas which then seemed refractory to such treatment.[137] Though he criticized the most mathematical of social sciences—economics—for its neglect of the importance of psychology, he felt that quantification and measurement could become important in the framework of his own social psychology. Mindful perhaps of the failure of Bentham's hedonistic calculus, Tarde did not himself seek to develop the possibilities he had nonetheless envisioned.

Though, like most of his contemporaries, he freely used biological metaphors, even insisting that they were useful, Tarde was not tempted to build his sociology on a biological foundation, perhaps because he had seen the absurdities it could lead to in Lombroso's criminology.[138] Social phenomena, he insisted, were *sui generis* and had to be studied as such. There was, of course, a biological component in human behavior which could not be ignored, but Tarde was convinced that social behavior could not be understood by trying to connect it to its biological roots. If the organic theory of differentiation seemed useful in explaining the modern division of labor, it was helpless to explain the concomitant growth of modern egalitarianism.[139] Whatever the connections between the physis and the psyche, social phenomena were essentially psychic phenomena and had to be studied as such. Social phenomena were what Tarde called "intermental" phenomena and, although individual psychology was a legitimate field of scientific enquiry, sociology could only be a social psychology. Here, he parted company with Espinas by insisting that social psychology does not require the existence of any collective mind in order to distinguish it from individual psychology. Durkheim would push the independence of sociology still further by attempting to study the "social fact" independently of its psychological foundations. This drive to set sociology apart was perhaps the distinctive grandeur of his thought and ultimate source of his failure; it was an attitude which formed the unbridgeable gap separating Durkheim from Tarde.[140]

Tarde was a *grand intuitif* whose mind operated primarily by analogical reasoning, but unlike many romantics he was careful to organize and render coherent the multitude of inspirations in which he was fertile. He established the fundamental principles of his sociology or social psychology at an early date, and most of his later work was devoted to drawing out the consequences and perfecting the formulation of those early insights. None of his later investigations seem to have caused him to modify his initial principles significantly. This fixity may seem unusual in a would-be science, though it was a good deal less so to most people in the nineteenth century,[141] and for Tarde it was perfectly in accord with his ideas about how intellectual progress was made. He saw new truths as the products of individual invention and discovery; their reception and ultimate acceptance and spread—or their rejection and disappearance—was a social process. The inventive individual could not exist in a vacuum and was dependent on the accumulated experience and knowledge of his society, but the creative act was nonetheless an individual one.

The most important principles of Tarde's social psychology can be summarized in brief compass. Some familiarity with them is essential to the understanding of his political thought. The whole edifice of his thought rested on the belief that human social behavior was basically logical, or perhaps better, that it was understandable in terms of a specifically social logic which he was the first to formulate. The belief was very different from the rationalism underlying most eighteenth-century social-contract thinking, which tended to make man a rational calculator. Tarde's social logic was meant to apply to even the least reflective social action. He expressed this logic in the form of a syllogism whose major premise was a *desire* (which might be conscious or unconscious, social or biological in origin), whose minor premise was a *belief* (again conscious or unconscious, but always social rather than vital in origin), and whose conclusion was an obligation to act in a certain fashion.[142] The term "obligation" should not make us think this was a normative syllogism, describing only how men ought to behave; rather it was meant to be descriptive, describing how they do in fact behave, but more than that, enabling us to understand why. Thus, in order to understand social behavior, Tarde invited us to examine men's desires and beliefs, both of which are socially conditioned.

Tarde's observation of society convinced him that the most common intermental action in society was *imitation*.[143] On this intuition he built what he called the laws (for want of a better word) of imitation. The general phenomenon of imitation was governed by a number of secondary laws, such as the law that the actions and ideas of those of higher social status are always imitated by those of lower status, or the law that external behavior is imitated before the inner ideas on which it rests are also assimilated. Such "laws" do indeed seem often to be confirmed broadly by general observation, but they also tend to resist any kind of rigorous demonstration. In less scrupulous hands than Tarde's, this method lends itself to the use of tautological argument to dispose of inconvenient data. The term "imitation" itself seems to invite facility and misuse, but Tarde rightly insisted that it also has its advantages because it evokes images of both conscious and unconscious activity and because it emphasizes the mental character of human society.

It is reasonably evident that there could be no society whose members were not in large degree similar. The important question is how to account for this similarity, and Tarde insisted that the purely biological similarities of men do not offer a sufficient explanation. A human society could exist only where its members had a measure of common attitudes and ideas, and Tarde held that only mutual imitation could account for the existence of such common mental states. Thus, without imitation there could be no society. Basic as it was to the formation of societies, imitation alone could not account for the character of the societies that exist today. The essential counterpart of imitation was thus *invention;* without invention, man would never have escaped his primitive beginnings. Inventions and discoveries, taken broadly, were the motor of all social change, but the invention that was not imitated remained sterile; it might as well never have been. Thus the interplay of invention and imitation made up the drama of human history. All men, Tarde insisted, were imitators; only a few were inventive to any significant degree. These few were the leavening in the lump, and Tarde was an open admirer of great men.[144] He heaped scorn on the idea that progress was somehow the working of the masses:

> If one adopts the common but empty phrases on the inefficacy of individual genius and the creative virtue of the masses, if one adopts the reputedly profound but absurd viewpoint that individuals do not make history, that crowds—inspired by who knows what all-powerful Unconscious—are its makers, then one ought logically to conclude that the importance of languages, religions, arts, industries, sciences, civilizing ideas, is in proportion to the size and life-span of the human masses wherein they have developed.[145]

And no one, he thought, would dare go that far.

Those who are familiar only with the invention-imitation interplay may suspect Tarde of having an edulcorated view of man's historical experience, of propounding a social theory that ignored conflict. But in fact he was far from ignoring conflict of all kinds—including class conflict—in his picture of past, present, and future. Against the sociobiologists he denied much social importance to the conflict of biological urges; even much sexual conflict had been socialized to become more a conflict of ideas than of bare vital urges. For Tarde, social conflict was a conflict of ideas, whether it took place in the minds of a few *savants* or on the bloody battlefields of war. Thus the idea of imitation had to be complemented by the idea of opposition, and Tarde devoted an entire book to the analysis of the modalities of opposition and their relations to the process of imitation.[146]

Tarde also insisted that the discussion of imitation and opposition needed to be complemented by the idea of adaptation, in order to round out his social theory. His stress on adaptation was revealing of his conviction that harmony was somehow the ultimate end, the purpose, the final goal of human relations and human efforts. But even theorists who stress conflict in the past and present may believe in its future elimination; and it is true that Tarde did oppose conflict theories of history on the grounds that they accounted for only a part of man's experience: without understanding man's ability to agree as well as to disagree, we could not make sense of his history. Tarde was not only opposed to Marxism but also thought that Durkheim's emphasis on constraint in his definition of social acts ignored the free interaction of equals.[147]

When looking at societies as wholes, Tarde discerned two basic varieties of imitation, which he called *imitation-contume* and *imitation-mode*.[148] In the former case, the imitation of models respected primarily for their antiquity predominated, in the latter, the imitation of current inventions, especially those originating in other countries. Both kinds of imitation were present in almost all societies, but one or the other was overwhelmingly dominant. Modern European nations offered the prime example of *imitation-mode,* he thought, and doubtless he would think so more forcefully today. This consideration was fundamental to Tarde's political outlook.

The neophilia characteristic of contemporary Western society made a deep impression on Tarde, who drew most of his inspiration for the laws of imitation from observing the rapidity with which ideas, crazes, fashions, and even seemingly basic wants were formed and circulated from social group to social group, from country to country, even from continent to continent. He saw how important this was for economic life—and took the economists, both classical and Marxist, to task for ignoring the tremendous importance of psychological factors in economic behavior. Though he did not live to see the day of the annual model change or planned obsolescence, Tarde would have understood them perfectly; he was already pointing to the vast importance of advertising for the economy of *imitation-mode*.

The prevalence of the psychology of *imitation-mode* could not but have a profound effect on political life. The spread of democracy in the Western world seemed to Tarde a prime example of the working of imitation, presenting as it did examples of the diffusion of ideas originating in the upper classes and of the copying of foreign institutions without understanding their spirit (he disliked in particular the mimicking of English parliamentarism). Tarde did not think that democracy was by any means a passing fad—but neither did he consider it the predestined end of political evolution. Democracy did not mean that there would be any lessening of the importance of imitation in political life; the aspiration to have a voice in government which had filtered down from the aristocracy through the bourgeoisie to the working class did not mean that the mass of people had ceased to be primarily imitative. The average man now had the opportunity to participate in the choice of his leaders; but the distinction between leaders and followers, between the governors and the governed was not thereby attenuated, let alone eliminated.

The prevalence of *imitation-mode* in democratic societies did, however, have an impact which could not be ignored. It was a great force, Tarde thought, for the generation of political instability. Not only were the bonds of custom loosened; there was a constant incitement to regard the new as worth more than the old, the untried as necessarily better than the familiar. Instability was also made greater by the fact that people were becoming more alike over ever larger areas and in ever larger numbers, so that the potential field of propagation of each invention was increasingly greater than in the days of provincial dialects and pedal locomotion. Tarde could see this process going on not merely in France, where regional differences were steadily declining, but also throughout the world as the spread of Western influence and the rapidity of communications marked the beginning stages of the formation of a world civilization. The political ideas that came to light in the American colonies or in the Parisian salons of the eighteenth century were changing the political conceptions of Arabs and Tonkinese; the process was beginning to accelerate. One day, currents of influence would begin to flow in the other direction, too. The more people throughout the world shared the same enthusiasms, desires, fears, hopes, the greater would be the world's political instability. Tarde foresaw unprecedented upheavals ahead.

Tarde's seemingly inexhaustible fertility in ideas and observations, his capacity to stimulate reflection, his vigorous manner of expression, all make it difficult to seize the exact nuance of his political thought and to present it systematically. There can be no doubt that he was with the other sociologists in defending the growing importance of the state and the value of other social institutions, in finding philosophical debate over free will irrelevant while valuing liberty, in accepting democracy while stressing the need for elites and leadership.

For Tarde, the growth of government was a natural consequence of the progress of civilization, and the growth of the centralized state was not hostile to liberty, even in France. At the same time, he recognized the historic trend toward imposing limitations on sovereignty and saw evidences of a trend toward decentralization of power in France. He seems to have believed that the forms of political institutions were less important than the people who held the reins of power. The impersonality of government was a democratic illusion, and freedom did not depend on constitutional devices but on the internal harmony of the ruling elite: "A truly free state is a state where one is sure of the morrow, a state where accord may not reign among the wills of the citizens, but where it always reigns among the wills and the ideas of those who govern."[149] He found in the desire of leaders to be consistent with themselves a greater protection for liberty than in the separation of powers. The real separation of powers—as he expressed it in the terms of his psychology—was that between the beliefs and the desires of the rulers.

Leadership was no less vital in a democracy; it was in the nature of the mass of men that they had to follow something and somebody.

These will be changed, but the need remained constant, and fortunately so, Tarde thought: "A people which was not born copyist would not be governable, even though it would feel very strongly the need to be governed."[150] The political equivalent of imitation is obedience. Tarde's social-psychological method thus led him to a position in some ways closer to the philosophers than to the other sociologists because he stressed the classic question of authority. The relation of leaders and led was for him a moral question as well as a factual one. Organismic analogies shed no light on this problem of the nature of authority nor on the practical questions of what strengthens and weakens authority. The fact that people felt the need for an authority over them was not enough to guarantee the stability of governments, for governments could and sometimes did lose the respect of their peoples, often with fatal consequences.

The state was, Tarde pointed out, not the only institution which exercised authority in society. The church, the school, the workshop, the regiment were all foci of authority. Even more important was the family, and Tarde was aligned with the philosophers in thinking that the state should do its best to protect the family. Indeed, in general, the state should promote those institutions which had a moralizing effect, that is, which promoted a concern for others. Seeing that some of the basic trends of modern society tended to promote individualism, Tarde was concerned to balance that creative individuality which was necessary for all progress with that solidarity which was necessary for stability.

More clearly than any of the other thinkers in this study, Tarde was working toward the creation of a sociology of politics, a social psychology of political behavior. Rather than focusing on the crowd psychology which LeBon was trying to make the foundation for a critique of democracy, Tarde turned toward the study of political parties.[151] Modern parties, he thought, were the product of the increasingly intense network of communications which strengthened the influence that people have on each others' ideas. For the locus of every party was an idea, a conviction shared by a group whose relations tended to a reinforcement of that conviction. For Tarde, beliefs were more important than material interests in the formation of parties, despite the commonplace materialism of modern society:

> I believe there are reasons for thinking that in spite of the utilitarian debasement of social struggles in times of crisis like our own, the formation of great parties—those which most stir the passions— is always more influenced by the antagonism of contradictory convictions than by the clash of interests.[152]

Political conflicts were essentially conflicts of ideas, affirmations versus negations. The most logical of all divisions, which drew his favor for that reason, was the opposition between a governmental party and an opposition. In contrast, he signaled the danger to the state and society of parties based on a region or a class. The class party advocated by the socialists was, he insisted, a retrograde idea, a throwback to the violent politics of the ancient Greek polis or the renaissance city-state of Italy.[153]

In general, Tarde believed, ideas played an increasing role in political life. Insofar as political authority was successful in detaching itself from religion, it had tended to put itself in the place of religion, and for that it needed a new set of beliefs. Theocracy was only an important subspecies of a much larger genre which he called *idéocratie*. From Plato to Auguste Comte the history of Western political thought was marked by the *logocraties* dreamed by the philosophers.[154] Tarde did not intend to add his personal dream to this long list; but he did see the world as tending toward the increasing rule of reason, the "dominant empire of logic,"[155] and his hope for a more harmonious world in the future clearly placed its hopes on reason. The liberal sociologists were projectors of trends—which depended on a certain necessity in the world, for how else could they be projected?—rather than builders of *logocraties*. Perhaps projections play the same role in sociological thought as rationalist utopias do in philosophy: they express the desire to move from what is to what is not. They are sometimes a way for the sociologist—perhaps unconsciously—to shed the burden of his self-imposed objectivity and to confuse what he wants with what he sees.

Like the other sociologists Tarde believed that it was important to rebuild the moral unity of France, but he offered no shortcut, no panacea like Izoulet's civic religion. Perhaps the problem seemed less acute from Sarlat than from Paris. Certainly, Tarde was able to nourish his originality in the heart of his province more easily than he could have done in the intellectual confines of Paris. He accepted the move to Paris with great reluctance and was never at home there; he recognized the role of the capital in French life and wrote about the authority exercised by great cities; perhaps that was why he avoided it. Perhaps that avoidance was what saved him from constructing a *logocratie* of his own.

None of the sociologists studied in this chapter built a large following of disciples to carry on their work and perpetuate their influence. None of them seems to have cared much; Izoulet was perhaps the most disappointed. They lacked the will to build a school, a will that was fully developed only in Durkheim. But also, their philosophies— and the word is not inappropriate here—did not easily lend themselves to the division of labor that is necessary to the construction of a science. To the extent that sociology on the whole has failed to become a science, this failing on their part seems less serious than it did a generation ago. Their contribution to the defense of liberalism was less in providing a new intellectual foundation—though no doubt they did strengthen the convictions of some liberals—than in their diffusion of the understanding that social science was not hostile to liberty.

·VI·

Alfred Fouillée: Science and Liberal Democracy

La philosophie est la religion des démocraties, et nous avouons que nous n'aurons pas grande confiance dans l'avenir d'une république sans philosophie. Si prêtre et roi vont bien ensemble, toujours aussi on a rapproché ces deux titres: philosophe et citoyen. *La propriété sociale et la démocratie*, p. 231

Alfred Fouillée (1838–1912) was one of the most original thinkers of the later nineteenth century, but he managed to avoid the extremes of eccentricity which had characterized the most original minds of the early century. As is often the case with original minds, Fouillée was largely self-taught as a philosopher; in this, as in the rest of his career, he would resemble Renouvier more than any of the other thinkers covered in this work. Fouillée might have received a more conventional education had not fate intervened.[1] He was born on 18 October 1838 at Pouèze (Maine-et-Loire), where his father operated a small slate quarry. Alfred was able to attend the lycée at Laval, but the failure of the quarry in which all the family's resources had been invested and the death of his father which followed soon afterward combined to force Fouillée to undertake the support of his family. Armed with only the *licence*, he began his career as a secondary-school teacher of rhetoric and philosophy at the age of nineteen. Beginning at the collège of Ernée, Fouillée progressed through the lycées of Louhans, Dôle, and Auxerre, becoming professor of philosophy at the lycée of Carcassonne.

By this time Fouillée had become sufficiently sure of his talent to aspire to a university career. Since the family's financial problems had prevented him from entering the Ecole normale supérieure, which was the surest path to a university post, he began to prepare himself for the competitive examination for the *agrégation* in rhetoric. When the *agrégation* in philosophy was restored, he switched his preparation to that program, working largely on his own, with some advice and encouragement from senior lycée professors. Knowing that he would

129

have to do better than the graduates of the Ecole normale, Fouillée unleashed the effort which carried him to the top of the list in the *agrégation* examination of 1864. This was an extraordinary achievement for an unknown lycée professor from the provinces, and it changed the course of his life.

For the first time, Fouillée was able to meet the leading philosophers of the university, especially Franck and Caro, and even the elderly Victor Cousin. The way was now opened for him to teach at more prestigious lycées, and he passed through Douai and Montpellier to Bordeaux, where he also had the opportunity to offer a course at the Faculty of Letters. Feeling the need to demonstrate clearly his mastery of the classical tradition, Fouillée was hard at work during these years on his first two books, both of which would be honored by the Académie française: his *Philosophie de Platon* with the Prix Bordin in 1867 and his *Philosophie de Socrate* with the Prix Cousin in 1868. While waiting for a suitable university position to become available, Fouillée prepared his principal doctoral thesis in which he would develop his most original concept, the *idée-force,* and the synthetic method which would shape all of his later work. In 1872 he successfully defended his thesis, *La liberté et le déterminisme,* winning praise for his skillful handling of an unexpectedly vigorous attack from Adolphe Franck.

The potential value of Fouillée's talent and his philosophy for the republican cause was not lost on one member of the audience that day, Léon Gambetta. Gambetta's praise attracted the hostility of the clerical Right, but a threatened interpellation of the education minister by Msgr Dupanloup, one of the intellectual leaders of Catholic monarchism, came to naught. As we shall see, Fouillée's philosophy did have important political implications, but he quickly made it clear that he had no desire to become personally involved in political life. The brief controversy faded and he was appointed a Maître de conférences at the Ecole normale, an uncommon honor for one who was not an *ancien élève* of the "maison" on the rue d'Ulm.

Fouillée's rise from obscurity had been achieved by a nearly superhuman effort of will; the physical price soon had to be paid. After only three years at the Ecole normale, his health failed; a combination of circulatory troubles, visual disturbances, and vertigo put an end to his teaching career. Fouillée's long retirement was spent mostly in the Midi, where he finally found at Menton the physical tranquillity his body needed and the intellectual companionship of his stepson, the philosopher and poet Jean-Marie Guyau, who was also suffering from poor health.

Retirement seems hardly the right word for the last thirty-seven years of Fouillée's life; it was "a hard-working retirement if there ever was one," for he published nearly a book a year in addition to numerous articles for the *Revue des deux mondes* and the *Revue philosophique*. By conserving his physical and emotional forces Fouillée was able to secure the time to apply his synthetic method to practically all of the philosophical, social, and political issues of the day, before he died on a visit to Lyons in 1912. In this chapter we are going to consider only those aspects of his work which relate to the evolution of French liberalism; it is unfortunate that Fouillée has not received the more general study he deserves.

I. The Philosophy of idées-forces

While the antiliberal social and political philosophies of the nineteenth century from Saint-Simon onwards had mostly called themselves "scientific" and had considered this claim a decisive challenge to liberalism, it was not until the latter part of the century that liberals fully appreciated the danger of such a challenge and began to make a major effort to establish the scientific validity of liberalism as distinguished from its philosophical truth. The decline of the prestige of philosophical modes of thought, whether justified by the achievements of scientists or not, was a fact of intellectual life in the nineteenth century. Renouvier's phenomenological Kantianism was no more freighted with nonscientific metaphysical assumptions than Auguste Comte's positivism, but the latter more nearly conformed with what most people had come to think of as science. In order to gain acceptance as scientific, liberalism would have to become more closely identified with the new intellectual currents of the century, especially evolutionism and, in France, positivism. The man who most clearly grasped this necessity and made the most explicit and determined effort to bridge the gap between the philosophical tradition and the scientific spirit of the age was Alfred Fouillée.

Fouillée acquired a knowledge of Western thought, from the pre-Socratics to his own time, that was almost without peer in his time or any other; yet this historical expertise fed rather than dampened his own originality: self-consciously standing at a turning point in the history of Western thought, respectful of a wisdom laboriously acquired from the time of the Greeks to the present, aware of the emergence of something like Comte's "third age," Fouillée was determined that nothing good from the past should be lost and that no hopeful possibility for the future should be neglected. Toward that end he became what can only be described as a compulsive synthesizer. No body of thought was entirely devoid of truth any more than it was entirely devoid of error; wisdom lay in discovering the respective truths of opposing views and in showing how they could be reconciled—a task which never seems to have exhausted Fouillée's dialectical ingenuity. Describing his method as the synthesis of opposites, he disclaimed any resemblance to the Hegelian dialectic which he criticized as too rationalistic.[2] Synthesis was not merely Fouillée's method; it was his vision of man's historic development, and he argued that man was headed not toward Comte's positive age but toward an era in which the theological, philosophical, and scientific ages would be synthesized.[3]

This mania for synthesis may account for the neglect into which Fouillée's work has fallen. Not only are positions which cling to one extreme or another easier for most people to assimilate, they also lend themselves more readily to the sloganeering of the marketplace of ideas in modern democratic societies. Moreover, such synthesizing is easily tainted as intellectual opportunism, as an effort to have the best of all worlds, or as a weakness for compromise; it is more difficult to recognize as what it certainly was in Fouillée's case—an uncompromising search for truth.[4] If sometimes too easily satisfied, he was not more so than other philosophers; he regularly had to defend himself against informed critics, and his age was very demanding of coherent thought. Indeed, the synthetic method as Fouillée practiced it demanded a high degree of critical self-awareness; the validity of our knowledge and its limits were among his constant preoccupations.

The synthetic approach made it impossible for the philosopher to take refuge in some narrow specialization; Fouillée could not stop short of the construction of a complete philosophical system which would endeavor to establish all of our knowledge on the most secure scientific grounds. The main task which Fouillée set for himself was nothing less than the reconciliation of science and philosophy—"The positivism of Comte, the evolutionism of Darwin and of Spencer, the idealism of Kant and of Hegel are perfectly reconcilable"—of idealism and materialism, of free will and determinism.[5] Early in his career Fouillée developed the concept which was the key to this vast enterprise of synthesis, the concept of the *idée-force*.[6] There is no English equivalent for the term "idée-force"; power-idea has too many wrong connotations. For Fouillée, all ideas contain elements of volition and emotion, all ideas are the commencements of action; but idées-forces are special cases, ideas which by their very nature have a power to drive men to seek their realization: beauty, justice, freedom.[7] The philosophy of idées-forces is not a Platonic idealism; the very term is an expression of Fouillée's determination to synthesize the materialist and idealist viewpoints, to reconcile the facts that determinism rules the world but men are not mechanical automatons.[8] With the concept of idées-forces, he set out in a long series of works, from *La liberté et le déterminisme* (1872) to *La pensée et les nouvelles écoles anti-intel-*

lectualistes (1911), to examine all the major philosophical questions that have bedeviled Western man.[9]

The most fundamental and persistent of those questions focus on the antinomy of freedom and determinism; it appeared in Fouillée's earliest works and was the subject of his doctoral dissertation.[10] The reconciliation of freedom and determinism was the first great task of his synthetic philosophy, and his solution laid the foundation for all his subsequent work. Fouillée examined the arguments of the modern pro- and anti-determinists (concentrating on the French), showing them all to be in part illogical or inadequate. The growth of scientific knowledge was making it increasingly apparent that everything is determined, but not, as some naively claimed, that the modes of determination are uniform, the same for man as for inanimate objects. Mechanistic determinism was wholly inadequate when it came to living things, especially to man; for it led to the ludicrous position of treating consciousness as a mere epiphenomenon, an idea which could not be held without self-contradiction.[11] On the other hand, absolute free will is impossible because everything has a cause; indeed, we cannot even conceive of an event without a cause.[12] Even the proponents of freedom must believe in causality: otherwise chance would rule and the world would be unknowable, unintelligible; without causality we could not anticipate the consequences of our acts—there could be no freedom.

The resolution of this antinomy becomes possible, Fouillée thought, when we recognize that freedom is an idea, an idea that has the power to determine action. You offer me a dollar to raise my right hand; I raise my left because I place a greater value on the expression of my freedom. That I may accept your offer if you raise it high enough does not negate my freedom; it does show that freedom does not operate outside the realm of causality: if it did, I would be equally as likely to accept one dollar as a thousand. The value of the dollar to me is also an idea; however many factors you may adduce as affecting my choice between competing ideas, you cannot eliminate the power of the idea of freedom.[13] It is, par excellence, an idée-force.

The existence of the idée-force of freedom demonstrates that if we want to advance the scientific understanding of man we must abandon merely physical concepts of determinism and seek to understand the higher, psychic determinism which shaped his actions.[14] This did not mean for Fouillée the substitution of an intellectualist determinism in place of a mechanistic one; it transcended that position as well. He recognized three varieties of determinism in the Western intellectual tradition: (1) mechanistic and intellectualistic determinism, (2) finalist determinism, and (3) moral determinism. The latter he considered the high point of determinist thought, so far; for he proposed to elevate them all by the introduction of *moyens-termes* between them and their opposites:

(1) Rectification of mechanistic and intellectualistic determinism by the introduction of the idea of liberty and its influence.—The idea of liberty is the equivalent of liberty in the mechanical order.
(2) Rectification of finalistic determinism by the desire for liberty.—The desire for liberty is the equivalent of liberty in the teleological and esthetic order.
(3) Rectification of moral determinism by the love of liberty.—The love of liberty is the equivalent of liberty in the moral order.[15]

For Fouillée, the idea of liberty, the desire for liberty, and the love of liberty could be distinguished as concepts but were inseparable in reality. Without the desire for liberty the idea of liberty would never have become the idée-force capable of changing man's behavior that history so clearly shows it to be; without the love of liberty, man could not lift himself to the aspiration for the universal good necessary to morality.

This union was also essential to Fouillée for the solution of the problem left by Kant's dualism, the problem of bringing morals from the unreachable noumenal world into the phenomenal world of our lives.[16] Completely rejecting Renouvier's efforts to relocate Kant's axioms in the phenomenal world, Fouillée argued that it was not necessary to show that freedom is inherent in the nature of man and the phenomenal world—a claim that went against the teachings of modern science—for the idea of freedom suffices to establish morals.[17] His solution is closer to that of the German neo-Kantians such as Windelband who founded morality in man's striving to transcend the *is* in pursuit of the *ought,* the ought being a self-determined value.[18] The natural necessity of this movement seemed demonstrated to Fouillée by the reality of evolution. Man has evolved, is evolving, psychically as well as physically.

Coming to terms with evolution was essential to Fouillée if he was to consider his philosophy scientific. Rightly critical of the misuses of Darwin in contemporary social science,[19] he was perhaps too ready to believe that all problems had been solved in the biology of evolution; in any case he seems to have been as much a Lamarckian as a Darwinist in his view of man's moral evolution. The idea of evolution, as Fouillée said, "makes determinism more flexible," and made purposeful change conceivable.[20] It introduces the teleological element essential to his concept of freedom. The finalism which directs the world either through the will of God or the cunning of Hegel's reason was unacceptable to Fouillée; it had to lie within man, to be the self-directed pursuit of a self-created ideal.[21]

The ideal, however, could not be merely the subjective creation of the individual, for such an ideal would lack universal validity and scientific demonstrability. Fouillée had, therefore, to find the genesis of the universal in the minds of particulars.[22] This he accomplished by analysis of the fact, the phenomenon of consciousness. The fact of consciousness was the base of all our knowledge; indeed, without it there would be no other facts, for they all necessarily involve the interaction of the mind and the material world. Both determinism and freedom are rooted in consciousness. But Fouillée's initial certainty was not quite identical to the Cartesian *cogito* (I think, therefore I am); rather, he insisted, our knowledge begins with a *Cogito ergo sumus* (I think, therefore we are). Consciousness of self is inseparable from consciousness of the existence of other selves comparable to our own.[23] This was not for Fouillée a metaphysical construction or an a priori assumption; it was a scientifically demonstrable fact.

On this foundation Fouillée erected his ideas of liberty and of determinism, his moral philosophy, his sociology, and his political philosophy. It was this foundation which enabled him to construct a social and political philosophy which would reconcile the individual and the group, which would protect the dignity of man and guide the reform of his social world.

What is true and just in individualism is that the human person, conceived as endowed with "reason" and "liberty," has a moral value incommensurable with all material values which confers on him a right to respect and love. For our part we go even farther. We do not believe it necessary in order to establish rights that man should be endowed with "reason," as Platonic, Cartesian, or Kantian spiritualism understands it, nor with "liberty," understood as free will or contingent will, or as a transcendental and "noumenal" faculty in the manner of Kant. According to us, it is sufficient to confer on man his true rights that he should have the *idea* itself of reason as a power of raising himself to the understanding of the universal, and the *idea* itself of liberty as a power to act in view of the universal. In effect, a being who acts under the influence of these two *idées-forces* of reason and liberty by that very act begins to make the world of reason and liberty real within himself. He thereby renders himself sacred and inviolable by virtue of the force inherent in that idea. All individuals, past, present, and future, have these same idées-forces; therefore they have the same rights and—for that reason—form a truly human rather than a merely animal society.[24]

Thus equipped with the concept of idée-force and the method of synthesis, Fouillée was prepared to examine the most important social and political questions of his day with an openness that enabled him to learn from every point of view and a self-assurance that enabled him to integrate everything he learned into his own original synthesis. The result was a socialized liberalism which we will now examine in greater detail.

II. Socialism and Materialism

Fouillée's general philosophical effort to find a middle ground between freedom and determinism, idealism and materialism, was paralleled in his social and political philosophy by an effort to find a middle ground between individualism and socialism. The correspondence between philosophical and political positions was not universally the same: there were idealist socialists, like Jaurès, and materialist individualists. But the main battle lines were drawn between materialist socialists and idealist liberals. Both views contained elements of value in Fouillée's opinion, but carried them to untenable extremes. What was needed was a real social science.

The generation which separated Fouillée from Renouvier brought an important change in the relations between liberalism and socialism. For Renouvier, socialism meant primarily the utopians he had known in his youth; for Fouillée, it meant the Marxist international. Utopianism was still an issue, for the utopianism of the Marxists had become a more pressing practical question than that of their predecessors had been. While political liberalism was still struggling with the support given to authoritarian government by the Roman Catholic church, a new authoritarian threat had emerged in the form of Marxian socialism. While Fouillée was as firmly anticlerical in his politics as Renouvier,[25] he was more worried by the threat of the future posed by authoritarian socialism. He was equally worried by the inability of laissez-faire liberalism to counter that threat or to meet the need for social reforms in the present. In this section we will consider his critique of socialism, in the next, his critique of individualist liberalism.

In any anthology of the French critics of Marxism, Fouillée would occupy an important place. He was especially well informed, in an era in which many professed Marxists knew little beyond the Manifesto of 1848. More than that, his approach to the subject was sympathetic and dispassionate; he was neither condescending nor outraged. Many of his criticisms have thus retained their validity. To Fouillée, socialism was a natural response to the developments that were transforming Western society, and it pointed to serious problems with which society would have to deal; but socialists were wrong in supposing they had discovered the solution to all those problems. They were wrong especially in believing they had established a science of society.

Marx's pretentions to scientific rigor were no more justified than those of Fourier, and Marxism could only be understood as a prescientific philosophy, a metaphysical theory of social change. For most of its adherents it might better be described as a religion than as a philosophy. In the first place, materialism was not a scientific position but a metaphysical opinion, one increasingly rendered untenable by the march of modern science. While Fouillée attributed to Marx a mechanistic materialism which might more fairly be associated with his followers, he was right in seeing Marx's materialism as a major source of error in his social philosophy.

Philosophical materialism, by neglecting the epistemological issues raised by Kant, failed to develop a critical method by which to judge the validity of its own propositions. Thus even valid ideas may become errors through a lack of understanding of their limits. When philosophical materialism was translated into historical materialism it was unable to avoid exaggerating the material and unconscious factors in the development of human society. It was not that such factors did not exist; rather, materialism provided no grounds for seeing their limits or the influence of other factors. Science, it was true, required abstraction from the messiness of reality, but materialism's penchant for oversimplification led to the substitution of ideological conformity for the search for truth. Marxist insistence on class struggle doctrine in the face of all the evidence for the interdependence of social groups was an example of this fatal inclination which undermined Marxism's claim to scientific status.[26]

The class struggle doctrine also pointed, in Fouillée's opinion, to the failure of Marxian socialism to develop a viable *morale*. It was this failure which led Marxists to take refuge in the illusion that changing institutions would transform men. The future man of the socialist ideal was not perhaps too far distant from that of the liberal ideal: both sought a harmony between the interests of the individual and those of society. Socialists, Fouillée insisted, did not possess a philosophy which would enable them to reconcile individual happiness and collective good.[27] The socialists' belief that private property in the instruments of production was the sole obstacle to the establishment of the harmony of interests was as utopian as the opposite point of view expressed in Bastiat's *Harmonies économiques*:

> According to M. G. Deville, in a socialist regime, "the material conditions needed to achieve *individual well-being* will *also* be the conditions of *social well-being*." There will be, in other words, a

concordance between personal interests and universal interest.— But one or the other of two things must be true: either that concordance will be true only on the average and in a general way (in which case private conflicts will not have disappeared and it will remain possible to seek one's own good at the expense of the good of all) or that concordance will be a complete harmony (but then you are falling back into those dreams of paradise which render "morals" absolutely useless). In this second hypothesis we would not have any choices to make or initiatives to take: our good would always be *one* with the universal good; every centripetal tendency would *ipso facto* coincide with a centrifugal tendency. This social astronomy is pure fantasy, and we doubt that the collectivist *fiat* can work the miracle of bringing it out of the void.[28]

Fouillée understood that socialism's insistence on working miracles would lead to tyrannical government; it did not break so radically with the past as its supporters imagined.

Fouillée reproached Marxists with an excessive reliance on the state as the instrument of social change, though he blamed this more on Engels than on Marx, whom he credited with a preference for federalism. Not only did this over-reliance lead toward dictatorship, it was bad social science, ignoring what we already know of the role of social groups other than the state.

Fouillée also charged the Marxists with bad economics, derived, ironically, from the errors of some liberal economists.[29] The most fundamental of these erroneous conceptions was the labor theory of value which vitiated all of Marx's economic theory—though not all of his criticisms of the existing order.[30] Labor is not the sole source of value, even if capital is considered a sort of congealed labor, and it does not explain the relative values which men place on goods and services in fact; neither can it serve to explain which values they ought to so place. Value is subjective as well as objective, and the greater our economic development, the greater the role of subjective values. At best, the labor theory was a useful polemical weapon for the socialists, especially as modified by their tendency to exalt manual labor at the expense of intellectual labor. Originally an expression of the socialist dislike for the entrepreneur and the merchant, the exaltation of manual labor would become a weakness, as Fouillée clearly saw, at a time when mental labor would increasingly supplant manual work.

Materialist philosophy was certainly in part responsible for leading the socialists into such pitfalls; it also contributed to their failure to develop a viable *morale*. This failure was fatal to their hopes of effective action in this world. All they offered was the chimerical goal of establishing distributive justice—a society in which each person is rewarded according to his merits—which was at best a cruel hoax, at worst an excuse for tyranny.[31] The liberal goal of commutative justice—a society in which equal opportunity is offered to all—was more desirable and more nearly attainable, in Fouillée's opinion, but not completely adequate.[32] He offered in its place a concept that would become one of the key elements in twentieth-century welfare liberalism: reparative justice.[33]

Fouillée credited socialism with pointing the way toward a viable *morale* by the stress it laid on man's social nature; here it was closer to the truth than the individualist philosophers of liberalism. But their materialism prevented the socialists from giving an adequate explanation of man's social nature; while proclaiming solidarity in theory, they often repudiated it in practice, either through class-warfare doctrine or by subjecting the individual to an all-powerful state.[34] As social theorists, the Marxists were in the same position as the late Ptolemaic astronomers: finding it increasingly difficult to reconcile theory and observation, unable to admit the need for a new theoretical foundation.

III. Individualist Liberalism and Idealism

In Fouillée's opinion the traditional liberals were no more successful than the socialists in solving either the theoretical or the practical problems of the relationship between the individual and society. Liberal rebellion against the constraints of old-regime society had led to an untenable emphasis on the isolated individual,[35] untenable not merely in a philosophical or scientific sense but in a practical one as well: while individualism had proved a powerful weapon against the privileged castes of the ancien régime, it was increasingly ineffective against the new social movements of the nineteenth century. Liberal thinkers responded to the new situation by attempting to reforge the social bond, but their initial concept of the individual doomed all such efforts to failure. One result was the utopianism of the doctrine of the natural harmony of interests, which many liberals espoused as theory, but which few were prepared to attempt to implement in practice. Another result of this failure, and a much more threatening one for the future of liberalism, was the flight toward Social Darwinism and all the comforts it offered the successful.[36]

Fouillée's critique, however, paid much less attention to these easily refuted tendencies than to the rise of neo-Kantian idealism, whose importance we have already examined.[37] Fouillée shared many of the practical aims of the liberal idealists but found their justification inadequate. He agreed that political practice must rest on the foundation of moral philosophy but insisted that moral philosophy must have a scientific basis more secure than the metaphysical propositions of the idealists.

The moral and political problems faced by the idealist liberals were closely intertwined; both involved the question of the obligations of the individual to others. The neo-Kantian solution was rationalist: the obligations imposed by reason—because man is a rational animal—in morals, the sovereignty of reason in politics. Kant's emphasis on the primacy of the practical reason dominated their thought, though some, like Renouvier, attempted to abolish the gulf between pure and practical reason. Fouillée insisted on the need for a scientific rather than a rationalist solution, deeming the latter arbitrary and ahistorical. He thought that the Kantian categorical imperative was weak in two ways: (1) While purporting to aim at the autonomy of the individual, it was in fact a standard imposed from outside, in Kant's terms, heteronomous; (2) it claimed a greater certainty than was scientifically justifiable. The moral maxims of the categorical imperative were basically sound, in Fouillée's view, but they rested on the wrong ground. The doctrine of idées-forces enabled us to see them as standards we impose upon ourselves, as truly autonomous creations, inherent not just in reason, but in the whole nature of man—his volition and his feelings as well as his reason. It also accepted the scientific relativity of our knowledge, and instead of attempting to achieve an impossible certainty which would alone justify its categorical character, it led us to accept what Fouillée called a *persuasif suprême*.[38] This was the foundation on which Fouillée would build his political synthesis.

IV. The Liberal Synthesis: Libéralisme réformiste

After refuting the extreme claims of the collectivists and the libertarians, Fouillée attempted to show that a middle ground between them could be justified on philosophical and not merely empirical considerations. It was not hard for him to turn the arguments of the liberals against the socialists, though his critique was more probing and coherent than that of most liberals, since he took the socialists seriously, and scarcely more difficult to use the arguments of the sociologists (and to some extent of the socialists) against the unfounded claims of the liberal individualists. The problem was rather to show that his use of these arguments was not contradictory or inconsistent, that he was not pushing synthesis for the sake of conciliation, but that there was an intellectually defensible middle ground. His political synthesis thus depended for its strength on his prior philosophical synthesis of positivism and idealism.[39]

Fouillée called his political synthesis a *libéralisme réformiste*.[40] He believed that it offered a reconciliation of individual freedom and social necessity which rested on a scientific understanding of man and society and which at the same time responded most directly to pressing present needs. Calling his position scientific did not mean that Fouillée believed that he had certain answers to all important social and political questions or even that his method would enable man to pass directly from his present difficulties to a utopia of his own making. His understanding of the rigors of scientific proof, his respect for the difficulties of applying scientific method to that most complex of subject matters, human society, his acceptance—however reluctant—of the deeply rooted nature of evil in mankind, all restrained his optimistic temperament from flying too far into an ideal future.

It was to sociology that Fouillée looked for the knowledge and the method which would guide us from where we are to where we want to be.[41] Reformist liberalism would rest on the intellectual base of a *sociologie réformiste*. If he was aware of the danger that in such a sociology the zeal for reform might overwhelm the search for truth, he brushed it aside with the assumption that reform is in the nature of things, that what sociology is studying is an evolutionary process which can be called progress. Fouillée was aware that sociology was in its infancy, that it had not yet jelled. While paying his respects to several sociologists, most notably Tarde and Durkheim (that they represented the main opposing wings of French sociology presented no problems to his synthesizing temperament), Fouillée clearly thought that he was offering the catalyst around which sociology would jell, a sociology of idées-forces which would be the practical wing of the philosophy of idées-forces.[42]

The sociology of idées-forces was based on the same search for synthesis which formed the rest of Fouillée's philosophy. In particular it sought to establish a middle ground between the individual and society, a middle ground which would furnish a base from which to formulate policy and a concept to orient further research. That middle ground was the idée-force of solidarity. Socialists and some sociologists had sought to build their political positions on the *fact* of solidarity. In addition to objecting to his emphasis on the ways men are materially dependent upon one another—as distinguished from the no less important ways in which they are psychologically and morally interdependent—Fouillée insisted that the mere fact of solidarity was an inadequate ground for political and social obligation.[43] It was inadequate and indeed dangerous, because those who relied on it—as many socialists demonstrated—tended to undervalue the individual and to take a mechanistic view of society which treated men as no more than interchangeable cogs in the machine. Solidarity as an idée-force, on the other hand, he conceived as an inspiration even more than a reality: idées-forces are expressions of becoming—they are rooted in experience, but they transcend it, they are a part of the is, but a part which reaches out toward the ought.[44] The idée-force of solidarity was an expression of man's moral interdependence and could thus furnish a needed ground of obligation.

The idée-force of solidarity was compatible only with a certain view of the nature of human society; and, not surprisingly, Fouillée's view of society was developed through a similar process of synthesizing opposite views. Between the extremes of voluntaristic social-contract theory on the one hand and biologistic organicism on the other, Fouillée found that human society was indeed an organism, but an organism sui generis, which contained a growing contractual element: an *organisme contractuel*.[45] French sociology in general was tending toward a view of society as an organism but was fearful of the antiliberal conclusions which could be, and were being, drawn from this concept. Fouillée was not just trying to wriggle out of a difficult practical position; the whole form as well as the content of his thought led in this direction. He was convinced that society both transcends the individual and is within him, is both natural and voluntary, and cannot be understood by treating it as if it were only the one or the other. Individual wills do matter, and yet society is not simply the aggregate of individual wills.

Society is an organism, comparable to other organisms, insofar as it is a complex whole, more than the sum of its parts. But there is a danger in placing too much reliance on this analogy, for "reasoning by analogy, dear to constructors of social systems (and the sociologists themselves have not always managed to avoid using it), is a means of supporting all theses and of giving them a pseudo-scientific appearance."[46] Fouillée was prepared to accept a larger dose of social-contract philosophy than most sociologists—even to the point of arguing that there is some historical foundation for it—but he thought it obvious that the social bond is not simply a voluntary contract which imposes on individuals only the obligations they explicitly choose. Society no doubt has biological roots, but it is also—or at least has also become—an object of man's consciousness, and therefore it is a bond to which man gives his reasoned as well as his instinctive assent—"the organic and voluntary solidarity of individuals in the group."[47]

The synthetic nature of this view of society led to the concept by which it could be translated into practice: the quasi-contract.[48] The idea of the quasi-contract furnished the justification for legislation which obliged the individual to make sacrifices for the good of the group; it was capable of supporting a wide range of welfare programs. Fouillée thus offered a welcome tool to liberals who saw the need for social welfare programs but feared they were of necessity illiberal. These new liberals had abandoned the expectation that the pursuit of private goods guaranteed the attainment of the general good, but they found it difficult to conceive a way to directly promote the general good without thereby leaving the door open for the return of the tyranny of the group, whether exercised by a despot or by the majority. The idea of the quasi-contract offered an escape from this dilemma because, on the one hand, the individual citizen could be held to have voluntarily accepted certain obligations because such acceptance was part of the very nature of man in society—and man in society is the only kind of man there is—while on the other hand those obligations were strictly limited to what the nature of man in society required, a matter of scientific judgment, not of political whim.

These ideas also justified the liberals' continuing attachment to the nation. Fouillée insisted that the nation was an *organisme contractuel,* indeed a vitally important one.[49] The *patrie* furnished the means by which the individual participated in an experience which transcended his own life; it was a necessary bridge between the individual and universal humanity. The *patrie* appeared as a synthesis between the extremes of ultranationalism and ultrainternationalism.[50] Fouillée condemned both socialist and libertarian internationalisms as leading to despotism or anarchy; man's slow ascent to freedom was possible only within the framework of the nation, and nations would continue to exist and play an important role in the harmonious united Europe of the future.[51] Fouillée wrote extensively on the question of national character, and while not rejecting everything that came from outside, was acutely aware of the existence of a French philosophic tradition with which he associated himself.[52] Unlike those authoritarians for whom the nation was a convenient tool with which to manipulate the masses, Fouillée recognized the rich complexity of the sentiment of nationality and its value to the members of all the strata of the national society.[53]

More important for the evolution of liberalism than his views on the nation and nationalism was Fouillée's interpretation of the role of the state in modern society. Without becoming an idolator of the "organic" state, he was able to escape the fears occasioned in most liberals by any growth in the power and attributions of the state. It was useless to lament that growth, which was a necessary part of the development of modern society; as men became increasingly interdependent, there was more need for those forms of social organization which expressed that interdependence, and the state was certainly one of the more important of these organizations. What Fouillée tried to show the liberals was that, contrary to laissez-faire doctrine, the growth of the state did not mean a corresponding decline in individual freedom. Any serious observation of recent experience showed that the contrary was true: more men are more free in the most advanced states—where government was far from withering away—than in any other time or place. Freedom was not what would be called today a zero-sum game. The private and public sectors of life were both growing.[54]

It was the sociological approach, Fouillée thought, which enabled us to understand this phenomenon that would have seemed impossible in the light of the philosophical conceptions of the old liberalism. The changing character of the relations between the individual and the group as manifested, for example, in the increasing division of labor, was the main source of this dual development. As the individual became a member of a growing number of sub-societies, he was less dominated by the integrating force of any one of them. Even the most inclusive had its limits: "Even when associations combine various special objects in a single group, even when they absorb all the material activity of group members, they do not absorb the individual member's inexhaustible juridical personality."[55] The nature of labor, always a major part of man's experience, also showed this simultaneous development of apparent contraries. It was becoming more socialized as each individual became less and less self-sufficient economically, yet at the same time it was becoming more individualized.[56] These contraries, far from being contradictory, were inseparable: when men were individual in the sense of self-sufficiency, they were also more alike— doing the same things, thinking the same thoughts. The growing difference in their labors was the basis of the growing difference in their personalities, and, as work itself came to play a smaller part in their lives, the possibilities for individual development grew even more.

It was this analysis of the changing relations between the individual and the society which more than any other insight marked the emerging importance of sociology in political thought. It demonstrated the growing acceptance of observation over ratiocination as a foundation for political philosophy. Observers of the political scene such as Machiavelli and Guicciardini had appeared to be cynics at best, immoralists at worst; now moralism and science could and would be combined. Fouillée was not destined to be regarded as one of the founders of modern sociology; he lacked the academic base from which to build a school, and his thought no doubt seemed too "philosophical" to those who would follow Durkheim.[57] But Fouillée appears to have had the greatest influence on liberal thought in his day and to have probed the relations between sociological and political thought more deeply than any of his contemporaries.

Fouillée was by no means an apologist for the unbounded growth of the state. Even while recognizing the necessary character of its growth, he stressed the importance of determining what state action was and what was not compatible with liberty. He thought that there was a clear line—but not an arbitrary or a fixed one—between what the state ought to do and what it ought not to do. It was not possible to draw up a list of universally valid prohibitions or requirements, for the limits of legitimate state action varied with circumstances.[58] The principal variable was the state of society and what it could do at a given moment without the intervention of the state: "Intervention by the state is therefore justified in those cases where private initiative and voluntary association show themselves radically impotent either to assure the exercise of individual rights or to perform an indispensable work of social justice and collective social interest."[59] State action beyond this necessity was an evil because it diminished individual responsibility.[60] By this standard there could be no doubt that under modern conditions the state had charitable obligations, for private and voluntary group charity was clearly insufficient to meet society's needs.[61] The state was also under a moral obligation to attempt to repair any harm it might do to individuals by its own legislation.[62]

It was a matter of pressing importance for liberals to develop a theory of state action appropriate to contemporary problems. Their failure to do so had practical consequences at the level of national government in France. Increasingly dominant in the legislature and the administration, yet fearful of implementing obviously needed reforms, the liberals hesitated to enact measures that had long been in their program. The political leaders of liberalism seemed to fear that reforms, however desirable in themselves, would open the door to socialism, or at least mean an abandonment of liberal principles. Fouillée thus found himself arguing, for example, that "the payments which the law obliges employers to make to the workers' insurance fund are not 'budding socialism'; they are only the application of the principles of existing law,"[63] and, in general, the implementation of needed reforms was the fulfillment of liberalism, not its negation. His view of what was necessary was characteristic of the new liberalism by its insistence on comprehending the aspirations of the working classes, insofar as these were aspirations toward liberty—economic as well as political.[64] The problems of freedom and of welfare could not be solved as quickly or by such simplistic methods as the socialists believed, and Fouillée held it morally wrong to offer panaceas—which were illusory at best—to the working classes,[65] but he did believe they could be solved by a reformist politics based on a liberal sociology.

Liberals were concerned that increased government activity threatened the institution of private property. For Fouillée, as for other liberals, old and new, private property remained essential to the development of human personality and to the protection of individual liberty: "in fact, a person is not free when his liberty does not lead to the ownership of things, of instruments and of products. From the day that the public collectivity administers all things it will also rule all persons."[66] But property rights were not superior to all other considerations; the power of use and abuse had to yield to the public interest in certain cases.[67] Virtually no one had ever denied this; the problem was to know in which cases and how to determine when such a public interest existed. The rule of law required principles on which such decisions could be made; as we have seen, Fouillée was trying to respond to this need. Rejecting socialist criticisms, he defended the right of inheritance and the right to bequeath by testament as essential to individual freedom.[68] On the other hand, he defended against some liberals the taxation necessary to meet the state's social obligations.[69]

Fouillée was particularly concerned to defend the right of private property in the "instruments of production" against the collectivists. The state could fulfill its proper role without replacing individuals and private groups in the organization of production. Such action would be not only unnecessary but harmful. It would bring inefficiency and a decline in the production of wealth, a decline which would harm workers as much as capitalists. The socialist argument that profits belonged to society because they were the production of social forces was as one-sided and false as the individualist claim that the entrepreneur is alone responsible for the achievements of his enterprise. In fact, progress contains social and individual elements, both of which must be recognized and rewarded if it is to continue. The right way for society to assure itself of its share of the benefits is through taxation rather than the ownership of enterprise.[70]

While closing this field to collective ownership, Fouillée concluded that there is nonetheless a domain of "social property" which is, and should be, growing. Fortunately, this could happen without its usurping the place of individual property.[71] Different needs called for different modalities; the state would do what fell into its area of responsibility. The growth of private wealth and social action would be complementary, not antagonistic.[72]

While defending the growth of state action, Fouillée was as sensitive as other liberals to the corresponding dangers, the greatest of which was the remaking of society on the model of the bureaucracy. While bureaucracy was a phenomenon of modern society, it was a particular problem in France because of the important historical role of the national administration. The French complained continually of bureaucratic rule but seemed wedded to it. Fouillée insisted that bureaucracy tended by its very nature to arbitrariness and despotism,[73] but he hoped only to reform, not to abolish it.[74] The necessity for state action to take place through bureaucratic modes of organization was another reason for confining the state to its proper sphere; the bureaucratization of society would bring stagnation and the triumph of mediocrity, it would dry up the wellsprings of progress in individual initiative (he accepted Tarde's model of invention and imitation in part). Fouillée's opposition to the socialists rested on his understanding that their vision of society was one of universal bureaucracy.

Fouillée's examination of the role and limits of the state, while standing in its own right, was not totally independent of his views on the political organization of the state. His appeals for reform were not addressed to an enlightened despot but to the political leadership of a republic. Fouillée's acceptance of the republic was not halfhearted; he proclaimed it as the form of government most conducive to the development of the moral individual and a moral society. It alone could guarantee liberty.[75] Or rather it alone could guarantee the opportunity for liberty; it still mattered what use was made of that opportunity.[76] Even though republican governments might go astray, they had the inherent advantage of being reformable.[77]

Although the republic was not a new form of government, two developments made the modern republic distinctly different from that of antiquity: the end of slavery and the rise of democracy. Fouillée, like other new liberals, was fully committed to democracy, but not without a sensitivity, sharpened by his classical education, to the twin dangers that loomed on either side: anarchy and despotism.[78] Just as his social policy rejected economic leveling, his politics was critical of the atomistic individualist democracy in which numbers alone count.[79] This atomism was an offspring of the old philosophical liberalism—even though many old liberals feared and rejected democracy—and reflected a view of man and society which sociology had shown to be wrong.[80] Here Fouillée had to confront one of the main dilemmas of modern democracy: democracy needs a natural elite if it is to avoid anarchy or despotism, but it tends to destroy such an elite.[81] The problem becomes especially acute in a society in which there is no longer an aristocracy of birth or of fortune[82]—and he believed this to be the case with France. What was needed was a "moral and intellectual elite."[83] "If universal suffrage presupposes men at the bottom capable of choosing, it especially presupposes men at the top worthy of being chosen."[84]

The nature of that elite was most clearly expressed in Fouillée's defense of the traditional classical secondary education. Liberals were divided over the issues of educational reform at the turn of the century, but it may seem strange to find the advocate of reformist sociology among the defenders of traditionalism. Sociology's importance for Fouillée was as a means to an end, and its utility, though great, was far from universal. It was certainly not (yet) adequate for the training of a political elite. A political elite needed to be able to put the long-range general good over those particular and present interests which democracy tends to favor; only liberal studies could produce such an elite.[85] Indeed, such an education was appropriate only for an elite. Fouillée recognized that the very structure of the lycée system was elitist but insisted that it still mattered what was in the curriculum. Latin was important, not for the training of scholars, but because it remained the best preparation for leadership in modern society:

> It is important above all in secondary education to maintain and increase esthetic, poetic, literary, historical, and philosophical culture which is the only culture that promotes morality by essence and purpose. For this reason, the "humanities" are an absolute necessity for the leaders of our French democracy (we do not say ruling *classes*). These studies are not necessarily a condition for *individual* morality, but—and this is different—they are a condition for *national* morality as well as for national greatness.[86]

This call for the formation of a moral elite was, of course, characteristic of almost all French social thought in the nineteenth century.

The question of whether or not it was the state's responsibility to undertake the moral education of the elite—indeed, of society as a whole—was increasingly resolved in the positive by liberals after the foundation of the Third Republic. While the elite and the mass did not require the same training, they did need to have a certain moral education in common in order for democracy to function.[87] Fouillée thought that a state program of moral education could provide the necessary bond if it were based on sociology.[88] Early republican efforts to base moral education on spiritualist philosophy seemed to him to be doomed to failure, but the state had to prepare its own program, for the only possible alternative in France was to allow the Catholic church to dictate it. A sociological approach would allow the state to fulfill its obligation to teach a religiously neutral *morale*.[89] Fouillée was willing to face Catholic opposition to the *morale laïque;* he would not follow some liberals in using that opposition to justify the establishment of a state monopoly.[90] On the whole, Fouillée's concern for moral education put him with the reformers of primary education and with the traditionalists in secondary education.

Fouillée's views on political reform were also shaped by his sociological viewpoint; he was by no means wedded to the contemporary structure of parliamentary government. His main concern was to make government reflect more accurately the nature and interests of society. The fact that society is an *organisme contractuel* suggested a reorganization in which the Chamber would represent the contractual aspect of society and the Senate the organismic. While the former might continue to be a geographically based representation, it was especially important to develop some sort of functional representation of the permanent and general interests of society.[91] He recognized that such a development was not likely in the short run; indeed, the increasing predominance of the Chamber over the other branches of government was the opposite of what was needed.[92] Republican government would have to adapt to the changing character of modern society:

> the University, the army, the navy, the scholarly associations, the agricultural, industrial, and labor associations are more important organs [of society] than the city council of Carpentras or even that of Toulouse, which worships its dead. In our increasingly complex societies social, intellectual, and economic groupings are increasingly more important than geographical groupings.[93]

Even within the framework of geographical representation some reform seemed necessary to Fouillée.

The most basic of those reforms was proportional representation, then enjoying an international vogue. While recognizing the inconveniences of this mode of election—difficulty of securing a durable majority and continuity of leadership, tendency to favor the coalition of anticonstitutional parties—Fouillée thought that its virtues would outweigh its risks: "Proportional representation would be a more sincere expression of the facts, a means of publicly recognizing them and, as a result, of remedying our ills."[94] It would at least mitigate that oppression of minorities by the majority which was one of the dangers of democratic government. Proportional representation was for Fouillée not the panacea some made of it; for him, it was part of a larger package of reforms aimed at strengthening national government by divorcing it from local politics and, conversely, at strengthening local government by diminishing the hand of national government in local politics.[95] To focus attention on national issues in national elections, he called for a smaller chamber with its members chosen from substantially larger districts and even for a certain number of nationwide at-large seats, in addition to the use of proportional representation. The natural response of the sociologist to the problems of the democratic republic was to call for more fully representative government.[96]

Fouillée's immediate political program seems to have been shaped by his observation of contemporary society, rather than by any a priori conceptions about human rights. But he was not an empiricist or a pragmatist (though closer to the latter than to the former), and his political views must be seen in the context of his overall philosophy and of his long-term hopes for mankind. He constantly interpreted contemporary developments in terms of the philosophy of idées-forces, and he thought in terms of that philosophy when developing his reform proposals. The philosophy of idées-forces inescapably supported a politics of evolutionary change, rejecting revolution almost to the point of denying its possibility.[97] Consciously or not, revolutionaries believe in the possibility of the radical elimination of evil; despite his optimism about long-run improvement in the human lot, Fouillée understood that evil is not just in our social organization.[98]

In Fouillée's synthetic philosophy, the philosophy of idées-forces provided the basic understanding of man, while the sociology of idées-forces provided the practical guidance needed to direct human affairs. The former, though subject to modification, was somewhat more developed than the latter; Fouillée was conscious of being in at the birth of sociology and of the corresponding need for caution.[99] He saw his own contribution to the development of sociology as bridging the gap between Tarde and Durkheim: it was necessary to combine the concrete psychological and the abstract sociological viewpoints.[100] Thus understood, sociology could become the instrument of progress he so ardently desired.[101] The philosophy of idées-forces transformed the foundations of liberalism; the sociology of idées-forces would transform liberal politics.[102]

·VII·

Durkheim's Sociology and the New Liberalism

Quant à moi, je ne vois pas dans la religion le mystère de l'Incarnation, mais le *mystère de l'ordre social.* Napoléon Ier

*T*he importance of Emile Durkheim (1858–1917) and his school in the development of French sociology is too well known to need emphasis here, but the significance of his work for the development of French political thought is less clearly understood.[1] Indeed, Durkheim's own political position has been so little understood that he has been diversely called a conservative, a liberal, and a socialist.[2] Such uncertainty has been possible because Durkheim was not a political activist or a political theorist and seldom addressed himself to obviously political questions. His fundamental liberalism would have been more generally recognized, nonetheless, had observers been more aware of the movement we have called the "new liberalism." For Durkheim rejected traditionalist conservatism, laissez-faire liberalism, and collectivist socialism, while much of his thought was occupied with the main problem of the new liberalism: how to combine adequate social integration with individual freedom.[3] What his sociology offered—as others we have studied in this work tried to offer—was a science of society which would support liberal values.

Political issues influenced the development of his intellectual concerns from the beginning of Durkheim's career. The humiliating defeat which France suffered when he was in his early teens was the foundation of his interest in social science.[4] Without that stimulus from the world of politics, he would probably have followed his family tradition and entered the rabbinate.[5] He decided instead that he must follow a career which would contribute to the national revival and, with his characteristic methodicalness, decided that it was first necessary to have a scientific understanding of what had gone wrong. Durkheim's search would lead him to as far afield as the study of Australian totemism but never so close as the study of the Franco-Prussian war itself. His vocation was to be a sociologist, not a historian.

Durkheim believed that France was suffering the natural ills, so to speak, of a protracted transition from the traditional society of the old regime to a new society that was democratic and individualist, scientific and industrial.[6] The difficulty of this transition had been manifested in the political realm by the inability of any regime since 1789 to last as long as twenty years. For Durkheim, the explanation of these convulsions was not to be found by studying them directly; historians would only show us events too distinct to furnish the foundations for a general understanding.[7] To comprehend the deeper movement of the society, he thought, we must look for the general, social causes. But this sociological perspective did not prevent Durkheim from reacting to the main political events of the past century as well as to those of his own time, much as most French liberals did. As a sociologist he saw the developments which had originated with the Revolution as largely inescapable, but he also saw them as basically good. Not only did he feel at home in the liberal tradition issuing from the Revolution, he also saw the intellectual tradition with which he identified—that of scientific rationalism applied to the study of society—as stemming from the same roots. His science and his politics were in natural harmony.

Durkheim's one venture into political activity demonstrated his immersion in the liberal tradition. Like many other academics he was moved to political action by the Dreyfus affair, in which he saw a direct challenge to the values on which the Third Republic rested. A very early member of the Ligue des droits de l'homme, he felt constrained from taking much public action by the hostile atmosphere of Bordeaux, where he was then teaching. He was moved to take a more public stand in the national forum by Ferdinand Brunetière's attack on the intellectual defenders of Dreyfus in his "Après le procès."[8] Both rationalism and liberty were under attack, and under attack in a way which stressed their solidarity. It was characteristic of Durkheim's outlook that he would defend them together.

Durkheim's whole career was tied to the newly founded Third Republic. Born at Epinal in the Vosges, his early intellectual promise led him to Paris to prepare for the Ecole normale supérieure, which he entered in 1879, impressing both faculty and fellow students as one of the intellectual leaders of his generation.[9] He was successful in the competition for the *agrégation* in philosophy in 1882 and spent three years teaching philosophy in various lycées before securing a grant to spend 1885–86 studying contemporary social philosophy in Germany. In 1887 he was named chargé de cours of social science and pedagogy in the

Faculty of Letters at Bordeaux, one of the first social science positions in the French university system.[10] After completion of his doctorate, Durkheim became titular holder of a chair in social science at Bordeaux; but the conservatism of the Sorbonne was such that when he was at last called to Paris in 1902, it was as chargé de cours of the Science of Education, succeeding Ferdinand Buisson. Durkheim became titular professor in 1906, and the title of his chair was changed to Science of Education and Sociology only in 1913. This grudging recognition of the rising status of sociology would no doubt have bothered Durkheim more had he not found his position as professor of education one in which he could make an important contribution to the consolidation of the republic.[11]

For several years Durkheim taught the only course at the Sorbonne which was required of all prospective teachers. He was thus able to continue in a wider arena the work he had started at Bordeaux of convincing the young teachers of France of the high moral importance of their mission. He did not try to indoctrinate them with the tenets of his sociology but drew primarily on the history of education in France to demonstrate the importance of the public schools and to show them how much difference they could make for the country's future. In this fashion, even more than in the formation of future sociologists, Durkheim believed he was in a position to influence the political future of the country. More direct involvement in politics did not tempt him:

> Even those whose vocation is to meditate on societies, such as historians and sociologists, do not seem to me much more qualified for these active roles than men of letters or naturalists; for one can have the genius which discovers the general laws that explain social facts in the past without really having the practical sense which discovers the measures needed by a given people at a given moment in their history. Just as a great physiologist is usually a mediocre clinician, a sociologist is likely to make a quite inadequate statesman.[12]

The comparison of the sociologist with the physician here was not accidental; Durkheim envisioned the role of sociology as a sort of social medicine, an image which conveyed both something of its utility and its limits.[13]

Durkheim felt acutely the need for a better social medicine than liberal philosophy or any of its rivals on the Right or Left had been able to produce. To succeed where they had failed, sociology had to develop a scientific basis for the understanding of present problems. By raising important questions out of the arena of competing opinions and dogmas, social science could also furnish the unifying force so obviously lacking in French social life:

> we are living precisely in one of those revolutionary and critical epochs when the naturally weakened authority of traditional discipline can easily give birth to the spirit of anarchy. This is the origin of those consciously or unconsciously anarchical tendencies which are found today not only in the particular sect bearing that name, but also in the very diverse doctrines which, though in conflict on other points, meet in a common rejection of everything that is governed by rules.[14]

The immediacy and seriousness of the crisis pulled the sociologist in conflicting directions: because the science was in its infancy, he had to admit that it could not offer ready solutions to all pressing questions; yet at the same time he had to argue that not only would it be able to provide much help in the long run, but it was of some immediate use.[15]

Since men cannot wait until their understanding is perfect before they take action, they will act. But, Durkheim thought, they ought to try to act on the basis of the best knowledge currently available, and here sociology could be of some help. First of all it could be helpful through its critique of rival forms of social thought.[16] In so doing, it could help wean men from a blind adherence to traditions that no longer met current needs, as well as armor them against the seductions of utopian hopes for a radical leap into a better future. This was not enough, but it was certainly a great deal in an age when so many ideas were competing for men's allegiances.

Durkheim did not think that sociology's contribution was primarily negative, even in the short run. It was already able to diagnose the main ill from which society was suffering, and this diagnosis enabled it to direct its research to the area which would bear the most immediate fruit. He had no doubt about what this area was: "Our first duty at the present moment is to make a moral science for ourselves."[17] The science of morals was by no means the whole of sociology in Durkheim's conception, but it was that part of sociology which was most urgently needed and to which he devoted his entire career.

For Durkheim, the science of morals offered the unique advantage over moral philosophy of being adaptable to the changes which necessarily took place in all societies. This was an advantage which he stressed in his campaign to implant a secular morality in the education system of the Third Republic.[18] Republican politicians, in attempting to win public acceptance of the secularization of moral education, had stressed that their moral values were not different from those of their fathers, that they merely had new grounds on which to support them. Durkheim rightly observed that this was correct but that it was not enough; the secular moral teaching would need to be able to innovate in accord with changing social circumstances and social needs.[19] The effort of the philosophers to supplant religion had been weakened by their commitment to a timeless and universal moral code and by their attempts to found morality on individual liberty instead of social solidarity.[20] Durkheim's attachment to the Western moral tradition prevented him from seeing the difficulty of establishing a defensible border between this desirable adaptability and a destructive moral relativism.

Moral science was not for Durkheim simply an instrument, still less a method for remaking society to suit our wishes. Society was not indefinitely plastic, and no science could mold it to our arbitrary will.[21] As a social scientist he could see that one could hope to steer the development of a society only in accord with its innermost trends; it would be futile to attempt to go against them. As a man, he could not accept this constraint as mere necessity; he had to be able to consider it also as just.[22] Thus, for Durkheim, as for Marx, being right meant being right with history. Being right with history meant, for Durkheim, accepting rationalism, democracy, and individualism because they were the current products of the centuries of development of Western society.[23] Moral relativism did not mean for him that the individual could choose his own moral code; man was pretty much stuck with whatever was offered by his society and his time. Sociology offered only one way out: the opportunity to work toward the better moral code of the future.

Durkheim was not satisfied with the prospect of a sociology which could show us how to get what we wanted; it must also be able to show us what we should desire. Certainly, he did not regard the *is* and the *ought* as identical, but he did think that the study of the *is* (and of the *has been*) would be sufficient to lead us to the *ought*.[24] Moralists in the philosophical tradition—even a Kant or a Renouvier—had retired to their studies and eventually emerged with more or less logically coherent systems of morals, which invariably proved powerless to affect human behavior. The direct study of human moral behavior could hardly, Durkheim thought, produce less effective results. Sociology would make a difference.

Of course, other social thinkers had also believed that a new understanding of man and society—which they alone had reached— would make possible in the near future a substantial improvement in the human condition, not to say the arrival of the millennium. They had invariably found that moving from the realm of ideas to that of practice was more difficult than they had at first imagined. On the one hand, there were those who believed that men are guided and moved by ideas, and that, therefore, if you discover the true ideas, men will, either rapidly or eventually, depending upon your degree of optimism, come to follow them. The more sophisticated holders of this intellectualistic viewpoint realized that an idea could triumph only if the time and circumstances were ripe for it, and like Louis Blanc, they constructed vast histories to show how the time had arrived for the triumph of their ideas. Failure of these hopes to be realized never proved that the ideas were wrong, only that the times were not yet ripe.

On the other hand, those who believed that men are moved and guided by material conditions and that ideas are merely reflections of the hard facts of material existence ran into difficulties of their own. If the forces that move men are in their biological makeup or the structure of their societies, where is the lever the reformer can move to forward his cause? Here again the common response was to find that biological evolution or the logic of history was working to realize the thinker's expectations. But no more than the intellectualists could the materialists escape the temptation to do the one thing open to them— attempt to influence men's ideas directly. Durkheim's belief in the predominance of collective forces over the thoughts of individuals did not incline him to quietism. The tenets of his sociology were framed to make action possible.

Durkheim was sensitive to the existence of that vicious circle in which it is necessary to change ideas in order to change circumstances, and necessary to change circumstances in order to change ideas, but he argued that in practice the circle could be broken by the cumulative and reciprocal effect of small attacks on both the material and intellectual fronts. He was able to reach this position without inconsistency because in his conception of nature, the relationship of cause and effect was not unilinear; they had a reciprocal effect on each other.[25] Social science was of course a means of acting on men's ideas and could influence institutions only indirectly; it was possible to expect it would make a difference without believing that it could do a great deal. Where existing ideas were an obstacle in the search for solutions to social problems, sociology could help reorient men's thinking in more useful directions. Thus it was worthwhile to attack the intellectual foundations of the atomistic individualism so popular in France. The facts about the individual's relations to his society obviously did not automatically penetrate his consciousness, but they were accessible to his reason.

An understanding of the problem of solidarity, in Durkheim's opinion, like the understanding of any moral question, could only come through the creation of a science of morals. He dismissed the efforts of moral philosophers—even those who had some influence on his own views, such as Kant—as so much idle speculation, resting on assumptions that were either demonstrably false or unverifiable.[26] What was needed was the empirical investigation of what morals actually have been and presently are. Only by applying the comparative method could the true nature of morals be discovered. It was difficult, Durkheim recognized, for most people even to admit the possibility of a science of morals.[27] Moral questions necessarily had that touch of the sacred about them which made it difficult to approach them with the objectivity of science.[28] For the social scientist that very sacredness became an important part of the phenomenon to be examined. A related obstacle to the development of a science of morals was the need to escape from our habitual ethnocentrism; it was necessary to study the moral behavior of all of mankind to discover the basis of morals. Comparative and historical study, not introspection, was the only way to escape the errors of past philosophy.

The examination of a variety of societies convinced Durkheim that the common characteristic of their moral systems was the obligation they imposed on the individual to obey rules of conduct whose source transcended his interests or his will. The content of that obligation was highly variable, and there was no point in trying to decide whether there were any moral maxims, such as "Thou shalt not kill," honored in all societies. There was one universal and that was fundamental: the fact of obligation. Acts which were guided simply by the desires and interests of the individual or group of individuals were never—or virtually never—regarded as moral in any society. Morals and religion were indeed closely linked in their origins, since both expressed an awareness that there is something which transcends the individual.

In Durkheim's view, the common origin of religion and morals did not mean that in one's own age religious belief was a necessary foundation for moral behavior. This was fortunate, since religious belief had clearly been on the wane in Western society for some time; religion was losing—for many, had lost—its powers of conviction over modern rationalist man, whose science had exposed its errors. But while science could undermine religion, it could not banish the importance of transcendence in men's lives; it could only lead us to understand that what transcends us, what is the source of the obligations that shape our moral lives, is not some God created in our image, but Society. In the past, religion had expressed the truth of this transcendence in symbolic form, but for Durkheim, this symbolism was no longer necessary, and men could be guided by their direct knowledge of society.[29] It was a mark of man's progress that he no longer saw through a glass darkly but could regard reality face to face. Religion's role and its value to man were largely in the past; now it was mainly an obstruction to the diffusion of scientific understanding.[30]

For Durkheim, sociology was not so much the enemy of religion and of philosophy as their heir, a somewhat impatient heir to be sure, irritated that the ghosts of its ancestors were reluctant to leave the stage. He was confident that sociology could do what they had done or attempted to do in the past. This was a dual task which involved reaching both men's minds and hearts: the true nature of their social obligations had to be demonstrated, and the spirit, the moral will to fulfill those obligations had to be created and sustained. Durkheim was not especially successful in explaining why, if moral obligation was the product of society, men did not obey it automatically, making moralists superfluous. He did think that the efforts of religious and philosophical moralists had been largely ineffectual, but that was because they had failed to understand the foundations of morals. The science of morals would offer society for the first time the opportunity to work its own temporal salvation; the sociologists would not be the priests of a new cult, but Durkheim expected their students, the schoolteachers of republican France, would have a truly priestly mission.[31] It was not necessary, or even possible, for sociology to create a new cult to replace the old—as Comte had tried to do with his Religion of Humanity; the main thing was to explain the real nature of the relationship between the individual and society.

Previous efforts to construct sociology had overturned the individualist, philosophical error of seeing society as merely an aggregate of individuals, but they had also tended to the opposite error of making the individual merely a cog in the machine. This was true whether they indulged in the unconscious metaphysics of a Comte, for whom the Grand Etre, Society, was alone real, or in the organic metaphor of the biosociologists who saw man as a subordinate part of the whole organism that was society. Durkheim was himself often accused of hypostatizing society, but his approach was designed to avoid that peril.[32] Society was for him a being *sui generis*, distinct from the individuals that composed it, but at the same time inseparable from them. His favorite analogy for this relationship was the relationship between the human mind and the brain: mental activity could not be reduced to the functioning of the brain cells, but neither could it exist without them. Durkheim rejected materialism because it led to this sort of reductionism; he denied that you can explain the higher by the lower. While biology and psychology were important for understanding man, they were not sufficient and could not furnish the basis for sociology. Society had to be studied directly, and the science that did so would be a science of the spirit.

In Durkheim's view, attempts by other sociologists to explain the relations of the individual to society had failed because they did not allow for any change in the nature of those relations, either as a result of positing a fixed human nature or of relying on a simplistic biological analogy. But clearly the relation of modern man to his society was different from the relation in earlier societies, or the whole question of individualism would never have arisen. If sociology could explain how and why man's idea of his place in society had changed, it would lay the foundation for dealing with today's problems. Modern individualism was obviously not conceived by some inventor, as Tarde had to claim, but could only be the product of society itself. How could this have come about? The resolution of this problem was the theme of Durkheim's doctoral thesis, *De la division du travail social*, and his solution was the cornerstone of his subsequent work.[33]

Durkheim used the expression "division of social labor" to make it clear that he was referring to something broader than the kind of economic specialization described in Adam Smith's *Wealth of Nations;* the differentiation of social roles involved an increasing portion of human affairs, our amusements and cultural activities as well as our means of survival. Social relations are far from being merely material; however much men depend on each other for their very existence, their relations have a spiritual dimension even in the most primitive of societies. It was not, Durkheim thought, so much the concrete facts that govern men as it was their mental representations, representations which ultimately derived from the physical reality, but which have acquired such a degree of independence from it that any study of society must be based on the study of these representations rather than on the physical substratum.[34] The mental relations which bind men together in modern society were much more complex, indeed of a different kind, than those of earlier times.

Durkheim characterized the solidarity of modern societies as "organic," in contrast to the solidarity of primitive societies, which was "mechanical." Awkward as these terms are for us—since we associate the organic with the more "natural" character of primitive societies and think of modern societies as artificial and mechanical—they adequately convey the fundamental distinction which was basic to Durkheim's argument.[35] While social solidarity was a moral phenomenon, the product of men's ideas and feelings, its form in any particular society was shaped by the material structure of that society to the extent that it determined which of the two forms of solidarity was predominant. In primitive societies where almost all men had the same social and economic functions, their solidarity was the product of their sameness; they all had the same interests and therefore tended to think alike.[36] The *conscience collective*—society in its mental aspects—was also a *conscience commune*. From the beginnings of civilization, and *a fortiori* in modern times, such social conditions have ceased to exist and the "conscience commune" has occupied a smaller and smaller place in our minds, yet social solidarity has not ceased to exist. Solidarity must therefore have taken on a new form, Durkheim argued, one based on differentiation instead of similarity. Men's awareness—which could be unconscious—of their interdependence supplied the mental basis of the new solidarity.[37]

This new form of solidarity seemed to Durkheim to be by its very nature more powerful than the older form—for men needed each other more than ever—but at the same time it was also more fragile—men were so different that they could lose that essential awareness of their solidarity, even cease to believe in it.[38] The mere fact of interdependence was evidently insufficient to hold a society together; the utilitarian motives of individuals who consider themselves distinct from society can form only the most tenuous of bonds. But it was precisely this growing individualism which was the characteristic moral expression of a society dominated by organic solidarity. Were such societies then inherently self-destructive? Durkheim could not believe so.

Modern individualism was the natural mental product of a society in which an increasing differentiation of roles was being produced by increased numbers and social density. But like anything in nature, this tendency could be carried to excess, with pathological results. The existence of atrophy and hypertrophy in nature were not incompatible with the continued existence of normal development. Modern society was, thus, not menaced by individualism, which was the healthy product of its normal development, but rather by a hypertrophy of individualism. If individualism were not kept within bounds, society would be threatened by the dissolution of a solidarity which could degenerate into anarchy, which was likely to be only the prelude to the domination of the strongest and the end of liberty.[39] It was even possible that the fear of anarchy would become strong enough to produce a reaction against the growth of modern liberties. Thus, social scientific knowledge of the origins, nature, and problems of modern individualism was essential if the liberty which Durkheim valued highly was to be preserved.

While excessive solidarity could still be a problem in certain segments of modern society, such as the army, the main social problems stemmed from inadequate solidarity, inadequate integration of the individual into the social order. One index of this development to which

Durkheim devoted considerable attention was the growth of what he called anomic suicide. *Anomie*, or normlessness, was a state of disorientation in which the individual had become so detached from the constraints of society that he had no guide to living, and might, indeed, find suicide the only way out. The rate and distribution of suicide in a given society would thus be social phenomena and not merely the product of individual failings. In showing that suicide, a problem usually regarded as purely individual, was primarily a social phenomenon, Durkheim hoped both to demonstrate the nature of the problem of solidarity in modern society and the capacity of sociology to help us understand it.

In concluding that the tensions in the relations of the individual to the group are part of the inescapable price we must pay for the benefits of modern society, Durkheim showed that sociology offered no panacea.[40] Because society transcends the individual and men are subject to the obligations it imposes on them, living in society will always present difficulties. At the same time those obligations are necessary to the individual's well-being because man is a being that requires externally sanctioned limits in order to function.[41] Human existence has thus a tragic dimension which has been recognized by religion, but which philosophy, especially social and moral philosophy, has tried to deny. Durkheim explicitly agreed with Kant that the essential ingredient of moral action is obligation but thought that Kant's effort to establish obligation on reason alone led to the divorce of his moral philosophy from all contact with human reality. In trying to establish a morals of pure obligation, Kant separated it from all idea of benefit—social as will as individual. The Utilitarians went to the opposite extreme, seeking to devise a moral code based on enlightened self-interest, rejecting the idea of obligation. For Durkheim, this was an even greater error than Kant's.[42] The sociological viewpoint, he thought, allowed us to see what was valid as well as what was defective in both points of view.

Although he thought that Kant had failed to see the social origins of individual autonomy, having to posit a world of noumena to explain its possibility, Durkheim's idea of freedom was very close to Kant's. Like Kant, he saw no way out of the conclusion that the reign of causality which is observable everywhere in nature must apply to society as well.[43] Man's freedom cannot therefore mean that he has the power to violate or to exempt himself from the laws of nature. Rather, his freedom consists in his ability—unique among living creatures—to understand and give his rational consent to the laws which govern his existence, although he did not make them.[44] Durkheim considered the eternal debate over free will versus determinism to be a metaphysical issue of no interest to science; what the social scientist could observe was that men seem always to have believed in both.[45] Man's liberty is clearly limited by nature's laws; it is merely absurd to speak of his right to violate them. For Durkheim, man's position with respect to society is comparable; freedom of thought was compatible with rational authority.[46] He even drew from this view the argument that democratic government was the superior form of political authority because it rested on the informed consent of the governed to the laws which rule them.[47] It is, so to speak, the adulthood of the group, comparable to the adulthood of the individual who has learned to understand and accept the rules which he passively obeyed as a child.[48]

Society was thus for Durkheim both the empirical source and the moral foundation of individual liberty. All attempts to found a doctrine of liberty on the individual were thus bound to fail in the future as they had in the past. Fortunately, thought Durkheim, there was a tradition of individualism in France which had never fallen into the extremes of a Spencer or the English Utilitarians:

> [This tradition] has been taught for the last century by the great majority of thinkers: it is the tradition of Kant and Rousseau, of the spiritualists, the tradition that the Declaration of the Rights of Man tried more or less successfully to translate into formulas, the tradition that is currently taught in our schools and which has become the basis of our moral catechism.[49]

That tradition had tended to present the liberties too negatively, and, Durkheim argued, the contradictions in Kant and Rousseau (and repeated in their successors) stemmed from their failure to recognize that the values of individualism come themselves from society, not from the individual.[50] The liberal tradition had tended to oppose the individual and society despite its basic conviction of the importance of both; this contradiction could be overcome by recognizing that social solidarity is one of the prerequisites of individual feedom.[51] The maximum liberty of which man is capable escapes man in isolation; it is attainable only in society.

From the sociologist's point of view the desire to be an autonomous individual, the aspiration for individual liberty, did not itself depend on or derive from the individual. It was rather a force of nature, the result of "an ineluctable law against which it would be absurd to rebel."[52] To be a free individual was an obligation which modern society imposed on everyone whether it was wanted it or not, and, indeed, many were obviously reluctant to accept what was perhaps the most difficult moral obligation in man's long experience: "Today no one contests the obligatory character of the rule which commands one to be, and to be more and more, an individual."[53] Durkheim's aim was not to crush the individual under the weight of society but to cut the grounds from under the claims of extreme individualism in order to show the true nature of modern individualism. Sociology and history would show, not that individualism was either good or evil in itself, but that it was a historical growth rather than an eternal truth, that it was a socially created value. This meant that sociology need not be— could not be—anti-individualist. By showing that individualism itself derives from society, it shows there is no necessary conflict between the individual and society. By the same token it showed that the individual had no grounds for shedding his moral obligations to society. Society made possible the independence from the *conscience commune*, and unless he recognized this, he risked destroying the foundations of his freedom in the very attempt to preserve it.

Durkheim would never attempt to pursue in any historical detail the process by which the changes in Western society had led from a social demand for mental conformity to a social demand for individuality. The fact that it was the result of social processes and not the accomplishment of individuals was the main thing. Of the three milieux which shaped man—his organism, the material world, society—only society had changed sufficiently to account for the rise of individualism.[54] The mechanisms by which society exercised this influence were of secondary importance, and Durkheim treated them very abstractly. The rise of rationalism was explained in the same fashion: it was not the cause of the rise of individualism but a parallel growth, itself having the same causes. The increasing variety of human experiences that resulted from the division of labor made the dictates of the *conscience commune* less and less imperative; men had to call on their reason for the guidance that had once come automatically from the group mind.[55]

The sociological explanation of individualism not only explained the relations of the individual to society, it also offered a means to understand the relations of the individual and the state. It eliminated the antagonism between the individual and the state which seemed inherent in the approach of philosophical liberalism. The state was for Durkheim a particularly important organ of society and to a large extent represented society to the individual:

> The only way to get around this difficulty is to reject the postulate according to which the individual's rights are derived from the individual and to admit that the establishment of rights is the work of the state. Then, in effect, everything becomes explicable. We understand that the functions of the state expand without caus-

163

ing a diminution of the individual or that the individual can develop without causing the state to regress, since the individual
would, in certain respects, be himself the product of the state and
since the activity of the state would essentially tend to liberate the
individual. Indeed, history effectively authorizes the acceptance of
this cause-and-effect relation between the growth of individualism
and the growth of the state; this conclusion springs obviously from
the facts. Except in those abnormal cases of which we will have
occasion to speak, the stronger the state, the more the individual
is respected.[56]

At the end of his life Durkheim would indeed have to deal with what
he could only consider an abnormal case if he was to preserve his
belief in the liberal character of his doctrine: the case of modern Germany. The main item of his wartime writings was an attack on Treitschke's
doctrine of the primacy of the state.[57] It remained true that the rise of
individualism and the rise of the modern state had gone on at the same
time in Western society and that a liberal theory would have to account for this to be viable in the twentieth century. For sociological
liberalism, this was an easier task than for philosophical liberalism, but
could sociological liberalism furnish an adequate defense against the
potential hypertrophy of the state?

Durkheim evidently thought so, but in any case, this was not the immediate problem facing French society. That was, rather, to stave off
the opposite danger, a hypertrophied individualism. Sociology was
fitted to deal with this problem because it also illuminated the only
possible cure: education. This was not offered as a shortcut; it was only
the beginning of a long-term solution. Durkheim insisted that French
society would not know the solidarity it needed until there had been
some fundamental changes in its institutions. But those institutional
changes would come about only when enough people wanted them,
felt them to be necessary. This changed mentality could not be brought
about overnight; it could only be the work of future generations. Future generations would have to receive an education which pointed
them in that direction; this would not be an education in sociological
theory but a moral education for which sociology furnished the foundation on which the teachers were prepared. A new kind of moral education could come only from the state: the moral education offered by
the church was an obstacle to the development of rationalism and solidarity; the moral authority of the family had declined to the point
where it could not do the job. The state was the only organism capable
of shaking off the inertia of society and providing the leadership to do
something new.[58]

Durkheim's view of the importance of a laic, public moral education was thus not fundamentally different from that of the philosophers. Nor did he differ with them significantly on the content of the moral code to be taught. No one, whether sociologist or philosopher, could invent a new moral code; these were generated by society. This was one reason why Durkheim thought that conservative fears about the teaching of a laic *morale* were unfounded; on the things that mattered, they could not be very far apart without falling into irrelevance. Why, then, should one bother with the development of a sociologically based *morale*? What practical effect could sociology have that was different from that of religion or philosophy? This was indeed a key point for Durkheim, one that helps us understand the motivation behind his effort to establish a science of morals. His sociology hoped— and this was one of the main reasons why his later work was devoted to primitive religion—through its understanding of the origins and nature of the religious impulse which Durkheim thought to be a permanent feature of man's nature, to be able to harness that inner force as effectively as religions had done in simpler societies.[59] Philosophers could show men the right; they always had trouble motivating them to pursue it within the framework of their intellectual conceptions. Sociology could admit, more easily than philosophy, that men are no more governed by rational calculations in modern society than they were in earlier times. Consciousness of irrationality did not mean giving in to it but was rather the only hope of achieving some mastery over it.

When the new liberals discussed the importance of the relations between the individual and society, the society they had in mind was the nation. Durkheim did not question this view; throughout most of his career he considered the nation to be the largest intelligible unit of social organization that had yet emerged, and therefore the main unit of study for sociology. For him, the nation was the normal milieu in which a truly human life could be lived, playing the same role that the *polis* had for Aristotle.[60] To this extent, sociological liberalism had a more nationalistic bias than philosophical liberalism; while most of the philosophic liberals were nationalists—with a tinge of internationalism— their moral philosophies tended to embrace the whole of humanity, making it difficult to provide a consistent defense of the individual's obligations to the nation. Durkheim agreed that in the very long run the individual's relation to humanity might supplant his relation to the nation, but to seek this as a goal was to ignore the needs of today—and of the foreseeable future.[61] This continuing importance of the nation was one reason why the new liberalism had to focus its attention on the role of the state; the state, Durkheim observed, was the only social institution which embraced the entire nation.

When it came to describing the relations of the state to the nation, Durkheim tended to fall back on organicist metaphor: "The state is, rigorously speaking, the very organ of social thought."[62] More particularly, it was the organ of practical, rather than speculative, thought. One of the principal concerns of its thought was the promotion and maintenance of the solidarity of society; it was in a better position to judge the interests of the community than any individual could be.[63] The role of the state was thus not simply to execute the will of society, as many individualistic liberals had tended to believe; indeed, Durkheim saw its mission as more reflective than executive—the function of the legislator was predominant.[64] The state's role was one of leadership, an organ whose decisions committed the community but were not the work of the community.[65] Yet, for Durkheim, the state did not absorb society; it was not the incarnation of the *conscience collective* but rather a limited part of that conscience, albeit the highest, most self-conscious part.[66] Pierre Birnbaum goes too far in arguing that for Durkheim the state became a "pure incarnation of the rational spirit," but when Durkheim was discussing the state, he seemed more often to be talking about what it ought to be rather than what it was, to be speaking more as a philosopher than as a sociologist.[67]

On the other hand, Durkheim did use sociological arguments to solve one of the basic problems of the new liberalism: justifying the growing importance of the state. "Everything obliges us to see it as a normal phenomenon which is inherent in the structure of higher societies, since it consistently advances in proportion to the degree to which societies approach this type."[68] In other words, one of the effects of the progress of the division of labor was an increase in the extent of state activity. Growth in activity required a growth in the size and variety of the organs of the state.[69] Since this development was inevitable, it was futile to complain about it. Durkheim does not seem to have shared the common liberal concern of his time with the growth of bureaucracy.[70] Nor did he deny that the growth of state activity meant that citizens were more dependent on the state than ever before.[71] This, too, was inescapable, but it was not necessarily a threat to individual liberty. It would become such a threat, however, if the society did not develop the larger complex of institutions needed in an era of organic solidarity. The role of the state would be to guide the development of those institutions. An organ of society capable of filling this role was essential in Durkheim's view because of the growing dysfunctionality of the habits and practices we have inherited from the past; the pace of adaptation needed to be speeded up, and only more social knowledge could make this possible.[72] Since men were mostly governed by habit, a specific organ of reflection was essential.[73]

Durkheim was, however, no believer in the omnicompetent state. His basic inclination was in the direction of an institutional pluralism, but he did not carry out a systematic development of the kind we will see in the next chapter in the work of Léon Duguit. While Durkheim did say that it was impossible to assign any definite limit to the growth of the state, he explained this in a way characteristic of the new liberalism of the twentieth century: "Individual rights are evolving; they advance unceasingly, and it is impossible to assign them an upper limit. What yesterday seemed a luxury will become an absolute right tomorrow. No limit, therefore, can be ascribed to the tasks of the state."[74] The growth of the state and the growth of individual freedom were not, then, merely parallel phenomena; they were interdependent. The state was the instrument that had freed the individual from the domination of other social organisms—family, commune, feudal power, guild, and so forth—and the growth of these freedoms generated the demand for further liberations.[75] For all its importance to Durkheim, the state was not some mystical entity through which the logic of history imposed itself on man. In his view of social processes, cause and effect were interdependent.[76]

There was one important area of social life in which Durkheim thought that the state was particularly incompetent to act: the economy. He did not find it surprising that when things were not going well in the economy, the state should be tempted to intervene, but experience showed that "its intervention, when it is not simply impotent, only causes problems of a different nature."[77] At the same time he was far from the view of the classical economists that the economy could be left to the self-regulating operations of the market. The economy needed to be rationally organized, but the state by its very nature was ill fitted to take on this task. The problems of economic life are detailed and specific; the state can only act in a simple and general fashion:

> The state is not close enough to these complex manifestations to be able to find the special solution which suits each case. It is a ponderous machine which is only made to deal with general and simple needs. Its action—always uniform—cannot bend and adjust itself to the infinite diversity of particular circumstances. As a result, it is necessarily oppressive and leveling [in its impact].... Whether it is a question of working hours or of hygiene, or of wages, or of insurance and assistance, the best of intentions meets the same difficulties everywhere. As soon as one tries to establish a few rules, they are found inapplicable to actual experience because they are not adequately flexible.[78]

Durkheim thought that it was a fundamental error of the socialists to believe that the role of the state ever could or should be the central direction of economic life.[79] One of the central problems of the new liberalism would be how to arrange the needed social intervention in economic life without giving the state a role it could not handle or a role that would menace individual freedom.

If the state was to play the role which Durkheim thought natural to it, some substantial changes would be required. The existing political structure of France was a "deviant form of democracy" in his eyes.[80] In the French democracy there was not enough distance between the government and the citizens, with the result that both sides suffered. The state was unable to fulfill its role as the reflective organ because it was too representative of the interests of the electors. This was not a situation to be blamed on the greed of the voters or the corruption of the representatives; the nation was simply a more powerful collective force than the deputies, so that when they were brought into direct contact, it had to prevail.[81] But the citizen was also a loser in this arrangement; he was deprived of the governmental leadership he needed, and he was impeded in the conduct of his own affairs by the wrong sort of state intervention.[82]

The essential political reform was therefore the creation of intermediate bodies between the state and the atomized mass of individuals. This was not simply a political reform for Durkheim, but a moral and social one as well. He could see only one sort of intermediate body as viable in modern (that is, governed by the division of labor) society: the professional association, or *corporation*.[83] Territorial organization, which still supplied the formal framework of political life, had had some validity in a simpler, predominantly agricultural, society, but the rise of the nation-state had increasingly undermined it.[84] In modern society men were more influenced by their occupations than by where they happened to live; this was true at all levels of society.[85] The national government would have more meaning to a man if he was represented in his capacity as a coal miner rather than in his capacity as resident of the department of the Nord.[86] But this was not the most important thing for Durkheim; even the reformed state based on occupational representation could not supply the solidarity needed by society. The occupational group itself, properly organized, could become the locus of the individual's integration into society.[87] It was sufficiently above the individual to generate that feeling of obligation which is the essence of morals, but not so far above that the feeling of belonging becomes too dilute. It was the only answer he could see to the moral crisis of modern society.

While Durkheim did not describe in detail how a political system based on occupational representation should be organized or, indeed, how the corporations themselves should be structured, he did lay out some general criteria.[88] The corporations had to be autonomous; they furnished the means by which occupational groups could govern themselves, subject to the overriding interests of the nation guarded by the state. They were not to be organs of the state administration. The corporations should be national in scale; they would group all participants in a given occupation and thus avoid the parochialism which was a major weakness of the guilds of the ancien régime.[89] Membership would be voluntary, but the advantages were so great that few would opt out. The corporations had to bring together in one organization capital, management, and labor. Durkheim by no means simply thought of this as a means of disciplining labor; it was also a means of disciplining capital. He considered the trade union movement a natural and legitimate effort on the part of workers to protect their interests in an unorganized economy, but it did not offer a long-term solution.[90]

Durkheim's corporatism did not express a nostalgia for the integration of medieval society nor was it a form of socialism in the manner of English guild socialism or French *syndicalisme révolutionnaire*.[91] Still less should it be considered a forerunner of the fascist corporation of the 1920s and 1930s.[92] It was the expression of Durkheim's conviction that the social problem of modern society was essentially a moral problem. The liberating effect of the social changes connected with the division of labor was on the whole a benefit in his opinion, but it was also a burden because the lack of rules led to demoralization.[93] The old sources of authority could not be revived, so new sources had to be discovered. The sociologist might expect new authorities to emerge by themselves in the long run if it were necessary. But sociology offers the possibility of accelerating this process, enabling us to see what is needed and to favor its development. Durkheim's observations remained at a high level of generality because only experience could show what would work. What matters most was his argument for the need for intermediate bodies to restore solidarity to modern society.[94]

New liberals were not particularly distressed to be called socialists by the old laissez-faire liberals because it was a natural misconception from the point of view of those extreme individualists. But while, for some individuals, the new liberalism might be a way station in the personal journey toward socialism, most new liberals saw their own position as a coherent and enduring one, better adapted than socialism to the realities of modern society. Durkheim's view of the state was one of the things which most clearly separated him from many of the socialists of his day. Not even in the long run was the state destined to be replaced by the economic organization of society. One of the chief objections that he constantly raised against the socialists was their economism and its belief that the government of men could be replaced by the administration of things. Still less did he accept the revolutionary syndicalist argument that the syndicate would replace the state. No doubt he was closer to the democratic socialism of Jean Jaurès, who was juggling with great skill a rather unstable mixture of neo-Kantian individualism and Marxist collectivism. Jaurès was a good friend and he drew into the SFIO a good many of the Durkheimian circle. Durkheim did not follow them simply because he was reticent about becoming involved in politics but because of fundamental differences about goals and methods. It was a friendly disagreement among men with the same education and, to a large extent, the same values. Like most new liberals he sympathized with certain aspects of the socialist program, but he dissociated himself from socialism in terms that could hardly be clearer.[95]

For Durkheim, socialism was not the solution to the problems of modern society; it was, rather, an important symptom of the existence and character of those problems.[96] It was, for this reason, an important object of study for the sociologist who wanted to believe that his work could make a difference. Socialism's relation to the problems of man in society was similar to that of religion: it was a symbolic interpretation.[97] And, as we have seen, the mission of sociology was to replace symbolic understanding with the direct scientific confrontation of reality. The reaction of many socialists to the Durkheimian analysis was analogous to the reaction of many Catholics: the accusation of sacrilege. In the case of the socialists the reaction was all the more acute because of Durkheim's explicit rejection of their claim to be scientific.[98] As far as he was concerned, socialism's claim to present a comprehensive system of society, explaining past, present, and future, was prima facie evidence of a lack of scientific rigor.[99] At best, socialism was a philosophical construction, and the philosophy on which it rested was often a version of the individualism whose foundations sociology had already undermined.[100]

Socialists have often tried to discredit sociology—are still trying to do so—by arguing that it appeared as a reaction to socialism and therefore is no more than a clever smoke screen for the defense of bourgeois interests, like liberalism in politics. There can be no doubt that one of the motivations behind the rise of sociology was a desire to respond to the rise of socialism, but whether this justifies the ideological unmasking is another question. The appeal of sociology in some political circles probably did derive from its apparent potential as a weapon against socialism, but there were at least as many supporters of the bourgeois order who, if they could distinguish sociology from socialism at all, suspected the former as a stalking horse for the latter. By his very effort to explain socialism, seen as a social phenomenon, Durkheim took a position that made his sociology a rival of socialism. But it certainly did not make him a defender of the status quo.

Unfortunately, Durkheim never completed the detailed investigation of socialism that he began in a series of lectures at Bordeaux.[101] We would be able to understand his position in the Third Republic better had he gotten beyond Saint-Simon and the Saint-Simonians. Durkheim began his investigation with his now-famous definitions of socialism and communism,[102] which have led some to think that he was socialist, or that he considered himself a socialist within the terms of his own definition.[103] Those definitions were certainly inadequate to explain the socialism of his day, but they are important as an effort to study the phenomenon of socialism sociologically. Durkheim saw communism and socialism as belonging to two distinct phases in the development of Western society: communism was a phenomenon which appeared in societies dominated by mechanical solidarity; socialism was characteristic of society dominated by the division of labor. Communism, like religion, was inappropriate to today's needs but expressed a deeply rooted feeling which was likely to persist in one form or another. Socialism, while not destined to permanence if social science could do what he thought it could, was much newer; it began not with the steam engine but with the French Revolution.[104] Like all social phenomena it was a mental phenomenon which could not be reduced to any material substratum but could be studied like other social phenomena.

Durkheim's criticisms of socialism were often paired with his criticisms of classical liberal economics, and he stressed their similarities. He repeatedly attacked the labor theories of value and of the origins of property. Value, he insisted, was a partially subjective judgment made by society largely on the basis of perceived utility.[105] It was a qualitative more than a quantitative judgment. Likewise, respect for property was not based on an evaluation of incorporated labor; like morals, it had an essentially religious origin. In tracing the origins of property in the earliest societies, Durkheim found it first appearing in the concept of that which belongs to the gods.[106] The sacred quality which men have found in property was not transferred from men but originated in the things themselves:

> Respect for property is not—as is often said—an extension to things of the respect we must have for the human personality, both individual and collective. It has an entirely different source, exterior to the person. To understand that source we must seek to discover how things or men acquire a sacred character.[107]

The concept of the sacred, which Durkheim found at the source of all

religion, was thus also the source of property; both were social phenomena and could only be understood through the application of sociological methods.

Durkheim's approach enabled liberals to defend individual property against collectivism while divorcing themselves from the tendency
to invest absolute property rights in individuals, which was inherent in
the old liberalism. Property, he thought, was an indispensable adjunct
to the role the individual was expected by society to play in an age of
the division of labor:

> Our moral organization implies that a large initiative should be
> left to the individual. But in order for that initiative to be possible
> there must be a sphere in which the individual is his own master,
> where he can act with a total independence and withdraw, shel-
> tered from all external pressures in order to be truly himself.[108]

When he concluded that "private property is the material condition for
the cult of the individual," Durkheim agreed with the eclectics on the
relationship between property and liberty, but with an important difference. Private property was justified because of its support for a social
value—the cult of the individual—rather than because of any right inherent in the individual. This social viewpoint could lead to limitations
on property rights which would not be justified under the older individualist conception.

There was another way in which the collectivist socialists and laissez-faire liberals shared, from Durkheim's point of view, the same error. Both considered economic life to be essentially self-regulating: the
liberals thought that harmony was achieved through the automatic
workings of the market (Adam Smith's invisible hand), while the socialists thought that perfect harmony would flow automatically from one
basic change—collective ownership of the instruments of production.[109]
Durkheim considered both views to be rationalizations of the existing
state of affairs, a state which he considered pathological rather than
normal. What was missing from the present society, and would be missing from the ideal societies of the economists or the socialists, was a
social discipline. Collectivism would not solve current economic problems; neither would it reduce anomie.[110] The human appetites which
economic activity tries to satisfy contain no basis for self-regulation:
"they are by nature infinite, insatiable, and if nothing regulates them,
they cannot regulate themselves."[111] The problems of modern society
could not be solved by the divorce of economics and morals.

In claiming to satisfy men's material desires, the main competing
ideologies of the nineteenth century were undertaking the task of

Sisyphus. The disparity between what men desire and what is possible for them to achieve can never be closed by increasing production. Durkheim was not among those class-bound liberals who condemned the growing acquisitiveness of the lower classes which was so obvious in the nineteenth century but who failed to see it as a result of the spread of their own values. The acquisitiveness of the aristocracy and of the new bourgeoisie demonstrated how insatiable men's desires were and thus exposed the folly of believing that any economic measures could ever satisfy the mass of society. Durkheim's sociological analysis, then, showed that what was needed was to put a damper on the growth of men's material desires, and this could obviously only be achieved by moral reform, by a social reorganization whose main function was the moral disciplining of the individual. It may be going too far to see Durkheim as a forerunner of the "small is beautiful" movement of our time or of the zero-growth program of the Club of Rome, but certainly economic growth was not something he considered a good in its own right.

Nevertheless, we should not imagine that Durkheim was a satisfied conservative preaching restraint to the less well off, a common type in his day. It was not unusual for the middle class, liberal and otherwise, to believe that its success derived from its moral qualities, the absence of which qualities explained the failure of the lower orders. But from Durkheim's viewpoint all levels of modern society were suffering from a lack of moral discipline. The morals of the bourgeoisie were a kind of practical utilitarianism which lacked the character of a genuine morality: it did not bring much satisfaction to the bourgeoisie, and it certainly stimulated the discontents of the working classes. The occupational groupings—corporations—which he had proposed seemed to Durkheim the only sort of institution which could meet this need of the new age, this need for a common moral discipline over all levels of society.

If the present society, despite the growing division of labor, had not yet produced the organic solidarity which Durkheim thought inherent in it, what reason did he have to hope that it ever would? Most importantly, he believed that there was a growing thirst for justice and for equality, a thirst which could only be satisfied by the working out of the inherent character of organic solidarity. The conflicts of social life would only be appeased—to the imperfect extent that they ever could be—when each individual had the position he deserved.[112] Durkheim's ideal was, after all, like that of the liberal economists and the socialists, that of a society of spontaneous harmony, one in which the only inequalities recognized as just are the natural inequalities.[113] With the rise of the cult of the individual, "it is not enough for everyone to have his task; it is also necessary for that task to suit him."[114] Only in such a society would most men be able to find the satisfaction that comes from the harmony of one's desires and one's means for realizing them. Thus the utopian element in liberalism was not missing even in Durkheim's sociological construction of it. The struggle toward this ideal would be a long one, but he thought it essential for the very survival of modern society.[115]

The relation of this view to the socializing of individualism should be evident: the individual should have that position in society which fits him, not because of any right inherent in his person, but because the moral purpose of society demands it. This forced Durkheim to confront one of the persistent practical problems of liberalism: the meaning of equality of opportunity. Every person in his place did not mean every person in the place assigned by some external authority; only if each individual is faced with the choice of a wide range of possibilities could we know whether he wound up in the right place for him. Liberals have often stressed the difference between equality of opportunity and equality of result, but the closer their examination of the question, the more they have had to acknowledge that the former is difficult to obtain without the latter as a prerequisite. In practice it appears that we can only hope to attenuate inequalities of opportunity. Durkheim was prepared to go a considerable way in this direction, calling for the abolition of inheritance.[116] He even suggested that the social impact of natural inequalities—intelligence, beauty, strength— would someday be moderated by that charity which derives from our sympathy for our moral equals.[117]

We must remember that it is moral equality which is essential to liberalism. The sociologist of the division of labor could hardly have desired a society of dull uniformity, though he certainly hoped for a less-marked inequality of wealth. For Durkheim, moral equality could only be achieved in a society based on individual merit, and his ideal, like that of most twentieth-century liberals, can fairly be described as a meritocracy. Durkheim's sociological liberalism was a liberalism of the *boursiers*, the scholarship boys, as distinct from the liberalism of the *héritiers*, the inheritors. This is, I suspect, one of the reasons why the sociological new liberalism has prevailed over the philosophical in the twentieth century.

Durkheim's relations to the liberalism of his time and the legacy of his sociology for the liberalism of the twentieth century were not without their ambiguities. He was trying to offer liberalism the new concepts it needed to adapt to the demands of a society in transition, but the changes which he thought necessary were so great as to require a long time for their implementation. As a result his ideas did not have as much immediate popularity in liberal circles as did those of Alfred Fouillée, whose synthetic approach did not break so radically with the past. Durkheim's long-term influence, however, was destined to be greater because he alone among the sociologists succeeded in founding a "school" and in implanting his method into the state educational system. That this influence did not lead to the implementation of Durkheim's most specific reform proposals should not make us underestimate its importance. Since the old liberalism became increasingly the doctrine of only a small sect, it was indeed important that there was in France a new liberalism which combined a dedication to individual freedom with a recognition of the individual's obligation to the community and of the legitimacy of an increasing sphere of state action.

Durkheim was most at one with the liberals of his day in his commitment to the defense of the basic liberties which he, like them, identified with France's contribution to the modern world. His acceptance of democracy was as complete as any liberal's can be, as was his opposition to economic collectivism. His sociological interpretation of the "cult of the individual" sought to put individualism on more solid ground, to save it from ruin in the collapse of the religious and metaphysical views on which it had rested. On the other hand, his dissatisfaction with the existing political structure of the liberal state was likely to discomfort liberals and give comfort to the opposition on both Right and Left. Most new liberals were agreed on the need for the moral reform of the nation, but Durkheim's insistence that this could only be achieved through the establishment of occupational corporations seemed to most a risky plunge into the unknown. The conservative bias which Nisbet and others have found in his sociology certainly did not prevent Durkheim from being very critical of contemporary mores and institutions.[118]

It is, perhaps, one of the strengths of sociology that it allows its practitioners to look backward and forward at the same time, to combine the acceptance of social realities with the advocacy of social reforms. While, as we shall see in the next chapter, some of the Durkheimians worked out the social and political consequences of his sociology more clearly than did Durkheim himself, his own position demonstrated some of the characteristic problems of the new liberalism. One of the most striking of these was the somewhat unstable combination of the penchants for meritocracy and for an extreme egalitarianism. Insofar as sociology is an ideology, it is an ideology not of the bourgeoisie but of the intelligentsia.[119] Durkheim's meritocratic convictions went to the extreme of holding that the only natural society, under a regime of organic solidarity, was one in which everyone had the place he merited. At the same time he acknowledged egalitarianism as the most irresistible social force of our day and felt that his sociology could offer no objections, even to its most extreme forms.[120] He observed, and subsequent experience seems to bear out his observation, that egalitarian sentiment was not content to accept even natural inequalities. While he did not think that natural inequalities could all be eliminated by social action—better education would never make all people equal in intelligence—he did think that social action to minimize the effects of natural inequalities was legitimate, if perhaps not strictly obligatory.[121] He likened its role to that of charity in the religious world view of the past. It would certainly be hard to deny that the charitable impulse has found an important outlet in the twentieth century in the drive to overcome natural inequalities.

Durkheim believed, as had many liberals, that egalitarianism posed a threat to liberty in France because of the historical circumstances which had produced a strongly centralized government while undermining the traditional checks on its authority. The combination of atomistic individualism and an emotionally charged egalitarianism presented the greatest opportunities for tyranny in the name of the group. Since, in the sociologist's view, the individual derived his rights from society through the state, he was not in an effective position to defend those rights if they were attacked by the state. The old liberalism tried to protect the individual by making him the source of his own rights, but since the claim was false, in Durkheim's opinion, it could not offer much of a bulwark in practice. Individual rights could only be safeguarded by the creation of countervailing social forces.[122] A student of Montesquieu, on whom he wrote his Latin thesis, Durkheim tried to conceive a balance of powers appropriate to modern industrial civilization.[123] He thus advocated that form of liberalism which is usually called pluralism, a branch of liberalism with many ramifications. Pluralism has been a way in which liberals have tried to face the realities of political power, recognizing that to defend liberty it is often necessary to oppose power to power. Durkheim did little more than sketch the outlines of his corporatism, and it has proved an abortive direction for liberalism, especially after it was co-opted by some fascists. Much liberal practice in this last half of the twentieth century has been based, consciously or otherwise, on the pluralism to which Durkheim's sociology gave the first important impetus.

Durkheimian sociology also showed liberals one way in which to combine acceptance of the apparent course of history with the determination to shape human existence through the pursuit of ideals. This is exactly what Jean Jaurès was trying to do for French socialism at that time, and we may safely assume that it was one of the dominant features of the spirit of the age (without postulating the existence of a zeitgeist). Jaurès and Durkheim differed over what constituted a scientific understanding of the workings and direction of modern society, and those differences explain why the former was a socialist and the latter a liberal. Durkheim lacked Jaurès' oratorical eloquence in proclaiming how the *is* provides a foundation from which we can reach toward the *ought*. Was Durkheim more successful than the Great Tribune in building the intellectual construction which would justify their common confidence in the possibility of that leap? Can what we know tell us what we should desire?

Clearly, Durkheim thought that it could, even if we restrict the meaning of "what we know" to what we know through science.[124] Even though what was currently known was not enough to answer all the meaningful questions, the experience of science made him confident that the correct path to future solutions had been found. In the field of morals, which had occupied Durkheim's particular attention, the argument which he sometimes left implicit was worked out in detail by his collaborator, Lucien Lévy-Bruhl, in his *La morale et la science des moeurs*.[125] As far as the more general study of society is concerned, Durkheim tried to bridge the gap from the *is* to the *ought* with a line of argument whose unscientific character he would never recognize. His argument was at best an unacknowledged metaphysical conception, at worst a merely rhetorical device. The strain of functionalist anthropology descending from Durkheim's sociology has often caused people to see only that side of his thought which stressed that every institution and practice which exists has a purpose and therefore a meaning. He was, on the contrary, far from thinking that what *is* is right, and, indeed, the closer the society under investigation came to his own time, the less likely he was to defend such a view. He could with consistency describe the growth of the division of labor as a natural, inevitable, and, indeed, largely beneficial social process and at the same time denounce the way that process had been going in France and in the industrial West generally, as abnormal, as pathological.

Not surprisingly, Durkheim's attempt to divide social facts into the normal or healthy and the abnormal or pathological has come in for a great deal of criticism from the beginning. In his effort to distinguish between the healthy and the morbid on some objective grounds, he was led to adopt statistical normality as his standard of value.[126] This would seem to have involved him in a circular argument and to have cast doubt on the validity of his conviction that science can help us in our moral decisions in the choice of ends as well as means. It compelled him to assert that pathological behavior is always an exception to the rule, always a minority phenomenon.[127] Yet we can feel certain that Durkheim would never have accepted *anomie* as normal no matter how common it became; he would surely have replied that a society in which it was prevalent would cease to exist.[128] While the concept of statistical normality did play a useful role in his sociology, it could not save his science in this critical area.

The method which Durkheim was actually following in his would-be scientific value judgments was one he never acknowledged, perhaps not even to himself, because it smacked too much of *a priori* philosophizing. Clearly, he had constructed a mental image of what a society dominated by the division of social labor would have to be like in order to have the solidarity necessary for a viable and satisfying life for its members.[129] Insofar as societies had not developed, in fact, the necessary features of this organic solidarity, their condition was morbid and unnatural. He could convince himself that this was a judgment based on observation and analysis because its initial premise, the division of labor, was an observed fact. Durkheim could not admit to himself that his image of organic solidarity was only a heuristic model, akin to the ideal types being developed by his contemporary, Max Weber, because Durkheim's idea of science did not admit of that kind of argument which could not reach the certainty of knowledge he thought essential. Durkheim's failure here has been that of Western social science generally, which has never found a satisfactory reconciliation of its ambition to be scientific and its desire to support liberal values.

Durkheim was aware that a genuine science can never have answers to all the questions it raises, still less a science in its infancy, but he had a deep faith in scientific progress. Sociology would never be able to give an adequate explanation of every social phenomenon—there was no final state of perfection beyond which it could not go—but he was confident that it would tend to approach this state as a limit. The greatest possible perfection of man's knowledge would not lead to an earthly paradise, for there were inescapable difficulties and contradictions inherent in any advanced society. The division of labor was, on the whole, a condition of progress, and many of its current drawbacks could be remedied, but some of the difficulties it causes, some of the strains it puts on man, are permanent.[130] The "whole man" of Marx's early philosophic writings would have been dismissed by Durkheim as just another utopian dream; without the division of labor, men could not coexist. Civilization also requires the repression of man's instinctual drives; sociology, along with psychology, could only show how to soften the impact of necessity, and Durkheim's moral theory sought to promote the internalization of this repression as much as possible.[131] This tempered optimism and sober realism were among the important reasons why Durkheim's sociology would seem to many a viable foundation for political thinking amid the trials of the twentieth century, especially for those who were looking for a way to continue to defend liberal values.[132]

Without doubt there will continue to be a measure of disagreement about the significance of Durkheim's social and moral thought for the political philosophy of his time, but certain conclusions would seem to impose themselves. Durkheim's sociology offered democratic liberalism intellectual weapons useful on several fronts at once. It provided a defense against those socialists who sought to use the argument of man's interdependence and debt to society as a justification for collectivism. It offered a defense against those conservatives who sought to promote the social value of the family over that of the individual or who insisted on man's need for a guidance which transcended his rational understanding. It enabled liberalism to separate itself more clearly from the anarchism which held man accountable only to his own desires and denied that society would disintegrate if man were not subject to any external obligations. And, indeed, sociology helped defend liberalism against some of its own internal weaknesses: simplistic rationalism, the tendency to an exaggerated individualism, the neglect of civic responsibility, a disregard for the fate of the less successful, a naive internationalism, a tendency to find reasons to be content with the status quo. We have seen a steady effort of the new liberals to divorce themselves from laissez-faire economics; Durkheim's sociology strongly supported that effort. Most important of all, it would compel liberals to take a new look at society and to realize that as society changed, so must liberalism change. Liberalism was born in the conviction that man could undertake through reason the control of his own affairs, and sociology would help restore this original impulse by showing that the activities of society, led by, but not absorbed by, the state, could be expanded without the diminution of individual freedom.

The political implications of Durkheimian sociology can be seen even more clearly in the work of some of the Durkheimians than in Durkheim himself. In the next chapter we will look at two men—Bouglé and Duguit—who, though somewhat heterodox in their interpretations of Durkheim's sociology, illustrate its impact on liberalism. They will show us not to look for his influence in the arena of political action, where there was often much noise and few results, but in other areas whose importance for the development of twentieth-century French society was fundamental. Bouglé's influence was felt throughout the highly centralized educational system, but especially in the training of the elite; Duguit's influence was not confined to the provincial law faculty where he taught but touched all French thinking about public law. The Durkheimians would have a lasting impact on the thinking of many within the educational and legal institutions of the nation.

·VIII·

Durkheimian Liberalism: Bouglé and Duguit

*M*any of the ways in which Durkheim's sociology contributed to the evolution of French liberalism can be seen more clearly in the work of other Durkheimians. Not surprisingly, this is especially true in those cases where they were more directly involved—in their lives as well as in their work—in political matters. The Durkheimians were not simply mirrors of the master's thought; the unity of the Durkheimian group was not a uniformity but depended on the sense of a common outlook which permitted considerable individual variations.[1] The two figures considered in this chapter were heterodox Durkheimians in quite definite, and different, ways. Both illustrate possible routes for the attempt to make sociology the foundation of a new liberalism.

The careers of Célestin Bouglé and Léon Duguit were similar only in that both were highly successful academics whose brief forays into politics were disappointing. Both came into close personal contact with Durkheim at a time in their lives which permitted him to have a considerable influence on them, but neither was ever in any sense his pupil. Otherwise, Bouglé and Duguit did not have a great deal in common. Bouglé became a professional sociologist whose career was centered in Paris and the Ecole normale; Duguit was a law professor whose life was spent almost entirely in Bordeaux. It is, however, not these differences but the differences in their contributions to the development of sociological liberalism that make it necessary to treat them separately in this chapter.

The transition from philosophy to sociology which shaped the character of French liberalism was also one of the principal themes in the intellectual life of Célestin Bouglé (1870–1940).[2] After his outstanding success as a philosophy student at the Ecole normale supérieure and a year studying contemporary social philosophy in Germany, Bouglé entered the circle of Durkheim's collaborators and became part of the crusading team which brought out the *Année sociologique* in the years before World War I.[3] He also began work on his doctoral theses, his principal thesis being a rather straightforward application of the concepts laid down in Durkheim's *De la division du travail social* to the study of the origins and development of egalitarian ideas in Western society.[4] But even after he had completed his conversion from philosopher to sociologist, Bouglé was never to abandon altogether the fruits of his earlier training, and he persisted in regarding philosophy and sociology as complementary rather than as antithetical. Both in his work and in his personal contacts, he was to be a lifelong mediator between one of the oldest and one of the newest of the vital currents in French intellectual life.[5]

The intellectual appeal of sociology for Bouglé lay primarily in its claim to be a science in the process of formation. As a student of the history of social ideas he was particularly conscious of how modern sociology differed from the social theorizing of its nineteenth-century precursors and from most contemporary schools of thought: sociology conformed more closely to the ideals and methods of modern scientific rationalism. Durkheim had realized that what sociology needed was not another grand synthesis à la Comte or Spencer but a method and a discipline, a definition of its field of inquiry, and sources of data. Truth was not the starting point but the goal. As Lévy-Bruhl remarked, "The sociologists now think that almost everything remains to be done."[6] Sociology would only become a science when it was possible for many men working within a generally accepted framework over many years, indeed, many generations, to accumulate the knowledge, formulate and test hypotheses, and demonstrate the results of their common and collaborative effort.[7] As Bouglé observed: "What alone matters is that the age of general and philosophical sociology, which has almost certainly rendered most of the services we can expect of it, should finally be succeeded by the age of specific and positive sociology."[8] The age of the prophets had been necessary, but it had to be surpassed.

The scientific modesty of Durkheimian sociology seemed to Bouglé the only position compatible with the modern consciousness, which could not accept dogmatism in ideas any more than in politics.[9] The Durkheimian approach offered the modern consciousness an alternative to the opposing dangers of skepticism and resignation on the one hand and doctrinaire self-blinkering on the other. It also had the advantage of adapting sociology to the processes of institutionalization and professionalization, for it did not call on the sociologist to be the priest of a new order or the prophet of doom of an old one. Furthermore, it had the facility of adapting itself well to the ideological needs of the republic.

The idea of doing something for the republic and the *patrie* stood very high among Bouglé's motivations as a sociologist. It could be said of him what he said of Durkheim: "Behind the scientist, the moralist still lives."[10] Bouglé did not think that sociology was in a position to offer a scientifically certified program of social reform, but he did think that what it could do ought to be done.[11] As a teacher he saw that the educational system offered a means of exposing the middle-class youth to the sociological mode of thought and thus of modifying their excessive individualism (which was rather encouraged by both the content and style of their present schooling).[12] In his later career as an educational administrator, he was in a position to help introduce elements of sociology into the curriculum, not only at the Sorbonne and the Ecole normale, where he continued to teach, but also throughout the system, where the influence of the Normale was great.[13] Bouglé was also able to promote the expansion of sociological research and its institutionalization through his founding at the Ecole normale of the Centre de documentation sociale (1920). He would also attempt to carry his sociological insights into the political arena as a Radical-Socialist candidate for the Chamber of Deputies.[14]

In all of these activities he remained conscious of sociology's limitations as well as its potential. While social science was useful to men in the choice of means, it could not be used for the determination of ends.[15] Even in this instrumental role sociology remained in its infancy, and to demand policy guidance from it too soon could endanger its development as a science (as this pressure had aborted the efforts of the great precursors). Bouglé thought that in its present condition sociology could offer evidence on this or that specific point and provide some principles so general as to offer more emotional comfort than practical guidance.[16] It was certainly in no position to supplant the metaphysical basis of ethics and to provide a rational, scientific *morale*.

Could sociology when it reached maturity in some unspecified future provide such a scientific *morale?* Proudhon had thought so.[17] Durkheim appeared to have thought so, and Lucien Lévy-Bruhl had made the most coherent case yet for the possibility. Bouglé, while prudently avoiding outright rejection of the possibility, continued to doubt it. At best, sociology could establish probabilities.[18] He did think that sociology could contribute to the development of the laic *morale* called for by defenders of the republic, because knowledge and the sentiments can have a reciprocal influence.[19] "Sociology does not seem to us ready—if indeed it ever will be—to take the place of ethics. But one has doubtless become aware that the former can henceforth render services to the latter."[20] Knowledge could not, however, totally replace the role of the sentiments, and Bouglé, as his continued interest in philosophy demonstrated, thought also that a metaphysics—whether tacit or explicit—would remain necessary.[21] This reservation would save him from some of the excesses of twentieth-century sociologism; he would remain a transitional figure.

Bouglé's intellectual contributions to the development of sociology were slender compared to those of other Durkheimians such as François Simiand and Marcel Mauss, but he furnishes a clearer example of the political implications of that sociology.[22] None of the other Durkheimians could rival his knowledge of the history of social thought or his familiarity with contemporary social and political issues, on which he wrote extensively. While some have seen in Durkheim's concern for social solidarity and his insistence on moral discipline the foundations of a conservative world view, Bouglé's lifework demonstrates how such sociological views can be compatible with a respect for individual freedom and a commitment to gradualist, noncollectivist social reform which were characteristic of the new liberalism.

In 1902 Bouglé published an article in the *Revue de métaphysique et de morale* which furnishes an important key to the understanding of his political thought and of what was happening to French liberalism. It was entitled "La crise du libéralisme," and the crisis which he identified was a crisis in the core of liberalism—freedom of thought.[23] He explicitly rejected the idea that liberalism still had anything to do with what contemporary French usage called "libéralisme," that is, laissez-faire economics of the school of J.-B. Say.[24] On the contrary, it was freedom of thought which was the cornerstone both of liberalism and of liberty in the modern world; Bouglé was convinced that it was under attack from both Right and Left. What made the situation of 1902 a crisis was not merely this attack—which was not exactly new—but the increasing feebleness of the liberals in their defense of freedom of thought.

Bouglé believed that liberals of earlier generations had been uncompromising in their advocacy of liberty because they did not fear its excesses, and the reason they did not fear its excesses was that, consciously or not, they were relying on the age-old constraints of religion and religiously based morality to prevent such excesses. Most liberals had not seen the need to build any constraints on the exercise of liberty into liberalism itself; paradoxically, the growing popularity of this uncompromising liberalism tended to undermine the authority of those traditional constraints on which liberals relied.[25] When the consequences of this were seen, many liberals began to doubt the practical validity of liberal solutions to the ensuing problems. Doubt about the effectiveness of liberal solutions was generated, according to Bouglé, by three main developments: (1) the rise of anarchist violence in the 1890s, (2) the Dreyfus affair, and (3) the assault on liberty by ultramontane clericalism.[26] These symptoms of social disintegration called forth from the liberals an appeal to "restore the moral unity" of France, and to do so by whatever means were necessary. If these means did violence to freedom of thought, this was a necessary and—they hoped—temporary sacrifice to a higher good.

For his part, Bouglé felt that his fellow liberals were overreacting. They tended to underestimate the stability of society; anarchy remained a lesser danger than the excesses of governmental authority.[27] The liberals' efforts to strengthen government control over thought were bound to be harmful to liberty, more harmful indeed than the existing disorder. As an educator, Bouglé had been trained in the republican tradition of the social mission of education—his whole life showed how seriously he took that mission—but he opposed the growing demand that the state education system be given monopoly powers in order to build a uniformity of consciousness on a laic basis.[28] The liberals were divided on this question, and Bouglé found himself in opposition to many of his closest associates, who insisted that the tenets of a democratic liberalism were not violated by the proposed reforms.[29]

From the point of view of our interest here, Bouglé's position in the educational debate of 1902 is of less interest than his analysis of why liberals were spurning liberalism, which in turn led him to a sociological analysis of liberalism itself. Lacking such an analysis, he argued, most liberals tended to misunderstand the very nature of their own faith: they thought of it as a pure individualism, a la Robinson Crusoe, when in fact it had very definite social foundations.[30] Liberalism, he said, is always predicated on a view of man as a social animal whose moral code is a given of his society. The claims of freedom which liberalism makes central to its doctrine are always set against a background of constraint. But that background always remained unacknowledged, and French liberals had doubted the liberalism of anyone who overtly recognized the importance of social restraints; hence, their uneasiness with Alexis de Tocqueville when he pointed to the importance of religion for liberty in America.[31] If liberals would come to recognize the social foundations of liberalism, they could learn how to reinforce the restraints which, as they were coming to realize, were essential to society, while at the same time preserving the liberties which they no longer knew how to defend with the traditional arms of philosophical liberalism. In recognizing the social character of liberalism, Bouglé's sociology not only helped explain the problems of the older liberalism but also played a part in the process by which the new liberalism based on sociology came increasingly to supplant the old liberalism based on philosophy.[32]

The shift in the intellectual foundations of liberalism from philosophy to sociology corresponded to the beginnings of a shift in liberal politics from an antistatist individualism toward a (still somewhat timid) state welfare program. The principal manifestation of this new orientation was the movement known as *solidarisme*.[33] Bouglé did not endorse every aspect of the solidarist program, which was given its most popular form in Léon Bourgeois' famous pamphlet, but he clearly regarded it as an important move in the right direction.[34] The emergence of solidarism was evidence that some liberals now saw that individualism required collective and state action to bring its full benefits to society.[35] The character of social development in an industrializing society and the individualist ethos which continued to dominate the French national character needed to be brought into harmony: "it can be affirmed that our production increasingly takes on a collective character and our morals an individualistic character. Solidarism throws a bridge across the gap between these two affirmations; it is on these two pillars that it builds for modern societies the declaration of duties."[36] Solidarism was one of the great disappointments of the Belle Epoque; it acquired the status of the quasi-official philosophy of the Radical and Radical-Socialist party (with which Bouglé was affiliated), but it was translated into legislative action very hesitantly during the period of the party's dominance.[37] Like sociology, solidarism stressed the fact of human interdependence, that interdependence characteristic of advanced societies which Durkheim had called organic solidarity.[38] This fact of solidarity was to provide the intellectual basis for a policy of social reform without collectivism—the elimination of poverty and oppression and the creation of a greater equality while preserving most (but not all) forms of private property.[39] Solidarism was aimed at a middle-class audience, in an effort to show that there was an alternative to the increasingly ineffective liberalism of the nineteenth century on the one hand and the menace of socialism on the other.[40] Bouglé called solidarism a rectification of individualism by the *idée sociale* and a link between collectivism and individualism, better adapted than either to the modern consciousness.[41]

Solidarism offered the Radicals a rationale—the ideas of social debt and quasi-contract—whereby the action of the state, especially its intervention in the economy, could be used to undo some of the results of laissez-faire, but Bouglé did not expect such action to have full effect until those institutional changes necessary for the development of a new social consciousness took place.[42] Greater economic security for the masses—the first aim of the solidarist legislative program—was necessary if liberty was to become meaningful for all levels of society, but it was not enough; indeed, there was always a danger that the state might offer people security in exchange for their freedom. Insistent though he was on the importance of the state—against both Marxist claims of the predominance of the economic order and against those pluralists who reduced it to one institution among others—Bouglé also stressed the need for initiative from below to create a freer society. Only through social action embodying their own initiative could people become more truly human.[43] Bouglé's liberalism thus combined solidarist political action and Proudhonian self-help.

Though he honored Saint-Simon as the founder of positivist sociology and Comte as its greatest propagandist, Bouglé found the most pertinent lessons for the present in the complex, shifting, and apparently ambiguous work of Pierre-Joseph Proudhon.[44] Proudhon's message, he claimed, was fundamentally similar to Durkheim's: "to force collective reason to consecrate individual rights."[45] Bouglé considered Proudhon a sociologist, and attempted to show that the essential unity of Proudhon's vast work could be seen through his sociological ideas.[46] Bouglé wrote a lengthy (for him) volume on Proudhon's sociology and contributed to another which attempted to assess Proudhon's influence and the continuing vitality of his ideas.[47]

From the time of the Revolution onward, French liberalism had attempted to eliminate the groupings which stood between the individual and the state; it had not recognized that the nation alone was not a sufficient social bond. Even the much-admired example of English local self-government and voluntary association did not free the French liberals from their distrust of "intermediate bodies" in society.[48] Against this abstraction, Proudhon, whose sense of society and human relations was very concrete, redirected attention to the need for all kinds of small-scale and voluntary associations—economic or other—to humanize man's existence. He offered, thought Bouglé, a kind of "solidarité avant la lettre."[49] Bouglé saw in the main lines of this approach, if not in every explicit program, the means by which a new *morale*, an ethic of cooperation and solidarity, might come to replace the ethic of competition, thus providing a means of adding a social policy to the laic policy which formed the core of Radicalism.[50]

Although solidarism was primarily a doctrine of state action and middle-class duty, it would help create a state which—unlike the existing one—would cooperate with the new forms of working-class organization:

> Is not the solidarist doctrine, based on the double theories of social debt and quasi-contract, well made to support and to justify those sentiments which help us to avoid the excesses of both anarchism and monarchism, whatever forms they may take?
> It offers a meeting ground, an area of understanding, for all those who today wish for political democracy to lead to social democracy through the coordinated efforts of labor unions, cooperatives, and the organs of the state.[51]

The voluntarist message of Proudhon continued to be felt in France in two areas of working-class initiative: the trade-union movement and the cooperative movement.[52] Bouglé was sympathetic to both of these movements and considered himself committed to the "emancipation of those who suffer from our economic organization," but he was especially active throughout his life in behalf of the cooperative movement.[53]

Bouglé was repelled by that part of the syndicalist movement which sought a violent and revolutionary upheaval, but he did not consider it a serious threat.[54] He opposed those syndicalist leaders who thought the syndicate was the only legitimate form of social organization, but he continued to believe that union activity was a school of social education and of individual development as well as a means of bettering the economic position of the worker.[55] The cooperative movement had the advantage of favoring these desirable goals in a manner that conformed with the demands of modern democracy and avoided the dangers of revolution.[56] Bouglé was willing to agree that revolution, like war, fostered certain social virtues, but he insisted that those virtues could be developed in peacetime, too, escaping the concomitant evils of violence, whose total impact was dehumanizing rather than liberating.[57] The revolutionary syndicalists, he thought, demonstrated a certain "nostalgia for violence" similar to that of the Right.[58] On the other hand, Bouglé's support for trade unionism was not shallow: he favored collective bargaining, though he wanted to minimize strikes through the use of conciliation, and he even opposed Durkheim by defending the *syndicats de fonctionnaires* (government employees' unions).[59] This support of a moderate trade unionism was, of course, one of the ways in which the welfare-state liberalism of the twentieth century has differed from the laissez-faire liberalism of the nineteenth. Bouglé was merely ahead of his time in stressing that Radicalism and syndicalism had important affinities.[60]

Bouglé tried to serve as an intermediary between the cooperative movement and the intellectual community. He believed that the Dreyfus affair had promoted a greater communication between intellectuals and manual workers, and he wanted to preserve this contact.[61] Such contact was especially important for the intellectuals and for the middle-class youth of the university, whose sense of social solidarity needed cultivating.[62] Bouglé thought that a knowledge of the cooperative movement could be a valuable part of that moral education which the republic sought to give its youth; the formation of cooperators would also be the formation of good republicans.[63] He also sought in his articles for the cooperative press to bring the working-class cooperators into contact with the larger world of social ideas and national issues. Though his role was perhaps not as important as that of the great intellectual promoter of cooperatives, the economist Charles Gide, Bouglé did win the respect of the cooperators.[64] This was as much, perhaps, because of his personality as because of his ideas, for Bouglé was an all too rare example of an intellectual who could deal with workers on a basis of mutual respect and equality.

Bouglé's activism and his intellectual support for solidarism were in full accord with his sociologically based liberalism. This liberalism went beyond the confines of solidarism; they were rather overlapping expressions of a common effort to renew and redefine liberalism to fit the conditions of the twentieth century.

Despite Durkheim's own liberal orientation, the new liberalism of Bouglé was not the path taken by most of the team of the *Année sociologique,* who became reformist socialists.[65] The socialism of Lucien Herr and Jean Jaurès which most of these sociologists followed was, however reformist, distinct from solidarism or welfare-state liberalism. Though he respected Herr and Jaurès, Bouglé differed from them on fundamental issues.[66] What he found most sympathetic in French socialism was that "socialisme libéral" he had seen in Proudhon and even in Jaurès, whose remark—"Socialism is logical and complete individualism"—he was fond of quoting.[67] After the formation of the unified SFIO in 1905, Bouglé was discouraged by the socialists' apparent adherence to a dogmatic Marxism.[68] Like most Radical-Socialists, Bouglé campaigned against the socialists but never severed his personal ties with them or ceased to feel that he and they had much in common.

Unlike the old liberals, who rejected the idea of class conflict and who preferred to deny that there were any longer such things as classes in French society, Bouglé recognized the existence of class conflict. Like Durkheim, he considered it a symptom of weakened social solidarity, produced by the development of modern industrial society. Material progress, now affecting all levels of society, threatened to undermine the sense of natural solidarity present in traditional society without replacing it with a sense of the solidarity inherent in the greater interdependence of men in industrial society.[69] For the sociologists, class conflict was thus a natural development in that it grew out of given social circumstances, but it was also a pathological condition in which the normal state of the social organism was disturbed. In other words, it was a social fact, which could only be understood and treated by a science of social facts.

Bouglé and Durkheim equally rejected the Marxist claim that class struggles are the motive force of all history, a claim based on a pre-scientific philosophy of history. In general, Bouglé's objections to Marxism were similar to Durkheim's. Despite the sociological insights of its founder, Marxism had never become more than a pseudoscience, typical of the mid-nineteenth-century urge to system building; it remained a pseudoscience because it failed to liberate itself from the discredited metaphysical materialism of the late eighteenth century.[70] While rejecting the "spiritualism" of the French socialist tradition, Bouglé was especially critical of Marxism's insistence that "représentations collectives" were mere epiphenomena.[71] Along with philosophical materialism went another kind of materialism in the undue stress given by Marxism to economic activity; with Durkheim and Max Weber, Bouglé found religion to be more important than economics in the basic organization of society.[72]

While socialism was not the science of society its adherents claimed it to be, sociology and socialism shared the conviction that the science of society holds the key to the shaping of man's future, and one can say of sociology, as Max Nomad and Lewis Feuer have done of socialism, that it is an ideology of the intelligentsia, which seeks to substitute the rule of talent for the rule of property.[73] Sociology and socialism have thus been in a certain sense, competitors, and the triumph of Durkheimian sociology in the West has been, as Alvin Gouldner shows, the welfare state.[74] Obviously, this result has not been exactly what Durkheim or the Durkheimians—whether liberal or socialist—intended, and Bouglé would certainly be disappointed with the persistence of the French tradition of state centralism. But we should not be surprised that that tradition has shaped the impact of sociological liberalism in the twentieth century, just as it shaped the impact of the philosophical liberalism of the nineteenth century.[75] Bouglé was certainly right in thinking that sociology could be a reformist force in society.[76]

Bouglé's sense of a crisis of liberalism which called for a new orientation of its political program was underpinned by his belief that such a change also called for a shift in the intellectual foundations of liberalism, where sociology could come to the rescue of a philosophy which had lost its efficacy. In particular, it could help liberalism come to terms with democracy. Unlike the conservative critics of liberalism, Bouglé did not much regret the passing of the traditional forms of solidarity, destroyed by modern egalitarianism, for he believed that a new solidarity, compatible with that egalitarianism, was now possible. His thesis, *Les idées égalitaires*, was not only a landmark in his personal commitment to sociology but also a statement of the intellectual's commitment to democracy. The rise of egalitarianism was an evident fact which Bouglé sought to explain in terms of the ramifications for the psychology of individuals of purely social forces—especially social density and the division of labor—but this egalitarianism was not merely a fact, toward which the observer could remain indifferent. Democracy was also the wave of the future, a foundation for the moral valuations of modern societies, which the sociologist had to endorse if he was to avoid a sterile isolation from reality—the pitfall of traditional moral philosophy.

Bouglé surely did not become a democrat for purely intellectual reasons or from an ambition to ride the wave of the future; it is more likely that his democratic sentiments were formed during his provincial youth and that they helped focus his attention on the utility of sociology.[77] Democracy had long been the subject of intellectual controversy in France, and more than one branch of early French sociology was decidedly anti-democratic.[78] It was thus natural for Bouglé's defense of Durkheimian sociology to be also a defense of French democracy. For example, biological sociology had grown in France, like Social Darwinism in America, to justify the privileges of certain social groups which seemed to have been favored in the struggle for existence.[79] As we have seen, not all of French biosociology was illiberal or anti-democratic, but one of its most popular wings, that which focused on crowd psychology, certainly was.[80] The sociology of the *Année sociologique*—despite Durkheim's personal weakness for biological metaphor—devoted much of its critical effort to the refutation of the biological sociologists, and this theme was also prominent in Bouglé's popular writing and lecturing. The goal of Bouglé's sociology was, from the beginning, not merely to gather knowledge about society but to apply that knowledge for the advancement of democracy in France and for the development of that moral education necessary for the success of a secular, and secularist, society. Democracy was the most socially progressive of ideas, while at the same time the most soundly grounded in the European past, and Bouglé saw that it was the best guarantee for social peace and the best means to effective social reform—two terms which were not contradictory but in necessary harmony.

Bouglé's early career as a teacher was distinguished more by his social activism than by his scholarly research. One of the ablest orators ever to come out of the Ecole normale, he was especially success-ful in establishing rapport with a variety of audiences.[81] Whether addressing a lycée class, a women's club, or a gathering of workers at the Montpellier Bourse du Travail, he could adjust to the interests and level of comprehension of his hearers, without condescension or vulgarity. He did not pretend to be other than an intellectual, but his evident sincerity and goodwill overcame any distance between him and his audience. Bouglé was very active during the Dreyfus affair, which brought a special urgency to his idea that the educator had a duty to civic action outside and in addition to his responsibilities in the classroom.[82] The defense of Dreyfus was, he thought, in the tradition of '89, and after it was successful, he continued to speak out in defense of the republic and of democracy against the intellectual critics of the Right.[83] The favorite theme of his public message was how the findings of Durkheimian sociology favored democracy and how they suggested certain paths by which it might be improved.

The title of one of his books from this period, *La démocratie devant la science (Democracy in the Light of Science)* (1904), summed up Bouglé's message. In it he elaborated and popularized his thesis on egalitarianism.[84] Science, he argued, had replaced theology as the most commonly accepted validator of ideas in the nineteenth century.[85] The failure of liberalism to adjust to this development seemed to Bouglé to be the root of its crisis. The liberals believed in science, but their system of morals depended on religion, and this incoherence was destroying their effectiveness and their self-confidence. Their belief in science had failed to serve them well in social matters, largely because the majority had an inadequate understanding of what science was. As a result, they tended either to accept the conclusions put forward in the name of science with the same blind acceptance they had once accorded the teachings of the church—or to reject those conclusions with the same uncritical skepticism with which they had once rejected the dogmas of the faith. Neither attitude was scientific. One of the goals of republican education should therefore be to teach some understanding of the scientific method: Bouglé thought that such teaching would have moral as well as intellectual value.[86] But until such education became widespread, he and the other sociologists would have to combat the prophets of false social science.

Among the commonest claims of such false science were that "science" showed that democracy and/or socialism (often not clearly distinguished by their opponents) were impossible because they were against the laws of nature and that, therefore, any attempt to establish them would result in the decadence of society.[87] Fearing that such propaganda would undermine popular confidence in the democratic republic and make people vulnerable to authoritarian movements, Bouglé undertook to expose its fallacies and to show that on the contrary a genuine social science supported the aspirations of democracy.[88] False social science was asking the wrong question, for "if you want to judge whether egalitarian demands are well or ill-founded, the right question to ask is not 'do they conform to the laws of nature?' but 'are they in conformity with the ends of society?' "[89] He was also concerned to refute the claims to scientific standing of the "sociological" racism of Edouard Drumont, the foremost anti-Semitic publicist.[90] Bouglé had thus to make himself a propagandist both for democracy and for sociology; he had to defend the claims of Durkheimian sociology to be really scientific and to explain its position with respect to the other social sciences, real and false.[91] He waged this dual campaign on two levels: one was through his popular oratory, mostly throughout the southern *départements* close to his posts at the universities of Montpellier and Toulouse; the other was addressed to a national audience, a part of the educated middle classes, through the book-review section of the *Année sociologique*. Bouglé was in charge of the section dealing primarily with works of general sociology and methodology; his distribution of praise or blame to the varied trends of sociological thought in Europe and America made him an important figure in the Durkheimian group. Questions of science naturally played a larger role in his reviews for the *Année* than in his popular speeches, but the cause of democracy was not forgotten in this scholarly work.[92]

Even Bouglé's major work of sociological research—his study of the caste system of India (1908)—was closely related to this dual concern.[93] An analysis of one of the fundamental types of nondemocratic society, it was also, perhaps even mainly, a vindication of the sociological method. The techniques that traced the rise of democracy in the West could also be used to explain why something quite different happened in the East.[94]

Bouglé's defense of democratic liberalism is demonstrative of the effect that the sociological approach would have on the character of liberalism. What was new was not so much the democratic strain—though much of nineteenth-century French liberalism had distrusted political democracy—but the attempt to justify liberalism on the basis of observed social facts rather than on hypotheses about human nature or philosophical deductions.[95] Such a change can be considered progressive insofar as the sociologists' insistence on scientific rigor of thought helped stem the proliferation of social pseudosciences.[96] But implicit (indeed, often explicit) in the sociological devotion to social facts was the assumption that study of those facts would guide us to a better world. Bouglé was more aware than the other Durkheimians of the dangers of such an assumption, for "every effort to claim that such and such a social reform is demanded by the facts should be suspected of arbitrariness."[97] Durkheimian sociology, with its general avoidance of questions of value, had had a considerable impact favoring the relativistic trend of twentieth-century political thought.[98] The moral relativism inherent in sociology, like the anarchism inherent in the old liberalism, is no longer held in check as it was in Bouglé's day by the moral absolutes of the Judeo-Christian tradition; sociological liberalism is today suffering from the same crisis as had philosophical liberalism, the crisis Bouglé had so accurately diagnosed. This was a consequence which Bouglé had not expected, since he shared Durkheim's conviction that the "unmasking" character of sociology where it touched on morals was not a practical danger; on the contrary, "baring the realities whose force is rendered symbolically by religious myths, it [sociology] prepares man's conscience to be directly attached to the group which opens to him the possibilities of a spiritual life."[99] Looking back on the experience of the Great War, Bouglé would be satisfied that the *école laïque* had demonstrated its ability to build a moral unity in a democratic society.[100] Perhaps he was not giving enough credit to the survival of older habits.

As the most active of the Durkheimians in public affairs, Bouglé demonstrated that the practical implications of modern sociology do not have to be centralist, elitist, and anti-democratic. In adapting Durkheimian sociology to the needs of public education under the Third Republic, he made use not only of those elements in sociology that promoted stability in a disturbed society but also of those elements which could help generate aspirations for a better future. He was especially concerned that the educational system do more than it had done to promote equality of opportunity, and he recognized that this would require sacrifices on the part of the bourgeoisie.[101] He once told a group of students that sociological training should develop three qualities: "a concern for objectivity, a sense of the relative, a sentiment of solidarity."[102] The dominance of his practical social concerns was evident throughout his career. The monarchist Right often denounced the republic as a moral wasteland, and Bouglé wanted to show that it could be, on the contrary, the seedbed from which mankind would develop its human potentialities more fully than ever before.[103]

Bouglé believed in the possibility not merely of others rising within the existing order through their abilities, as he himself had done, but of others shaping new social forms which would correspond to the needs of modern egalitarianism. It seemed to him that egalitarianism and an enhanced desire for social justice were the natural consequences of Western development:

From this point of view, it is apparent that the only individualism which is sociologically justified today—an individualism both democratic and rationalist—is precisely that which asks that the collectivity know how and when to intervene and that individuals control themselves. That is why we can say that by allowing itself to be guided by sociology, solidarism would recover the meaning of and, in order to enlarge it, would continue the work of classical individualism.[104]

Bouglé tried, as he thought Proudhon had tried, to reconcile *l'esprit sociologique* with the *sentiment individualiste*.[105]

The spread of evolutionistic and sociological ideas was almost as rapid—though less pervasive—in the world of legal scholarship as elsewhere. Given the innate conservatism of this milieu, where thinking tended to be dominated by texts and precedents, there could be no clearer testimony to the impact of the new modes of thought. Moreover, thought and practice were more clearly related here than in the academic disciplines, for the legal thinker was more bound to take account of what was going on in the realms of legislation and jurisprudence in his own society than he was to become immersed in the study of animal societies or the religions of Australian aborigines. Of course this did not prevent him from seeing what he wanted to see, but it put that vision to a more immediate practical test.

The legal scholar, involved day to day in the preparation of young people for careers in the legal profession, was not only obliged not to stray too far from contemporary realities but also to grasp the intellectual significance of those realities. His interpretation might in its turn influence those realities when (and if) it came to shape the briefs of lawyers, the decisions of judges, the votes of legislators. That ideas and experience have a reciprocal influence was thus more easily seen in this domain of thought than in most others. This is a good moment, therefore, to remember that we have not been proposing any direct, simple cause and effect relation between the evolution of liberal ideas traced in this work and the social legislation of the Third Republic. These were two realms which interpenetrated at many points but which were nonetheless distinct.

It should not be surprising that the teachers of law remained close to the vision of the character of the state and the relations of the state to the individual which had emerged in the Revolution and became deeply rooted in the course of the following century. Neither should it be surprising to see develop during the Third Republic a legal theory which was dissatisfied with this tradition and found it inadequate for the defense of liberal society. The leading exponent of the traditional view, based on the natural rights of the individual and the indivisible, inalienable sovereignty of the state was Adhémar Esmein (1848–1913), holder of the chair of constitutional law at the Sorbonne. In any history of the legal thought of the Third Republic he would surely occupy the most prominent position.[106]

Here we are concerned, however, with the emergence of a challenge to that legal tradition, a challenge directly inspired by the sociological movement of the nineteenth century.[107] The law schools were perhaps the most effectively decentralized part of French higher education; this permitted a greater diversity of views to achieve respectability than in most areas, where the domination of Paris was complete. It was thus that the sociological theory of Léon Duguit (1859–1928) was able to develop and spread its nationwide influence from the law faculty of Bordeaux.[108] After growing up amid the legal community of Bordeaux, Duguit had entered that faculty as a student in 1876 at age seventeen and received his doctorate at age twenty-two; he soon returned there as a professor, in 1886. He remained at Bordeaux, being elected doyen of the faculty in 1919, for the rest of his career.[109]

How early in that career his positivist convictions were formed is unclear. One suspects that his decision to go into teaching rather than to follow his father's footsteps in the practice of law was shaped by an awareness that he had something new to say, for which students and not clients were the appropriate audience. It took Duguit a little while to discover the true path of his mind. From the beginning he meant to apply a social scientific method to the study of law, but which method? His first impulse was to follow Espinas on the path opened by Herbert Spencer, and he published an "orthodox" organicist interpretation of the nature of the state, but his determination to pursue a purely scientific method soon turned him in another direction.[110] He became convinced that the organicist approach rested on a priori conceptions rather than on observation, and he abandoned it totally.[111]

Duguit was thus led into an effort to discover the facts of the political order as distinguished from the ideas people had developed about it.[112] His was not an effort to apply a sociological system— Durkheim's or any other's—to the study of law, but rather a parallel effort—closer to Durkheim's than to any other's—to build a science of public law on a purely "experimental" foundation.[113] His effort to exclude all a priori—whether theological or metaphysical—concepts from his thought was pursued with all the rigor of a powerful dialectical mind.[114] Duguit even balked at the jump so many would-be social scientists were not able to refuse: he denied the possibility of deducing any obligation from the facts he observed.[115] He was content that citizens had to obey the state as a matter of fact rather than as a matter of obligation. What legal theorists had long regarded as the central problem, the most difficult of problems, was dismissed by Duguit as irrelevant. He would be even more positivist than Comte. But even Duguit could not keep all a priori concepts from his thought; his very determination to do so can be taken to demonstrate the futility of his approach. If a sociologist who could accuse Durkheim of resorting to metaphysical concepts would yet not avoid them himself, who could?[116]

Duguit's attack on what he considered to be the metaphysical legal theories of his day focused on two central concepts: natural law and sovereignty. The facts his observations offered for the construction of a counter-theory hinged around one center: social solidarity. Like the sociologists, Duguit attacked the natural law conception of liberalism not merely because it was "unscientific" but also because it did not offer an adequate defense of the liberty to which he, too, was committed.[117] On the one hand, it offered only a shield of words against the de facto violations of rights by the sovereign state; on the other hand, its extreme individualist consequences offered no adequate rationale for the limitation of individual rights and hence was antisocial, anarchistic.[118] Only a philosophy founded in facts could, he thought, escape these extremes.

Duguit found the essential fact to be that of social solidarity, ignored in all individualist philosophies. That men were born free and equal in rights was an a priori assumption; that they were born members of a collectivity was a fact.[119] It must therefore be possible, he thought, to establish rights on the foundation of solidarity. Duguit perhaps came closer to success in this task than other sociological thinkers; this possibility was certainly necessary to his whole system. Solidarity as a fact seemed to him the only possible *règle de droit*. Men were compelled, he argued, by the conditions of their existence in society to work for the preservation of this society, which was also the preservation of themselves, since they were unable to exist outside it.[120] The fact therefore established the duty, a duty deriving from the very nature of the human condition, and also sanctioned by society.[121] His claim to have made this connection without recourse to metaphysical concepts has often been disputed and was perhaps the decisive weakness of his philosophical position.[122]

From the duty to preserve society all rights were derived, since men could not without injustice be prevented from doing what they had to do. Men therefore had the right to defend and promote social solidarity.[123] Rights extended only so far as duties. This did not, Duguit insisted, lead to a narrow subordination of the individual to society,

for the ways in which the individual could contribute to the preservation of solidarity were many. Indeed the basic duty—and thus the
basic right—which Duguit discerned in this view was the free and full
development of the individual's necessarily highly varied capacities.[124]
The very definition limited this development to capacities which were
not antisocial by character, one of the problems which advocates of
the free and full development of the individual often overlooked in
their assumption that man is basically good.[125] For Duguit, the deriva-
tion of rights from duties was not merely a rhetorical device, as it
tended to be in individualist philosophies (though there were exceptions, such as Fouillée). For Duguit, rights derived from duties in the
most concrete manner possible.

The conception of the state which Duguit derived from his observations was integrated with his conception of the origins and nature
of rights. Where natural rights theorists undertook to defend the individual against the power of the sovereign state, he undertook to de-
molish the very idea of sovereignty, even rejecting its most attenuated
form, the sovereignty of reason. Sovereignty, he insisted, was not a
fact, it was merely a metaphysical concept which carried in its train
all sorts of other fictions on which the legal thought of the nineteenth
century had rested, such as that of the personality of the state.[126] The
rise of democracy, the acceptance of the idea that the state is a manifestation of the will of the people seemed to Duguit a greater menace
to the liberties of individuals than even the divine-right monarchy had
been. There was indeed no fundamental difference between the two
except that a sovereign democracy was potentially even more oppressive, the majority being less likely to be restrained by scruples than
any individual ruler.[127]

What observation revealed, he insisted, was not sovereignty but
the existence of rulers and ruled.[128] Since that was all there is, legal and
political thought must build upon this base: government was the domination of the strongest.[129] Moreover, this was true always and everywhere, though the nature of that superiority was obviously variable.
In modern democratic societies, it was the majority which was the
strongest and the minority which had to obey.[130] Unfortunately,
Duguit did not analyze this conception in any detail or attempt to
show how it actually worked in modern society, where, to say the
least, such a broad statement tells us very little.[131] Duguit, in any case,
appeared interested only in the consequences he could draw from this
observation for his political theory. The principal of these was that
since there was no sovereignty, no personality of the state, there was
no essential difference between rulers and ruled with respect to the
fundamental *règle de droit* of social solidarity. The rulers were equally

bound by it; indeed, because of their power, they had even greater opportunities and therefore greater responsibilities to promote it.[132] Without recourse to the "fiction" of natural law it became possible, Duguit thought, to determine that rights were prior to the state, that the state was entirely subordinate to the rule of law.[133]

Thus Duguit argued that recognition of the rule of the strongest, far from justifying the ancient doctrine of might makes right, offered the greatest possible protection to individual liberties.[134] And not just at the level of theory, for he insisted that the governors, knowing that they were not above the law, lacking the psychological reinforcement of the idea of sovereignty, would be more apt to restrain themselves in the light of his ideas than they had shown themselves to be under the existing system.[135] The objectively determined rule of social solidarity constrained them further because it offered a justification for resistance to oppression.[136] There being no moral obligation of obedience, but only a duty—mutual for rulers and ruled—to promote solidarity, there could be no gulf between the individual and the state.[137]

What are the consequences of this view for individual liberty? Critics of Duguit are almost as divided as critics of Rousseau on whether his view leads to tyranny or to anarchy.[138] Duguit himself maintained that it was a sound liberal position because liberty was the best means—from the point of view of governors and governed—to promote solidarity. His views on the nature of social solidarity were essentially similar to Durkheim's.[139] He recognized the existence of two types: solidarity as a result of similarity (which Durkheim called mechanical) and solidarity as a result of the division of labor (which Durkheim called organic), though he did not employ Durkheim's terminology.[140] Duguit agreed that in modern society the second type of solidarity was increasingly predominant, and he drew sociopolitical conclusions similar to Durkheim's.

Duguit saw the path to integrate liberty and solidarity in the associationist movement, of which syndicalism was the principal branch.[141] His choice of the word *syndicalisme* risked causing some confusion about Duguit's political ideas, for although he saw the contemporary syndicalist movement as part of the trend he discerned in society, that movement was largely shaped by principles contrary to his own and would remain, even when it became more reformist, a stranger to his conceptions. Duguit utterly repudiated a syndicalism based on the Marxist idea of class struggle.[142] His syndicalism, like Durkheim's corporatism, was a movement of conciliation, not of conflict.

Observing that the division of society into two warring classes was utterly contrary to fact, and that the division of labor had on the contrary tended to multiply the classes of society along professional lines, Duguit looked forward to a corporatist restructuring of society in which the common interests of each profession would lead to the formation of *syndicats* grouping everyone—capitalists, cadres, workers—into the common regulation of their lives and protection of their interests.[143] If existing organizations did not correspond to this wish, he saw them as nonetheless stemming from an aspiration which would eventually lead in that direction.[144] It would bring both an increase in self-government and in social solidarity. Like Durkheim, Duguit considered this restructuring especially urgent because the family was in decline and something was needed to carry on its moral role.[145] Happily, he thought, the time was not far distant when everyone would be integrated in a professional association, and many people in more than one. Duguit was extrapolating rather venturesomely from the development he thought merely to observe. This temptation seems inherent in the sociological approach.

Like Durkheim, but less cautiously, Duguit proposed the introduction of a system of professional representation into the government of France, a system which would have made sense only if society had already been organized along the syndicalist lines he proposed.[146] Political realism was in any case not Duguit's strong point, as his personal ventures into politics in 1908 and 1914 amply demonstrated.[147] He proposed to replace the Senate, representing the communes of France—an anarchic and artificial grouping—with a professional chamber which would enjoy the same powers as the existing Senate.[148] Such a chamber would, he thought, represent the increasingly important interests of all groups in the actions of the national government, interests which were neglected in the traditional liberal order.[149] Corporatism enjoyed something of a vogue in Europe between the wars, though nothing even remotely resembling Duguit's model was ever attempted, despite an occasional kind word—later repudiated—from both the Soviet Union and fascist Italy.[150] Duguit was undoubtedly right when he observed that in individualist France the practice of voluntary association had made great strides in the nineteenth century, and he expected that trend to continue.[151] He was equally right in seeing in association one of the vital protections for individual liberty in the modern world. But his proposals betrayed an impatience to arrive at a definitive solution, to find an equilibrium which would have risked becoming a stagnation.[152]

Separated from its rigidity and comprehensiveness, Duguit's syndicalism appears in retrospect a forerunner of the pluralist version of liberalism which has become so prevalent in the West, where experience has indeed shown that the individual may be better protected against the state through his membership in organized groups, while on other occasions he remains better protected against the sometimes repressive action of other organized groups—even those of which he is a member—by the power of the centralized state.[153] Duguit was aware of this problem and never proposed—unlike some revolutionary syndicalists—that the *syndicat* would entirely replace the state. The political state remained necessary for internal as well as external reasons.[154] But in Duguit's vision it was destined to become a very different state from what the nineteenth century had known.

Duguit's rejection of the idea of sovereignty led him to propose a conception of the state as a collection of public services.[155] The idea of the state as authority, he argued, may have made some sense when its functions were largely limited to external defense, internal order, and the provision of a system of justice.[156] But it was scarcely relevant to the enormous and growing variety of activities of the modern state: postal service, roads and bridges, sanitation, protection of orphans, education, regulation of child labor, museums, and so forth. Their justification could be found, however, in the *règle de droit* of promoting social solidarity which he advanced. Not only existing services, but also those which people might come to desire in the future, could be justified by this standard. This concept of the state also rendered null and void all the traditional arguments against women's suffrage.[157]

Furthermore, the idea of public services was able to furnish a guide for the organization and regulation of state activities. The habits of sovereignty were of no use in determining the relations of, say, public health services with their clientele. For Duguit, this was not merely a speculative calculation; a close study of the evolution of administrative jurisprudence convinced him that the very nature of things was pushing the actual operation of the French state in this direction.[158] He could therefore view himself as the observing scientist, drawing theoretical conclusions from the data of experience. Duguit was, indeed, one of the most respected interpreters of administrative jurisprudence, and his views were of influence on its evolution.[159] While the idea of public services was not applied in all its potential *ampleur*, it no doubt shaped many aspects of the relation between the French state and its citizens.

Public services by nature possessed a certain autonomy, and Duguit sought to stress this quality as a means to the decentralization of state power, a decentralization which he thought all the more necessary if the continuing growth of state activity was to remain compatible with individual liberty.[160] The state was going to have an increasing role in the economy, and Duguit was aware that centralized economic power was a sure path to the greatest tyranny ever.[161] While guarding against this danger, he did not mean to completely splinter the state, for a central political element would remain necessary.

The growth of the syndicalist movement among state employees *(fonctionnaires)* seemed to Duguit to point the way toward a new organization.[162] Stimulated by reaction against the abuse of sovereign political power in their lives—lack of job security, lack of an independent system of evaluation and advancement, often miserable salaries— fonctionnaires were organizing to protect themselves from arbitrary treatment. In this movement, he saw also the way to protect citizens from the arbitrary practices of the administration and to improve the quality of the services provided.[163] It would be in the name of their obligations to the public that fonctionnaires would be freed from political control and endowed with the organs of self-regulation. In return for this large autonomy the syndicats of fonctionnaires would have to recognize their obligations to the public; this meant, among other things, that it would never be legitimate for them to strike.[164] The kind of judicial recourse which the jurisprudence of the Conseil d'Etat was increasingly providing against the abuses of administration would also serve as an adequate check on the actions of such autonomous *services publics*.[165]

There can be little doubt that Duguit put his finger on one of the most important trends of the day, even though he sometimes bent his picture to suit his preconceived ideas. Where he went furthest astray was in thinking that things have to work themselves out to their logical conclusions. The state has proved capable of living with a rather less logical hybrid of new and old attitudes than Duguit thought possible.

Liberals were naturally concerned with the question of what Duguit's rejection of natural law would do to the concept of property. Even though, as we have seen, no one regarded it as an absolute right, property might seem unprotected in Duguit's system. But his position was that property, like liberty, was socially functional.[166] This function determined the limits of property rights; there could be no right beyond what contributed to social solidarity.[167] Such a limitation did not, he thought, leave property at the mercy of government, since solidarity offered an objective standard of right, a standard on which to resist arbitrary encroachments. While objective, this standard was not fixed and eternal, since it hinged on what the mass of people at any time felt to be right. Duguit thought that this was an adequate protection; in any case it was all there was.

The standard of solidarity which Duguit proposed would serve to justify a considerable expansion of governmental activity beyond what the old liberalism could have accepted. But government action was by no means the only solution he saw to contemporary social problems. He put a high value on private and voluntary action and was himself very active in several charitable organizations, especially hospitals, of the Bordeaux region.[168] Though an ardent Dreyfusard, he drew the hostility of republicans after the Affair by insisting that many anticlerical measures were illiberal and, indeed, illegal.[169] As a promoter of the right of association, Duguit was less afraid than many liberals of the abuse of that right, even by Catholics. For him, the whole future of society rested on its development.

Like many, perhaps most, social theorists, Duguit was more effective in his criticisms—especially of the regalian state—than in his constructions, more accurate in his analysis of existing developments than in his extrapolations and projections of the future.[170] The insufficiency of his sociological "realism" as a basis for a science of society did not prevent him from being in many ways a clear anticipation of how the liberalism of the twentieth century would differ from that of the nineteenth, and a clear demonstration of the manner in which the sociological approach to the great questions of society, state, and the individual was of decisive importance in that transformation.[171] There results from Duguit's concept of democracy "a constant reopening of the question of the social order by a constant reopening of the question of social values and of their respective priorities, within the framework of the social structures."[172] Just as a search for secure absolutes had characterized the old liberalism of the nineteenth century, so has a value relativism resting mainly on sociological concepts characterized the new liberalism of the twentieth century.[173] This new attitude was a prime constituent of that "modern consciousness" of which much was heard, from Duguit as well as others, in the last prewar decades. His thought was a good example of what that expression meant.

Taken together, Bouglé and Duguit demonstrate the emergence of most of the characteristics of the new liberalism which distinguish it from earlier nineteenth-century liberalism. Most fundamental, perhaps, is the shift of emphasis from the demand that state and society interfere as little as possible with the activities of the individual, to a concern with the moral integration of the individual within society. The liberalism of the Enlightenment had always seen man as bound by a network of moral obligations which were not so much constraints on the exercise of his liberty but rather guidelines which enabled the individual to distinguish the exercise of his freedom from the mere pursuit of license. In the nineteenth century the rise of an extreme individualism had threatened to convert liberalism into a doctrine of might makes right, giving the practices of the successful a philosophical or pseudoscientific veneer. The inability of philosophical liberals to stem this tide had contributed to the rise of sociological liberalism.

By attacking what seemed to them the false dichotomy between the individual and the group, the Durkheimian liberals strove to restore social solidarity; by showing that society is prior to the individual, they hoped to reopen a path toward individuality without egoism and solidarity without oppression.

The effort of the sociological liberals to rebuild social solidarity was not an effort to preserve the status quo; it was indeed in reaction to the tendency of the old liberalism to become merely a means of defending the advantages of the successful. As we have seen, both Bouglé and Duguit were proposing substantial structural changes in French society. Their sociology pointed in the direction of a democratization of liberalism and suggested ways in which individual liberty could come to have practical meaning in the lives of all men and women. During the course of the nineteenth century the universality of liberal aspirations had taken a formalized quality which defined rights in ways that prevented the majority from taking advantage of them. The new liberalism dreamed of a liberty that would be meaningful to everyone.

This did not mean that the new liberalism was in opposition to traditional liberal values, or even that it thought that formal liberties were useless. Rather, it arose from a belief that liberal values were being endangered not merely by socialist collectivism but also by those liberals who contributed to the popular impression that liberalism was simply the ideology of the bourgeois ruling class. Despite their efforts, the philosophical liberals had not been able to overcome the various pseudoscientific doctrines which sought to justify unrestrained egoism or to submerge the individual in the mass. Men like Bouglé and Duguit were convinced that only a social science which raised men to a true consciousness of the relations of the individual and the group could show the way to a viable conciliation of liberty and solidarity. By recognizing the social bases of individual rights they hoped to find the ways to establish those rights on an unshakable foundation.

These concerns with the relations of the individual and society were, I think, more fundamental to the new sociological liberals than the question of the relations of the individual and the state. It is true that they sought to purge liberalism of the idea that state intervention is always, and of necessity, bad by observing that the growth of individual rights and state activity had coexisted over the last century. They tried to show that both these developments were products of the increasingly complex nature of modern societies and to show that, on occasion at least, the state had been an instrument of expanding individual rights. New liberals, like any liberals, had to admit that state and society could be oppressors of individual rights, but unless it could be shown that they were not intrinsically enemies of the individual, there would be no hope for the future of liberalism.

Both Bouglé and Duguit preferred private collective activity to that of the state where possible and tended to see the state as one social organ among others, though perhaps privileged in certain respects. Their direct involvement in politics shows how important they thought state action was for bringing about social reform. They would both certainly regret the degree to which the moral activity of the welfare state has become bureaucratized. For despite the efforts of the new liberals, the liberalism of the welfare state has tended to become based on the sum of individual egoisms; they had certainly hoped to lead us to a conception of the general interest which the old liberalism had vainly sought. Science has not proved more effective than philosophy in this quest.

In their separate ways, Bouglé and Duguit exemplified the determination of the new liberalism not merely to build a party platform from which to launch reformist action dealing with the social needs of the present, but more basically to discover the intellectual grounds on which individual liberty could stand unshaken by the loss of belief in the philosophical concepts of the past century and by the efforts to undermine it in the name of a pseudo-social science. This, rather than their specific reform proposals, would be the lasting heritage of Durkheimian liberalism.

·IX·

Afterword

*T*he historical account of the evolution of French liberalism which has been developed in the preceding chapters was of necessity more schematic, more clear-cut than the reality. Ultimately such an interpretation rests on the historian's judgment, which can never be based on the whole of that reality and which must depend on a sincere determination to achieve—and to transmit—an understanding of it. The student of nineteenth- and twentieth-century ideas soon learns that once he gets past the textbook summaries, with their inevitable effort to categorize and to render comprehensible, the reality does not conform to any neat developmental scheme, that ideas which have been "refuted" do not at once disappear from everyone's mind. Social and political ideas tend logically to a mutual extermination but—unless they also possess the secular arm, and not always even then—are radically powerless to bring that extermination about. An apparently illogical coexistence of the most contradictory views is what reality shows us. As citizens, we should rejoice in this diversity: it is a sign of freedom and a sign of life. For the historian of ideas it imposes a responsibility of judgment which one can never be sure of having adequately fulfilled. It is possible to take a sampling of that reality which would support almost any preconceived schema of interpretation, but such forced interpretations can triumph only in isolation. The approach to truth is—must be—a collective effort. This brief study cannot claim to offer the last word on French liberalism, but it does hope to have contributed to reopening the study of a wrongly neglected subject of great importance.

The evolution of liberalism from a philosophical to a sociological foundation was not merely a French experience, but it is doubtful that the issues were ever spelled out more clearly elsewhere. One of the particular fascinations of the intellectual history of the Belle Epoque is the extent to which the intellectual issues of the twentieth century were laid out and the main lines of controversy opened. In some cases those issues have been explored more thoroughly in subsequent decades; in others we scarcely seem to have maintained the level of nineteenth-century debate. I want to draw attention in this afterword to certain aspects of that debate which were of central importance then and which seem to me to have a continued importance for free peoples. What follows is not meant to exhaust the subject so much as to show its continued relevance.

There were four basic questions confronting French liberalism at the end of the nineteenth century, questions to which sociology and philosophy brought differing yet partially overlapping answers: (1) What should be the attitude of liberalism toward the growth, not so much in the power as in the range of activities, of the modern state? (2) How should liberalism adapt itself to the growth of democracy? (3) How best could liberalism continue to defend the rights of the individual? (4) How should liberalism conceive of the reciprocal obligations of society and the individual? Each of these questions could be the subject of a treatise in its own right, but what I propose to do here is to develop the contrasts and similarities of the philosophical and sociological viewpoints as propounded by the thinkers we have studied in the previous chapters.

I. The Growth of the Modern State

Both the philosophers and the sociologists took this growth to be an established fact. Even those philosophers like Jules Simon who expressed the most hostility to this development did not expect to be able to roll it back. At best they sought to define its proper limits, to try to turn it into liberal channels. Thus Simon himself would contribute to the growth of the French state through his efforts on behalf of public education.

Unless one took the pessimistic position that this growth was necessarily at the expense of individual freedom, the question for liberals became one of which kinds of growth to support as compatible with or even useful to the growth of liberty and which kinds to resist as manifestations of arbitrary authority. The liberals we have studied clearly rejected the idea that this was a zero-sum game in which everything added to the state was taken from the individual. For the philosophers the purpose of the state remained the service of the ends of the individual and the only foundation for its legitimacy lay in its commitment to that purpose. They wanted the state to be strong but to mind its own business. Liberals had long been aware of the inherent practical conflict in this position: the stronger the state, the less likely it was to simply mind its own business.

The eighteenth-century solution to this problem, given its definitive form in France by the Revolution, was to pose on the one hand a declaration of human rights founded on the idea of natural law and on the other hand the idea of national sovereignty. National sovereignty offered the grounds for a strong state—potentially stronger than under the old regime; the rights of man defined the limits of that state power. The theoretical foundation of this political system was an atomistic individualism. But the French society on which the liberalism of the Revolution was superimposed was by no means a "poussière d'individus," an amorphous mass of equals, even after the destruction of the class system of the old regime. In its naked abstraction, the liberal program did not offer a viable formula for social and political life any more than the social science of the eighteenth century offered the image of a viable society. Its relation to reality was about that of Condillac's "living" statue to a real human being. But when taken out of that abstraction and used for a guide to action in the French society that really existed, the liberal philosophy had a real efficacity. The network of ties which held French society together was perfectly strong enough to do without the *encadrement* provided by the aristocracy—largely a fiction by 1789 in any case—and the *encadrement* provided by the church was, if anything, strengthened by the revolutionary tribulations it had passed through. Economic integration was beginning to grow and would make rapid progress in the nineteenth century. The solidity of local culture would gradually give way to a national culture of nearly equal strength.

In short, individualism could flourish because its dissolving effects on society were counterbalanced by the secular accumulation of social bonds. The fear—more than the reality—that all bonds would be dissolved by liberal philosophy can be seen reflected in Balzac's *Comédie humaine*, a sort of multivolume commentary on Edmund Burke's *Reflections on the French Revolution*. Whereas the philosophes of the eighteenth century had taken the bonds of society for granted in the formulation of liberalism and had felt free to express it in absolutes because they knew how those absolutes would be tempered in reality, the liberal philosophers of the nineteenth century were increasingly forced to confront the antisocial character of the raw liberal creed. They did not for a minute believe that liberalism deserved to survive if it were really antisocial, and they set out to prove—a task that had been superfluous in the eighteenth century—that it was not antisocial.

The reasoning by which the laissez-faire economists attempted to reach this same objective seemed to the philosophers both false and immoral.

To find another path presented difficulties for the preservation of the liberal credo. The basic tactic of the philosophers was to turn to moral philosophy; if morals mean anything at all, they are concerned with the relations of the individual to other individuals, to groups, to society. Thus through moral obligations the isolation of the individual in liberal political philosophy could be overcome. This was surely one of the reasons the French so consistently rejected English utilitarianism, connected though it was to certain strands of French Enlightenment thought: utilitarianism could not bridge the gulf between the individual and society. Sensing that moral philosophy lacked the means of directly influencing the mass of society, the eclectics tended to seek the support of religion for morals. While Cousin tried to make philosophy's peace with Catholicism, the next generation of eclectics feared that liberty would be compromised by moving so far in that direction, and they tried to promote a sort of natural religion, acceptable to everyone but atheists. Even Renouvier, despite his scorn for the eclectics, would eventually come to a similar position for similar reasons. While the tendency of the philosophers was to void religion of all but its moral content, the sincerity of their religious sentiments should not be put in doubt. But while liberal society could draw benefits from the existing Judeo-Christian tradition, liberalism tended to undermine that tradition and to find itself more alone in the world.

If moral philosophy offered a way of connecting the individual and his society, how did it help cover the distance between the individual and the state? The idea of national sovereignty and, even more effectively, republicanism, offered one possible connection. If the state was a creature of society, then it could be connected to the individual through the intermediary of society. Its functions remained, however, hard to justify except in terms of necessity. And while necessity might furnish grounds for accepting the expansion of state activity, this was too negative for most liberals, and on that basis they found it hard to accept much change. Renouvier pointed to one possible way out of this problem: to recognize, as philosophers had before the nineteenth century, that the state possessed a moral mission and that its citizens had an obligation to promote that moral mission.

The revival of this opinion would surely be of great importance in turning liberalism away from laissez-faire. This would be all the easier in France, where liberalism had never completely severed its connection with the idea of a moral state. The resistance of French sociology to the Social Darwinian temptation is evidence of the prolongation of this moralistic attitude; the sociologists were not altogether unfaithful to their philosophic mentors.

In its arguments, however, sociological liberalism offered an altogether different sort of justification for the growth in the activity of the modern state. First of all, it explained this growth as an empirical reality, the political consequence of the changes that were taking place in society. The state was not a demon to be exorcised by brandishing the Declaration of the Rights of Man. Only sociological study could reveal whether—and how—liberty was served—or damaged— by the growth of the state; a priori suppositions only obstructed this understanding. Secondly, by presenting the state as one of the organs of society, sociology offered a means to end the radical otherness of the state, a view which liberal philosophy rather tended to promote. The gap could then be closed by the sociological integration of the individual into society.

Arguing that society was the source rather than the product of individual freedom, it was easier for the sociologists than for the philosophers to conceive of the state as an instrument which could be used by society to advance its freedom. The sociologists did not advocate—or even foresee—the enormous growth of state power and activity that would characterize the twentieth century. The Durkheimians looked forward rather to a proliferation of intermediary bodies in society over which the state would exercise an important, but essentially tutelary, power. The failure of other kinds of association to grow as rapidly and as effectively as desired and expected left the sociologists—pragmatic by temperament and conviction—open to an increasingly uncritical acceptance of the welfare state.

Both the philosophical-moralist and the sociological-liberal positions were essentially liberal on this question of the state. Both accorded the primacy of civil society over the state; both saw the state as serving the ends of society as a whole and not its own ends or those of some fraction of the society. Outside these parameters there could be no liberalism. Abuses of either view could lead outside liberalism: sociological liberalism could degenerate into a bureaucratic statism, the self-sanctified rule of an "intellectual" elite; philosophical liberalism could degenerate into the antipolitical paranoia of an Alain. Given a certain irreducible ambivalence in the relations of the individual and the state, liberalism will probably always oscillate between these extremes; the definitive triumph of either one would destroy it.

II. The Rise of Democracy

The acceptance of democracy by liberals in the nineteenth century was by no means unanimous; distrust of the masses found its most effective spokesman in Gustave LeBon, whose crowd psychology tried to found that distrust on a scientific basis. But for all his popularity LeBon remained outside the mainstream of Third Republic liberalism; his determination and his considerable talent for self-promotion could not overcome the basic repugnance of his philosophy to the reigning democratic liberalism. Philosophic and sociological liberals approached democracy from radically different positions and justified its acceptance on completely different grounds. How important were those differences for the direction taken by liberalism in the twentieth century?

Democracy is in a certain sense inherent in philosophical liberalism since it begins with the assumption that "men are born equal in rights." This *de jure* equality was the foundation of liberal politics in the eighteenth century, the basis on which the old regime—the regime of special privileges, of legal inequality—was attacked and overthrown. The justification of human rights, the very idea that rights beyond those existing *de facto* in a given society at a given moment also really existed, could only be founded on qualities presumed to belong to all men as men. This was essentially a moral argument, which opposed that which ought to be against that which is, how men should act against how they do act. It was also a profoundly revolutionary position, going against what had been the dominant tide of European thought for centuries.

But liberty and equality are both composite notions rather than simple ones. Men, who were equal in rights, were obviously very different in virtually every other respect, and for the liberals those differences were as natural as was that equality. Liberal opinion was sharply divided on the origins of inequality as it was united on the origin of equality. Some attributed inequality to heredity; some attributed it to the action of society. Either view could be accommodated to liberalism; a penchant for unitary explanations kept (and continues to keep) most people from accepting that both factors are at work. The tendency of the philosophical liberals was toward the view that physical, mental, and moral inequalities are basically products of heredity. But the liberal belief in man's basic freedom, his moral free will, led to the conclusion that moral inequalities were essentially the result of individual character, that however much heredity and environment bore on the individual, he remained responsible for his acts, for the quality of his life.

Liberals who were seduced by the idea of "economic man" fell into the trap of equating economic success and personal worth. This was not quite the new phenomenon that enemies of "capitalism" have made it out to be. Individual liberals might succumb to the sin of pride; French liberal philosophy did not. While believing in the basic inequality of talents, the liberal philosophers were aware that all material inequalities did not result from this cause. From the beginning, one sense of the term "liberalism" was the removal of obstacles to the development of individual talents, and in the nineteenth century liberals came increasingly to recognize that equality before the laws did not remove all the social obstacles to individual development. To be sure, they remained hostile to anything that smacked of leveling or that sought to reduce material inequalities by attacking the property of those who had it.

It was in this arena that liberty and democracy seemed to come into conflict. The use of public authority to reduce inequalities seemed to the philosophic liberals to be a direct threat to liberty, not fundamentally different from the acts of the old regime monarchy when it subsidized the court nobility, but potentially more dangerous since there were so many more poor. But that society should undertake to develop institutions which would reduce inequalities was clearly acceptable. And the liberals increasingly came to accept that the state should intervene—not to prevent coalitions in the manner of the Le Chapelier law of 1791—but to protect formal equality where inequality of wealth threatened to undermine it. Thus Renouvier urged state action to ensure justice in contracts between individuals. The liberals' encouragement of cooperatives and other forms of self-help among the workers was no doubt sometimes tinged with the smug moralism of the successful; it did not offer—as the socialists rightly charged—a means for the radical "liberation" of the working classes from their slavery. But from this latter point of view the socialists' remedies were even more worthless. Only the triumph of industrialization—which most French socialists opposed until near the end of the century—would make possible the end of misery. And, so far, that process of industrialization has fully triumphed only in liberal societies (although on occasion its success has been confiscated for other purposes, as by Hitler). The experience offers powerful arguments for the philosophical liberals' contention that to sacrifice liberty in the search for equality would be a mistake—even from the point of view of those who favored greater equality.

Philosophical liberals had an easier time coming to terms with political democracy—on the practical level. The idea of natural rights superior to the state seemed to offer as much protection against a democratic state's excesses as against those of an absolute monarchy. Moreover, despite the upheavals of the century, the introduction of democracy was gradually losing its violent character; if the masses still lacked the political maturity of the middle classes, they were already showing that they were capable of acquiring it. The middle classes came to realize that they could hasten this process by the spread of public education. The intellectual problem for philosophical liberalism was in some ways more difficult than the practical one. The idea of national sovereignty developed in the eighteenth century could be accommodated to the idea of majority rule either by assuming for the majority a right to speak for the whole or by considering this a practical necessity though not a theoretical right. Neither view explained how the majority was to be made to respect the rights of the minority. As long as most liberals were unwilling to follow Benjamin Constant in his denial of national sovereignty, this problem would trouble them.

Sociological liberalism would offer a couple of ways out of this problem and toward a reconciliation of liberalism and democracy. Biological sociology, with its emphasis on elites and the importance of leadership, might seem at first hostile to democracy, but rather it was hostile to a certain vision of democracy, one which stressed not equality of rights but the leveling of conditions and the elimination of social distinctions. Of course this biologistic viewpoint might be turned, and was turned, to antidemocratic uses, and that is no doubt one of the major reasons why it did not succeed in dominating the liberal movement. Was a man like Espinas, then, a liberal democrat in spite of, rather than because of, his sociological convictions? Probably his basic liberalism came from elsewhere, while his sociology served the important purpose of reconciling equality of rights with the inequality of positions necessary to the functioning of any society, even the most democratic. This would perhaps have been a viable foundation for liberal practice despite its intellectual fragility had not other thinkers so obviously turned biologism to antidemocratic purposes.

But if this evolutionary reconstruction of the development of humanity drew attention more readily to the differences among men than to their equality as men, a more genuinely empirical sociology like that of Durkheim and the Durkheimians could integrate both phenomena with equal force. Democracy and the division of labor were equally real when one looked at present society and its modern history. Evolutionary theory offered a kind of prehistory of man that could explain the changes in the historic era only by an abusive manipulation of concepts detached from the data of observation. Neither the democratic movement nor the modern division of labor could be explained in terms of an organic evolution whose natural time-scale of action was millions of years, not decades or centuries. A look at modern history showed the Durkheimians that the movements of diversification and for equality had virtually grown up together in Western society, creating at least a presumption that they were not incompatible, even that they went naturally together. By shedding the search for organismic analogies and by focusing instead on the development of collective mentalities, Durkheimian sociology could embrace egalitarianism *and* social differentiation, making the latter the social foundation of individual liberty. It could unite liberalism and democracy without subjecting itself to the inner tensions which the same attempt produced among philosophical liberals.

III. The Rights of the Individual

The contrasts between the philosophical and the sociological positions were nowhere more striking than on the question of the foundations of individual rights. As we have seen, the liberals did not differ fundamentally on what those rights were; there was only a gradual evolution of opinion on how to translate them in practice. But on the question of the origins and nature of those rights, there appeared to be a *solution de continuité* which even the synthetic genius of Fouillée could not close. For the philosophers, rights were inherent in the human person, being rationally deductible from the very concept of the person. For the sociologists, rights were a product of social forces; the individual was their beneficiary rather than their origin.

The shock of this clash at the theoretical level was somewhat attenuated at the practical level, for in practice the philosophical liberals recognized that the realization of what they considered to be timeless and universal rights was conditioned by the social and political circumstances, while the sociologists acknowledged that it would be impolitic to publicly proclaim the full force of their contempt for the metaphysical concept of rights. But even at the practical level, that fundamental difference of starting points was not without effect.

For the philosophical liberals the problem was one of adapting absolute formulas to relative possibilities. There were essentially two ways of doing this (not counting the absolute rejection of politics by quietism on the one extreme and anarchism on the other): (1) a politics of the *juste milieu*, which made moderation in the struggle for rights a higher value than the rights themselves; (2) the "radical" politics as Jules Simon defined it in the 1860s: a continual reference to the absolutes combined with a willingness to accept what seems attainable without disorder in the present. These two attitudes defined the conservative and the progressive wings of French liberalism. Both were expressions of a rationalist politics, rationalist not only in its definition of ends but in the correlation of ends and means. Indeed, in this sense liberalism is rationalist politics.

Even while recognizing the difficulties of translating absolute ideals into practical realities, the philosophical liberals remained convinced of the practical need for their absolutes. Unless rights were lodged in the human person, they saw no way to make them superior to society and the state. Whether that foundation was conceived as deriving from an act of God (as for Caro) or as a logical consequence of human nature needing no other reference (as for Renouvier), they thought liberty impossible without the concept of the person as subject of rights. This did not lead the philosophical liberals to a rejection of society; man was a social being and he had duties toward his fellow men. But he did not exist for the sake of society; the very purpose of society was the defense and advancement of the individual. Any retreat from this position seemed to the philosophers to entail the return of arbitrary authority or the subjection of the individual to irrational forces.

Under the influence of the positivistic idea of science, the sociological liberals saw only an illusion where the philosophers saw irrefutable first principles. Not only were natural rights a mere metaphysical conception, they rested on a dualistic conception of the person or the soul, which was untenable in the light of modern science. The philosophic view was good enough for an earlier age; the arrival of Comte's third stage had relegated it to the dustbin of history. Man and his social world were regulated by laws as necessary in their working as those governing the physical universe, if more complex and harder to discover. Must one draw from this the conclusion that freedom does not exist? That conclusion seemed inescapable, and the sociologists did not hesitate to deny what philosophers had called "free will" existed. But the sociologists could not fail to observe the existence of a phenomenon which men called "freedom" and an aspiration which they called "rights." Was this no more than a kind of sinister comedy, a black joke of the universe?

The sociological liberals could not think so. The individual's freedom of action was a great deal more limited than the philosophers believed, but it existed. For the biological sociologists, the necessary laws of evolution had produced a being of such complexity as to be partly liberated from that necessity and to be governed by a mixture of conscious ideas and vital forces. For some, the laws of society were statistical in nature, determining the action of social wholes rather than of each individual member. For others, society was essentially a network of mutual relationships in which the needs of the whole could be obtained while leaving an increasingly large margin of individual choice, choice whose determinations were so complex as to be equivalent to freedom.

In all of these sociological views liberties appear not as the product of the nature of the individual but as the result of the character of society. Far from being absolutes, they are strictly relative to that character. What to the philosophers appeared a practical weakness, a manifestation of the imperfect realization of the ideal, was for the sociologists a strength, a rooting of liberties in the real instead of the imaginary. Liberty was not merely the product of social relations; it was on the increase because of the historical evolution of those relations. That evolution had produced societies in which a large measure of individual freedom was a functional good for the society as a whole. While this left society as the judge of individual rights, it defended those rights more securely than any abstraction could, and it provided a barrier against the inherently antisocial tendency of the individualist philosophers.

There was no reason why in a given society at a given moment philosophical and sociological liberals could not be pursuing the same practical goals. As philosophical liberals adjusted themselves to a greater recognition of collective needs, they might even advocate the same methods. And in practice individual thinkers might have a foot in both camps despite their differences. Does this mean that these apparently fundamental intellectual differences were of little practical consequence? The answer to that question will become clearer in the next section.

IV. Individual Duty and Social Obligation

There was certainly a considerable overlapping of practical views between the sociologists and the philosophers. Otherwise we would not be speaking of them both as liberals. In the period under discussion both placed an increasing stress on the obligations of the individual to society, with the distinction that the philosophers tended to justify this in moral terms and the sociologists in functional ones. Both encouraged voluntary association as a means of dealing with social and economic problems, though again with somewhat different rationales, the philosophers seeing such associations as schools of morality, as lessons in freedom and self-reliance, the sociologists not repudiating this view but adding to it considerations of functional efficiency. Certainly the philosophers placed a higher value than the sociologists on purely individual social action, thinking of how such action improved the individual as well as it benefitted society. On the other hand, the sociologists were more ready to favor state action as the means for the execution of social responsibilities; but the pre-1914 sociologists were by no means so enamored of state action as later generations would be. It can be said that the sociological approach was much more conducive to this development than the philosophical view was.

The simple fact of approaching questions from the point of view of the ensemble inclined sociological liberalism to welfare statism. Of all the organs of society the state is clearly the one which embraces the whole. The more social problems seem to involve the functioning of the total organism, the more the state seems the logical, the necessary organ of direction. In part this penchant was a direct result of the positivist outlook, with its stress on functional rationality. Voluntary action seemed a remnant of free will philosophy; bureaucratic organization seemed more compatible with the scientific method. The more the operation of society seems to require a pooling of intelligences rather than a concert of wills, the more the statist view would prevail. Socialism was, of course, also a product of this mode of thought, which made it attractive to many sociologists; what we have sought to show here was that there was also a liberal sociology. Belief in the value of liberty proved to be a force for anchoring sociology in the real. When Lenin concluded that "freedom was unnecessary," he cut socialism's ties with reality, plunging it into the gnostic irreality which has destroyed Russian society without creating "socialism." Western sociology's liberal roots have helped save it, so far, from this catastrophe. Auguste Comte's motto of "order and progress" deliberately excluded liberty as an obstruction to both order and progress. Could sociology *prove* that liberty was, after all, functional?

Just as philosophical liberalism was held back from the brink of anarchism by the Christian heritage of Western society, so was sociological liberalism held back from the temptation of collective tyranny by the pervasive spirit of natural rights in Western civilization. Would either of these liberalisms be strong enough in the face of the new challenges of the twentieth century?

The evolutionist viewpoint which came to dominate French—and European—thought by the end of the nineteenth century conceived of the history of ideas as a series of ever more perfect adaptations. Any idea might be valid in its own time and place, but once something newer and better had evolved, the old was fated to extinction as surely as the dinosaurs. While this attitude may have had some validity in the physical sciences, it was as surely misplaced in the realm of social and political thought as was the condescension with which some sociologists treated the metaphysicians. In the interests of clarity of presentation, this book has made the evolution of French liberal ideas seem more uniform than it really was. Even the predominance of the sociological viewpoint in the construction of the twentieth-century welfare state has not caused philosophical liberalism to disappear. Though snubbed by the university intelligentsia, which has followed other gods after 1945, the influence of both the philosophical and sociological viewpoints has survived, in their strengths and in their weaknesses.

The main contribution of sociology to liberalism has been its demonstration that the organized action of society under the leadership of the state can expand without necessarily causing a diminution of individual liberty—indeed, that such action may be needed in order to bring the benefits of liberty to all elements of society. The main contribution of philosophy to liberalism was to show that for liberty to survive and to continue to grow in the face of new and old threats we must continue to believe in the human person as an end and to keep as tight a rein as possible on the ever-present temptation to treat him as a means to other ends, however noble in appearance.

Liberals of the Belle Epoque tended to emphasize either the importance of protecting the individual against the encroachments of society and the state or the importance of protecting the individual against anarchic egoism by reinforcing his integration into society and the nation. The persistence of the problems of individual freedom and of social integration into the later twentieth century shows that these two viewpoints are not so much opposed as related. Liberal society requires both the protection and the integration of the individual; either view, taken to its extremes, becomes destructive of that society. At the same time no stable synthesis of these approaches has been found, and none seems likely ever to be discovered. But it is the strength of Western society as well as its weakness that it offers us no easy solutions to such vital and persistent problems. Even if the intellectual effort to establish liberalism on an unshakable foundation has not succeeded, liberty has survived despite great and repeated threats. Its very flexibility has proved to be an invaluable strong point. On the other hand, liberal society remains subject to the risk of losing sight of its ultimate values either in the pursuit of short-term material goals or in the search for a more comfortable stability. Liberal politics remains a difficult art, but no more so in modern democratic society than earlier. It is the refusal of simplistic solutions which has made possible the survival and growth of liberty.

But is it not true that Western liberal society faces greater threats to its survival now than it did a hundred years ago? It is certainly difficult to escape the feeling that this is so. Despite the changing times there has been a considerable continuity in the nature of the threats facing liberalism. But there remains in the twentieth century a threat which did not exist in the Belle Epoque, which would have been scarcely conceivable to either the philosophers or the sociologists of that age, which we have trouble understanding even today: totalitarianism. The liberalism of the turn of the century was a political doctrine of the Center, facing a traditional authoritarianism on its Right and an emergent socialism on its Left. In France, at least, that socialism was in many ways a stepchild of liberalism, separated from it by a rather wavering and uncertain line. The problem began to change radically in 1917 with the rise of Soviet communism, which at first appeared to be a further development of Western socialism. It took a long time before it became apparent to most Westerners that communism was not to be found to the extreme Left of liberalism, but elsewhere. The habit of thinking in terms of a political spectrum whose origins were in the French Revolutionary assemblies has proved not merely inadequate to grasp the realities of the twentieth century but positively dangerous insofar as it masks the radical disjunction between Western social-democracy and Russian communism. It was almost equally difficult to see that radical disjunction between German Nazism and traditional German authoritarianism.

Liberalism has developed through the elaboration and interchange of ideas. But there was and is no common ground for discussion with Nazism or communism because both are entirely closed systems of thought, ideologies which live in a different world—a world which does not exist. Where liberalism was firmly planted, the ideologies have never succeeded in winning over more than a minority of the population or of the intelligentsia. But the position of liberalism remains precarious because ideology needs to cover the entire world in order to prevent its surreality from being exposed. It has been argued that there are more people in Western Europe who believe in communism than there are on the other side of the Iron Curtain, that one has to live in a totalitarian society for one's understanding to pierce through the hollow shell of ideology. The moderate temperament of Western liberalism certainly makes it difficult for liberals to comprehend the otherness of a regime which talks so constantly in what look like Western terms: peace, freedom, democracy, prosperity. But unless liberals can learn to do so, liberty will be in increasing danger. Such a *redressement* is possible because liberalism has deep roots from which it can draw strength. It will not be enough to try to further elaborate the sociological approach; not only has sociology disappointed the great hopes placed in it by the pioneers of the turn of the century, it seems stuck in that pre-scientific stage of evolution from which they thought they had at last rescued it. It will not be enough to attempt to revive the philosophical tradition though we can certainly use a large dose of the effort toward rigorous thought which distinguished the philosophers of liberalism. Both views still have their value—and liberalism does not require a monolithic foundation—but liberalism needs also to draw on its spiritual heritage, which has long been one of its hidden strengths. What liberalism needs most at the end of the twentieth century is a return to the serious discussion of the meaning of liberty, equality, and fraternity, a discussion which has largely been replaced in our time by hollow sloganeering, the pursuit of successive intellectual fads, and the search for recognition in the mass media. Reflection on the history of liberal thought in the nineteenth century can perform a valuable service by stimulating our interest in the fundamental ideas of liberalism and by allowing us to see those ideas more clearly. Such humanistic inquiry is needed today more than ever.

Notes

e

·I·

1. *Les idées politiques de la France* (Paris: Stock, 1932), p. 49.

2. The comparable phenomenon in Britain has received considerable attention. See, for example, Michael Freeden, *The New Liberalism: An Ideology of Social Reform* (Oxford: Clarendon Press, 1978).

3. *L'idée de l'Etat: essai critique sur l'histoire des théories sociales et politiques en France depuis la Révolution* (Paris: Hachette, 1895).

4. The Jacobin strain has been identified with the Catholic heritage of the French Left by, among others, Charles Renouvier: "what is involved everywhere and in every manner is authority; what is expected is a miracle; the Catholic spirit reigns." *La critique philosophique* (1873–II), p. 148.

5. Jean-Jacques Chevallier, *Cours d'histoire des idées politiques* (Paris: Les cours de droit, 1967), p. 106: "We will rediscover in the 19th century the *aristocratic liberalism* of Montesquieu, confronted by the *bourgeois* liberalism which opposes it even though descended from it, while we await a truly democratic liberalism."

6. Chevallier, p. 207, begged the question: "The term liberalism is, in sum, a synonym for *liberal* individualism in France."

7. On the liberal reaction to the press laws of the Second Empire see Jules Simon, *La liberté* (Paris: Hachette, 1859), II: 64.

8. The argument that this has been one of the basic weaknesses of French liberalism has been recently revived by Alain Peyrefitte, *Le mal français* (Paris: Plon, 1976).

9. For a comprehensive discussion of the communal movement see Louis Greenberg, *Sisters of Liberty: Marseille, Lyon, Paris and the Reaction to a Centralized State, 1868-1871* (Cambridge: Harvard University Press, 1971).

10. See Jacques Droz, *Histoire des doctrines politiques en France* (Paris: Presses universitaires de France, 1948), p. 106.

11. Léon Duguit, *Les transformations du droit public* (Paris: Colin, 1913), p. 135, noted that decrees of 1899 established maximum hours and minimum wages in all firms operating under concessions from the state. He also

pointed (*Traité de droit constitutionnel* (Paris: Boccard, 1921-26), I: 142-43) to other examples of social legislation: "support of children on welfare (27.VI.1904), free medical care (15.VII.1893), obligatory aid to the aged or infirm (14.VII.1905), workers' retirement (5.IV.1910)." One can also mention insurance against work-related accidents (9.IV.1898, amended 31.III.1905, 12.IV.1906, 18.VII.1907); laws regulating women's and children's labor (2.XI.1892, amended 1900, 1908, 1909, 1911); the *loi Siegfried* (30.XI.1894) and *loi Ribot* (10.IV.1908) to aid workers and peasants to acquire housing and small plots of land; the expansion of the Caisse Nationale d'Assurances (17.VII.1897, 19.VII.1907); the regulation of the hours of work for adult males (30.III.1900); the obligation to provide workers a weekly day of rest (13.VII.1906); the creation of the Ministère du Travail et de la Prévoyance sociale (23.XI.1906); the codification of the labor law (28.XII.1910, 26.XI.1912). As Bertrand de Jouvenel, *Cours d'histoire des idées politiques à partir du XIXe siècle* (Paris: Les cours de droit, 1967), p. 285, has rightly said, the philosophy behind most of this legislation could be called *solidarisme*.

12. We are going to study the period from a rather different point of view than that of Claude Digeon, *La crise allemande de la pensée française (1870-1914)* (Paris: Presses universitaires de France, 1959), though I am largely in accord with him on the importance of the defeat of 1870.

13. See Chevallier, p. 275.

14. Even the Catholic political philosopher Michel Halbecq, *L'Etat, son autorité, son pouvoir (1880-1962)* (Paris: Librairie générale de droit et de jurisprudence, 1964), p. 11, admits that late 19th-century liberalism placed the individual "in a natural *social environment*."

15. Thus I differ with Grangé, *Les doctrines politiques du parti républicain à la fin du Second Empire* (Bordeaux: Cadoret, 1903), p. 74, although he is more right about politicians than about intellectuals.

16. See Halbecq's praise of René Waldeck-Rousseau (premier, 1899-1902) in this connection (p. 54).

17. See Halbecq, p. 281.

18. Compare Digeon, p. 112: "the ideological structure developed under Napoleon III by the opposition between spiritualism and realism will be replaced after 1870 by a new structure which can be defined by the opposition between a rationalist idealism (Kantian influence) and a renewed realism (Taine)." Taine's positivism led in a different direction from that of the liberal sociologists and, indeed, to a rapid dead end.

19. On how little they have been studied see André-Jean Tudesq, *La démocratie en France depuis 1815* (Paris: Presses universitaires de France, 1971), pp. 73-74.

20. Maurice Agulhon and André Nouschi, *La France de 1914 à 1940* (Paris: Nathan-Université, 1974), p. 49.

·II·

1. For the most complete summation of the eclectic philosophy see Adolphe Franck, ed., *Dictionnaire des sciences philosophiques*, par une Société de professeurs de philosophie, 6 vols. (Paris: Hachette, 1844-52), and for a brief summary, pp. vi-ix. Another good summary is Paul Janet, *Les problèmes du XIXe siècle: la politique, la littérature, la science, la philosophie, la religion* (Paris: Michel Lévy frères, 1872), pp. 376-409. General histories of philosophy are not much help; for example, Emile Bréhier, *Histoire*

de la philosophie, vol. II: *La philosophie moderne* (Paris: Presses universitaires de France, 1946), pp. 656-67, deals only with Cousin.

2. Jules Simon, *Liberté*, II: 231.

3. For Franck's views of Maistre and Bonald see his *Essais de critique philosophique* (Paris: Hachette, 1885), pp. 193-237.

4. Adolphe Franck, *Nouveaux essais de critique philosophique* (Paris: Hachette, 1890), pp. 28-29.

5. See Simon, *Liberté*, I: 30-31, and Adolphe Franck, *Philosophie du droit civil* (Paris: Alcan, 1886), p. 105.

6. See Adolphe Franck, *Moralistes et philosophes* (Paris: Didier, 1872), pp. 306-8; cf. the criticism of Bréhier, II: 656-67.

7. On Cousin's independence see Franck, *Nouveaux essais*, pp. 42-43.

8. Reconciliation did not mean that the distinctions between philosophy and religion should become blurred: see Janet, *Problèmes*, pp. 340-41, and Adolphe Franck, *Philosophie et religion* (Paris: Didier, 1867), pp. 341-55. Franck (*Moralistes*, p. 319) did reproach Cousin with a tendency to favor religion at the expense of philosophy.

9. As Franck (*Philosophie et religion*, p. 358) observed: "If it is true, as is continually being repeated, that the religious spirit is lacking in our century, one will at least agree that it hasn't been lacking in religions."

10. See Janet, *Problèmes*, p. 489.

11. See Franck, "Victor Cousin," in *Moralistes*, pp. 291-321.

12. The following material on Franck's career was derived mainly from *A la memoire d'Adolphe Franck: discours et articles* (Paris: J. Montorier, 1893), and Institut de France, Académie des sciences morales et politiques, *Funérailles de M. Franck*, discours prononcés par M. Dareste et M. G. Boissier (Paris, 1893). See also the *Grande Encyclopédie* and the *Encyclopedia Judaica*.

13. Published as *La vraie et la fausse égalité*, "Conférences populaires faites à l'Asile impérial de Vincennes" (Paris: Hachette, 1867).

14. C. B. Macpherson, *The Political Theory of Possessive Individualism* (Oxford: Clarendon Press, 1962). But Franck repudiated Locke's empiricism: see his *Moralistes*, p. 296.

15. *Egalité*, pp. 49-50.

16. See Franck, *Philosophie et religion*, p. 421.

17. *Droit civil*, p. 4. In general the eclectics thought that English Utilitarianism undermined the sense of personal responsibility: for example, see Elme-Marie Caro, *Problèmes de morale sociale* (2d ed.; Paris: Hachette, 1887), 278-79.

18. *Droit civil*, p. 7.

19. *Essais*, p. xvi; later he came to fear that Jean-Marie Guyau's *L'irreligion de l'avenir* might become the monument to "an age of dissolution" (*Nouveaux essais*, p. 164).

20. *Droit civil*, p. 7.

21. See ibid., pp. 265-76 and Chap. 2.

22. While the "human personality" was an abstraction, it did not exist apart from real individuals whose self-awareness of freedom is the basis of this philosophy: ibid., p. 6.

23. See Franck, *Le communisme jugé par l'histoire* (Paris: Joubert, 1848), pp. 22-23.

24. *Droit civil*, p. 7; see also Franck, *Moralistes*, p. 412.

25. *Nouveaux essais*, p. ix.

26. See *Egalité*, p. 21, for his attack on slavery.

27. *Droit civil*, p. 5. Free will is both man's strength and weakness since it makes him open to the influence of both good and evil: Franck, "Création," *Dictionnaire des sciences philosophiques*, I: 596. A similar view was expressed by Caro, *Etudes morales sur le temps présent* (5th ed.; Paris: Hachette, 1887), pp. 49–50.

28. Nor can there be law and justice without liberty: *Moralistes*, p. 408.

29. The two bases of morality are "le devoir et la liberté": *Essais*, pp. 332, 344–45.

30. *Egalité*, pp. 45–48.

31. *Droit civil*, p. 3.

32. Ibid., pp. 277–92: Franck argued that Alfred Fouillée's (see Chap. 6 below) attack on absolute individualism was an attack on a straw man, since no one held such a view with respect to property.

33. Ibid., pp. 117–19.

34. Ibid., p. 23.

35. Ibid., pp. 131–45; *Communisme*, p. 71.

36. He considered the labor theory only another version of the right of the strongest: *Nouveaux essais*, pp. 235–42; see also *Droit civil*, pp. 117–29.

37. *Egalité*, pp. 32–34.

38. Ibid., pp. 35–45.

39. Hence the importance of inheritance: *Droit civil*, pp. 193–203; see also p. 123.

40. *Egalité*, p. 40.

41. There is something of a working-class version of this to be found in Proudhon.

42. *Droit civil*, p. 167.

43. See ibid., pp. 75–87.

44. Ibid., p. 86.

45. *Liberté*, I: 386.

46. See also ibid., I: 376–77, 380, 383–84.

47. *De l'instruction obligatoire* (Paris: Raçon, 1862), p. 14.

48. See *Droit civil*, pp. 49–59, 61–65.

49. See ibid., pp. 89–101. This is an important point on which the later sociologists (esp. Durkheim) would sharply differ with the philosophers.

50. See also Simon, *Liberté*, I: 383.

51. *Droit civil*, pp. 98–99; see also *Instruction*, pp. 8–9.

52. *Instruction*, passim.

53. *Lettres sur la guerre de 1870* (Milan: Dumolard frères, 1871).

54. *Nouveaux essais*, pp. 214–15; government should be limited to doing what is necessary: *Droit civil*, p. 21.

55. *Droit civil*, p. 20.

56. *Nouveaux essais*, pp. 212–13, 214–15; this need was also recognized by Simon, *Liberté*, I: 374–75.

57. Franck, *Projet de constitution* (Paris: A. LeChevalier, s.d.), pp. 13–14.

58. Lectures delivered at the Collège de France during the academic year 1871–72, apparently published in 1872.

59. His views on women in public life had not changed. On the dangers of a single-chamber legislature see *Projet*, pp. 7–11. On suffrage as a right (as distinguished from a function) see Simon, *Liberté*, II: 243.

60. *Projet*, pp. 28–30. This is an idea which is usually assumed to have originated with the sociological school. In his survey of the antecedents of twentieth-century French corporatism Matthew H. Elbow (*French Corporative Theory, A Chapter in the History of Ideas* [New York: Columbia University Press, 1953]) does not mention Franck or any of the eclectics.

61. *Projet*, p. 33.

62. Ibid., p. 32.

63. Paris: Alcan, 1886.

64. *Nouveaux essais*, pp. 203–4.

65. *Philosophie et religion*, p. 422.

66. Material on Caro's career is derived mainly from the article by P. Leguay in the *Dictionnaire de biographie française* and the article by Henri Marion in the *Grande Encyclopédie*.

67. Institut de France, Académie française, *Funérailles de M. E. About, …le…19 janvier 1885; Discours de M. Caro* (Paris: Firmin-Didot, 1885). Caro's remarks may have been ill-timed, but they were fair and mildly expressed, in passing.

68. Caro himself pointed out that there have been no new ideas in metaphysics for a long time and that many who claimed originality were merely reviving very old ideas: *L'idée de Dieu et ses nouveaux critiques* (Paris: Hachette, 1864), pp. 480–89.

69. *Le matérialisme et la science*, 5th ed. (Paris: Hachette, 1890), pp. 79–86. Caro had considered theological intolerance still a problem in the 1850s: *Etudes morales*, pp. 1–5.

70. *Etudes morales*, p. 38.

71. *Matérialisme*, pp. 70–71.

72. *Dieu*, p. 479.

73. Hegel, for example, was leading us back to Protagoras: ibid., p. 14.

74. *Matérialisme*, pp. vii–viii; see also Franck, *Philosophie et religion*, pp. 372–73.

75. Science could neither replace nor suppress metaphysics: *Matérialisme*, p. iii; see also his *M. Littré et le positivisme* (Paris: Hachette, 1883), pp. 169–70.

76. *Matérialisme*, pp. 256, 281–82.

77. The eclectics all agreed that the existence of God could be demonstrated by reason alone. As a Catholic, Caro claimed also to be able to show the divinity of Christ (see *Dieu*, pp. 496–500), while, as a Jew, Franck rejected this conclusion (*Philosophie et religion*, p. 416).

78. See *Littré*, p. iv, and *Matérialisme*, p. 151.

79. *Etudes morales*, p. 87; but he recognized that Littré took positivism to a materialistic conclusion: *Littré*, pp. 143–54. Worth reading, too, is Franck's biographical sketch of Comte in *Philosophie et religion*, pp. 357–70, where, in the most sober and straightforward manner, he leaves no doubt that Comte was insane.

80. For a critique of this argument see Walter Kaufmann, *Critique of Religion and Philosophy* (Garden City: Doubleday, 1961).

81. See *Matérialisme*, p. v, where Caro distinguishes an "experimental school" from positivism and materialism.

82. See ibid., pp. 6–38, 219.

83. See *Dieu*, p. 203; Caro also fought against the antimetaphysical tendencies of Renouvier's neo-criticism: *Etudes morales*, pp. 16–21.

84. He was convinced that everybody wants the same thing from government: security in the exercise of his rights (*Problèmes*, p. 364).

85. *Les jours d'épreuve, 1870-1871* (Paris: Hachette, 1872), pp. 153-57.

86. Caro insisted that France was a democratic country *en droit* as well as *en fait*: *Jours*, pp. 260-61.

87. Ibid., pp. 96-97, 100-103, 116-23.

88. Ibid., pp. 141-42, 149-54.

89. Ibid., pp. 162-63, 302.

90. Ibid., pp. 195-96.

91. Caro underlined the contradiction in the position of those democrats who opposed allowing the people to vote on the question of the form of government (ibid., pp. 264-70).

92. Ibid., pp. 198-99, 205.

93. Ibid., p. 172.

94. Ibid., pp. 164-72.

95. Ibid., pp. 176-77.

96. Ibid., pp. 145-48.

97. Ibid., pp. 179-98; in *Problèmes*, p. 368, he described revolutions as exaggerations of individualism.

98. *Jours*, pp. 207-58: a chapter entitled "La fin de la bohème."

99. Caro, *Etudes morales*, p. 39, called moderation "the natural form of truth."

100. See *Problèmes*, pp. 358, 375-90, and *Etudes morales*, p. 58.

101. *Etudes morales*, p. 58; see *Problèmes*, pp. 294-349.

102. The philosopher Paul Janet (1823-1899) should be distinguished from his son, Paul Janet (1863-1937), who became a noted physicist, and from his nephew, Pierre Janet (1859-1947), one of the leading figures of the French school of experimental psychology. On the philosopher Janet's career see Emile Boutroux, *Notice sur Paul Janet* (Versailles: Cerf, 1900) and Georges Picot, *Paul Janet* (Paris: Hachette, 1903), which includes a comprehensive bibliography.

103. See Dominique Parodi, in Paul Janet and Gabriel Séailles, eds., *Histoire de la philosophie: les problèmes et les écoles*, Supplement: *Période contemporaine* (Paris: Delagrave, 1929), pp. 6-7, 1070.

104. *Problèmes du XIXe siecle*, pp. 284-85.

105. Ibid., pp. 327, 328-29.

106. *Histoire de la science politique dans ses rapports avec la morale*, 5th ed. (Paris: Alcan, [1924?]), I: x-xi, where he calls eclecticism the "summary of the work of centuries."

107. See ibid., pp. xi-xxxviii.

108. Ibid., p. xliii.

109. *Problèmes du XIXe siecle*, pp. 325-26.

110. Ibid., pp. 281-82.

111. *Science politique*, I: viii. Janet noted that while French philosophy was abandoning eclecticism for neo-criticism or positivism, French liberals remained united behind the Declaration of the Rights of Man.

112. Ibid., pp. xci-xcii.

113. Ibid., II: 727-39.

114. *Problèmes du XIXe siecle*, p. 39.

115. See ibid., pp. 37-130.

116. *Problèmes*, p. 389. See also *Jours*, pp. 286-91.

117. *Problèmes du XIXe siecle*, p. 59.
118. Ibid., p. 61.
119. Ibid., p. 59.
120. Ibid., pp. 85–87.
121. Ibid., p. 106.
122. See, for example, *Les origines du socialisme contemporaine* (Paris: Baillière, 1883), pp. 131, 149.
123. *Science politique*, I: xcix.
124. Ibid., p. lxxx.
125. Simon, *Liberté*, II: 380, would insist that the state could accept Natural Religion without infringing on the rights of the revealed religions.
126. *Science politique*, I: lxxxv, lxxxvii.
127. Ibid., p. xcvi: "Man is not born in order to be happy."
128. Ibid., p. lxx; see also *Problèmes du XIXe siecle*, p. 34.
129. There is, finally, a good study of Jules Simon: Philip A. Bertocci, *Jules Simon: Republican Anticlericalism and Cultural Politics in France, 1848–1886* (Columbia: University of Missouri Press, 1978). See also the *Grande Encyclopédie*.
130. For his complaints about the state's domination of the teaching of philosophy see *Liberté*, II: 213, 410–12.
131. Ibid., p. 245; a similar view was expressed by Janet, *Science politique*, I: lii: "the legal and constitutional forms of a country ought to be in harmony with its social condition."
132. *Liberté*, II: 280; see also his *La politique radicale* (Paris: Lacroix, Verboeckhoven, 1868), preface.
133. *Liberté*, II: 401.
134. See ibid., pp. 191–92.
135. Ibid., I: 150–51.
136. Ibid., I: 18–19, 147–48, 149; II: 398.
137. See ibid., II: 202; see also *Politique radicale*, pp. 34–35.
138. See *Liberté*, I: 4, 19, 379.
139. Ibid., p. 201; but government should strive to make itself unnecessary: *Politique radicale*, p. 35.
140. In *Liberté*, I: 61, he presented taxes as a kind of payment for protection, concluding that the rich should pay more because they receive more.
141. See *Politique radicale*, p. 29.
142. See *Liberté*, II: 154, 171, 182–83.
143. In ibid., I: 169, he parallels "traditional and monarchical communism with revolutionary communism."
144. Ibid., I: 284, 299.
145. Property which recognized no limits became itself a tyranny: ibid., p. 285. Janet, *Socialisme*, p. 66, linked the *mainmorte* of the church and communism.
146. For his definition of "liberté du travail" and how it differed from the socialists' "droit au travail" see *Liberté*, II: 41–42, 121–22.
147. Ibid., pp. 101–2.
148. *Politique radicale*, pp. 330–56.
149. Ibid., pp. 308–9.
150. In *Liberté*, I: 124, he quoted with approval Mirabeau's "War against the privileged and privileges!"
151. See Janet, *Socialisme*, pp. 2–3.

152. *Liberté*, I: 4-5.
153. Ibid., p. 252.
154. Ibid., p. 283; see also p. 212.
155. Ibid., I: 206.
156. Ibid., p. 227.
157. *Droit civil*, pp. 103-16; also pp. 23-30, 43-47.
158. Ibid., pp. 52, 67-73.
159. John Lukacs, *The Passing of the Modern Age* (New York: Harper & Row, 1970).
160. See Caro, *Dieu*, p. 480.
161. Franck argued that if sociology were really a science it would absorb the "science" of natural law: *Nouveaux essais*, p. 193; see also p. 195.
162. See Caro's observations on how the survivals of Christianity have masked the moral consequences of positivism: *Littré*, pp. 209-12, 215.
163. See Ernest Nolte, *Three Faces of Fascism* (New York: Holt, Rinehart and Winston, 1966), pp. 429-34, where he defines fascism as "resistance to transcendence."
164. See the last chapter of Caro's *Littré*. Franck, *Droit civil*, p. vi, argued that evolutionism and positivism were the philosophical equivalents of the modern political assault on liberty by collectivism.
165. On the other hand, Caro appreciated that the modern idea of equality was a late and complex product of civilization: *Littré*, pp. 154-85.
166. Socialism, Franck said (*Communisme*, p. 7), blamed all evils on social organization, none on individuals.
167. Caro, *Etudes morales*, p. 128, noted that Stirner made each man his own God while Comte stopped short of this, merely making humanity as a whole God. He also noted (*Dieu*, pp. 42-45, 52), that the idea of a progress inherent in Nature had become a substitute for God. Evolutionism seems to him to be a fatalism comparable to Comte's idea of progress: *Littré*, pp. 131-32.
168. Caro, *Problèmes*, p. 401.
169. Caro (ibid., pp. 180-99) drew a picture of what evolutionist politics would be like, which offers a striking forecast of the Nazi regime.

·III·

1. Henry Michel, "De l'histoire des doctrines politiques: sa nature, sa méthode, son esprit," *Revue du droit public* 7 (1897): 228-29.
2. Citation will be to the posthumous reedition of 1908 (2 vols.; Paris: Alcan). There is a slight ambiguity of terminology here which need not worry us: Kant's philosophy is known as criticism or critical philosophy because of the central role of his critiques of knowledge (Critique of Pure Reason, of Practical Reason, of Judgment). The prefix "neo-" implies both a revival and a difference. But Renouvier's main philosophical work was also a critique and can be called a critical philosophy without the prefix.
3. *L'idée de l'Etat: essai critique sur l'histoire des théories sociales et politiques en France depuis la Révolution* (Paris: Hachette, 1895).
4. *Manuel républicain de l'homme et du citoyen.* "Nouvelle édition publiée avec une notice sur Charles Renouvier, un commentaire et des extraits de ses oeuvres par Jules Thomas" (Paris: Colin, 1904).
5. Renouvier, *Manuel républicain*, pp. 298-99.
6. The following details of Renouvier's early life are taken largely from

the Abbé Louis Foucher, *La jeunesse de Renouvier et sa première philosophie (1815-1854), suivi d'une bibliographie chronologique de Charles Renouvier* (Paris: J. Vrin, 1927).

7. Just as he would preserve his hostility to Cousin's eclecticism, which he denounced as a vulgar, unphilosophic defense of a ruling caste: *Critique philosophique*, 1872-II, pp. 115-16.

8. Isaac Benrubi, *Contemporary Thought of France* (New York: Knopf, 1926), pp. 85-86, attributed Renouvier's antimetaphysical attitude to the influence of Comte. Perhaps Renouvier's effort to use mathematics against metaphysics was an example of this influence?

9. Certainly the *Manuel républicain* was more socialistic in tone than Renouvier's later writings, but Foucher, p. 153, is justified in saying that it was no more than a "vague christianisme social."

10. See *Critique philosophique*, 1873-I, p. 35.

11. Ibid., 1873-II, p. 145: "Criticism is in philosophy what Protestantism is in religion."

12. His bitter hostility to eclecticism was both philosophical and political; he saw the eclectics as supporters of the July Monarchy: ibid., 1876-I, pp. 371-72.

13. Ibid., 1873-II, pp. 154-55.

14. For a time (1879-85) he published a review, *La critique religieuse*, which advocated a Protestant reformation for France as the best way of eliminating the obstacles to liberty posed by the Catholic heritage. Eventually realizing this was chimerical, he rested his hopes on proselytizing *personnalisme* among the intelligentsia and thought that Henry Michel was the most capable of succeeding him in this task: Louis Prat, *Derniers entretiens avec Renouvier* (Paris: Colin, 1904), p. 106.

15. See Gabriel Séailles, *La philosophie de Charles Renouvier: introduction à l'étude du neo-criticisme* (Paris: Alcan, 1905), pp. 119-22. I have relied on Séailles in this section on neo-criticism. Brecht, *Political Theory: The Foundations of Twentieth-Century Political Thought* (Princeton: Princeton University Press, 1959), pp. 105-6, argues rightly that Kant's *a priori* principles do not conflict with the scientific method.

16. *Critique philosophique*, 1873-II, p. 297; Séailles, p. 58.

17. See Séailles, pp. 1-2, 20, 68-69.

18. See ibid., pp. 129, 197, and especially 209. Without freedom we could not choose between true and false answers in science itself (Brecht, p. 316); he also observes that this position has been stated by Simmel and by Heidegger.

19. See Séailles, p. 260.

20. In the end, he settled for a single, but nonetheless finite, God.

21. Louis Prat's account of Renouvier's last days is a moving account of the philosopher's devotion to his mission in life.

22. See *Science de la morale*, I: 115-16; II: 262.

23. Ibid., II: 261.

24. For a discussion of conscience as a basic concept of Renouvier's pure theory, see ibid., I: 116.

25. Ibid., I: 1-28: on the concept of duty toward oneself.

26. Ibid., I: 29-50. Renouvier worried about the bad effects on man of his exploitation of animals.

27. But obligations toward others could be analytically deduced from ob-

ligations toward oneself, which were the result of a synthetic, *a priori* judgment: ibid., I: 59.

28. This was Kant's term; Renouvier preferred "autonomy of reason": ibid., I: 115-16.

29. Michel, *L'idée de l'Etat*, pp. 617-18. J.-J. Chevallier, *Cours de principes du droit public* (Paris: Les cours de droit, 1951), p. 272, describes this as a "statist individualism, communitarian individualism"; Jacques Droz, p. 110, also insists on this link with the eighteenth century.

30. Joseph Cropsey, *Political Philosophy and the Issues of Politics* (Chicago: University of Chicago Press, 1977), pp. 124-25, insists that liberals always come back to this in one form or another.

31. *Science de la morale*, I: v.

32. If morals were not dependent on transcendental truths, then only critical philosophy could establish them: ibid., I: 10; any conception based on the end of man risked subordinating morals to other purposes: ibid., I: 151-53; religion drew its strength from morals, not vice versa: ibid., I: 207-11.

33. See ibid., I: 119-24; he also found that liberty and moral action can bring their own reward and happiness: ibid., I: 204.

34. Ibid., I: 58.

35. On the inadequacy, even dangers, of love: ibid., I: 204-7; duties of charity were rated below those of justice, on a par with duties to oneself: ibid., I: 96-99.

36. For his discussion of the State of Peace, see ibid., I: 219-27.

37. Rejection of moral relativism: *Critique philosophique*, 1872-I, pp. 4-5.

38. *Science de la morals*, I: 227.

39. It was especially important to avoid hatred in the exercise of the right of defense: ibid., I: 261-62; an individual's merit and responsibility must be judged relatively to circumstances, not absolutely: *Critique philosophique*, 1873-I, p. 104.

40. For his critique of utilitarianism in moral theory, see *Science de la morale*, I: 134-42; he gave the utilitarians credit for at least trying to make morals independent: ibid., I: 150.

41. Love easily became the basis for accepting the idea that the end justifies the means: *Critique philosophique*, 1873-I, p. 213.

42. For his exhaustive examination of the passions, see *Science de la morale*, I: 268-324; more briefly, *Critique philosophique*, 1873-I, pp. 216-18; 1878-I, pp. 33, 36-37.

43. He distinguished three categories in the right of defense: (1) protection against attack on the person, (2) protection of property, (3) power to compel observance of contracts: *Science de la morale*, I: 243-44.

44. Ibid., II: 2.

45. Ibid., I: 263-64; on property and personal independence, see ibid., I: 107-8, 264; II: 18.

46. The right of defense could not be used to justify slavery: ibid., I: 331-46. He even objected to domestic service: ibid., II: 98-105.

47. Ibid., I: 109-14; assistance was not a remedy for inequalities: ibid., II: 28.

48. Ibid., II: 13.

49. Ibid., II: 30, 35.

50. Ibid., II: 75.

51. Ibid., II: 30, 37, 74.
52. Ibid., II: 36-44, 74-75. See Chevallier's criticism, p. 282.
53. *Science de la morale*, II: 17.
54. Ibid., II: 123.
55. Ibid., II: 126-27; *Critique philosophique*, 1873-I, p. 35.
56. *Science de la morale*, II: 92.
57. He defended freedom of labor contracts but approved government intervention to insure equity: ibid., II: 58. Chevallier, p. 276, saw a parallel to T. H. Green here.
58. *Science de la morale*, II: 130-32.
59. Even with its faults, a free economy was preferable to an authoritarian one: ibid., II: 70. He held that in theory state intervention in commerce would be more justifiable than in production but found that in current society this would be to attack a class which was especially important in defending liberty: ibid., II: 85-86.
60. *Critique philosophique*, 1872-I, pp. 216-17. He was clearly more sympathetic to those socialists, such as Proudhon and Fourier, who did not have such hopes: *Science de la morale*, II: 355.
61. *Science de la morale*, II: 385.
62. This follows his moral theory: constraint is the opposite of justice: ibid., I: 78-79.
63. Ibid., II: 328; *Critique philosophique*, 1876-II, p. 217.
64. *Science de la morale*, I: 265.
65. This is a truth partially grasped by Rousseau in his *Contrat social*, but he oscillated between the pure and the practical realms without a clear consciousness of the distinction between them. Taken as a treatise of pure morals or pure politics, the *Contrat social* is very penetrating, while on the practical level it contains some dangerous equivocations. Renouvier's contractualism is clear evidence of his links to the eighteenth century.
66. *Science de la morale*, I: 325-26.
67. See ibid., II: 151-52.
68. Ibid., I: 328.
69. See ibid., I: 330.
70. Ibid., II: 137.
71. Ibid., II: 166. In practice this condition never fully existed, so the principle had to be modified: ibid., II: 166-67.
72. Ibid., II: 276; like individuals, oppressed nations had a right to seek their freedom: ibid., II: 288.
73. See his discussion of tyrannicide: ibid., II: 267-72; of insurrection: ibid., II: 272-80; of secession: ibid., II: 280-82.
74. See ibid., I: 351-52.
75. Ibid., II: 276-79.
76. See ibid., II: 266-67.
77. See his discussion of emigration: ibid., II: 263-65; of passive resistance: ibid., II: 265-67; of conscientious objection: ibid., II: 296.
78. Monarchy and aristocracy were not excluded by reason: ibid., II: 148-49.
79. For his defense of the practical superiority of democracy, see ibid., II: 141.
80. The alternatives were worse: *Critique philosophique*, 1873-II, pp. 1-2.
81. *Science de la morale*, II: 164.

82. Ibid., II: 162–64.
83. Majority rule was a sort of convention of war, to limit the use of actual violence: ibid., II: 165; *Critique philosophique*, 1873-II, pp. 7–8. Ruling elites were necessary in the present world, and he defended indirect election as a means of regularizing their inevitable influence: *Science de la morale*, II: 143–44, 158–62. Existing democracy was thus a sort of mixed government in the Aristotelian sense: ibid., II: 222.
84. Executive power was always a threat to freedom: ibid., II: 216–22.
85. Ibid., II: 173.
86. Ibid., II: 135; see also ibid., I: 240.
87. See, in partial support, ibid., I: 370.
88. Ibid., II: 223.
89. Ibid., II: 231.
90. On the importance—and limitations—of education: ibid., I: 415; II: 224.
91. Droz, p. 110, attributed solidarism to Renouvier's influence.
92. Renouvier, too, saw continuing danger from the old, discredited authorities: *Science de la morale*, II: 386; he was especially pessimistic about the implantation of liberty in a country of long Catholic tradition: ibid., II: 256–57.
93. Renouvier had long recognized the major change in the character of Western society which would affect all political calculations: "Doubtless the preponderance acquired in our time by labor and the anticipated supremacy of the working classes gives us—indeed promises us—reasons for and guarantees of tranquillity which the ancients lacked, for their free activity had totally different ideals than those of production and exchange": ibid., II: 297–98. Here was one point of agreement with Herbert Spencer.
94. No law of progress: ibid., II: 346–47; progress as a modern substitute for divine grace: ibid., II: 379–80.
95. For his critique of determinism, see ibid., II: 356–85.
96. *Critique philosophique*, 1872-I, p. 8.
97. History had a goal—"the progressive realization of logic"—but its attainment was not certain or automatic: *Science de la morale*, II: 139; the degree of liberty in a society was the measure of its progress: ibid., II: 329.
98. On the Middle Ages as a regression: ibid., II: 331–45; for his lack of sympathy for the medieval church, see ibid., I: 357–60.
99. Regression was easier than progress: ibid., II: 225; he feared we might be entering a sort of positivist Middle Ages: ibid., II: 387–88. Continued struggle was necessary: *Critique philosophique*, 1875-I, p. 253.
100. For a prescient critique of positivist politics, see *Science de la morale*, II: 196–98.
101. Ibid., II: 283–92, especially 286, 287–88.
102. Ibid., II: 379, 383–84.
103. Ibid., I: 217–18.
104. Ibid., I: 214.
105. Ibid., I: 331–46.
106. Ibid., I: 349–50, 353.
107. Claude Digeon, p. 106, said that their program, "both vast and specific," was admirably suited to the interests of the republican Left.
108. *Critique philosophique*, 1876-I, pp. 370–71.
109. But see ibid., 1873-I, p. 87 and pp. 241–42, where he quoted at length and approvingly from Emile Littré's critique of monarchy.
110. Ibid., 1873-I, p. 346; 1875-I, pp. 20–21.

111. Ibid., 1873-I, pp. 342-44; the only real alternatives were the republic or Caesarism; ibid., 1872-I, p. 115; 1878-II, p. 289.

112. Ibid., 1874-I, pp. 177-84, 371-80.

113. Ibid., 1875-I, pp. 69-70.

114. Ibid., 1876-I, pp. 81-90.

115. Ibid., 1878-I, p. 71.

116. Ibid., 1876-II, pp. 225-31. For the same reason he respected Thiers, but he considered that Thiers's reputation would be forever marred by the unnecessary violence with which the Commune was put down: ibid., 1873-I, p. 60.

117. Ibid., 1876-II, pp. 220-21.

118. Ibid., 1876-I, p. 404; 1877-I, pp. 385-96.

119. See, for example, ibid., 1873-II, p. 147.

120. He noted that the first time science had played a role was in nineteenth-century Germany: ibid., 1874-II, p. 65; but he claimed to have shed his youthful Saint-Simonian belief in the need for unity of faith in a modern society: ibid., 1877-II, p. 277.

121. Ibid., 1876-II, p. 199; the church was a main source of French backwardness: ibid., 1873-II, pp. 148-49.

122. Ibid., 1873-II, p. 150; 1878-II, pp. 302, 308.

123. See ibid., 1873-I, p. 149; he called the church hostile to civil society and to the family: ibid., 1877-II, p. 289.

124. Approving commentary on and quotations from William Gladstone's attack on the Vatican Council: ibid., 1874-II, pp. 401-5; he feared the church was becoming more political and less religious: ibid., 1876-I, pp. 355-59.

125. *Critique philosophique*, 1875-II, p. 22.

126. Ibid., 1876-I, pp. 161-63, 243: he called this not a question of rights but of material reforms.

127. That is to say, an antisocial morality: ibid., 1874-I, p. 35; he favored the use of the Bible in state moral education: ibid., 1873-I, p. 167; he did not want to leave its interpretation solely in the hands of the church: ibid., 1876-I, pp. 246, 257-67. Renouvier carried his offensive against the moral education of the church to the point of wishing to close the "petits seminaires" (false seminaries, called such only to evade certain legislative restrictions), allowing the church to train only people who were already adults: ibid., 1876-I, pp. 367-68; 1877-I, pp. 234-35; 1878-II, p. 302.

128. Ibid., 1878-II, pp. 345-58.

129. Ibid., 1873-II, p. 406; 1875-II, pp. 22-23, 49, 51.

130. Ibid., 1878-II, pp. 597-98.

131. Ibid., 1873-I, p. 84; 1875-II, p. 21. The state would try this, with limited success, in 1905.

132. Ibid., 1872-I, p. 167: reacting against the defeat of 1870-71, he argued that the Latin spirit in religion was more conducive to liberty than the Germanic spirit, even going so far as to say a good word for some Jesuits. See also ibid., 1872-I, p. 279.

133. See, for example, ibid., 1873-II, p. 355.

134. Examples of his criticism of the French bourgeoisie: ibid., 1872-I, pp. 82, 86, 119; 1873-I, pp. 83-84; of the National Assembly of 1871: ibid., 1875-II, pp. 386-87; of the ruling classes: ibid., 1877-II, pp. 81-87, 167-73.

135. Ibid., 1873-I, p. 247.

136. Ibid., 1873-II, p. 403. See ibid., 1872-I, p. 120; while the bourgeoisie, taken broadly, had furnished all the country's leadership, it had done poorly in

choosing political leaders: ibid., 1873-I, p. 86. He did acknowledge that it is difficult to shed oligarchic habits for democratic ones: ibid., 1876-II, p. 214.

137. Ibid., 1872-I, p. 87.

138. Ibid., 1873-II, pp. 355–56.

139. Ibid., 1875-II, p. 391; 1877-II, pp. 85, 163–64.

140. Ibid., 1872-I, p. 77; for a similar list, see ibid., 1873-II, pp. 403–10; 1876-I, p. 163. See also ibid., 1876-I, p. 92; 1877-I, pp. 51–55.

141. Ibid., 1873-I, pp. 86–87.

142. Ibid., 1873-II, p. 355.

·IV·

1. Ferdinand Buisson, though hostile to religion in the primary and secondary schools, defended the teaching of the history of religion at the university level; there did not need to be any taboos in the preparation of the elite: *La foi laïque* (2d ed.; Paris: Hachette, 1913), pp. 222–26.

2. Ferdinand Buisson, *Jules Ferry et l'Ecole laïque* (Rodez: Forveille, 1911), pp. 19–20.

3. Ibid., p. 8.

4. See Louis Legrand, *L'influence du positivisme dans l'oeuvre scolaire de Jules Ferry* (Paris: Rivière, 1961).

5. Buisson, *Ferry*, p. 22.

6. See Eugen Weber, *Peasants into Frenchmen* (1976).

7. Before the overthrow of the empire, republicans had been in principle favorable to the constitutional referendum: Ch.-A. Grangé, *Les doctrines politiques du parti républicain à la fin du Second Empire* (Bordeaux: Cadoret, 1903), pp. 115–19. For an important discussion of this liberal position, see Georges Burdeau, *Libéralisme* (Paris: Seuil, 1979), pp. 202–6.

8. Thus rightly drawing the praise of Marxist historian Sanford Elwitt, *The Making of the Third Republic* (Baton Rouge: Louisiana State University Press, 1975).

9. *La morale professionnelle: l'homme politique* (Paris: La Revue du mois, 1907), p. 22.

10. Ferdinand Buisson and Charles Wagner, *Libre-pensée et protestantisme libéral* (Paris: Fischbacher, 1903), p. 39.

11. Buisson, *L'avenir du sentiment religieux* (Paris: Fischbacher, 1923), pp. 5–6.

12. *La crise de "l'Anticléricalisme"* (Paris: Revue politique et parlementaire, n.d.), pp. 7–8.

13. He ridiculed Christians for wasting time debating such points as the divinity of Christ when they should be out working for social causes: *Le christianisme libéral* (Paris: Cherbuliez, 1865), p. 56.

14. Buisson, *La religion, la morale et la science, et leur conflit dans l'éducation contemporaine* (Paris: Fischbacher, 1900), pp. 128–30, 136–37.

15. *Avenir*, pp. 6–7. But like Durkheim he saw the source of religious sentiment in the individual's awareness that there is something which transcends him: *Foi laïque*, p. 182.

16. See, for example, *Foi laïque*, pp. 181–90.

17. See, for example, *Religion*, pp. 186–87. Buisson kept biblical metaphors out of his speech and urged liberal Protestants to do likewise, lest others take them too literally.

18. See Buisson, *Jules Ferry*, and, for the three principles, *Foi laïque*, pp.

15-24. See also Raymond Poincaré's fulsome praise of Buisson in his preface to ibid.

19. *Foi laïque*, pp. 6-8.

20. Buisson, *La politique radicale* (Paris: Giard et Brière, 1908), p. 86.

21. *Foi laïque*, pp. 39-49, 277-82.

22. See ibid. and, especially, *Crise*.

23. *Foi laïque*, pp. 114-16, 177-80.

24. See ibid., pp. 101-17, 118-28; *Politique radicale*, pp. 88-96, *L'école et la nation en France* (n.p., n.d.), p. 14.

25. *Foi laïque*, pp. 80-89.

26. See *Morale professionnelle*, p. 22.

27. See *Christianisme libéral, Libre-pensée*, pp. 77-79; *Foi laïque*, p. 150; and *L'instituteur et la République* (Paris, 1909), pp. 9-10. But cf. *Foi laïque*, pp. 289-92.

28. See *Foi laïque*, pp. 297-99, and Poincaré in ibid., p. ix.

29. *Ecole*, p. 8; *Foi laïque*, pp. 307-8; *Avenir*.

30. *Foi laïque*, pp. xi-xiii, 162-76, 313-26.

31. Ibid., pp. 194-95; *Politique radicale*, pp. vi, 206-55.

32. *Foi laïque*, p. 200.

33. Ibid., p. 195.

34. *Politique radicale*, pp. 99, 210-17.

35. Buisson, *Le vote des femmes* (Paris: Dunod et Pinat, 1911). On proportional representation, see his *La réforme des moeurs politiques par la réforme electorale* (Paris: n.d.).

36. But earlier he had advocated educating women to better fill their place in the home: *Foi laïque*, pp. 25-31.

37. His lectures on Kant were published in the *Revue des cours et conférences* 7 (1899): 258-65, 306-14, 490-500, 633-40; 8 (1900): 8-15, 201-7.

38. Paul Janet and Gabriel Séailles, *Histoire de la philosophie* (Paris: Delagrave, 1887); Séailles, *La philosophie de Charles Renouvier: introduction à l'étude du néo-criticisme* (Paris: Alcan, 1905).

39. *Les affirmations de la conscience moderne* (Paris: Colin, 1903), p. 104.

40. Ibid., p. 111.

41. *Les affirmations de la conscience moderne: Education ou révolution* (Paris: Colin, 1904), pp. 172-73, 239. This is a different work from that cited in note 39. Hereafter called *Education ou révolution*.

42. See Université Populaire: Coopération des Idées, *Histoire de douze ans (1898-1910)*. Preface by Gabriel Séailles. (Paris: La coopération du livre, 1910).

43. *Education et révolution* (Paris: La coopération des idées, [1899?], pp. 2-5. Do not confuse this with the work cited in note 41. See also *Affirmations*, p. 109.

44. Séailles, *La philosophie et l'éducation du peuple* (Paris: Union pour l'action morale, 1896), pp. 11-13.

45. Séailles, *Une affirmation de la conscience moderne: le vrai patriotisme* (Paris: Société française pour l'arbitrage entre nations, n.d.), p. 22.

46. *Affirmations*, pp. 69, 228, 247.

47. *Education et révolution*, p. 9; *Education du peuple*, p. 13; *Education ou révolution*, pp. 169-72; see also *L'enseignement primaire et la politique: l'affaire Guéry* (Paris: Courrier européen, 1906).

48. See *Affirmations*, pp. 164, 180; *Education et révolution*, pp. 11-12. Séailles was active in the Union pour l'action morale.

49. See *Affirmations,* pp. 129, 135-36, 254; *Education du peuple,* p. 16; *Education ou révolution,* p. 95.
50. "Pourquoi les dogmes ne renaissent pas," *Affirmations,* pp. 1-114.
51. Ibid., p. 168; see also pp. 187, 191-214.

·V·

1. Alfred Espinas, *Des sociétés animales* (2d ed.; Paris: Germer Baillière, 1878), pp. 57-58, credited Hegel's evolutionism with breaking down the radical opposition between the individual and the state.
2. Of the people studied, Jean Izoulet put the most emphasis on race conflict in history. See his *L'âme française et les universités nouvelles selon l'esprit de la Révolution* (Paris: Colin, 1892), p. 13.
3. Izoulet, *La cité moderne et la métaphysique de la sociologie* (Paris: Alcan, 1894), pp. 383-92.
4. Izoulet, *L'âme française,* pp. 34-37, lamented that Social Darwinism had the effect of making science odious even to freethinkers.
5. The triumph of new ideas is generally associated with the rise of a new generation of thinkers, as Izoulet, *Cité moderne,* p. 550, observed: "The *evolution of ideas* takes place only through the *revolution of generations.*"
6. André Lalande, *Notice sur la vie et les travaux de M. Alfred Espinas* (Paris: Institut de France, 1925), p. 3.
7. There was also an effort to make the new, scientific history contribute to the restoration of French unity: see William Keylor, *Academy and Community* (Cambridge: Harvard University Press, 1975). Izoulet, *Cité moderne,* pp. 245-46, claimed that biological sociology's influence extended to encouraging the rise of historical method in political and juridical studies.
8. Izoulet also considered society an organism; Durkheim recognized a distinctive collective consciousness but was more hesitant about calling society an organism.
9. Izoulet, *Cité moderne,* pp. 345-55.
10. The biographical information on Espinas is derived from Lalande.
11. All references to *Des sociétés animales* are to the definitive second edition.
12. See Roger L. Gieger, "The Development of French Sociology, 1871-1905" (Ph.D. diss., University of Michigan, 1972).
13. Lalande, p. 16, calls Espinas the source of Durkheim's "réalisme sociale"; and Georges Davy, "L'oeuvre d'Espinas," *Revue philosophique* 96 (1923) notes his influence on Durkheim, and, indeed, suggests (p. 269) that with just a few different ideas Espinas could have played Durkheim's role in the establishment of French sociology.
14. Lalande, p. 11. On the relations of the ideas of Comte and Spencer see Espinas, *Sociétés animales,* pp. 113-30.
15. Davy, pp. 215, 245. Spencer rejected the *conscience collective.*
16. See Davy, p. 214.
17. Espinas originally shared Spencer's conviction that the world was becoming more pacific, but he eventually concluded that the reverse was more nearly true and, therefore, French national revival remained as important at the turn of the century as it had been thirty years earlier: see his "Etre ou ne pas être, ou du postulat de la sociologie," *Revue philosophique* 51 (1901): 479.
18. He later (ibid., p. 449) suggested that the study of animal societies was sufficiently remote from any applicability to present concerns to be

pursued without any parti-pris.

19. Espinas, agreeing with Durkheim, would attack Tarde for confusing psychology with sociology. Espinas's own interest in psychology was considerable. He was a schoolmate of the founder of French experimental psychology, Théodule Ribot, at the Ecole normale supérieure, and later collaborated with him on several projects.

20. "Etre ou ne pas être," p. 422.

21. *Sociétés animales*, p. 530.

22. Lalande, p. 13, puts it another way, saying that we can hardly imagine the spiritualist reaction, so much have times changed. He also notes, pp. 15–16, the interest stimulated in political circles by Espinas's work. Espinas's examiners considered that the importance which he attributed to Comte in the lengthy (150 pp.) historical introduction to his dissertation was politically imprudent in 1877, but Espinas preferred to delete the entire introduction rather than denature it. He restored the introduction in the second edition, published the following year. For this story see that introduction, pp. 95–96, and Lalande, pp. 13–14.

23. On why sociology must include animal societies see *Sociétés animales*, pp. 210–11, 217, 218.

24. Ibid., p. 214.

25. On the nation as an individual see ibid., pp. 223–24.

26. According to Davy, he did not draw this out till some twenty years after the publication of *Des sociétés animales* (p. 230).

27. *Sociétés animales*, pp. 534, 541.

28. Ibid., p. 379.

29. See ibid., pp. 406–7.

30. Ibid., p. 298.

31. Ibid., p. 530.

32. Ibid., pp. 199, 201–2, 203. While agreeing ("Les études sociologiques en France," *Revue philosophique* 14 (1882): 518–19) that nations had only a limited control over their destinies, Espinas objected (*Sociétés animales*, pp. 131–32) to Spencer's tendency to erect a politics of immobilism on this foundation.

33. *Sociétés animales*, pp. 147–48, 149.

34. Ibid., pp. 152, 547, 550, 552–53, 558.

35. He praised Comte for his effort to marry "thought and love, mind and heart, science and morality" (ibid., p. 114).

36. Ibid., pp. 474–75.

37. Ibid., pp. 544, 545–46. According to Lalande, pp. 26–27, Espinas even tried to derive the division of labor from the attraction of likes.

38. The nation was basically an involuntary association: "Etudes sociologiques," pp. 355–56. He later complained that the rise of internationalism and pacifism, based as they were on the false idea that we were entering an era of peace, inhibited the acceptance of his sociology with its emphasis on the importance of the nation: "Etre ou ne pas être," p. 461.

39. *Sociétés animales*, pp. 367–68.

40. "Etre ou ne pas être," p. 470.

41. Ibid., pp. 466–69.

42. "Etudes sociologiques," pp. 507–8.

43. Ibid., p. 358.

44. Ibid., p. 362.

45. Ibid.
46. Ibid., pp. 361–62.
47. Ibid., p. 364.
48. Ibid., p. 513.
49. It even led liberals into inconsistency with their principles, for example, by denying political rights to women: ibid., p. 515.
50. By exposing the limits of human malleability sociology could offer a safeguard against attempts to remake society in the name of somebody's abstract ideas: *Sociétés animales*, p. 150.
51. "Etre ou ne pas être," pp. 459–60.
52. With this concept of the individual, he thought, society could only be justified in terms of utilitarian interests: ibid., p. 477.
53. See, for example, *Sociétés animales*, pp. 456–57, 542.
54. See, for example, "Etre ou ne pas être," pp. 461–62.
55. "Etudes sociologiques," p. 345.
56. *Sociétés animales*, p. 517.
57. Ibid., pp. 528–29.
58. "Etudes sociologiques," p. 514.
59. Espinas, *Histoire des doctrines économiques* (Paris: Colin, 1891), p. 306.
60. Ibid., pp. 316–20.
61. Ibid., pp. 328, 332; "Etudes sociologiques," pp. 520–21.
62. "Etre ou ne pas être," p. 460; *Doctrines économiques*, p. 348.
63. *Doctrines économiques*, p. 335: "Governments, too, have a considerable role to play in the economic and social crisis that modern nations are going through. Being in full possession of themselves, the latter can direct their legislation and their policy toward a more equitable distribution of burdens and a better organization of production."
64. See Davy, p. 252; "Etre ou ne pas être," p. 480.
65. "Etudes sociologiques," p. 512.
66. Ibid., pp. 511–12.
67. *Sociétés animales*, p. 520.
68. "Etudes sociologiques," pp. 519–20.
69. For example, ibid., pp. 523–24.
70. "Etre ou ne pas être," pp. 462–63.
71. This is one of the major themes of "Etre ou ne pas être," pp. 449–80.
72. Ibid., pp. 455–57.
73. On the persistence of their opposition see ibid., pp. 453–55.
74. For the ideas he considered essential to social science see ibid., pp. 450–51.
75. For a sample see Davy, p. 255. Contemporary sociobiology is trying to avoid the errors of its ancestors: see Edward O. Wilson, *On Human Nature* (Cambridge: Harvard University Press, 1978).
76. "Etudes sociologiques," p. 528.
77. *Sociétés animales*, p. 139.
78. For Izoulet's biography see Emile Bocquillon, *Izoulet et son oeuvre* (Paris: Baudinière, 1943). A mark of the fleeting quality of Izoulet's fame is that there was an entry for him in the *Larousse du XXe siècle* (1931) but not in any later Larousse encyclopedia.
79. Bocquillon, p. 8.
80. Ibid., pp. 29–31.

81. Izoulet defended his dissertation in January 1895 before a committee headed by Paul Janet.

82. He thanked them publicly in his inaugural lecture, published as *Les quatre problèmes sociaux* (Paris: Armand Colin, 1898), p. 5.

83. Izoulet understood Durkheim to be saying that modern society was hell, but that nonetheless it must be the focus of all of man's moral obligations. See *Cité moderne*, pp. 607, 611-12, 614ff.; Bocquillon, pp. 152-55.

84. Bocquillon, p. 23.

85. According to ibid., p. 7; see Izoulet, *La rentrée de Dieu dans l'Ecole et dans l'Etat* (Paris: Fayard, 1925).

86. Izoulet tried, without much success, to distinguish between a *culte de la cité* (which he advocated) and a *culte de la patrie* (which he rejected): *Cité moderne*, pp. 456-68.

87. Capable, too, of ending the religious division which plagued France, acc. Bocquillon, p. 99.

88. See ibid., pp. 97-98, 224.

89. *Cité moderne*, p. 611.

90. Ibid., pp. 540-41; Izoulet denied that Nature could be "wrong" or "immoral": ibid., pp. 515-23.

91. Ibid., pp. 506, 507, 637. Bocquillon, pp. 303-5, claimed that because of his advocacy of a civic religion Izoulet became known as the "Confucius of the West."

92. *Cité moderne*, pp. 9-12.

93. Ibid., p. 79: "*Human civilization* is a chapter of *natural history,* which is, in its turn, a chapter of *cosmic evolution.*"

94. As Bocquillon, p. 193, put it: "Three bodies: the *animal* body, the *social* body, the *universal* body and three heads: Brain,   State,   God."

95. Ibid., p. 213.

96. *Quatre problèmes*, p. 12.

97. *Cité moderne*, pp. 222-51.

98. Ibid., p. 59.

99. On the division of labor: ibid., pp. 34-38; on the benefits of increasing specialization: ibid., pp. 104-5.

100. Ibid., pp. 69-70.

101. Ibid., p. 100.

102. Ibid., pp. 209-14. His *Ame française (The French Spirit)* was particularly marked by the defeat of 1870.

103. For the theorists of the elite, especially Vilfredo Pareto and Robert Michels, see H. Stuart Hughes, *Consciousness and Society: The Reorientation of European Social Thought, 1890-1930* (New York: Vintage, 1958), pp. 249-77.

104. *Cité moderne*, p. 355; see also pp. vii-ix.

105. Ibid., pp. viii, 444-46.

106. *Ame française*, p. 79.

107. Izoulet proposed to restore the feeling of solidarity by restoring the dignity of labor: *Cité moderne*, pp. 194-221.

108. Ibid., p. 122.

109. Ibid., p. 315.

110. Ibid., p. 324; see also pp. 434-46.

111. Ibid., pp. 411-24, 425-33. His effort to demonstrate the transition from animal appetite to human aspiration was rather embarrassed: ibid.,

pp. 310-30.

112. Ibid., pp. 134, 135-42.

113. Ibid., pp. 358, 153-61.

114. Ibid., pp. 331-44, 152-53, 149.

115. Ibid., pp. 447-55, 469-85.

116. Ibid., p. 556.

117. Liberal egalitarianism risked leading to an-archy: ibid., p. 354; see also p. 639.

118. *Quatre problèmes*, pp. 15-17.

119. Ibid., pp. 18-19; *Ame française*, p. 56.

120. *Cité moderne*, pp. 252-63.

121. Ibid., pp. 379, 557, 640ff.

122. Ibid., pp. 645, 647-50. See Bocquillon, p. 13.

123. See *Cité moderne*, pp. 524-41.

124. Like other social scientists of his day, Izoulet sometimes despaired of his countrymen's lack of aptitude for scientific thinking. He found the bourgeoisie little better than the mob in this respect and compared them unfavorably to the Germans: ibid., pp. 222-51. Nonetheless he looked to science to help revitalize the bourgeoisie: *Ame française*, p. 39.

125. *Civisme et sur-civisme* (Angoulême: Coquemond, 1958), pp. 34-45.

126. Human progress, Izoulet pointed out, was neither linear nor isochronous: *Cité moderne*, pp. 71-83. The quotation (his emphasis) is on pp. 114-15.

127. For a summary of his career see Gabriel Tarde, *On Communication and Social Influence:* Selected papers edited and with and introduction by Terry N. Clark (Chicago: University of Chicago Press, 1969), pp. 2-7. See also *Gabriel Tarde: introduction et pages choisies par ses fils* (Paris: Louis-Michaud, 1909), pp. 7-67. The most important study is Jean Milet, *Gabriel Tarde et la philosophie de l'histoire* (Paris: J. Vrin, 1970): see his "Introduction bio-bibliographique," pp. 11-57.

128. According to Milet, p. 85, contemporaries compared Tarde to Montesquieu and other great magistrates of the eighteenth century. On the persistence of his influence in the law faculties see Clark, *Tarde*, p. 69.

129. See Milet, p. 79.

130. Gabriel Tarde, *Les lois de l'imitation: étude sociologique* (Paris: Alcan, 1890), p. vi.

131. See Milet, p. 95.

132. Tarde, *La logique sociale*, 4th ed. (Paris: Alcan, 1913), p. xv: the progress of criminality was evidence that we were not headed toward some terrestrial paradise.

133. In *L'opinion et la foule* (Paris: Alcan, 1901), pp. 159-60, Tarde criticized purely individualistic conceptions of responsibility.

134. Ibid., p. 160.

135. Ibid., p. 207.

136. See Milet, p. 254. Tarde probably misunderstood what Durkheim meant in describing crime as normal. Durkheim certainly thought there was too much of it in his day, but he also thought societies could go too far in their efforts to stamp it out; crime was part of the price we pay for a freer society. Durkheim was undoubtedly right in this observation, but his attitude can lead to a moral relativism which in turn may favor an increase in crime.

137. Tarde, *Imitation*, pp. 148-55; Clark, *Tarde*, pp. 39-41; Tarde, *Psy-*

chologie économique (Paris: Alcan, 1902), I: 13.

138. *Imitation*, p. v, for his defense of analogies; pp. 1–40, for examples of biological metaphor; pp. 76–77, for examples of physical metaphor.

139. *Logique sociale*, p. 128.

140. Durkheim, like Espinas, would not recognize Tarde's psychology as genuinely *social* psychology because Tarde denied the existence of a *conscience collective.*

141. Thomas Kuhn, *The Structure of Scientific Revolutions* (Chicago: University of Chicago Press, 1962), has shown this to be normal in the natural sciences, so I guess we should not be surprised to find it in the social sciences.

142. See Milet, pp. 197–98.

143. See *Les lois de l'imitation,* cited above.

144. Tarde's idea of the great man was not so narrowly conceived as Izoulet's.

145. Tarde, *Les transformations du pouvoir* (Paris: Alcan, 1899), p. 182.

146. *L'opposition universelle, essai d'une théorie des contraires* (Paris: Alcan, 1897).

147. *Logique sociale*, pp. vii–viii.

148. He developed this distinction at length in *Imitation*, pp. 267–396.

149. *Tranformations du pouvoir*, p. 167.

150. Ibid., p. 119.

151. See Robert A. Nye, *The Origins of Crowd Psychology: Gustave LeBon and the Crisis of Mass Democracy in the Third Republic* (London: Sage, 1975).

152. *Transformation du pouvoir*, p. 157.

153. Ibid., pp. 140, 258.

154. Ibid., p. 212.

155. Ibid.

·VI·

1. See the biographical sketch by his grandson, Augustin Guyau, in his *La philosophie et la sociologie d'Alfred Fouillée* (Paris: Alcan, 1913).

2. For Fouillée's description of his method see *La liberté et le déterminisme* (Paris: Alcan, 1890), p. vi; see also his *Le socialisme et la sociologie réformiste*, 2d ed. (Paris: Alcan, 1909), pp. 359–60, 365.

3. See Fouillée, *Le mouvement positiviste et la conception sociologique du monde* (Paris: Alcan, 1896), pp. 262–63 and esp. p. 272.

4. On the difficulty of holding synthetic views see Fouillée, *Socialisme*, p. 64.

5. *Mouvement positiviste*, p. 337.

6. On the origins of the concept see Guyau, Ier Partie, Chap. 1.

7. For a more extensive definition of idée-force see Guyau, pp. 59–60.

8. While rejecting the idea that there can be such a thing as pure will or pure intelligence, Fouillée was inclined to the view that ultimate reality was psychic rather than physical: Guyau, pp. 25, 68.

9. For an overview see the bibliography.

10. *La liberté et le déterminisme* (Paris: Ladrange, 1872).

11. See his "Critique du matérialisme historique..." in *Socialisme*, Book I, Chap. 5, and also Chap. 6; see also *Mouvement positiviste*, pp. 86–87.

12. See Guyau, p. 54. Fouillée totally rejected Renouvier's argument for

the creation of the universe and the theory of numbers on which it rested: *Mouvement positiviste*, p. 42.

13. "Determinists have wrongly neglected to include the idea of free will among the forces that determine things" (*Liberté*, p. 225).

14. On psychic determinism see Guyau, p. 89; on the idée-force of freedom see ibid., pp. 36-37, 38-39. On how the idée-force of freedom conforms to both reason and experience see Fouillée, *La morale des idées-forces* (Paris: Alcan, 1907), IIe Partie, Book II, Chap. 1.

15. *Liberté*, p. 349.

16. For a systematic discussion of Fouillée's moral philosophy see his *Morale des idées-forces*.

17. Guyau, with some justice, calls Fouillée's debates with Renouvier over determinism "heroic struggles": p. 90.

18. On the Germans see Thomas E. Willey, *Back to Kant: The Revival of Kantianism in German Social and Historical Thought, 1860-1914* (Detroit: Wayne State University Press, 1978).

19. Fouillée criticized the reduction of sociology to biology as a reduction of the more complex to the more simple: *Mouvement positiviste*, p. 235.

20. Ibid., p. 30. Does Fouillée's evolutionism bear some resemblance to that of Julian Huxley?

21. See Guyau, pp. 82-83, 90-91, 93-94, 109.

22. See *Mouvement positiviste*, pp. 306-7, for Fouillée's summary of the theses of his *La psychologie des idées-forces* , 2 vols. (Paris: Alcan, 1893).

23. See his *Morale des idées-forces*, Ier Partie, Book I, Chap. 1.

24. Fouillée, *La démocratie politique et sociale en France* (Paris: Alcan, 1910), pp. 14-15.

25. For a minor example of his anticlericalism see his *Les études classiques et la démocratie* (Paris: Colin, 1898), p. 210.

26. For example, it blinds Marxists to the fact that progress has benefitted the working classes, too (*Socialisme*, pp. 281-82).

27. See ibid., pp. 125, 150-51.

28. Ibid., pp. 99-100.

29. Fouillée equally denied that "économisme" was scientific: ibid., Chap. 3.

30. For his critique of the labor theory of value see ibid., p. 238.

31. Fouillée, *La propriété sociale et la démocratie* (Paris: Hachette, 1884), p. 64; see also *Mouvement positiviste*, p. 252, and *Socialisme*, p. 76. For a thorough critique of the concept of distributive justice see F. A. Hayek, *The Constitution of Liberty* (Chicago: University of Chicago Press, 1960).

32. For example, the state may intervene to promote commutative justice in the area of the distribution of goods: *Propriété sociale*, Book I, Chap. 2.

33. For a discussion of reparative justice see Fouillée, *La science sociale contemporaine*, 2d ed. (Paris: Hachette, 1885), Book V, Chap. 3.

34. See *Socialisme*, p. 59.

35. "I can neither feel alone, nor think alone, nor talk alone, nor will alone, nor exist alone. And why should I complain about a law which, understood and accepted by our intelligence, becomes the law of solidarity, the law of universal fraternity?" (*Mouvement positiviste*, p. 192.)

36. How well did Fouillée know the Utilitarians? Did he neglect the social elements in utilitarianism?

37. For Fouillée's views on Renouvier see his *Critique des systèmes de morale contemporaines* (Paris: Baillière, 1883), Chap. 4.

38. On the theory of the *persuasif suprême* see *Morale des idées-forces*, Ier Partie, Book III, Chap. 2, and esp. p. 305. Fouillée rejected the search for certainty in morals as leading to monstrous results; *la morale* was necessarily problematic: *Critique*, p. xii.

39. This latter synthesis was the main theme of his *Mouvement positiviste;* see esp. pp. 1–2.

40. *Socialisme*, p. 30. Fouillée also insisted that political science must become independent, i.e., it must become a *science morale* in its own right and not merely the servant of some external *science morale: Démocratie politique*, introduction.

41. The new liberalism was more sanguine than the old about the possibility of getting where we want to be. Fouillée's expression of that goal—"For me to be totally free, everyone must be free"—was not new, but he thought mankind had at last found, through science, the path that would lead it as close as possible to the goal (*Liberté*, p. 299).

42. For his views of the sociologists, see *Mouvement positiviste*, p. 240.

43. In general, he argued, a purely positivist morals must fail because obligation cannot be founded on facts alone: ibid., pp. 329–32.

44. See *Socialisme*, p. 192.

45. For Fouillée's argument that society is an *organisme contractuel* see his introduction to *Démocratie politique*.

46. *Socialisme*, p. 52.

47. *Démocratie politique*, p. 19.

48. Paul Vogt has pointed out to me that Fouillée was at pains to defend his authorship of these terms in his *Les éléments sociologiques de la morale* (Paris: Alcan, 1905).

49. *Socialisme*, p. 126. On the combination of the organic and the voluntary in the nation see *Démocratie politique*, p. 84.

50. *Démocratie politique*, p. 116.

51. See ibid., Book II, on the nation, nationalism, and internationalism. Fouillée observed that the socialists' internationalism gave them no grounds on which to reject a claim to an equal share of the product of French industry on the part of the poor of Africa or Asia, thus anticipating one of the issues of the late twentieth century.

52. On national character see his *Psychologie du peuple français* (Paris: Alcan, 1898) and *Esquisse psychologique des peuples européens* (Paris: Alcan, 1903). His comments on the French philosophic tradition appear throughout his work.

53. A similar view was reflected in Mme Fouillée's children's classic, *Le tour du monde par deux enfants.*

54. *Socialisme*, Book III, Chap. 4, and esp. p. 301.

55. *Démocratie politique*, p. 194. Fouillée was hostile to any tendency, whether socialist or Durkheimian, to absorb people in their professional categories: ibid., pp. 47–48.

56. *Socialisme*, p. 180.

57. Some of these Durkheimians would be open to the same charge.

58. See *Mouvement positiviste*, p. 251.

59. *Socialisme*, p. 300. He agreed that the state should take over those functions which were necessary to society but not profitable, e.g., the post

office, education, workers' retirement: ibid., Book III, Chap. 4; see also Book IV, concl., part 5.

60. *Socialisme*, p. 105.

61. *Démocratie politique*, p. 196.

62. *Socialisme*, p. 156.

63. Ibid., p. 367. In general Fouillée argued that intervention by the state to redress the effects of the inequality of workers and employers is *not* socialism: ibid., Book II, Chap. 2, part 3. On social insurance see *Propriété sociale*, Book II, Chap. 4.

64. *Socialisme*, p. 79.

65. Ibid., p. 60.

66. *Démocratie politique*, p. 207. See also *Propriété sociale*, p. 38.

67. See *Propriété sociale*, Book I, Chap. 1.

68. *Socialisme*, Book IV, Chap. 2; these rights could, however, be regulated: *Propriété sociale*, Book I, Chap. 3.

69. Where the social element was preponderant over the individual, the state could intervene more extensively; for example, municipalities could buy and lease out all vacant terrain within their limits in order to prevent property speculation: *Propriété sociale*, Book I, Chap. 3. Taxation was legitimate to help those unable—temporarily or permanently—to help themselves, but it was even better for the state to seek to diminish social problems by more equitable taxation, establishment of labor exchanges, and the stimulation of enterprise: ibid., Book II, Chap. 4.

70. *Socialisme*, Book II, Chap. 2.

71. Examples of social property in advanced societies included: (1) collective capital and public services, (2) political power, (3) moral and intellectual instruction: *Propriété sociale*, preface.

72. "Les deux modes de propriété, particulière et collective, sont également nécessaires; l'un complète et corrige l'autre." *Socialisme*, p. 343. "On pourrait résumer le libéralisme économique dans cette formule:—Les individus libres propriétaires dans l'état libre propriétaire." *Propriété sociale*, p. 66.

73. See *Démocratie politique*, Book I, Chap. 3; Book III, Chap. 4.

74. Ibid., Book I, Chap. 4.

75. Ibid., avant-propos.

76. *Socialisme*, p. 42.

77. *Démocratie politique*, Book I, Chap. I, part 4.

78. On the danger of anarchy see ibid., p. 24. Fouillée was also concerned with democracy as a source of mediocrity.

79. Ibid., Book I, Chap. 1, parts 1-2.

80. On the right to vote as a complex of individual, contractual, and social elements see *Propriété sociale*, Book III, Chap. 1; and esp. pp. 168-69.

81. *Démocratie politique*, Book I, Chap. 5.

82. *Etudes classiques*, p. 3.

83. *Démocratie politique*, p. 78.

84. *Propriété sociale*, p. 289.

85. Scientific education could not be an adequate substitute because it was too practically oriented: *Etudes classiques*, pp. 6-7.

86. Ibid., pp. 7-8, 21. For a briefer summary of his views on secondary education see *Propriété sociale*, Book IV, Chap. 2.

87. He considered equality of education to be no more desirable than

the leveling of fortunes: *Etudes classiques,* p. 231. For a summary of his views of primary education see *Propriété sociale,* Book IV, Chap. 1.

88. See *Démocratie politique,* pp. 138–39, 157–58.

89. See ibid., p. 146.

90. See ibid., Book III, Chap. 2.

91. Ibid., Book I, Chap. 3.

92. *Etudes classiques,* p. 67.

93. *Démocratie politique,* p. 63.

94. Ibid., p. 45; but in *Propriété sociale,* Book III, Chap. 3, he inclined to the belief that proportional representation was too dangerous for present-day France; *scrutin de liste* was the best possibility under the circumstances.

95. *Démocratie politique,* Book I, Chap. 2; and also Chap. I, part 3.

96. Like most contemporaries he remained hostile to women's suffrage in a Catholic country: ibid., p. 54; see also *Propriété sociale,* Book III, Chap. 3.

97. On Fouillée's gradualism see *Mouvement positiviste,* pp. 256–57, and on his reformism see *Socialisme,* p. 62.

98. *Socialisme,* p. 100.

99. *Mouvement positiviste,* pp. 230, 248.

100. Ibid., preface, p. 10.

101. On Fouillée's belief in intellectual progress see ibid., p. 6.

102. Sociology, he thought, would advance a new "positive" idea of liberty as a *pouvoir effectif: Socialisme,* p. 8.

·VII·

1. The best appreciation is that of Anthony Giddens, "Durkheim's Political Sociology," *Sociological Review,* N.S. 19 (1971): 477–519, and *Capitalism and Modern Social Theory: An Analysis of the Writings of Marx, Durkheim and Max Weber* (Cambridge: Cambridge University Press, 1971). Since completing this chapter I have read the very important study by Bernard Lacroix, *Durkheim et la politique* (Paris: Fondation Nationale des Sciences Politiques, 1981) and find that it supports my interpretation.

2. Conservative: Talcott Parsons, Alvin Gouldner, Irving Zeitlin; Liberal: W. Paul Vogt, J.-C. Filloux, A. Giddens; Socialist: Steven Lukes, Annie Kriegel; Politically liberal but socially conservative: Lewis Coser, Robert Nisbet.

3. Giddens, "Durkheim's Political Sociology," p. 513; on his relations with the solidarist version of the new liberalism, see Steven Lukes, *Emile Durkheim: His Life and Work* (New York: Harper & Row, 1972), p. 351.

4. See Geiger, p. 135.

5. The most comprehensive biography is that by Steven Lukes, cited above.

6. See Giddens, "Durkheim's Political Sociology," pp. 479–80.

7. Durkheim, *Pragmatisme et sociologie,* ed. A. Cuvillier (Paris: J. Vrin, 1955), p. 163.

8. See Durkheim, "L'individualisme et les intellectuelles," *Revue bleue,* 4th series, 10 (1898); reprinted in *La science sociale et l'action,* ed. Jean-Claude Filloux (Paris: Presses universitaires de France, 1970), pp. 261–78. Geiger, p. 159, is wrong in seeing here "a casuistical redefinition of his old bête-noire, individualism."

9. Georges Davy, *L'homme, le fait social et le fait politique* (Paris: Mouton, 1973), p. 18.

10. On the political significance of Durkheim's nomination, see Geiger,

p. 148. See also Lukes, pp. 365–66.

11. See Giddens, "Durkheim's Political Sociology," p. 482.

12. *Science social et l'action*, p. 279.

13. He compares the role of the statesman to that of the physician: *Les règles de la méthode sociologique* (Paris: Alcan, 1895), p. 93.

14. *L'éducation morale* (Paris: Alcan, 1925), p. 62.

15. See his *Sociologie et philosophie*, ed. C. Bouglé (Paris: Alcan, 1924), p. 89, and *De la division du travail social* (Paris: Alcan, 1893), pp. 379–80.

16. For example, see his critique of other types of moral theory at the beginning of *Division du travail*, pp. 4–15.

17. Ibid., p. 460. On the identity of morality and social solidarity, see ibid., pp. 447–48. Cf. Bernard Lacroix, "La vocation originelle d'Emile Durkheim," *Revue française de sociologie* 17 (1976): 245: "Durkheim invented political science while seeking to establish a moral science."

18. On the fixed character of religious morality: *Education morale*, p. 121. On the moral role of the state: *Leçons de sociologie: physique des moeurs et du droit* (Paris: Presses universitaires de France, 1950), pp. 87–89.

19. *Education morale*, pp. 9–10: when throwing out religion, care is needed not to throw out morals.

20. *Division du travail*, pp. 447–48.

21. This is one point on which Durkheim agreed with Marx.

22. *Division du travail*, p. 380.

23. Is the idea of historical necessity an attempt to escape from the perils of moral relativism? For a critique of the tendency to confuse the is and the ought see W. Y. Elliott, *The Pragmatic Revolt in Politics: Syndicalism, Fascism, and the Constitutional State* (New York: Fertig, 1968), p. 23.

24. *Division du travail*, p. iv; *Règles*, pp. 60–61; *Sociologie et philosophie*, p. 89.

25. *Règles*, pp. 118–19, cited in *Pragmatisme*, p. 196.

26. See *Sociologie et philosophie*, pp. 57–58, 65.

27. See *Education morale*, pp. 4–6.

28. *Sociologie et philosophie*, pp. 69–70; see also *Education morale*, pp. 138–39.

29. *Education morale*, pp. 12–13.

30. Ibid., p. 79; *Division du travail*, p. 183: "la religion embrasse une portion de plus en plus petite de la vie sociale."

31. Alessandro Pizzorno, "Lecture actuelle de Durkheim," *Archives européennes de sociologie*, 4 (1963): 34, notes that while Durkheim repudiated the Comtean cult of humanity, he creates something similar in his "rendering sacred the cult of the human person."

32. See his "Représentations individuelles et représentations collectives," *Revue de métaphysique et de morale*, 6 (1898); reprinted in *Sociologie et philosophie*, pp. 1–48.

33. I agree with Giddens, "Durkheim's Political Sociology," pp. 477–78, on this, against Parsons and Nisbet, who see Durkheim's later work as moving away from this foundation.

34. *Division du travail*, p. 375.

35. Durkheim's language here clearly rejects the nostalgia implicit in Toennies' division of the two types of society into, respectively, *Gemeinschaft* and *Gesellschaft*.

36. See especially *Division du travail*, p. 139, for his definition.

37. See especially ibid., pp. 140–41, for his definition. Pizzorno, "Lecture actuelle," pp. 31–32, notes the parallel between Durkheim's passage from mechanical to organic solidarity and the evolutionist theory of the passage from homogeneity to heterogeneity, with the distinction that Durkheim tried to make social rather than biological factors dominant in this change.

38. *Division du travail*, pp. 160–63; on the delicacy of modern societies, see *Leçons*, p. 86.

39. *Division du travail* (2d ed.), p. iii; without a moral authority which people respect, society degenerates into the rule of the strongest.

40. *Science sociale et l'action*, pp. 331–32.

41. *Le suicide: étude de sociologie* (Paris: Alcan, 1893), pp. 272–82.

42. *Journal sociologique*, ed. Jean Duvignaud (Paris: Presses universitaires de France, 1969), pp. 266–67, 570.

43. *Règles*, pp. 172–73.

44. *Leçons*, p. 110.

45. Ibid., p. 241; *Science sociale et l'action*, p. 83.

46. *Science sociale et l'action*, pp. 268–69.

47. *Leçons*, p. 110.

48. See *Education morale*, p. 133.

49. *Science sociale et l'action*, p. 263. Bouglé, preface to *Sociologie et philosophie*, p. xv, remarked that "Durkheimian sociology is, on the contrary, an effort to establish and justify spiritualist tendencies in a new manner."

50. *Science sociale et l'action*, pp. 275–76.

51. Ibid., p. 203; on how state action is essential to individual freedom, see *Division du travail* (2d ed.), pp. iii–iv.

52. *Division du travail*, p. 186.

53. Ibid., p. 455. See Pizzorno, "Lecture actuelle," p. 9.

54. *Division du travail*, pp. 388–89.

55. See ibid., p. 322.

56. *Leçons*, pp. 70–71. Lukes, pp. 271–72, noted a parallel between Durkheim's view here and that of T. H. Green.

57. *L'Allemagne au-dessus de tout: la mentalité allemande et la guerre* (Paris: Colin, 1915). M. Marion Mitchell, "Emile Durkheim and the Philosophy of Nationalism," *Political Science Quarterly* 46 (1931): 104–6, is quite mistaken in seeing Durkheim's view as a transition from nineteenth-century humanitarianism toward Charles Maurras' integral nationalism.

58. Durkheim's views on this subject are found throughout his pedagogical lectures, published posthumously as *L'éducation morale* (1925).

59. See ibid.

60. Ibid., p. 86; *Science sociale et l'action*, pp. 299–300.

61. *Leçons*, pp. 88, 91; *Science sociale et l'action* p. 299.

62. *Leçons*, pp. 62–63.

63. *Science sociale et l'action*, pp. 207–8.

64. He stressed the importance of respect for the impersonal authority of the law: *Education morale*, p. 179.

65. *Leçons*, p. 61.

66. Ibid.

67. Birnbaum, "La conception durkheimienne de l'Etat: l'apolitisme des fonctionnaires," *Revue française de sociologie* 17 (1976): 248, 254. I do not find Birnbaum's argument about why Durkheim failed to develop a political

sociology convincing. See Lacroix, *Durkheim et la politique.*
68. *Division du travail,* p. 243.
69. *Leçons,* p. 65.
70. Note the sharp contrast with Max Weber.
71. *Division du travail,* p. 249.
72. *Leçons,* p. 101.
73. See *Science sociale et l'action,* pp. 196–97.
74. *Leçons,* pp. 82–83.
75. Ibid., p. 78.
76. For a comparison of this view with Marx's dialectic, see Armand Cuvillier, "Durkheim et Marx," *Cahiers internationaux de sociologie* 4 (1948): 75–97.
77. *Leçons,* pp. 38–39.
78. *Suicide,* pp. 436–37.
79. *Leçons,* p. 87.
80. Ibid., p. 114. *Division du travail* (2d ed.), pp. xxxii–xxxiii: "A society made up of an infinitely fine dust of unorganized individuals whom a hypertrophied state tries to encompass and to contain would constitute a veritable sociological monstrosity."
81. *Leçons,* pp. 114–15.
82. Ibid., p. 119.
83. Ibid., pp. 116–17. For the influence of Schaeffle on Durkheim's corporatism see Geiger, pp. 136–38.
84. *Division du travail,* p. 207.
85. Ibid. (2d ed.), pp. iv–v.
86. On the widespread interest in economic and professional representation in government see Harry Elmer Barnes, "Durkheim's Contribution to the Reconstruction of Political Theory," *Political Science Quarterly* 35 (1920): 236–54.
87. See his discussion in *Suicide,* pp. 434–42, and *Division du travail* (2d ed.), pp. xi–xii. Giddens, "Durkheim's Political Sociology," p. 487, links Durkheim's corporatism to *solidarisme.*
88. See *Division du travail* (2d ed.), pp. vi, xxx–xxxi.
89. Ibid., p. xxvii.
90. *Leçons,* pp. 49–50. Durkheim thought that the conflict of interest between workers and capitalists was such that the two groups should choose their representatives separately within the corporation.
91. Barnes, "Durkheim's Contribution," p. 251.
92. Lukes, p. 268.
93. *Suicide,* p. 448.
94. See Robert A. Nisbet, ed., *Emile Durkheim* (Englewood Cliffs: Prentice-Hall, 1965), pp. 68–69.
95. See W. Paul Vogt, "Anatomy of a 'Fin-de-siecle' Sociologist," *Reviews in European History* 1 (1975): 567–68. Cf. Lukes, pp. 76–77, 322, 546.
96. *Science sociale et l'action,* p. 244.
97. Ibid.
98. Not surprisingly, this struggle has continued to the present.
99. *Science sociale et l'action,* pp. 242–43.
100. Ibid.
101. *Socialism,* ed. Alvin W. Gouldner (New York: Collier, 1962). These lectures were originally edited and published by Marcel Mauss (Paris: Alcan,

1928). A useful recent edition is *Le socialisme: sa definition—ses débuts—la doctrine saint-simonienne*, Pref. Annie Kriegel (Paris: Les classiques des sciences humaines, 1978).

102. "We denote as socialist every doctrine which demands the connection of all economic functions, or of certain among them, which are at present time diffuse, to the directing and conscious centers of society" (*Socialism*, p. 54). "The fundamental communist idea—everywhere the same under scarcely different forms—is that private property is the source of selfishness and that from selfishness springs immorality" (ibid., p. 73).

103. Geiger, pp. 169, 335. Annie Kriegel (*Le socialisme*, p. 14), who thinks Durkheim to have been a socialist in pre-1917 terms, perhaps closest to the German Kathedersozialisten, has explained the significance of his definitions in a fine metaphor: "a reality too often ignored: socialism and communism are not even two distinct strong branches springing at the same height from a common trunk which is marxism; they are in their own right two distinct trunks from which certain branches come together and intermingle their leaves" (ibid., p. 15). Durkheim, on the contrary, attributed a position similar to the Kathedersozialisten to Fouillée: *Science sociale et l'action*, pp. 181–82. The influence of the Kathedersozialisten on Durkheim is analyzed thoroughly by Lacroix, *Durkheim et la politique*.

104. *Science sociale et l'action*, p. 289; *Socialism*, pp. 104–5.

105. *Leçons*, p. 253.

106. Ibid., pp. 170–71, 186–87, 202.

107. Ibid., p. 187.

108. Ibid., p. 202.

109. Ibid., p. 16.

110. Ibid., p. 39.

111. Ibid., p. 16.

112. See *Division du travail*, p. 423.

113. Ibid., p. 426.

114. Ibid., p. 420.

115. Ibid., p. 426.

116. *Leçons*, p. 250.

117. Ibid., pp. 258–59.

118. Pointed out by Lacroix, "Vocation originelle," p. 236. See also Nisbet, *Durkheim*, pp. 26–27.

119. Geiger, p. 126, says the same of Tarde's sociology.

120. See, for example, his letter to Bouglé, 9 mai 1899, in *Textes*, pp. 431–32.

121. On the declining importance of heredity: *Division du travail*, pp. 338–66.

122. Giddens, "Durkheim's Political Sociology," p. 497.

123. *Quid secundatus politicae scientiae instituendae contulerit* (Bordeaux: Gounouilhou, 1892). English trans. *Montesquieu and Rousseau: Forerunners of Sociology* (Ann Arbor: University of Michigan Press, 1960).

124. Especially as he considered the fundamental subject matter of sociology to be "systèmes de valeurs": *Sociologie et philosophie*, pp. 140–41.

125. This was an epoch-making work which cut off for many any possible return to the older tradition of moral philosophy by giving a sociological interpretation of that tradition which effectively undermined its premises. Lucien Lévy-Bruhl (1857–1939) also carried out a spirited defense of the

new sociological position by methodically refuting all the major arguments that had been raised against it. Extremely influential in its day, his work remains essential to any study of moral thought.

Lévy-Bruhl's main thesis was that all older moral philosophy is and has always been useless, since it is no more than an elaborate rationalization of the prevailing moral code. In spite of their differences over theory, philosophers in a given time and place always agree on almost every detail of practical morals; this practical convergence demonstrated the unimportance of their theories. Philosophy fails because it seeks to explain morals from within the human person—taken as a universal constant—when morals are really of social origin and vary from society to society.

What was needed, he insisted, was a *science* of morals which would treat moral codes and behavior not as ideals but as social facts. Only then would it be possible to discover the laws of moral life. Such a science was only in its infancy, and Lévy-Bruhl readily admitted that centuries might pass before it could reach the stage of practical application. While not seeking to minimize the obstacles to be overcome, he remained confident of ultimate success. This confidence was based on the elaborate analogies which he drew between the science of morals and the natural sciences. His analogies made an effective argument, the force of which can still be felt today, but he cannot really prove that they are valid analogies. That men have treated physical facts in the way we now treat social facts strongly suggests that our current attitude toward social facts may be in error, but it does not prove that social facts are, or ever will be, subject to the same kind of treatment that we now give physical facts.

The inability of this moral science to supply current remedies did not bother Lévy-Bruhl as it did Bouglé and most other Durkheimians. Men always have to act on the basis of current knowledge and under the pressure of current moral beliefs; sociological relativism may not help much in the present, but neither would it destroy moral conduct. Despite the modesty of his claims for the current state of the *science des moeurs*, Lévy-Bruhl did think there had been some progress and that current sociology could at least help men to adjust to change. In this it was an advance over moral philosophy's search for timeless truths. The pressure for immediately useful knowledge will always weigh heavily on sociology. While Lévy-Bruhl showed that it was possible to break even more clearly than Durkheim had done from the orientation of the past, he could not keep all his fellow Durkheimians on the narrow path of science.

126. See *Division du travail*, pp. 33–38. Giddens, "Durkheim's Political Sociology," pp. 506–7.

127. But things were not pathological simply because they were minority phenomena; the current economy was pathological because lacking in moral discipline: *Leçons*, p. 16.

128. *Division du travail*, p. 221: "In reality, everywhere that it is normal, social life is spontaneous; and where it is abnormal it cannot endure."

129. Geiger, p. 165, is right in seeing organic solidarity as an *a priori* ideal.

130. *Division du travail*, p. 409: "It is not necessary or even possible for social life to be without conflicts."

131. *Education morale*, p. 58: "Discipline . . . seems to us to be demanded by Nature itself." He also thought that, fortunately, the role of instinct in human affairs was declining: *Division du travail*, p. 360.

132. On Durkheim's sense of the long-range character of his goals: *Division du travail*, pp. 458–59. Durkheim's importance comes from the fact that he posed questions that are still with us: Pizzorno, "Lecture actuelle," p. 2.

·VIII·

1. See Philippe Besnard, "La formation de l'équipe de l'*Année sociologique*," *Revue française de sociologie* 20 (1979): 7–31.

2. The section of this chapter on Bouglé is largely taken from my article, "Sociologie et politique: le libéralisme de Célestin Bouglé," *Revue française de sociologie* 20 (1979): 141–61. Used with permission.

3. Bouglé published a report on his studies in Germany as *Les sciences sociales en Allemagne: les méthodes actuelles* (Paris: Alcan, 1896). On his involvement with the *Année* see his *Humanisme, sociologie, philosophie: remarques sur la conception française de la culture générale* (Paris: Hermann, 1938), p. 23. He appeared as a public defender of Durkheimian sociology with Durkheim's enthusiastic support: see Bouglé's rebuttal to Charles Andler in "Sociologie, psychologie et histoire," *Revue de métaphysique et de morale* 4 (1896): 362–71, and Durkheim's comments on the same in *Textes*, Vol. II: *Religion, morale, anomie*, Victor Karady, ed. (Paris: Editions de minuit [1975]), p. 392 (lettre à Bouglé, 16 mai 1896).

4. The thesis was published as *Les idées égalitaires: étude sociologique* (Paris: Alcan, 1899). See Durkheim's comments in *Textes*, II, 403–4; he expressed his approval of (and his reservations about) the finished work in a letter to Bouglé, 9 mai 1899, in ibid., pp. 430–32. Bouglé later linked this work with Durkheim's by describing them both as works of "morphologie sociale": *Bilan de la sociologie française contemporaine*, Nouv. ed. (Paris: Alcan, 1938), Chap. 3.

5. Durkheim was aware of Bouglé's reputation for being able to bridge the two groups and found it useful: see *Textes*, II: 420 (lettre à Bouglé, 1898–1899?). Bouglé observed that most of the *équipe* of the *Année* were, like himself, agrégés de philosophie (*Humanisme*, p. 30). His continued interest in contemporary philosophy and its relations to sociology was shown at the end of his life in his *Les maîtres de la philosophie universitaire en France* (Paris: Maloine, 1938), especially in the chapters on his contemporaries, Frédéric Rauh, Xavier Léon, and Dominique Parodi. The persisting influence of neo-Kantian philosophy on Bouglé's thought is examined by W. Paul Vogt, "Un durkheimien ambivalent: Célestin Bouglé," *Revue française de sociologie* 20 (1979): 123–39. See also Maurice Halbwachs, "Célestin Bouglé sociologue," *Revue de métaphysique et de morale*, 48 (1941): 28.

6. According to Bouglé, *Année sociologique* 4 (1901): 151.

7. See Durkheim's introduction to the first volume of the *Année sociologique*.

8. *Année sociologique* 1 (1898): 126.

9. The idea of a "modern consciousness" was very popular at that time; see the discussion by Gabriel Séailles, *Les affirmations de la conscience moderne*. See chapter IV above.

10. *Humanisme*, p. 31.

11. Bouglé's doubt that a *morale scientifique* was possible persisted throughout his life: *Bilan*, pp. 159–69. He had pointed out that the early advocates of a scientific morale were anti-democrats, see his *La démocratie devant la science: études critiques sur l'hérédité, la concurrence et la différen-*

ciation, 3d ed. (Paris: Alcan, 1923), pp. 1-20. See also Bouglé, *Leçons de sociologie sur l'évolution des valeurs,* 2d ed. (Paris: Colin, 1929), pp. 235-38.

12. See his *Syndicalisme et démocratie: impressions et réflexions* (Paris: Cornély, 1908), pp. 176-80. On the importance of education, see Bouglé, *Le solidarisme,* 2d ed. (Paris: Marcel Giard, 1924), pp. 182-204.

13. Elements of sociology were added to the program of the *classes de philosophie* (final year of the lycée) and the primary program: Bouglé, "La philosophie sociale et la pédagogie," preface added to the 4th ed. (1921) of his *Qu'est-ce que la sociologie?* See also the brief comments of M. Prevost in the *Dictionnaire de biographie française,* Vol. 6, col. 1294. For an example of Bouglé's postwar teaching at the Sorbonne see *Leçons* (cited in note 11 above).

14. I would like to thank W. Paul Vogt and Philippe Besnard for this information.

15. *Les idées égalitaires,* pp. 12-14. Durkheim thought that sociology could discover ends, while means belonged to the realm of practical politics.

16. But see Bouglé, *Pour la démocratie francaise: conférences populaires* (Paris: Cornély, [1900]), pp. 114-15; see also *Année sociologique* 10 (1907):185.

17. Bouglé, *La sociologie de Proudhon* (Paris: Colin, 1911), pp. 191-222.

18. *Allemagne,* p. 70; see also *Démocratie devant la science,* p. 228; *Année sociologique* 4 (1901): 112: "in order to prove the necessity of sociology it is important to show that certain special problems have so far remained unsolved, not that certain solutions are the only true ones." On the other hand, he thought that sociology could provide knowledge of the mechanisms of society which would be needed for any effective social reform: *Solidarisme,* p. 59.

19. *Solidarisme,* pp. 55-70.

20. *Qu'est-ce que la sociologie?* (Paris: Alcan, 1907), p. 143.

21. See *Démocratie devant la science,* pp. 301-2. Note also the observations of Arnold Brecht, *Political Theory,* pp. 171, 312. See also Bouglé, *Cours de sociologie: sociologie juridique, politique, religieuse, morale* ("Les cours de Sorbonne"; Paris: Centre de Documentation Universitaire, n.d.), p. 20.

22. "The most critical and most qualified of our comrades," says Hubert Bourgin, "considered him less a scholar than as a vulgariser of sociology. It's easy to understand why such a temperament should have been attracted by politics" (*L'Ecole normale et la politique* [Paris: Fayard, 1938]), p. 468. Despite Bourgin's animus against his former comrades, the observation is not unfounded. Another companion, Maurice Halbwachs, put it better: "Bouglé has been an alert propagandist for the sociologists—always in the breech, indefatigible." ("Célestin Bouglé sociologue," p. 47.)

23. *Revue de métaphysique et de morale* 10 (1902): 635-52. Based on a speech given at the Université Populaire of Montauban and reprinted in his *Vie spirituelle et action sociale* (Paris: Cornély, 1902), pp. 39-70. Cf. Durkheim, *La science sociale et l'action,* p. 269: "liberty of thought is the first of liberties."

24. "Crise du libéralisme," pp. 635-36.

25. Critics of Bouglé's article mistakenly saw him as taking a similarly absolutist stand about freedom of thought; see Paul Lapie, "La crise du libéralisme," *Revue de métaphysique et de morale* 10 (1902): 764-72, and D.

Parodi, "La crise du libéralisme," ibid., pp. 773-83.

26. Ibid., pp. 642-44.

27. These remain the two dangers of modern times: Bouglé, *Solidarisme.*

28. For a general discussion of this issue, see John E. Talbott, *The Politics of Educational Reform in France, 1918-1940* (Princeton: Princeton University Press, 1969), introduction.

29. In addition to the articles cited in note 6 above, see the following articles appearing in the *Revue de métaphysique et de morale:* Gustave Lanson, "A propos de la 'crise du libéralisme,'" 10 (1902): 748-63; B. Jacob, "La crise du libéralisme," 11 (1903): 110-20; D. Parodi, "Encore la crise du libéralisme," ibid., pp. 263-79.

30. See Nisbet, *Durkheim,* p. 58, for how closely this resembles Durkheim's views.

31. See Doris Goldstein, *Trial of Faith: Religion and Politics in Tocqueville's Thought* (New York: Elsevier, 1975).

32. For an interesting contemporary discussion see Gaston Richard, *La question sociale et le mouvement philosophique au XIXe siècle* (Paris: Colin, 1914).

33. See Bouglé's discussion in *Solidarisme;* see also his "Note sur les origines chrétiennes du solidarisme," *Revue de métaphysique et de morale* 14 (1906): 251-64; in *Syndicalisme,* pp. 212-25, he described solidarism as a rationalism of the Revolution by way of a positivism which has become more scientifically sophisticated. The best study of solidarism is the excellent series of articles by J. E. S. Hayward, "Solidarity: The Social History of an Idea in Nineteenth Century France," *International Review of Social History* 4 (1959): 261-84; "The Official Social Philosophy of the French Third Republic: Léon Bourgeois and Solidarisme," ibid., 6 (1961): 19-48; "Educational Pressure Groups and the Indoctrination of the Radical Ideology of Solidarism, 1895-1914," ibid., 8 (1963): 1-17. The extensive discussion in John A. Scott, *Republican Ideas and the Liberal Tradition in France, 1870-1914* (New York: Octagon, 1966 [orig. 1951]), pp. 157-86, is of little value.

34. *Solidarité* (Paris: Colin, 1896).

35. Bouglé in Bouglé et al., *Du sage antique au citoyen moderne: études sur la culture morale* (Paris: Colin, 1921), pp. 204-8.

36. Bouglé, *Démocratie devant la science,* p. 280.

37. See Hayward, "Official Social Philosophy," p. 19.

38. Bouglé found that many of the solidarists were too fond of organicist arguments: *Démocratie devant la science,* pp. 251-81. Solidarism and sociological liberalism both rest on the logical fallacy that because the members of a society are in fact in a state of mutual dependence, the individual has a moral obligation to fulfill his social function: see Brecht, p. 126.

39. See Bouglé, *Solidarisme,* pp. 140-81.

40. Ibid., p. 109. See also Lukes, *Durkheim,* p. 351.

41. *Démocratie devant la science,* pp. 279-80. Cf. Durkheim, *Textes,* II: 423 (lettre à Bouglé, 22 mars 1898): "It is necessary to show that whatever one does individualism is our only collective end, and that far from scattering us it is the only possible center around which we can rally, that it is already the whole positive content, the only real and durable achievement of Christianity." See also Alvin Gouldner, *The Coming Crisis of Western Sociology* (New York: Basic Books, 1970), p. 121.

42. There is a positive statement on the value of these ideas in *Soli-*

darisme, p. 6. Bouglé says that Marx and the sociologists agree that you do not change men by preaching, only by changing social conditions: *Chez les prophètes socialistes* (Paris: Alcan, 1918), pp. 196-207.

43. See *Vie spirituelle,* pp. 1-20, and also *Démocratie devant la science,* p. 132.

44. Bouglé did disagree with Proudhon on major points, e.g., Proudhon's insistence that religion and metaphysics were harmful to morality: *Sociologie de Proudhon,* pp. 191-222.

45. Ibid., p. 329.

46. Ibid., pp. v–xviii.

47. *Proudhon et notre temps* (Paris: Etienne Chiron, 1920). Scholars are indebted to Bouglé for his work with H. Moysset in editing a scholarly edition of Proudhon's *Oeuvres complètes,* 12 vols. (Paris: Marcel Rivière, 1923-61), unfortunately likely to remain uncompleted.

48. For comment on Durkheim's emphasis on these *corps intermédiaires,* see Nisbet, *Durkheim,* p. 62. Bouglé linked Durkheim with Constant and Tocqueville in his concern for the *corps intermédiaires,* "Crise du libéralisme," p. 649.

49. See *Sociologie de Proudhon,* pp. 29-81.

50. *Syndicalisme,* pp. 212-25. Though Radicalism needed to be modified by solidarism, it remained closest to the Principles of '89 and the Rights of Man, according to Bouglé, *Socialismes français: du "socialisme utopique" à la "démocratie industrielle"* (Paris: Colin, 1932), Chap. 4.

51. *Solidarisme,* p. 6.

52. Bouglé, *Socialismes français,* Chap. 10, on Proudhon and syndicalism.

53. *Vie spirituelle,* p. 20.

54. *Syndicalisme,* pp. 31-32, 119-203.

55. See his criticism of Victor Griffuelhes and Georges Sorel in ibid., pp. 90-95. Bouglé denied that Edouard Berth and Georges Sorel were authentic interpreters of syndicalism: *Socialismes français,* Chap. 10. For his praise of the German unions, see *Syndicalisme,* pp. 144-48; on his personal contacts with syndicalism, see ibid., p. vii; on the importance of syndicalism for women workers, see ibid., pp. 131-37.

56. He thought that many syndicalist leaders feared democracy: ibid., pp. 111-17. For Bouglé, democracy was the best means to effective and durable reforms: *Du sage antique,* pp. 230-42.

57. Bouglé managed to write a patriotic tract during World War I that was distinguished for its moderation and lack of hatred: Jean Breton [pseud.] *A l'arrière* (Paris: Delagrave, 1916). Bouglé opposed not only Hervé but also Jaurès on peace questions: *Syndicalisme,* pp. 83-89.

58. Ibid., pp. 102-7; see also *Vie spirituelle,* pp. 95-125.

59. "Les syndicats de fonctionnaires et les transformations de la puissance publique," in *Syndicalisme,* pp. 3-55; Bouglé cites (pp. 16-17) Durkheim in support of his own position. Bouglé also defended the *syndicats d'instituteurs*: ibid., pp. 193-98. See Pierre Birnbaum, "Conception durkheimienne," p. 252.

60. *Syndicalisme,* pp. 204-11. According to Bouglé, the Radical traditions of solidarism and federalism go hand in hand with syndicalism against the centralism and statism of the socialists.

61. *Démocratie devant la science,* p. 94.

62. Ibid., pp. 100-104.

63. See *Solidarisme*, pp. 182-204. He suggested that a collection of his speeches (on peace, cooperation, and feminism) would be useful in the Ecoles normales primaires: *De la sociologie à l'action sociale: Pacifisme—féminisme—coopération*, new ed. (Paris: Alcan, 1934), p. 6.

64. Bouglé asserted that Gide's social economy was separated from sociology by its normative tendencies: *Bilan*, Chap. 6. Shortly after his death in 1940, cooperative organizations brought out a memorial volume of Bouglé's cooperative writings: *Bienheureux les coopérateurs* (N.p.: Union suisse des coopératives de consommation [Bale]; Fédération nationale des coopératives de consommation [Paris]; Les propagateurs de la coopération [Bruxelles] [1940]).

65. Bouglé says that most of them were socialists: *Humanisme*, p. 34. He noted that Durkheim believed that sociology would be able to tell what was worthwhile in socialism: ibid., p. 33.

66. Bouglé dedicated his *Régime des castes* to Lucien Herr and *Chez les prophètes socialistes* to the memory of Jaurès: "I did not share all his hopes. I even had on more than on occasion publicly debated with him about them." See also *Démocratie devant la science*, pp. 160-86.

67. *Sociologie de Proudhon*, pp. 173, 189; see *Les idées égalitaires*, p. 35. He had expressed a sympathy for the socialists as early as 1896; see *Allemagne*, p. 16; see also *Solidarisme*, pp. 140-81.

68. See *Syndicalisme*, pp. 59-66.

69. *Pour la démocratie*, pp. 138-39.

70. "Did not the materialism which they [Marx and Engels] preferred get in their way and close off the sociological perspectives they had themselves opened?" (*Chez les prophètes*, p. 195).

71. Ibid., p. 245. On the French tradition, see *Allemagne*, p. 12; on Marxism, see ibid., p. 16. His most extensive critique of Marxism is in *Chez les prophètes*, pp. 185-246.

72. *Essais sur le régime des castes* (Paris: Alcan, 1908), p. 82: "Far from confirming the theses of 'materialist' philosophy, the sociological study of India tends rather to confirm what the most recent sociological research has demonstrated by all the means available to it: the preponderant role played by religion in the initial organization of societies."

73. "What socialism really aims at is merely a change from private capitalist to bureaucratic-managerial exploitation": Max Nomad, *Aspects of Revolt* (New York: Bookman, 1959), p. 69. Cf. Gouldner, *Coming Crisis*, p. 92: "Sociology was born, then, as the counterforce to the political economy of the middle class in the first quarter of the nineteenth century."

74. Cf. ibid., p. 230: "The academic sociologist still speaks from the standpoint and represents the claims of the educated nonpropertied sectors of the middle class, who now find the Welfare State a uniquely suitable fulfillment of their vested professional interests, their elite ambitions, and their liberalism—which is to say their social utilitarianism."

75. See Birnbaum, "Conception durkheimienne," pp. 247-58.

76. *Leçons*, p. 9. But he also points out that values are not arbitrary, changeable at will, because they come from society: ibid., pp. 12-16. Sociology could also help the teacher choose which values to promote (by showing what fits current society, not necessarily what is "right"): ibid., pp. 55-57.

77. Democracy was, after all, a social fact, one that all sociological sys-

tems had to account for. Bouglé showed that Spencer and Tarde, as well as Durkheim, did just this: "Sociologie et démocratie," *Revue de métaphysique et de morale* 4 (1896): 123–26.

78. See Susannah Barrows, "Crowd Psychology in Late 19th Century France: The Riddle of the Sphinx," (Ph.D. diss., Yale University, 1977).

79. For Bouglé's views of Social Darwinism, see *Démocratie devant la science*, pp. 187–92; on the anthropo-sociologists (Otto Ammon and Vacher de Lapouge) see "Anthropologie et démocratie," *Revue de métaphysique et de morale* 5 (1897): 443–61; on the bio-psycho-sociologie of Jacques Novicow, see *Année sociologique* 1 (1898): 135; on solidarism as a counteraction to "le pessimisme darwinien," see *Solidarisme*, p. 70.

80. See Barrows and Roger Geiger; see also Nye.

81. On Bouglé as an orator see Gabriel Séailles, preface to *Pour la démocratie*, p. iv; Bourgin, pp. 468–69; and Halbwachs, p. 47.

82. Like Durkheim, Bouglé was an early member of the Ligue des droits de l'homme; see *Textes*, II: 417–18 (lettre à Bouglé, 18 mars 1898); see also ibid., p. 428, where Durkheim praises Bouglé's Dreyfusard speeches.

83. See *Pour la démocratie*, pp. 1–39.

84. Halbwachs justly observed that Bouglé's "democratic individualism" and moralism did not lead him away from the sociological point of view (pp. 44–45). Bouglé continued this message after 1918: see *Action sociale*, pp. 55–63.

85. *Démocratie devant la science*, pp. 1–20.

86. *Vie spirituelle*, p. 12: "In the world of the mind as in the world of matter, force undergoes various transformations. Well guided intellectual light will produce moral heat, which will in turn produce economic movement." Between the wars Bouglé argued that while science had served all causes, both good and bad, it was now working for the moral unification of mankind, and the spread of scientific culture with its critical spirit among the masses would work for peace (*Action sociale*, pp. 46–49).

87. See *Démocratie devant la science*, pp. 1–20, and 111–15, where he attacks the argument that differentiation equals progress and that therefore democracy equals decadence. See also *Revue des cours et conférences* 9 (1900–1901): 328.

88. See *Démocratie devant la science*, p. 303.

89. *Revue de métaphysique et de morale* 5 (1897): 460.

90. See Bouglé, "Philosophie de l'antisemitisme: l'idée de race," in *Pour la démocratie*, pp. 41–71, esp. pp. 43–46.

91. On this latter, see especially *Qu'est-ce que la sociologie?*, pp. 3–32.

92. One example is in *Année sociologique* 10 (1907): 419; see also ibid., 12 (1913): 479, contra Robert Michaels. Other examples of Bouglé's articles in defense of sociology were collected in *Qu'est-ce que la sociologie?*

93. *Essais sur le régime des castes* (Paris: Alcan, 1908). Like most of the Durkheimians, Bouglé worked from printed sources rather than in the field. This work was essentially a synthesis based on monographic studies in French, German, and English. For a summary, see Halbwachs, pp. 39–42.

94. W. Paul Vogt, "Sociology and Political Commitment in the Third French Republic," paper presented at the Social Science History Association, 22 October 1977, argues that the last chapter of the *Régime des castes* is significantly different in methodology from *Les idées égalitaires*.

95. Parodi, "Crise du libéralisme," p. 776, wrongly suggests that Bouglé's

position is close to that of natural law theory.

96. It also enabled Bouglé to escape the older liberals' prejudice against women. See his defense of feminism and equality in *Action sociale*, pp. 95-111. Brecht, pp. 188-89, observes that "twentieth-century science has made perhaps its most important contribution by merely recognizing the nonscientific character of the unlimited trust in progress and science and of many specific predictions [by nineteenth-century social thinkers]."

97. *Année sociologique* 2 (1899): 167.

98. See Brecht, p. 174.

99. *Humanisme*, p. 33.

100. *Action sociale*, pp. 67-75.

101. *Syndicalisme*, pp. 169-75.

102. *Humanisme*, p. 38.

103. Ibid., p. 35: "Those among the Durkheimians who had to take on administrative functions in the University and to exercise a reforming influence on this or that branch of instruction could not fail to remember his lessons. It was almost inevitable that they would be tempted to lean on him [Durkheim] in the work of moral education with which they were involved." He lamented that criticism had persisted even after the Great War had demonstrated the moral strength of the generations trained in the Ecole laïque: *Leçons*, pp. 123-27. The *conscience collective*, he thought, was tending increasingly to exert itself directly without the intermediary of religion: ibid., pp. 153-56; this favored the development of liberty: ibid., pp. 203-4.

104. *Solidarisme*, p. 139.

105. *Sociologie de Proudhon*, p. 155.

106. See Michel Halbecq, *L'état, son autorité, son pouvoir (1880-1962)* (Paris: Librairie générale de droit et de jurisprudence, 1965), p. 165.

107. The magnitude of the challenge is reflected in an anonymous review in the *Revue du droit public* 30 (1913): 427.

108. For an analysis of his thought by a close disciple, see Roger Bonnard, *Léon Duguit, ses oeuvres, sa doctrine* (Paris: Marcel Giard, 1929); a more objective account is that of Paul Cintura, "La pensée politique de Léon Duguit," *Revue juridique et économique du Sud-Ouest: série juridique* 19 (1968): 67-98.

109. For Duguit's career, see Marcel Laborde-Lacoste, "La vie et la personnalité de Léon Duguit," *Revue juridique et économique du Sud-Ouest: série juridique* 10 (1959): 93-114.

110. Duguit, *Le droit constitutionnel et la sociologie* (Paris: Colin, 1889). According to Cintura, pp. 75-77, there were already some Durkheimian elements in this early work. See also Bonnard, pp. 8-12.

111. I am uncertain whether Durkheim had any influence on this change. While at Bordeaux he was a regular guest of the Duguits, along with the historian Camille Jullian and the philosopher of science Pierre Duhem: Laborde-Lacoste, pp. 110-14. Duguit admitted his error and agreed that the biological world and the social world are governed by different sorts of laws: *L'état, le droit objectif et la loi positive* (Paris: Fontemoing, 1901), p. 16.

112. It is important to distinguish Duguit's application of positivism to the study of law from what is commonly called "legal positivism," a view which holds that the only meaningful law is that enacted by legitimate authorities; see Halbecq, p. 61.

113. See *Droit constitutionnel*, p. 6; *L'état*, p. 19; *Les transformations du droit public* (Paris: Colin, 1913), pp. xv–xvi. On the relations of his ideas to Durkheim's see Milan P. Markovitch, *La doctrine sociale de Duguit: ses idées sur le syndicalisme et la représentation professionnelle* (Paris: Pierre Bossuet, 1933), pp. 119–21, 157–58.

114. Elliott, p. 255, argues that had Duguit succeeded, it would have meant leaving out large portions of human activity.

115. The authority of government derived from what it did, not from what it was: Duguit, *Traité de droit constitutionnel*, Vol. I: *Théorie générale de l'Etat* (Paris: Fontemoing, 1911), p. 24. See Bonnard, p. 39.

116. Halbecq, p. 63, argues that Duguit introduced more finality than Comte. Duguit called the *conscience collective* pure metaphysics: *L'état*, pp. 3–9. Bonnard defends Duguit's consistency, pp. 24–27, 32–33, 36. On the other hand, the Durkheimian Charles Eisenmann said that Duguit was not a sociologist but a "philosophe ou moraliste politique": "Deux théoriciens du droit: Duguit et Hauriou," *Revue philosophique* 110 (1930): 247. Other critics who found Duguit unable to maintain his purely positivist stance include Elliott, p. 301, and Louis Le Fur, "Le fondement du droit dans la doctrine de Léon Duguit," *Archives de philosophie du droit et de sociologie juridique* (1932), pp. 181, 200–203.

117. *Tranformations*, pp. xvi, 27–28.

118. *L'état*, p. 14. Elliott, p. 264, shows an unexpected parallel between Duguit and T. H. Green on the limitation of rights.

119. *Traité*, I: 11–13. See Cintura, p. 85.

120. See Cintura, p. 88.

121. The idea of duty seemed less metaphysical to Duguit than the idea of right: Le Fur, p. 190. See also Bonnard, p. 38; Eisenmann, pp. 237–38.

122. Halbecq, p. 219, thinks that Duguit sticks to his principles here, but Brecht, *Political Theory*, p. 126, shows that Duguit's argument requires additional premises which he claimed to have avoided.

123. See *Traité*, I: 18–19.

124. See ibid., I: 12.

125. See ibid., I: 19–20. Cropsey, *Political Philosophy*, pp. 124–25, shows this to be one of the basic problems of liberalism: the collapse of the distinction between duty and interest which results from liberal efforts to harmonize perfect freedom and perfect integration.

126. *Traité*, I: 293, 361; *L'état*, pp. 3–9.

127. *Traité*, I: 29, 33–34.

128. Ibid., pp. 37–38. See Harold J. Laski, "La conception de l'Etat de Léon Duguit," *Archives de philosophie du droit et de la sociologie juridique* (1932), pp. 121–34.

129. Halbecq, p. 242, observes that Duguit agreed with Treitschke, "Der Staat ist Macht."

130. Obedience to the law remained an obligation even though sovereignty was a fiction: *Transformations*, p. 75. See Cintura, p. 96.

131. Neither does Cintura's commentary, p. 161. Le Fur, pp. 196–99, argues that right and justice are simply matters of majority opinion for Duguit.

132. The *règle de droit* furnishes no clear guide as to whether a specific proposal in fact promotes solidarity. See Laski, pp. 129–30; Halbecq, p. 185.

133. Several commentators have argued that Duguit nonetheless put him-

self in the natural law tradition without realizing it: Le Fur, pp. 193-94; Elliott, p. 297; Halbecq, p. 16.

134. See *Transformations*, pp. 65-66.

135. Ibid., pp. 44-45; criticized by Eisenmann, p. 245.

136. *Traité*, I: 153; see Eisenmann, p. 244.

137. On the problems of this view, see Eisenmann, pp. 240-42; Elliott, pp. 297-98; Halbecq, p. 215.

138. Those two alternatives being, according to Duguit (*L'état*, p. 10), the two possible outcomes of the traditional view of the state. The parallel between Duguit and Rousseau is drawn by Cintura, pp. 182-83, 191. Le Fur, p. 206, and Maurice Hauriou (according to a review by Gaston Jèze in *Revue du droit public* 29 [1912]: 180-83) saw Duguit as tending to anarchy; Elliott, pp. 43, 267, finds support for fascism.

139. Though, as we have seen, he rejects the conscience collective: *L'état*, pp. 3-9.

140. *Traité*, I: 15.

141. See Duguit, "Le syndicalisme," *Revue politique et parlementaire* (10 June 1908), pp. 472-93. The most extensive discussion is that of Markovitch.

142. "Le syndicalisme," pp. 473-75.

143. Ibid., pp. 476-78, 479, 480.

144. *Traité*, I: 534-35; he considered anarchism just a growing pain.

145. "Le syndicalisme," pp. 480-81.

146. He assumed this development was irresistible: *Traité*, I: 294. In general he assumed a decline of the citizen and a rise of the producer to be characteristic of modern society: Cintura, p. 172.

147. See Laborde-Lacoste, pp. 106-7; Cintura, p. 69.

148. On occupational representation, see *Traité*, I: 388-92; "Le syndicalisme," p. 483. On continued need for a bicameral legislature: *Traité*, I: 367-71.

149. It would also give legislative representation to both kinds of solidarity: *Traité*, I: 297. For criticism, see Cintura, p. 184; Markovitch, pp. 222-50.

150. Cintura, pp. 69-70; Markovitch, pp. 171-72.

151. *Transformations*, pp. 121-29.

152. Like Buisson, he favored Proportional Representation because it was rational, even though its application in France would probably have had undesirable results: see *Traité*, I: 375-79.

153. "Le syndicalisme," p. 482. According to Halbecq, p. 234, Duguit went beyond Durkheim in seeing association as creative of liberty, not merely of integration, but Durkheim thought this too. Cropsey, p. 125, notes that twentieth-century liberalism turned to interest groups to avoid the old notion of a common good but then had to seek protection against the egoism of the interest groups by looking beyond property.

154. *Traité*, I: 462; Cintura, pp. 176-77.

155. *Transformations*, p. xix.

156. Ibid., p. xvii; *Traité*, I: 101-2.

157. *Traité*, I: 320-21.

158. See *Transformations*, pp. 33-72.

159. Respected even by people who rejected his philosophy, like François Gény and Gaston Jèze: Bonnard, p. 23.

160. *Traité*, I: 452, 457-67, esp. 465; *Transformations*, pp. 107-12.

161. "Le syndicalisme," p. 493; *Traité*, I: 466; *Tranformations*, pp. 128-29.

162. "Le syndicalisme," pp. 484-87.

163. *Traité*, I: 460; Duguit proposed that fonctionnaires should share in the profits brought about by their efficiency, for example, in the Post Office: ibid., pp. 462-63. See also "Le syndicalisme," p. 491.

164. Agreeing with Durkheim on this: *Traité*, I: 512-22; *Transformations*, p. 155; according to Markovitch, pp. 55-56, he opposed all strikes.

165. See *Transformations*, pp. 205, 222-25. See Charles E. Freedeman, *The Conseil d'Etat in Modern France* (New York: Columbia University Press, 1961).

166. "Le syndicalisme," p. 492. He considered the traditional defense of property an important breach in the doctrine of sovereignty: *Transformations*, pp. 227-28. See also Le Fur, p. 190, and Achille Mestre, "Remarques sur la notion de propriété d'après Duguit," *Archives de philosophie du droit et de la sociologie juridique* (1932), pp. 163-73.

167. The labor theory of the origins of property, adopted by many liberals, seemed to Duguit to lead to communism: *Traité*, I: 20.

168. See Laborde-Lacoste, pp. 108-10.

169. A.-J. Boye, "Souvenirs personnels sur Léon Duguit," *Revue juridique et économique du Sud-Ouest: série juridique* 10 (1959): 121-23.

170. See, for example, Markovitch, p. 220, and Halbecq, p. 117.

171. Duguit, *Droit constitutionnel*, p. 4, proposed converting the law schools into faculties of social science. Halbecq, p. 165, relates the rise of sociological jurisprudence, led by Duguit, to the rise of the Radicals in national politics.

172. Cintura, p. 166.

173. See, for example, Jean-François Revel, *Ni Marx, Ni Jésus.*

Bibliography

&

PRIMARY AUTHORS (in the order of their appearance in the text)

FRANCK, Adolphe. *Le communisme jugé par l'histoire.* Paris: Joubert, 1848.
  De l'instruction obligatoire, une leçon au Collège de France. Paris: Raçon, 1862.
  Essais de critique philosophique. Paris: Hachette, 1885.
  Lettres sur la guerre de 1870, à sa Majesté le roi Guillaume, aux populations allemandes, aux puissances neutres. Milan: Dumollard frères, 1871.
  Moralistes et philosophes. Paris: Didier, 1872.
  Nouveaux essais de critique philosophique. Paris: Hachette, 1890.
  Philosophie du droit civil. Paris: Alcan, 1886.
  Philosophie et religion. Paris: Didier, 1867.
  Projet de constitution: deuxième leçon du cours de droit naturel et de droit des gens au Collège de France. Paris: Le Chevalier, 1872.
  La vraie et la fausse égalité. Paris: Hachette, 1867.
  (Editor.) *Dictionnaire des sciences philosophiques, par une Société de professeurs de philosophie.* 6 vols. Paris: Hachette, 1844–52.
  Works about:
  A la mémoire d'Adolphe Franck: discours et articles. Paris: Montorier, 1893.
  Institut de France. Académie des sciences morales et politiques. *Funérailles de M. Franck: discours prononcés par M. Dareste et M. Gaston Boissier.* Paris, 1893.

CARO, Elme-Marie. *Etudes morales sur le temps présent.* 5th ed. Paris: Hachette, 1887 [1st ed. 1855].
  Funérailles de M. E. About,...le...19 janvier 1885: Discours de M. Caro. Paris: Firmin-Didot, 1885.

L'idée de Dieu et ses nouveaux critiques. 2d ed. Paris: Hachette, 1864 [1st ed. 1864?].

Les jours d'épreuve, 1870-1871. Paris: Hachette, 1872.

M. Littré et le positivisme. Paris: Hachette, 1883.

Le matérialisme et la science. 5th ed. Paris: Hachette, 1890 [1st ed. 1867].

Nouvelles études morales sur le temps présent. Paris: Hachette, 1869.

Problèmes de morale sociale. 2d ed. Paris: Hachette, 1887 [1st ed. 1876].

Works about:

Institut de France. Académie française. *Funérailles de M. Caro, le 15 juillet 1887: discours de M. Auguste Himly.* Paris, 1887.

Leguay, P. "Elme-Marie Caro," *Dictionnaire de biographie française,* vol. 7, pp. 1190-91.

Waddington, Charles. *Notice sur M. E. Caro.* Paris, 1889.

JANET, Paul. *Histoire de la science politique dans ses rapports avec la morale.* 5th ed. Paris: Alcan, 1924. [1st ed. titled *Histoire de la philosophie morale et politique, dans l'antiquité et les temps modernes.* Paris: Ladrange, 1858.]

Les problèmes du XIXᵉ siècle: la politique, la littérature, la science, la philosophie, la religion. Paris: Michel Lévy frères, 1872.

Les origines du socialisme contemporaine. Paris: Baillière, 1883.

(Editor, with Gabriel Séailles.) *Histoire de la philosophie.* Paris: Delagrave, 1887.

Works about:

Boutroux, Emile. *Notice sur Paul Janet.* (Extrait de l'Annuaire de l'Association des anciens élèves de l'Ecole normale pour 1900). N.p., n.d.

Picot, Georges. *Paul Janet: notice historique lue en séance publique le 6 decembre 1902.* Paris: Hachette, 1903 [bibliography].

Séailles, Gabriel, "M. Paul Janet: leçon d'inauguration de M. Gabriel Séailles, professeur à l'Université de Paris," *Revue des cours et conférences* 7 (1898-99): 647-65.

SIMON (François Jules SUISSE, called), Jules. *La liberté.* 2 vols. Paris: Hachette, 1859.

La politique radicale. Paris: Lacroix, Verboeckhoven, 1868.

Works about:

Bertocci, Philip A. *Jules Simon: Republican Anticlericalism and Cultural Politics in France, 1848-1886.* Columbia: University of Missouri Press, 1978.

RENOUVIER, Charles. *Essais de critique générale. Premier essai. Analyse générale de la connaissance. Bornes de la connaissance.* Paris: Ladrange, 1854.

Essais de critique générale. Deuxième essai. L'homme: la raison, la passion, la liberté, la certitude, la probabilité morale. Paris: Ladrange, 1858.

Essais de critique générale. Troisième essai. Les principes de la nature; Quatrième essai. Introduction à la philosophie analytique de l'histoire. 2 vols. Paris: Ladrange, 1864.

Les derniers entretiens recueillis par Louis Prat. Paris: Colin, 1904.

Manuel de philosophie moderne. Paris: Paulin, 1842.
Manuel républicain de l'homme et du citoyen. Nouvelle édition publiée avec une notice sur Charles Renouvier, un commentaire et des extraits de ses oeuvres par Jules Thomas. Paris: Colin, 1904 [1st ed. 1848].
La nouvelle monadologie. Paris: Colin, 1899.
Le personnalisme. Paris: Alcan, 1903.
Science de la morale. 2d ed. 2 vols. Paris: Alcan, 1908 [1st ed. Ladrange, 1869].
Uchronie: l'utopie dans l'histoire; esquisse historique du développement de la civilisation européenne, tel qu'il n'a pas été, tel qu'il aurait pu être. Paris: Critique philosophique, 1876.
(Editor.) *La critique philosophique.* 1872–1889.
(Editor.) *La critique religieuse.* 1879–1885.
Works about:
Cornwell, Irène. *Les principes du droit dans la philosophie de Charles Renouvier. Le droit international.* Paris: Presses universitaires de France, 1924.
Foucher, Louis. *La jeunesse de Renouvier et sa première philosophie, 1815-1854, suivi d'une bibliographie chronologique de Charles Renouvier.* Paris: Vrin, 1927 [bibliography covers entire life].
Hamelin, Octave. *Le système de Renouvier.* Paris: Vrin, 1927.
Milhaud, Gaston. *La philosophie de Charles Renouvier.* Paris: Vrin, 1927.
Picard, Roger. *Les idées sociales de Renouvier.* Paris: Rivière, 1908.
Platz, Wilhelm. *Charles Renouvier als Kritiker der französischen Kultur.* Bonn: Röhrscheid, 1934.
Séailles, Gabriel. *La philosophie de Charles Renouvier: introduction à l'étude du néo-criticisme.* Paris: Alcan, 1905.

BUISSON, Ferdinand. *Un moraliste laïque: Ferdinand Buisson. Pages choisies.* Précédées d'une introduction par C. Bouglé. Paris: Alcan, 1933.
L'avenir du sentiment religieux. Nécessité et conditions d'une union pour la culture morale: deux conférence faites en 1914 et 1923. Paris: Fischbacher, 1923.
Le christianisme libéral. Paris: Cherbuliez, 1865.
La crise de "l'Anticléricalisme." Paris: Revue politique et parlementaire, n.d. [1903?].
L'école et la nation en France. N.p., n.d.
La foi laïque: extraits de discours et d'écrits (1878-1911). Préface de Raymond Poincaré. 2d ed. Paris: Hachette, 1913.
L'instituteur et la République. Paris, 1909.
Jules Ferry et l'école laïque: conférence faite à Rodez le 28 mai 1911. Rodez: P. Forveille, 1911.
La morale professionnelle: l'homme politique. Paris: La Revue du mois, 1907.
La politique radicale: études sur les doctrines du parti radical et radical-socialiste. Précédée d'une lettre de M. Léon Bourgeois. Paris: Giard et Brière, 1908.
La réforme des moeurs politiques par la réforme électorale. Paris, n.d.
La religion, la morale et la science, et leur conflit dans l'éducation contemporaine: quatre conférences faites à l'aula de l'Université de

Genève (avril 1900). Paris: Fischbacher, 1900.

Le vote des femmes. Paris: Dunod et Pinat, 1911.

(Editor, with Frederick Farrington.) *French Educational Ideals of Today: An Anthology of the Molders of French Educational Thought of the Present*. New York: World, 1919.

(With Charles Wagner.) *Libre-pensée et protestantisme libéral*. Paris: Fischbacher, 1903.

SEAILLES, Gabriel. *Les affirmations de la conscience moderne*. 4th ed. Paris: Colin, 1909 [1st ed. 1903].

Education et révolution: conférence faite à l'inauguration de l'Université populaire, le 8 octobre 1899. Paris: La coopération des idées, [1899].

Education ou révolution: les affirmations de la conscience moderne. Paris: Colin, 1904.

L'enseignement primaire et la politique: l'affaire Guéry. Paris: Courrier européen, 1906.

Patrie et patriotisme: conférence faite à Troyes, le 19 mai 1910, à l'Assemblée générale des instituteurs et institutrices publics laïques de l'Aube. Troyes: Grande imprimerie, 1910.

La philosophie et l'éducation du peuple. Paris: Union pour l'action morale, 1896.

Le vrai patriotisme: une affirmation de la conscience moderne. Paris: Société française pour l'arbitrage entre nations, n.d.

(Preface to) Université Populaire: Coopération des Idées, *Histoire de douze ans (1898-1910)*. Paris: La coopération du livre, 1910.

ESPINAS, Alfred. *Des sociétés animales*. Deuxième édition, augmentée d'une introduction sur l'histoire de la sociologie en général. Paris: Baillière, 1878 [1st ed. 1877].

"Etre ou ne pas être," *Revue philosophique* 50 (1901): 449-80.

"Les études sociologiques en France," *Revue philosophique* 14 (1882): 337-67, 507-28.

Histoire des doctrines économiques. Paris: Colin, 1891.

La philosophie sociale du XVIIIᵉ siècle et la Révolution. Paris: Alcan, 1898.

Works about:

Davy, Georges. "L'oeuvre d'Espinas," *Revue philosophique* 96 (1923): 214-70.

Lalande, André. *Notice sur la vie et les travaux de M. Alfred Espinas*. Paris: Institut de France, 1925.

Ostrowski, Jan J. *Alfred Espinas, précurseur de la praxéologie (ses antécédents et ses successeurs)*. Paris: Librairie générale de droit et de jurisprudence, 1973.

IZOULET, Jean. *L'âme française et les universités nouvelles selon l'esprit de la Révolution*. Paris: Colin, 1892.

La cité moderne et la métaphysique de la sociologie. Paris: Alcan, 1894.

Les quatre problèmes sociaux. 2d ed. Paris: Colin, 1898.

La rentrée de Dieu dans l'école et dans l'Etat, ou la philosophie de l'histoire de France: le drame du Rhin et le drame du Christ. Paris:

Fayard, 1925.
Works about:
Bocquillon, Emile. *Civisme et sur-civisme*. Angoulême: Coquemard [1958].
Bocquillon, Emile. *Izoulet et son oeuvre*. Préface: Izoulet vu par Maurice Barrès. Paris: Baudinière, 1943.

TARDE, Gabriel. *Introduction et pages choisies par ses fils, suivies des poésies inédites de G. Tarde*. Préface de H. Bergson. Paris: Michaud, 1909.
La logique sociale. 4th ed. Paris: Alcan, 1913 [1st ed. 1895].
Les lois de l'imitation. Paris: Alcan, 1890.
Les lois sociales: esquisse d'une sociologie. Paris: Alcan, 1898.
L'opinion et la foule. Paris: Alcan, 1901.
L'opposition universelle: essai d'une théorie des contraires. Paris: Alcan, 1897.
Psychologie économique. 2 vols. Paris: Alcan, 1902.
Les transformations du droit: étude sociologique. Paris: Alcan, 1893.
Les transformations du pouvoir. Paris: Alcan, 1899.
Works about:
Clark, Terry N. *On Communication and Social Influence: Selected Papers* [of Gabriel Tarde]. Intro. by Terry N. Clark. Chicago: University of Chicago Press, 1969.
Milet, Jean. *Gabriel Tarde et la philosophie de l'histoire*. Paris: Vrin, 1970 [bibliography].

FOUILLEE, Alfred. *Critique des systèmes de morale contemporaines*. Paris: Baillière, 1883.
La démocratie politique et sociale en France. 2d ed. Paris: Alcan, 1910.
Les éléments sociologiques de la morale. Paris: Alcan, 1905.
Esquisse psychologique des peuples européens. Paris: Alcan, 1903.
Les études classiques et la démocratie. Paris: Colin, 1898.
La liberté et le déterminisme. 3d ed. Paris: Alcan, 1890 [1st ed. Ladrange, 1872].
La morale des idées-forces. Paris: Alcan, 1907.
Le mouvement positiviste et la conception sociologique du monde. Paris: Alcan, 1896.
La propriété sociale et la démocratie. Paris: Hachette, 1884.
La psychologie des idées-forces. 2 vols. Paris: Alcan, 1893.
Psychologie du peuple français. Paris: Alcan, 1898.
La science sociale contemporaine. 2d ed. Paris: Hachette, 1885 [1st ed. 1880].
Le socialisme et la sociologie réformiste. 2d ed. Paris: Alcan, 1909.
Works about:
Guyau, Augustin. *La philosophie et la sociologie d'Alfred Fouillée*. Paris: Alcan, 1913.

DURKHEIM, Emile. *L'Allemagne au-dessus de tout: la mentalité allemande et la guerre*. Paris: Colin, 1915.
De la division du travail social: étude sur l'organisation des sociétés supérieures. Paris: Alcan, 1893 [2d ed. with a new preface, 1902].

L'éducation morale. New ed. Paris: Alcan, 1934 [1st ed. 1925].

L'évolution et le role de l'enseignement secondaire en France. Paris: Revue politique et littéraire et Revue scientifique, n.d.

L'évolution pédagogique en France. 2 vols. Paris: Alcan, 1924.

Journal sociologique. Intro. et notes de Jean Duvignaud. Paris: Presses universitaires de France, 1969. [All of Durkheim's articles and many reviews from the *Année sociologique.*]

Leçons de sociologie: physique des moeurs et du droit. Paris: Presses universitaires de France, 1950.

Montesquieu and Rousseau: Forerunners of Sociology. Ann Arbor: University of Michigan Press, 1960.

Pragmatisme et sociologie. Cours inédit prononcé à la Sorbonne en 1913-14 et restitué d'après des notes d'étudiants et avec préface par A. Cuvillier. Paris: Vrin, 1955.

Les règles de la méthode sociologique. Paris: Alcan, 1895.

La science sociale et l'action. Intro. et présentation de Jean-Claude Filloux. Paris: Presses universitaires de France, 1970.

Sociologie et philosophie. Préface de C. Bouglé. New ed. Paris: Alcan, 1951 [1st ed. 1924].

Le socialisme: sa définition—ses débuts—la doctrine Saint-Simonienne. Préface de Annie Kriegel. Paris: Les classiques de sciences humaines, 1978 [1st ed. Préface de Marcel Mauss. Paris: Alcan, 1928].

Le suicide: étude de sociologie. Paris: Alcan, 1892.

Textes, Vol. I: *Eléments d'une théorie sociale.* Vol. II: *Religion, morale, anomie.* Présentation de Victor Karady. Paris: Editions de minuit, 1975.

Works about:

Aimard, Guy. *Durkheim et la science économique.* Paris: Presses universitaires de France, 1962.

Alpert, Harry. *Emile Durkheim and His Sociology.* New York: Russel & Russel, 1961.

Barnes, Harry Elmer. "Durkheim's Contribution to the Reconstruction of Political Theory," *Political Science Quarterly* 35 (1920): 236-54.

Birnbaum, Pierre. "La conception durkheimienne de l'Etat: l'apolitisme des fonctionnaires," *Revue française de sociologie* 17 (1976): 247-58.

Cuvillier, Armand. "Durkheim et Marx," *Cahiers internationaux de sociologie* 4 (1948): 75-97.

Filloux, Jean-Claude. "Démocratie et société socialiste chez Durkheim," *Cahiers Vilfrédo Pareto* 25 (1971): 29-48.

Giddens, Anthony. "Durkheim's Political Sociology," *Sociological Review,* n.s. 19 (1971): 477-519.

Lacroix, Bernard. *Durkheim et la politique.* Paris: Fondation nationale des sciences politiques, 1981.

Lacroix, Bernard. "La vocation originelle d'Emile Durkheim," *Revue française de sociologie* 17 (1976): 213-45.

Lukes, Steven. *Emile Durkheim: His Life and Work. A Historical and Critical Study.* New York: Harper & Row, 1972.

Mitchell, M. Marion. "Emile Durkheim and the Philosophy of Nationalism," *Political Science Quarterly* 46 (1931): 87-106.

Nisbet, Robert A. (ed.) *Emile Durkheim.* "Makers of Modern Social Science." Englewood Cliffs: Prentice-Hall, 1965.

Pizzorno, Alessandro. "Lecture actuelle de Durkheim," *Archives europé-
ennes de sociologie* 4 (1963): 1–36.
Vogt, W. Paul. "Anatomy of a 'Fin-de-siecle' Sociologist," *Reviews in
European History* 1 (1975): 565–69.
Wolff, Kurt H. (ed.) *Essays on Sociology and Philosophy.* [Emile Durk-
heim et al.]. New York: Harper & Row, 1960.

BOUGLE, Célestin. [Jean Breton, pseud.] *A l'arrière.* Paris: Delagrave, 1916.
Bienheureux les coopérateurs. Bruxelles: Les propagateurs de la coopéra-
tion; Paris: La fédération nationale des coopératives de consomma-
tion; Bâle: Union suisse des coopératives de consommation [1940].
Bilan de la sociologie française contemporaine. New ed. Paris: Alcan,
1938 [1st ed. 1935].
Ce que la guerre exige de la démocratie française. Paris: Foi et vie,
1918.
*Chez les prophètes socialistes: Saint-Simoniens et ouvriers. Le fémi-
nisme Saint-Simonien. L'alliance intellectuelle Franco-Allemand (1844).
Marxisme et sociologie.* Paris: Alcan, 1918.
Cours de sociologie: sociologie juridique, politique, religieuse, morale.
"Les cours de Sorbonne." Paris: Centre de Documentation Universi-
taire, n.d.
"La crise du libéralisme," *Revue de métaphysique et de morale* 10
(1902): 635–51.
De la sociologie à l'action sociale: pacifisme, féminisme, coopération.
New ed. Paris: Alcan, 1934 [1st ed. 1923].
*La démocratie devant la science: études critiques sur l'hérédité, la concur-
rence et la différenciation.* 3d ed. augmentée d'une préface sur la
sociologie monarchiste. Paris: Alcan, 1923 [1st ed. 1904].
*L'éducateur laïque: son attitude en matière de religion, de patriotisme,
de socialisme.* Paris: Rieder, 1921.
Essais sur le régime des castes. Paris: Alcan, 1908.
*Humanisme, sociologie, philosophie: remarques sur la conception fran-
çaise de la culture générale.* Paris: Hermann, 1938.
Les idées égalitaires: étude sociologique. Paris: Alcan, 1899.
Leçons de sociologie sur l'évolution des valeurs. 2d ed. Paris: Colin,
1929 [1st ed. 1922].
Les maîtres de la philosophie universitaire en France. Paris: Maloine,
1938.
Pour la démocratie française: conférences populaires. Préface de Gabriel
Séailles. Paris: Cornély, 1900.
"Proudhon fédéraliste." In Michel Augé-Laribé et al. (eds.) *Proudhon et
notre temps.* Préface de C. Bouglé. Paris: Chiron, 1920.
Qu'est-ce que la sociologie? Paris: Alcan, 1907.
Les sciences sociales en Allemagne: les méthodes actuelles. Paris: Alcan,
1896.
*Socialismes français: du "socialisme utopique" à la "démocratie indus-
trielle."* Paris: Colin, 1932.
La sociologie de Proudhon. Paris: Colin, 1911.
Le solidarisme. 2d ed. Paris: Giard et Brière, 1924 [1st ed. 1907].
Syndicalisme et démocratie: impressions et réflexions. Paris: Cornély,
1908.

Vie spirituelle et action sociale. Paris: Cornély, 1902.

(With others.) *Du sage antique au citoyen moderne: études sur la culture morale.* Préface de Paul Lapie. Paris: Colin, 1921.

Works about:

Halbwachs, Maurice. "Célestin Bouglé sociologue," *Revue de métaphysique et de morale* 48 (1941): 24–37.

Logue, William. "Sociologie et politique: le libéralisme de Célestin Bouglé," *Revue française de sociologie* 20 (1979): 141–61.

Vogt, W. Paul. "Un durkheimien ambivalent: Célestin Bouglé, 1870–1940," *Revue française de sociologie* 20 (1979): 123–39.

DUGUIT, Léon. *Des fonctions de l'Etat moderne: étude de sociologie juridique.* Paris: Giard, 1894.

Le droit constitutionnel et la sociologie. Paris: Colin, 1889.

L'Etat, le droit objectif et la loi positive. Paris: Fontemoing, 1901.

Manuel de droit constitutionnel, théorie générale de l'Etat, organisation politique. Paris: Fontemoing, 1907.

"Le syndicalisme," *Revue politique et parlementaire,* 10 June 1908, pp. 472–93.

Traité de droit constitutionnel. Vol. I: *Théorie générale de l'Etat (Les éléments, les fonctions, les organes de l'Etat, les agents publics).* Paris: Fontemoing, 1911.

Les transformations du droit public. Paris: Colin, 1913.

Works about:

Archives de philosophie du droit et de sociologie juridique. Cahiers nos. 1–2, 1932. [Special number on Léon Duguit.]

Bonnard, Roger. *Léon Duguit, ses oeuvres, sa doctrine.* Paris: Giard, 1929.

Boye, A.-J. "Souvenirs personnels sur Léon Duguit," *Revue juridique et économique du Sud-Ouest: série juridique* 10 (1959): 115–28.

Cintura, Paul. "La pensée politique de Léon Duguit," *Revue juridique et économique du Sud-Ouest: série juridique* 19 (1968): 67–98, 151–93.

Eisenmann, Charles. "Deux théoriciens du droit: Duguit et Hauriou," *Revue philosophique* 110 (1930): 231–79.

Laborde-Lacoste, Marcel. "La vie et la personnalité de Léon Duguit," *Revue juridique et économique du Sud-Ouest: serie juridique* 10 (1959): 93–114.

Markovitch, Milan P. *La doctrine sociale de Duguit: ses idées sur le syndicalisme et la représentation professionnelle.* Paris: Pierre Bossuet, 1933.

SECONDARY SOURCES

History of Political Thought

Chevallier, Jean Jacques. *Cours de principes du droit public.* Paris: Les cours de droit, 1951.

——. *Cours d'histoire des idées politiques rédigé d'après les notes...* Paris: Les cours de droit, 1967.

Crossman, R. H. S. *Government and the Governed: A History of Political Ideas and Political Practice.* New York: Pica Press, 1969.

Delbez, Louis. *Les grands courants de la pensée politique française depuis le XIXᵉ siècle.* Paris: Librairie générale de droit et de jurisprudence, 1970.

Droz, Jacques. *Histoire des doctrines politiques en France.* 2d ed. Paris: Presses universitaires de France, 1963.

Jouvenal, Bertrand de. *Cours d'histoire des idées politiques à partir du XIXᵉ siècle.* Paris: Les cours de droit, 1967.

Lavroff, D. G. *Histoire des idées politiques depuis le XIXᵉ siècle.* Paris: Dalloz, 1972.

Leroy, Maxime. *Histoire des idées sociales en France.* 3 vols. Paris: Gallimard, 1946-54.

Mayer, J. P. *Political Thought in France from the Revolution to the Fifth Republic.* 3d ed. London: Routledge & Kegan Paul, 1961.

Michel, Henry. "De l'histoire des doctrines politiques: sa nature, sa méthode, son esprit," *Revue du droit public* 7 (1897): 221-34.

———. *L'idée de l'Etat: essai critique sur l'histoire des théories sociales et politiques en France depuis la Révolution.* Paris: Hachette, 1895.

Ponteil, Felix. *La pensée politique depuis Montesquieu.* Paris: Sirey, 1960.

Prélot, Marcel. *Histoire des idées politiques.* 3d ed. Paris: Dalloz, 1966.

Soltau, Roger H. *French Political Ideas in the Nineteenth Century.* London: Benn, 1931.

Thibaudet, Albert. *Les idées politiques de la France.* Paris: Stock, Delamain et Boutelleau, 1932.

Touchard, Jean. *Histoire des idées politiques.* Vol. II: *Du XVIIIᵉ siècle à nos jours.* 5th ed. Paris: Presses universitaires de France, 1970.

French Liberalism

Bourgin, Hubert. *L'Ecole normale et la politique.* Paris: Fayard, 1938.

Digeon, Claude. *La crise allemande de la pensée française (1870-1914).* Paris: Presses universitaires de France, 1959.

Elbow, Matthew H. *French Corporative Theory, 1789-1948: A Chapter in the History of Ideas.* New York: Columbia University Press, 1953.

Grangé, Ch.-A. *Les doctrines politiques du parti républicain à la fin du Second Empire.* Bordeaux: Y. Cadoret, 1903.

Greenberg, Louis M. *Sisters of Liberty: Marseille, Lyon, Paris and the Reaction to a Centralized State, 1868-1871.* Cambridge: Harvard University Press, 1971.

Hayward, J. E. S. "Educational Pressure Groups and the Indoctrination of the Radical Ideology of Solidarism, 1895-1914," *International Review of Social History* 8 (1963): 1-17.

———. "The Official Social Philosophy of the French Third Republic: Léon Bourgeois and Solidarism," *International Review of Social History* 6 (1961): 19-48.

———. "Solidarity: The Social History of an Idea in Nineteenth Century France," *International Review of Social History* 4 (1959): 261-84.

Kayser, Jacques. *Les grandes batailles du radicalisme des origines aux portes du pouvoir, 1820-1901.* Paris: Marcel Rivière, 1962.

King, Preston. *Fear of Power: An Analysis of Anti-Statism in Three French Writers.* London: Cass, 1967.

Minnich, Lawrence A. "Social Problems and Political Alignments in France, 1893–1898: Léon Bourgeois and Solidarity." Ph.D. dissertation, Cornell University, 1948.

Nail, Hüseyin. *L'idée de l'Etat chez les précurseurs de l'école sociologique française*. Paris: Domat-Montchrestien, 1936.

Nordmann, Jean-Thomas. *Histoire des radicaux, 1820–1973*. Paris: La table ronde, 1974.

Reardon, Bernard. *Liberalism and Tradition: Aspects of Catholic Thought in Nineteenth-Century France*. Cambridge: Cambridge University Press, 1975.

Rémond, René. *L'anticléricalisme en France: de 1815 à nos jours*. Paris: Fayard, 1976.

Scott, John A. *Republican Ideas and the Liberal Tradition in France, 1870–1914*. New York: Octagon, 1966.

French Philosophy and Sociology

Aron, Raymond. *Les étapes de la pensée sociologique: Montesquieu, Comte, Marx, Tocqueville, Durkheim, Pareto, Weber*. Paris: Gallimard, 1967.

Barrows, Susanna. "Crowd Psychology in Late Nineteenth-Century France: The Riddle of the Sphinx." Ph.D. dissertation, Yale University, 1977.

Benrubi, Isaac. *Contemporary Thought of France*. Trans. Ernest B. Dicker. New York: Knopf, 1926.

Besnard, Philippe. "La formation de l'equipe de l'*Année sociologique*," *Revue française de sociologie* 20 (1979): 7–31.

Bréhier, Emile. *Histoire de la philosophie*. T. II: *La philosophie moderne*. Paris: Presses universitaires de France, 1946.

——. *Transformation de la philosophie française*. Paris: Flammarion, 1950.

Clark, Terry Nichols. *Prophets and Patrons: The French University and the Emergence of the Social Sciences*. Cambridge: Harvard University Press, 1973.

Davy, Georges. *L'homme, le fait social et le fait politique*. Paris: Mouton, 1973.

Geiger, Roger Lewis. "The Development of French Sociology, 1871–1905." Ph.D. dissertation, University of Michigan, 1972.

Gurvitch, Georges. *La vocation actuelle de la sociologie*. Vol. I: *Vers la sociologie différentielle*. 2d ed. Paris: Presses universitaires de France, 1957.

Leroux, Emmanuel. "La philosophie morale en France depuis la guerre," *Revue philosophique* 109 (1930): 43–78.

Lévy-Bruhl, Lucien. *La morale et la science des moeurs*. Paris: Alcan, 1903.

Nye, Robert A. *The Origins of Crowd Psychology: Gustave LeBon and the Crisis of Mass Democracy in the Third Republic*. Beverly Hills, Calif.: Sage, 1975.

Political Thought

Aron, Raymond. *Essai sur les libertés*. 2d ed. Paris: Calmann-Lévy, 1976.

——. *Etudes politiques*. Paris: Gallimard, 1972.

Brecht, Arnold. *Political Theory: The Foundations of Twentieth-Century Political Thought*. Princeton: Princeton University Press, 1959.

Burdeau, Georges. *Le libéralisme*. Paris: Seuil, 1979.

———. *Traité de science politique*. 2d ed. 10 vols. Paris: Librairie générale de droit et de jurisprudence, 1966–77.

Christophersen, Jens A. *The Meaning of "Democracy" as Used in European Ideologies from the French to the Russian Revolution: An Historical Study in Political Language*. New York: Humanities Press, 1966.

Crick, Bernard. *In Defense of Politics*. Rev. ed. Baltimore: Penguin, 1964.

Cropsey, Joseph. *Political Philosophy and the Issues of Politics*. Chicago: University of Chicago Press, 1977.

Cumming, Robert Denoon. *Human Nature and History: A Study of the Development of Liberal Political Thought*. 2 vols. Chicago: University of Chicago Press, 1969.

Elliott, William Y. *The Pragmatic Revolt in Politics: Syndicalism, Fascism, and the Constitutional State*. New ed. New York: Fertig, 1968.

Germino, Dante. *Beyond Ideology: The Revival of Political Theory*. New York: Harper & Row, 1967.

Halbecq, Michel. *L'Etat, son autorité, son pouvoir (1880–1962)*. Paris: Librairie générale de droit et de jurisprudence, 1965.

Hayek, F. A. *The Constitution of Liberty*. Chicago: University of Chicago Press, 1960.

Lowi, Theodore J. *The End of Liberalism: Ideology, Policy, and the Crisis of Public Authority*. New York: Norton, 1969.

Lukes, Steven. *Individualism*. "Key Concepts in the Social Sciences." New York: Harper & Row, 1973.

Nisbet, Robert. *Twilight of Authority*. New York: Oxford University Press, 1975.

Plamenatz, John. *Democracy and Illusion: An Examination of Certain Aspects of Modern Democratic Theory*. London: Longman, 1973.

Rawls, John. *A Theory of Justice*. Cambridge: Harvard University Press, 1971.

Shklar, Judith N. *After Utopia: The Decline of Political Faith*. Princeton: Princeton University Press, 1957.

Voegelin, Eric. *The New Science of Politics: An Introduction*. Chicago: University of Chicago Press, 1952.

Weldon, T. D. *The Vocabulary of Politics*. Baltimore: Penguin, 1953.

Liberalism

Ashcraft, Richard. "Marx and Weber on Liberalism as Bourgeois Ideology," *Comparative Studies in Society and History* 14 (1972): 130–68.

Barker, Rodney. *Political Ideas in Modern Britain*. London: Methuen, 1978.

Coker, F. W. *Organismic Theories of the State: Nineteenth Century Interpretations of the State as Organism or as Person*. New York: AMS Press, 1967 [orig. ed. 1910].

Collini, Stefan. *Liberalism and Sociology: L. T. Hobhouse and Political Argument in England, 1880–1914*. Cambridge: Cambridge University Press, 1979.

Emy, H. V. *Liberals, Radicals, and Social Politics, 1892–1914*. Cambridge: Cambridge University Press, 1973.

Freeden, Michael. *The New Liberalism: An Ideology of Social Reform*. New York: Oxford University Press, 1978.

Giddens, Anthony. *Capitalism and Modern Social Theory: An Analysis of the Writings of Marx, Durkheim and Max Weber.* Cambridge: Cambridge University Press, 1971.

Girvetz, Harry K. *The Evolution of Liberalism.* Rev. ed. New York: Collier, 1963.

Gouldner, Alvin W. *The Coming Crisis of Western Sociology.* New York: Basic Books, 1970.

Hughes, H. Stuart. *Consciousness and Society: The Reorientation of European Social Thought, 1890–1930.* New York: Knopf, 1958.

Macpherson, C. B. *The Political Theory of Possessive Individualism.* Oxford: Clarendon Press, 1962.

Masur, Gerhard. *Prophets of Yesterday: Studies in European Culture, 1890–1914.* New York: Macmillan, 1961.

Richard, Gaston. *La question sociale et le mouvement philosophique au XIXe siècle.* Paris: Colin, 1914.

Richter, Melvin. *The Politics of Conscience: T. H. Green and His Age.* Cambridge: Harvard University Press, 1964.

Ruggiero, Guido de. *The History of European Liberalism.* Trans. R. G. Collingwood. Boston: Beacon, 1959 [orig. ed. 1927].

Salvadori, Massimo. *The Liberal Heresy: Origins and Historical Development.* New York: St. Martin's, 1977.

Schultz, Harold J. (ed.) *English Liberalism and the State: Individualism or Collectivism?* Lexington, Mass.: Heath, 1972.

Willey, Thomas E. *Back to Kant: The Revival of Kantianism in German Social and Historical Thought, 1860–1914.* Detroit: Wayne State University Press, 1978.

272

Index

About, Edmond, Caro's remarks at funeral of, 31
Académie des sciences morales et politique, 30, 37, 53, 102, 119
Académie française, 30, 130
Affirmations de la conscience moderne (Séailles), 88
Agulhon, Maurice, 16
Alain (Emile Chartier), xii, 209
Alliance Israélite Universelle, 21
Année sociologique, 15, 16, 181, 188, 190, 192
Anomie, 161, 172, 177–78
Archives d'anthropologie criminelle, 118
L'argent (Zola), 25
Associationist movement. *See* Syndicalist movement

Balzac, Honoré de, 207
Barrès, Maurice, 106
Barthélemy Saint-Hilaire, Jules, 21
Barthou, Louis, 101
Bastiat, Frédéric, 5, 137
Bentham, Jeremy, 28, 120
Bergson, Henri, succession to Tarde's Collège de France chair by, 119
Bernard, Claude, 32
Bert, Paul, 112
Biological sociology, 102, 111; cell theory and evolutionism, as basis for, 96, 97; Espinas on, 102, 108; and Izoulet, 111, 112–13, 114; and racism, 96–97; Tarde's repudiation of, 117; Social Darwinism in, 97
Birnbaum, Pierre, 166
Blanc, Louis, 54, 61, 156
Bocquillon, Emile, 116
Bodin, Jean, 96
Bonald, Louis de, 18, 100
Bonaparte, Louis Napoléon, 8, 41, 99
Bouglé, Célestin, 15, 16, 179, 180, 181–94, 202, 203; use of Jean Breton pseudonym, in *A l'arrière,* 254n.57
Bourgeois, Léon, 80, 91, 112, 185
Bourges, Michel de, 37
Boutroux, Emile, 37
Broglie, duc de: and Seize Mai crisis, 69
Brunetière, Ferdinand, 152
Buisson, Ferdinand, 15, 37, 82, 87, 89–92, 93, 94, 153
Buloz, François, 30
Burke, Edmund, 18, 48, 207

Carlyle, Thomas: translated by Izoulet, 115
Carnot, Hippolyte, 53
Caro, Elme-Marie, 15, 20, 30–37, 39, 44, 50
Caro, Pauline (née Cassin), 30

273

Milton Keynes UK
Ingram Content Group UK Ltd.
UKHW052016140424
440953UK00009BA/85